INNOVATION IN MIXED METHODS RESEARCH

INNOVATION
IN MIXED
METHODS
RESEARCH

Cheryl N. Poth

A Practical Guide to
Integrative Thinking
with Complexity

Los Angeles | London | New Delhi
Singapore | Washington DC | Melbourne

Los Angeles | London | New Delhi
Singapore | Washington DC | Melbourne

SAGE Publications Ltd
1 Oliver's Yard
55 City Road
London EC1Y 1SP

SAGE Publications Inc.
2455 Teller Road
Thousand Oaks, California 91320

SAGE Publications India Pvt Ltd
B 1/I 1 Mohan Cooperative Industrial Area
Mathura Road
New Delhi 110 044

SAGE Publications Asia-Pacific Pte Ltd
3 Church Street
#10-04 Samsung Hub
Singapore 049483

Editor: Aly Owen
Assistant editor: Charlotte Bush
Production editor: Ian Antcliff
Copyeditor: Richard Leigh
Proofreader: Chris Bitten
Indexer: Martin Hargreaves
Marketing manager: Susheel Gokarakonda
Cover design: Shaun Mercier
Typeset by: C&M Digitals (P) Ltd, Chennai, India
Printed in the UK

Library of Congress Control Number: 2018938197

British Library Cataloguing in Publication data

A catalogue record for this book is available from the
British Library

ISBN 978-1-4739-0668-6
ISBN 978-1-4739-0669-3 (pbk)

At SAGE we take sustainability seriously. Most of our products are printed in the UK using responsibly sourced
papers and boards. When we print overseas we ensure sustainable papers are used as measured by the PREPS
grading system. We undertake an annual audit to monitor our sustainability.

To my husband, Damian J. Rogers.

Without his love, patience, and support during the writing of this book and in life, none of this would be possible.

CONTENTS

DETAILED CONTENTS

LIST OF TABLES

LIST OF FIGURES

💡 LIST OF RESEARCHER SPOTLIGHTS

⟳ LIST OF PRACTICE ALERTS

✈ LIST OF GUIDING TIPS

PEDAGOGICAL GUIDE

The learning features included in this book are intended to describe a complexity-sensitive approach that is relevant, accessible, and practical. Embedded throughout the book you will find:

Key questions that help orient you to the topics within each chapter. With a practical focus, the questions ensure you capture the skills you need and the knowledge necessary for executing those skills in a quick and accessible way.

New chapter terms that allow you a quick introduction; and definitions are provided in the Glossary (Appendix A).

Check-ins that make you pause for a moment at the end of each chapter. Taking time to assess the extent to which you have developed the intended knowledge and skills allows you to build confidence in your emerging mixed methods research capacity.

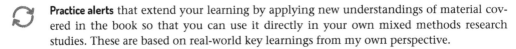 **Practice alerts** that extend your learning by applying new understandings of material covered in the book so that you can use it directly in your own mixed methods research studies. These are based on real-world key learnings from my own perspective.

Researcher spotlights that allow you to access the experiences and viewpoints of several prominent and emerging mixed methods researchers on key pressing and future challenges and possible ways we can better prepare mixed methods researchers for working under conditions of complexity. See also Appendix C for biographies of the researcher spotlight contributors from around the globe.

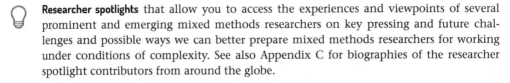 **Guiding tips** that offer you succinct advice from a variety of perspectives of mixed methods researchers from around the globe for navigating the complexity of mixed methods research.

Featured studies that are purposefully selected to represent a range of mixed methods article examples under conditions of complexity are introduced in Chapter 1 and revisited throughout the book as a means of bridging theory with real research projects. The articles are available on the companion website for the book.

Key chapter concepts that are concise summaries to guide your reflection on the content for each chapter. Recapped information about topics covered in the chapter ensures you capture the important points.

Further readings that allow you to go and explore further beyond the chapters. With up-to-date references and summarized information, they can begin to extend your understanding of the field of mixed methods research. The readings denoted with an asterisk are available on the companion website for this book.

Visual organizers that are used throughout the book for two purposes: to provide a 'roadmap' in advance of a written description, and to summarize text in a quick and accessible way. Templates are available for the practice innovations in Appendix B as well as editable versions on the companion website.

Instructor resources for supporting the use of this book are available on the companion website.

Online Resources

Innovation in Mixed Methods Research: A Practical Guide to Integrative Thinking with Complexity is supported by a wealth of online resources for both students and lecturers to aid studying and support teaching, which are available at https://study.sagepub.com/poth.

For students

Videos from author Cheryl N. Poth

Links to curated **further reading articles** on the **SAGE Journals** platform offer you the chance to broaden your understanding of mixed methods research.

Chapter-by-chapter **activities** enable you to review your knowledge of key terms, connect up the theory you've learnt with your own research practice and gain insight from experts in the field.

Downloadable templates empower you to implement research innovations in your own practice.

For lecturers

PowerPoint slides with key topics, tables and figures from the book can be downloaded and customised for use in your own teaching.

PREFACE

Along with increased recognition of varying conditions of complexity in our mixed methods research come demands for guiding practices for integrative thinking with complexity. This is because while our traditional (i.e., established) practices work well under some conditions, others require some rethinking when faced with greater complexity. Through adopting a complexity lens, I formed new connections with my understandings of complexity science, my practices as a developmental evaluator, and my experiences as a mixed methods researcher from learning about the dilemmas my colleagues, students, and I were encountering in mixed methods research. Using these new connections as a catalyst, I imagined how mixed methods researchers might mitigate some of the perceived limitations with traditional practice tendencies under some conditions of complexity. By recognizing the sources of complexity in mixed methods research, I began to see new possibilities for guiding adaptive practices where researchers become more responsive to the varying conditions of complexity.

In this book, I advance six adaptive practices that comprise a more complexity-sensitive approach to mixed methods research. These adaptive practices should be considered as evolving and as providing an essential starting point for further discussions and applications. Other resources focus on introducing the foundations of mixed methods research – designs and integration – and it is assumed that readers have some familiarity with these on which to build new understandings of research under complex conditions. All research takes place under conditions of complexity – regardless of whether we, as mixed methods researchers, recognize the dimensions of this complexity – and our responses to dynamic influences pose dilemmas and offer opportunities. All too often, our responses involve attempts to reduce, control, or simply ignore the effects of complexity, and these responses have become the basis for our traditional research practice tendencies over time. The need for this book reflects trends I have observed and adopted in my own mixed methods research teaching and advising. I advocate for researchers to assume responsibility for recognizing and making mindful decisions about how to deal with the varying conditions of complexity surrounding their research.

The text is set out in three parts:

- Part I provides essential foundations for getting started with mixed methods research under conditions of complexity.
- Part II describes six adaptive practices involved in conducting mixed methods research. The rationale for each practice is described along with opportunities and hazards, and procedures are illustrated with specific examples.
- Part III offers suggestions for how to realize a more complexity-sensitive approach to mixed methods research through adopting the six guiding practices.

This book is written for those with various roles and expertise in mixed methods research. The common element is an interest in adapting practices for mixed methods research under conditions of complexity. These include (but are not limited to) graduate students, instructors of mixed methods research courses or workshops, individual researchers or members of a mixed methods research team, research associations and communities, research managers, and reviewers of mixed methods research. Enjoy the journey!

ABOUT THE AUTHOR

Cheryl N. Poth, PhD, is an award-winning instructor and textbook author. She joined the University of Alberta in 2008 as a faculty member of the Centre for Research in Applied Measurement and Evaluation within the Department of Educational Psychology in the Faculty of Education. In this role, she has developed and taught graduate-level research methods and programme evaluation courses in addition to supervising and mentoring students, faculty, and community members in qualitative, quantitative, and mixed methods research. Dr. Poth has an adjunct appointment in the Faculty of Medicine and Dentistry and serves as the methodologist on several cross-disciplinary research teams. She has been principal investigator for projects and grants funded federally (e.g., Social Sciences and Humanities Research Council and Physiotherapy Foundation of Canada), provincially (e.g., Alberta Education, Policywise and Alberta Advisory Committee for Educational Studies), and locally (e.g., University of Alberta and school boards). In 2016, she was elected as the fourth president of the Mixed Methods International Research Association (MMIRA) and is active in the mixed methods groups within her other professional associations (e.g., the American Educational Research Association and American Evaluation Association) and an advisory board member of the International Institute of Qualitative Methods. She recently co-authored the fourth edition of *Qualitative Inquiry and Research Design* with John Creswell and was conferred the Sage Author Cornerstone Award and 2018 McGuffey Longevity Award from the Textbook & Academic Authors Association. In addition, she has authored over 30 peer-reviewed journal articles and served as guest co-editor of two special issues focused on mixed methods research in the *International Journal of Qualitative Methods*. She is currently an associate editor for the *Journal of Mixed Methods Research* and editorial board member of the *International Journal of Qualitative Methods* and *Canadian Journal of Program Evaluation*. She strives to model lifelong learning and enjoys creating situations in which learning occurs about mixed methods research. She is a contributor to the massive open online course launched by the Mixed Methods International Research Association (see mmira.org). In 2013, she was recognized with the University of Alberta's Provost's Award for Early Achievement of Excellence in teaching.

ACKNOWLEDGEMENTS

I am grateful to the students in my mixed methods classes at the University of Alberta and colleagues from around the globe who have influenced my thinking for this book. These students and colleagues, as well as members of the Department of Educational Psychology Mixed Methods Reading Group, and many workshop participants, have offered suggestions for book content and provided inspiration to keep me going.

I would like to acknowledge the influence of scholarly mentors I have had the good fortune to encounter – key among the global mixed methods research community are Drs. John Creswell, Burke Johnson, Tony Onwuegbuzie, Vicki Plano Clark, Sharlene Hesse-Biber, Pat Bazeley, Leslie Curry, Donna Mertens, Elizabeth Creamer, Nataliya Ivankova. Reading their work and collaborating with them has enriched my thinking and subsequent work in immeasurable ways.

Locally, I especially single out Drs. Jacqueline Pei and Lia Daniels and members of the Centre for Research in Applied Measurement and Evaluation as important influencers and supporters. Also, I am appreciative of my Department of Educational Psychology, Faculty of Education, and community at the University of Alberta. I am grateful to Adrienne Montgomery's close eye on all things related to conveying my ideas coherently and to Alexandra Aquilina for her contributions during the final stages of the book.

I am particularly indebted to the scholars who favourably reviewed the proposal for this book and then those who served as external reviewers for SAGE throughout the writing of this book. Thank you for your meticulous attention to the details of this book – I hope you will see the influence of your suggestions for content and references. I am thankful to Katie Metzler as my initial acquisition editor for her persistent pursuit of this book proposal as well as providing the opportunity to later work with the equally capable Mila Steele, Jai Seaman and finally Alysha Owen as editor during the writing and production processes. Key among the many others have contributed to bringing this manuscript to life include Ian Antcliff (Production editor), Richard Leigh (copyeditor), and Susheel Gokarakonda (marketing manager), and Charlotte Bush (Assistant editor).

To my many friends, locally and around the world, and family – Joyce, Brian, Andrea, Lisa, Dennis, Anna, Thomas, Madison and Jacob – thank you for your encouragement to pursue my dreams. To my dad, Richard, who left this world during the writing of this book and whose influences can be seen in the way I live my life and who is lovingly remembered every day.

Finally, to members of my Edmonton-based family – Damian, Avery and Jasper – thank you for providing me the time and space to create this book.

Thank you all.

PART I

Welcome to the field of mixed methods research, and I now invite you to join me on a learning journey. In the first three chapters I describe the essential foundations for the adaptive mixed methods research practices described in Part II of this book. When I first began describing these practices I realized the need to first familiarize readers with what I meant by complexity and mixed methods research under conditions of varying complexity, why innovations were necessary in mixed methods research, and what opportunities were afforded by integrative thinking with complexity for mixed methods researchers. In so doing, I provide access to a complexity-sensitive approach to readers with a wide range of familiarity with mixed methods research. Revisiting the essential foundations of mixed methods research will allow us all to begin on common ground.

Mixed methods research is well established in the literature yet there exists much diversity across many areas. Researchers trained in some research approaches and disciplines often express surprise (and even dismay) at what appears to be a lack of consensus within the field of mixed methods research. I come at this diversity with a sense of wonder. This is because the field of mixed methods research and understandings about how to conceptualize, design, and conduct mixed methods research continue to develop across many disciplines and are influenced by countless perspectives. I place a great deal of value on this diversity because I believe it helps advance mixed methods research practice. To that end, I welcome diverse disciplines, orientations, and perspectives because I believe they produce a more interesting and rich mixed methods research community! That said, I would be doing a disservice to the reader if I did not acknowledge that diversity can also be confounding – especially to those new to mixed methods research and those beginning to consider the varying conditions of research complexity. Hence the importance of the initial three chapters in this book.

Mixed methods research continues to experience unprecedented interest and demand as a mechanism for mitigating the inherent limitations with either qualitative or quantitative data alone. More recently, mixed methods research has been highlighted as useful in generating innovations for solving societal problems. For the most part, this is welcome news as researchers recognize the potential of mixed methods research to address societal problems where the solutions are not apparent and remain inaccessible by either qualitative and quantitative data alone. If the mixed methods research community is to position itself for effectively addressing societal problems, then we must shift the way we intellectually and methodologically respond under conditions of varying complexity. Essentially, harnessing the potential of mixed methods research means creating mixed methods research practices that are more complexity-sensitive – the theoretical underpinnings of such transformations informed by the principles of complexity science. Prior to delving into the thinking and actions behind the adaptive practices reflective of a more complexity-sensitive mixed methods research approach described in Part II of this book, it is important to introduce the essentials of mixed methods research.

GETTING STARTED WITH ESSENTIAL FOUNDATIONS

The three chapters in Part I are as follows:

EMBRACING COMPLEXITY IN MIXED METHODS RESEARCH

KEY CHAPTER QUESTIONS

By the end of this chapter, you will be able to answer the following questions:

- Why focus on complexity within mixed methods research?
- What experiences does the author draw upon?
- What is meant by complexity and innovation in mixed methods research?
- Who are the audiences for this book?
- How is this book organized for the reader?
- What are the six mixed methods research studies featured in this book?

NEW CHAPTER TERMS

By the end of this chapter, you will be familiar with the following terms:

- High complexity
- Complexity
- Innovation
- Complexity lens
- Integrative thinking
- Complexity science
- Low complexity

- Complexity-sensitive mixed methods research approach
- Mixed methods research
- Complex mixed methods research problems
- Moderate complexity
- Conditions of complexity
- Traditional mixed methods research practices

This chapter provides an introduction to this book. It speaks to the question: *Why focus on complexity and how can understandings about varying conditions of complexity inform my approach to mixed methods research?* The book was born out of necessity, and I am forever grateful to the students (as well as colleagues, editors, and others) who encouraged me to write it! A conversation about five years ago with a small group of graduate students seeking advice related to their individual mixed methods studies gave rise to the idea for the book. Common to these studies and at the heart of my own **mixed methods research** definition was the design of research to generate previously inaccessible insights from the integration of qualitative and quantitative data (see Chapter 2 for further discussion). What had led to this group conversation was being approached individually by four students, within the same month, with questions about the dilemmas they were facing in their mixed methods studies. Although the students were working independently, I realized that they could each benefit from having access to the discussions about one another's experiences. The students quickly agreed to my suggestion of meeting several times as a group. I confess that my primary motivation for the group approach was efficiency – I did not anticipate the emergence of new understandings from the group interactions that would not have been possible with those involved individually.

Through embracing a new way of **integrative thinking** – and questioning the utility of some **traditional mixed methods research practice** tendencies under certain research conditions – I began to conceptualize the need for more adaptive approaches to mixed methods research. To that end, this book advances a **complexity-sensitive mixed methods research approach** incorporating six adaptive practices to enhance researchers' capacity to respond to the unique and unfolding conditions under which mixed methods research studies are undertaken (see Chapter 3, Table 3.3). Through adopting a **complexity lens**, I formed new connections with my understandings of **complexity science**, my practices as a developmental evaluator, and my experiences as a mixed methods researcher from learning about the dilemmas these students were encountering in their mixed methods research. Using these new connections as a catalyst, I imagined how mixed methods researchers might mitigate some of the perceived limitations with traditional practice tendencies under some **conditions of complexity** (see Chapter 2 for fulsome discussion of traditional mixed methods research practice tendencies). By recognizing the sources of **complexity** in mixed methods research, I began to see new possibilities for guiding adaptive practices where researchers become more responsive to the varying conditions of complexity. But first, let me define what I mean by complexity – there is little consensus, and many definitions refer to complexity as a state or quality of being complex, which of course is not very helpful! Later in the chapter I distinguish complex from complicated and simple, but, for now, I see complexity as characterizing the behaviour of a research system whereby its components (such as research participants, researchers, their environments) interact in multiple, nonlinear ways without direction. The outcomes of these interactions are impossible to predict with any accuracy, yet patterns of behaviour from the system can be documented retrospectively.

This work, related to varying conditions of research complexity, was both challenging and rewarding because it required me to think creatively about mixed methods research practices. In so doing, I embody the words of the American psychiatrist and best-selling author M. Scott Peck who wrote in the introduction to his book, *Further along the Road Less Traveled*: 'abandon the urge to simplify everything, to look for formulas and easy answers, and begin to think multidimensionally, to glory in the mystery and paradoxes of life, not to be dismayed by the multitude of causes and consequences that are inherent in each experience – to appreciate the fact that life is complex' (1998, p. 14). To that end, in advancing six adaptive practices, I see these as a starting point and that our understandings of complexity-sensitive approaches to mixed methods research will naturally evolve over time (see Table 3.3). In Practice Alert 1.1, I consider the usefulness of integrative thinking as guiding my approach to mixed methods research under conditions of complexity and I invite you to begin doing the same. In so doing, I provide a framework for acknowledging the usefulness of many traditional mixed methods research practices but also opening the possibilities for practices that have yet to be developed for conditions of complexity that have yet to be encountered.

 **Practice Alert 1.1**

How can reflection on past experiences and readings of literature inform future mixed methods research practices?

My practices as a mixed methods researcher were initially guided by what I had read in the literature. As I began to read more about complexity science and learn about the dilemmas researchers were facing in their mixed methods research, I began to think about the need for more adaptive practices. My current thinking about adaptive mixed methods research

(Continued)

(Continued)

practice tendencies reflects bringing a complexity lens to bear on what works in traditional mixed methods research practice tendencies under varying conditions of complexity. In this way, my practices not only respond to varying conditions of complexity but also make the adaptations explicit so that researchers can begin to learn from the experiences of others.

Try this now – sketch your ideas about what have been the key practices in your approach as a mixed methods researcher and consider what practice tendencies have been easy to apply. What dilemmas have you experienced? How might you approach mixed methods research practices differently in the future?

As I shared my emerging thinking about how mixed methods research practices might be made more complexity-sensitive with students and colleagues, I engaged in discussions concerning how these practices might be applied, and imagined their effects under varying conditions of complexity. In some cases, I found literature confirming that others had already advanced ideas for mitigating some limitations that I had considered in these traditional practice tendencies (further discussed in Chapter 2); for example, Guest (2013) proposed a mixed methods research design approach based on succinct descriptions of the points of data interface, and Creswell and Plano Clark (2018) advanced complex mixed methods designs. However, what I did not find in the literature was a comprehensive approach for attending and then responding with adaptive practices to the dynamic influences within the varying conditions under which mixed methods research occurred. The lack of such an approach was at the heart of many of the dilemmas I had documented, and so I began to sketch the adaptive practices involved in a complexity-sensitive approach to mixed methods research. Around the same time a body of work began emerging to confirm my inklings that **complex mixed methods research problems** and dynamic conditions required new thinking. Particularly noteworthy for my own thinking was reading about the potential role for mixed methods in addressing wicked problems described by Donna Mertens in an editorial for the *Journal of Mixed Methods Research*. In this work, Mertens (2015, p. 3) referenced Rittel and Webber's (1973) definition of wicked problems as those that 'involve multiple interacting systems, are replete with social and institutional uncertainties, and for which only imperfect knowledge about their nature and solutions exist'. The differentiation of wicked problems was a critical event for me because it provided an adjective to distinguish some problems I had been grappling with in my research and evaluation projects such as service delivery for children affected with fetal alcohol spectrum disorder and enhancing teaching and learning experiences in large-sized class environments. For each of those problems there were multiple interacting systems involving individuals, groups, and society influenced by many, many changeable aspects.

I began to realize that there was a reason why working on wicked problems was hard! There was no recipe – conceptually, theoretically, or methodologically – for addressing them. I had felt like I was on a new path, and now I *knew* I was breaking new ground! I began by examining the conditions surrounding these problems in a way that intended to capture the interacting systems but did not try to reduce or simply them. Little did I know that I would begin to see many more problems as wicked than I had originally intended! I also came to see that the term 'wicked' had negative associations for some, so I decided simply to call them complex mixed methods research problems. I began making connections between my experiences as an evaluator and researcher with complex problems. Examine Researcher Spotlight 1.1, featuring the challenges wicked mixed methods research problems present and the need to prepare future mixed methods researchers for the pressing issues they will tackle, from the perspective of a pre-eminent mixed methods researcher and professor emeritus from Gallaudet University in Washington, DC.

 **Researcher Spotlight 1.1**

Donna Mertens on preparing for the challenges of tackling complex mixed methods research problems

Mixed methods researchers are faced with challenges that emanate from advances in technology, accessibility to big data, and the need to be responsive to wicked problems such as economic inequality, climate change, violence, and conflict. Responsiveness to these challenges necessitates an understanding of complexity, politics, and ethics. The ubiquity of mobile phones and the collection of big data through other types of technological capture raises issues of privacy and use of data collected for purposes other than those of the researcher. The challenge of the contribution of mixed methods researchers to understanding and developing solutions to wicked problems is most salient. These problems are urgent and there is no agreement on what the appropriate solutions are. Solutions will require coordinated efforts across multiple systems. How can researchers design studies that are inclusive of the diverse stakeholders needed to make a meaningful contribution to solving these problems? How can they incorporate elements of coalition building and social activism in their designs so that there is an increased probability of action being taken that enhances social and environmental justice? What needs to change in the preparation of researchers who choose to accept the responsibility to move forward an agenda of human rights?

Over time it became apparent that others could benefit from access to many of the adaptive practices, and so the purpose of this practical book was born – to provide access to the integrative thinking and actions underpinning six adaptive practices comprising a complexity-sensitive approach to mixed methods research. These adaptive practices reflect a new way of thinking about and responding to conditions of complexity, and transform traditional mixed methods research practice tendencies. Adaptive practices drawing upon insights gleaned from a complexity lens are not something that needs to be left to a mixed methods research expert; rather, those who are just learning about mixed methods research sometimes have the advantage that they are not constrained by traditional wisdom.

Throughout the development of this book, each of the adaptive mixed methods research practices has been continually shaped by the experiences shared with me by students and colleagues, as well as by my own mixed methods research experiences. To that end, this book is a tribute to everyone who has influenced my integrative thinking and actions as a mixed methods researcher, research team facilitator, and instructor, and to those that have taught me more than they can imagine. The writing of this book was guided by a single compelling question: *How can our responses, as mixed methods researchers, to varying conditions of complexity shape how we frame problems, define contexts, describe integrations, develop interactions, and assess outcomes of a study?*

Purpose and Need for the Book

All research takes place under conditions of complexity – regardless of whether we, as researchers, recognize the dimensions of this complexity – and our responses to dynamic influences pose dilemmas and offer opportunities. All too often, our responses involve attempts to reduce, control, or simply ignore the effects of complexity, and these responses have become the basis for our traditional research practice tendencies over time. The purpose of this book is serve as a guide for researchers to assume responsibility for recognizing and making mindful decisions about how to deal with the varying conditions of complexity surrounding their research. This is because how the researcher chooses to initially diagnose their research along a continuum of varying conditions has important implications for the possible outcomes. The need for this book reflects trends I have observed and adopted in my own mixed methods research teaching and advising and builds upon the concept of messiness of mixed methods research. According to Plano Clark and Ivankova (2016, pp. 276–277), this concept 'recognizes the inherent complex, dynamic, and undetermined nature of mixed methods research practice'. Like others (e.g., Freshwater, 2007; Plano Clark & Ivankova, 2016; Seltzer-Kelly, Westwood, & Peña-Guzman, 2012), I consider that many sources of complexity cannot be fully anticipated or predicted yet have implications for mixed methods research practices. When asked how mixed methods researchers can optimize their societal contributions, I talk about the need for our training initiatives to move beyond seeking answers to known problems and to pursue some of the most challenging and pressing societal issues. I believe that integrative thinking and adaptive practices can boost innovation in the field of mixed methods research and its yet-to-be-realized potential. In order to move the field forward we must support a developmental perspective that positions learning as a progression towards becoming a competent mixed methods researcher and the needs of the learner as the starting point. To that end, this book is intended to set the stage for an individualized learning journey about complexity within mixed methods research because:

- The connections you make with the book content are personal to your experience.
- Your readiness to consider the ideas around complexity is individualized; no two people are the same.
- The agreement you voice about the adaptive practices I advance may be low or high; differences are to be expected and welcomed because it creates a richer learning environment.
- The consideration you give to the book content presents an opportunity for shifting the assumptions underpinning your perspective of the world; for many this is a paradigm shift and can take time to reconcile, so be patient.
- The feedback you offer is necessary to move us all forward in our thinking, so feel free to get in touch with me at cheryl@poth.ca.

Most surprising to me, and the catalyst for writing this book, is that no author has yet adopted a complexity perspective that advances guiding practices specifically for mixed methods research under conditions of complexity. A complexity perspective recognizes that research conditions call into question six traditional mainstays of mixed methods research practice tendencies: stability of the research conditions can be assumed; mixing purposes can be identified; contextual study boundaries can be defined; expertise for necessary capacities can be predetermined; integration procedures can be fixed; and indicators of outcome legitimacy can be anticipated. Complexity-sensitive practices are well established across diverse disciplines (e.g., business, evaluation, and health) and without exception require rethinking and indeed transforming traditional practices. Among the key benefits of complexity-sensitive approaches is the capacity to respond and adapt to evolving conditions. A complexity-sensitive approach has emerged as guiding my own mixed methods research practices because it affords new opportunities for me to be creative in my work on challenging and pressing societal issues.

The need for this book specifically focused on mixed methods research is based on my experiences as a mixed methods instructor, graduate supervisor, researcher, and research team member and the need to address the demand for guidance that is currently lacking. In particular, the six adaptive practices aim to mitigate dilemmas experienced under mixed methods research conditions that are typically considered to have greater complexity than researchers might encounter in either qualitative or quantitative research alone (further discussed in Chapter 2). Dilemmas associated with the research process become intensified when using mixed methods research for several reasons. First, the inherent need for data integration in a mixed methods design requires collecting and analysing *more data sources* and thus greater time and resources than is usually the case for either qualitative or quantitative research alone. Second, the generation of mixed insights previously inaccessible by either qualitative or quantitative research draws upon *diverse researcher expertise* and thus more often necessitates a research team to address the research problem. Third, on-demand *access to mixed methods-specific expertise* remains generally limited, and thus the researcher is often self-directing their own advocacy of the approach and development as a competent researcher. Thus, mixed methods researchers need a practical resource to support their responses to the dynamic conditions of complexity they encounter. To that end, this resource guides the transformations of established mixed methods research practices to be more complexity-sensitive (further discussed in Chapter 3).

The primary intent of this book is to provide access to the integrative thinking and actions underpinning six adaptive mixed methods research practices (described in Chapter 4–9). The description of the integrative thinking processes as preceding actions is essential, as these practices are not intended to be prescriptive; rather, the researcher must adapt to their unique research conditions. By describing examples of applying these practices, hopefully this book will open up the multiplicity of options suitable for engaging in your own mixed methods research process. With so many books available that are focused on designing and conducting mixed methods research, mixed methods researchers are sometimes inundated with choices yet lack access to the thinking necessary for guiding actions under varying conditions of complexity. My hope is that, by reading this book, you will gain an understanding of the usefulness of a complexity perspective for transforming mixed methods research practices under conditions of complexity. To that end, my aim is to instil a new way of thinking about the mixed methods research process reflective of possibilities rather than limited by current understandings and established practices. In Guiding Tip 1.1, an assistant professor at the University of Michigan (USA) whose interdisciplinary work fosters a real passion for methodology offers new ways of thinking about mixed methods research.

 **Guiding Tip 1.1**

Tim Guetterman advising how to navigate the complexity of mixed methods research

Mixed methods research requires flexible thinking and creativity, reflective openness to disparate views, and seeing the value of mixed methods. At least, that is what I found in my own research about characteristics of mixed methods researchers. It might be helpful to think about when navigating complexity!

Positioning Myself

You need to know something of my background training, life experiences, and influential mentors in order to understand how I came to conceptualize a complexity-sensitive approach to mixed methods research and to write this guiding resource for adaptive practices. About 25 years ago, while I was training as a natural scientist in the area known as biological (or life) science, I used the tools for quantitative research that were common to my field to generate observational and empirical evidence. Then, in the 1990s, as I advanced my interests in global travel and natural phenomena as a secondary school classroom teacher in international and domestic educational contexts, I became concerned with the reliance on test scores to represent accurate and useful evidence of student learning. This led me to frequently record written comments describing evidence of learning alongside the individual numeric scores for my students in my grade book. Although I was required to produce a numeric score twice each term for report cards, I was surprised to find myself referring almost exclusively to the written comments in my other communications with students and parents. Subsequently, as a programme evaluator, I became even more convinced of the limitations of numeric data to capture the individual outcomes from participation in social programmes. These experiences led me to realize the need to seek additional expertise about research if I was to advocate for policy changes.

When I pursued graduate studies in the areas of educational assessment, evaluation, and measurement, I became aware of the usefulness of qualitative research for understanding human behaviour and investigating the why and how. At the same time, as I began to question the capacity for traditional approaches to programme evaluation to meet the informational needs of organizations operating in complex environments, I began to read about innovative theories that were being adopted within the discipline of organizational development. Over the years, as I delved into the worlds of qualitative inquiry and complexity science, I was mentored by experts such as Drs. Lyn Shulha, Nancy Hutchinson, Rena Uptis, Robert Stake, and Rebecca Luce-Kapler. A key implication from my qualitative case study dissertation in 2008, titled *Promoting Evaluation Use within Dynamic Organizations: A Case Study Examining Evaluator Behavior*, was reframing developmental evaluator practices to be more attentive and responsive to the complexity inherent in organizational environments (Poth, 2008).

Significantly, I also encountered the emerging field involving mixing qualitative and quantitative data during my graduate studies and sought to gain expertise by enrolling in a two-day workshop with Dr. John W. Creswell at the Annual *Qualitative Research Summer Intensive* (see researchtalk.com). I consider that fate played an important part in my development as a mixed methods researcher because, since that initial workshop in 2005, John and several members of the global mixed methods community have played an important mentorship role for me as a new faculty member at the University of Alberta. In particular, four experiences were key to developing my confidence and capacity to write this book: returning to teach the workshop in 2012 that I had initially taken at the Annual *Qualitative Research Summer Intensive* at the invitation of Research Talk's founder, Ray Maietta; working with John Creswell on the fourth edition of *Qualitative Inquiry & Research Design* (Creswell & Poth, 2017); co-guest-editing two mixed methods research-focused special issues of the *International Journal of Qualitative Methods* with Tony Onwuegbuzie (Poth & Onwuegbuzie, 2015, 2016); and being involved as a founding member of the Mixed Methods International Research Association (for historical descriptions, see Mertens, 2014; Poth, Fetters, & Molina-Azorin, 2018). As a result of having benefited from such mentorship, I have sought to 'pay it forward' over the past decade as a mixed methods researcher, instructor, and supervisor. Whenever opportunities arise, I have wanted to enhance methodological training in qualitative, quantitative, and mixed methods research by increasing the relevance of course and workshop content, the engagement in learning activities, and the alignment of assessments with what researchers need to know and do. I am surprised by the lack of accessible and practical guidance for researchers across the developmental learning progression, and I see the greatest need in the field of mixed methods research. I consider myself to be a pragmatist in my choice of research approaches and am aware of my own preferences as I strive to generate insights in ways that are appropriate to the research conditions.

This background explains how I have come to identify myself as an applied researcher working across diverse fields and research approaches with a commitment to enhancing access to practical guidance for mixed methods researchers working under varying conditions of complexity. It also provides a rationale for my definition of mixed methods research as requiring the integration of different types of data – quantitative and qualitative – and assumes that the collective contribution mitigates inherent weaknesses in either type of data. In writing this book, I have drawn on my background expertise in qualitative, quantitative, and mixed methods research approaches as an instructor, programme evaluator, and researcher undertaking studies as a lead, as a member of cross-disciplinary research teams, and as a supervisory mentor. Throughout this book, I include examples and have purposefully selected the featured studies from varied disciplines and perspectives in an effort to represent the diversity of the field. While my primary area of specialization is education, I have made concerted efforts to include literature and my own experiences beyond the areas of social and health sciences. In Practice Alert 1.2, I consider the key influences to my evolving thinking which underpin my interactions as a mixed methods researcher, and I invite you to do the same. In so doing, I have enhanced my understandings of how my instructional approaches to mixed methods research courses and workshops have been influenced by my reflections on traditional approaches to teaching about designing and conducting mixed methods research.

 **Practice Alert 1.2**

What influences your interactions as a mixed methods researcher?

My teaching of mixed methods research has been closely tied with my thinking and practice. More than a decade ago – as I developed and began to facilitate mixed methods research courses, workshops, and seminars – my initial efforts focused on the foundational mixed methods research concepts, that is, *what* distinguishes mixed methods research. This was because these opportunities represented, for the vast majority of my participants, their first access to formalized learning about mixed methods research. To that end, many of the intended learning outcomes and instructional activities compared the distinctive characteristics of mixed methods research with either qualitative or quantitative research. This remains foundational to my approach to teaching introductory research methods, which is similar to the approach adopted by some texts to juxtapose mixed methods research with qualitative and quantitative research (e.g., Creswell, 2014; Johnson & Christensen, 2016). This approach continues to serve an important purpose of introducing researchers to mixed methods research as a third methodological option. The focus on distinguishing mixed methods research knowledge and skills is essential because it is simply not enough to be competent in qualitative and quantitative research.

My current teaching approaches with researchers who are familiar or even experienced with mixed methods research reflects a focus on applying understandings of the research process to varying conditions, that is, *how* to engage in mixed methods research and *why* use mixed methods for discovering innovative solutions. In so doing, my efforts not only respond to researchers' demand for opportunities to develop expertise specific to mixed methods but also develop the capacity to respond appropriately under varying conditions of complexity. This is similar to the approach adopted by some newer texts; for example, Creswell and Plano Clark (2018) and others in particular disciplines (in the health sciences, see Curry & Nunez-Smith, 2015) and guiding challenging aspects of the research process (e.g., integration using a particular mixed analysis strategy; see Bazeley, 2018).

Try this now – sketch your ideas about what have been the key influences in your thinking and interactions as a mixed methods researcher and consider the effects on your current research interests, your philosophical orientation to research, or your approaches to working with others.

Defining Conditions of Complexity and Innovations for Practice

To consider the conditions under which our traditional mixed methods research practice tendencies are an appropriate fit and the conditions under which these practices may be limiting and require innovations, we must begin by defining what we mean by these terms. So far in this chapter, I have referred to terms with differing frequency; whereas conditions of complexity have been used a number of times, innovation has been mentioned only sparingly. These differences are attributable to what I see as the 'overuse' and even 'misuse' of the term 'innovation' in much of my reading. Of course, you will note I was not deterred from using 'innovation' in the book title because of its importance to the purpose of the book.

The definitions and concepts I introduce here are further discussed in this first part of the book. A complexity-sensitive approach guides mixed methods researchers' responses to emergent and dynamic realities under conditions of complexity while engaging in the research process. I advance an organic mixed methods research process as including five interconnected, traditional research practice tendencies: defining problems; situating contexts; establishing capacities; determining designs; and generating insights. I conceptualize my approach as middle ground between the process-oriented and methodologically oriented approach to mixed methods research described by Plano Clark and Ivankova (2016). This is because I consider the logistical considerations in the dilemmas I had personally experienced while engaging in the practices involved in mixed methods research processes. In so doing, I draw upon the experiences of others in my consideration of the literature surrounding complexity and identifying the need for more adaptive practice tendencies. By understanding the indicators for varying conditions of complexity and the implications for mixed methods researchers we can recognize those conditions for which new, more adaptive practice tendencies are needed. In so doing, I set the stage for creating an openness in understanding the key characteristics of a complexity-sensitive approach to mixed methods research featured in this book. An open mind to new possibilities is featured in Guiding Tip 1.2, where the vice chancellor of the University of Western Australia (Perth) and professor of mental health at the University of Leeds (UK) offers advice for navigating the complexity of mixed methods research.

 Guiding Tip 1.2

Dawn Freshwater advising openness to discovering new approaches to mixed methods research

Mixed methods research is built on a fundamental platform of openness to discovery, alternative and equally valid views, and entertains kaleidoscopic lenses through which to understand what it is to be human. That openness has never been more crucial.

Continuum of Complexity Conditions

You may already be familiar with some of the terms that have been advanced in the literature to describe the varying conditions under which research and evaluation can take place: simple, complicated, and complex. While I will use them here for illustrative purposes to begin our conversation, it is logical that I refute the use of these terms in this book because of my position that *all* research takes place under conditions of complexity. Instead I favour describing conditions along a continuum: low complexity, moderate complexity, and high complexity. Thus, I use 'low', 'moderate', and 'high' in this book to differentiate among varying levels of conditions of complexity. Examine Table 1.1 to learn about the indicators along the continuum of complexity conditions for six mainstays of mixed methods research practice. Our understandings of these indicators are naturally evolving, and the six traditional

Table 1.1 Indicators for continuum of complexity conditions for six mixed methods research practices

Research practices	Indicators for continuum of complexity conditions		
	Low	**Moderate**	**High**
Assessing conditions	Assumptions of stability and evidence of predictable influences	Some assumptions of stability and evidence of somewhat predictable influences	No assumption of stability and evidence of nonlinear influences
Articulating purposes	Identifiable mixing purpose and study need for integration can be grounded in literature	Discoverable mixing purpose and study need for integration can be somewhat grounded in literature	Yet-to-be-known mixing purpose and study need for integration can be difficult to pinpoint beyond innovation
Situating contexts	Definable and study boundaries describable	Generally definable and some study boundaries describable	Yet-to-be-defined systems and few boundaries describable
Establishing capacities	Identifiable expertise based on predetermined contributions	Typically known expertise based on collective contributions	Yet-to-be-known expertise based on emergent contributions
Implementing designs	High agreement for integration procedures and implemented as planned	Some agreement for integration procedures and some changes to plans during implementation	Yet-to-be-known integration procedures and implementation plans
Evaluating insights	Knowable outcomes produced by predictable legitimation strategies	Generally knowable outcomes produced by recognizable legitimation strategies	Unknowable outcomes produced by yet-to-be-known legitimation strategies

research practices may not capture all the tendencies that others have noted are important for mixed methods research.

In the literature, *simple* is a term used to describe conditions where 'knowledge and experience tell you what to do and there is widespread agreement about what to do' (Patton, 2010, p. 86). If a researcher assesses their study as having **low complexity**, several conditions have been met: the assumption of stability and evidence of predictable influences; the mixing purpose is identifiable and the study need for integration can be grounded in the literature; the research contexts are definable and describable; the necessary capacities involve identifiable expertise and predetermined contributions; the research design has high agreement for integration procedures and is implemented as planned; and the research outcomes are knowable and are generated using predictable integration strategies. In my experience, few studies are consistently assessed at low complexity, yet examples of such research problems are characterized as having established approaches for attaining predictable outcomes such as to distinguish among low- and high-ability readers. The study might rely on researchers with known expertise in using standardized assessments and experimental designs. In so doing, these procedures could be used again with a comparable study population within the same study boundaries with generally predictable results.

Complicated is a term used in the literature to describe conditions that are less predictable and whose outcomes and procedures for attaining the outcomes are less certain but still able to be known. **Moderate complexity** often dictates that 'more than one area of expertise is needed and these must therefore be coordinated and integrated' (Patton, 2010, p. 87). For a researcher to assess their study as having moderate complexity, many of the following conditions are evident: some assumptions of stability and evidence of somewhat predictable influences; the mixing purpose is discoverable and the study need for integration can be somewhat grounded in literature; the research contexts are generally definable and some study boundaries describable; the necessary capacities are typically known expertise based on collective contributions; the research design has some agreement for integration procedures and some changes to plans during implementation; and the research outcomes are generally knowable and are generated using recognizable integration strategies. In my experience, most studies are assessed as moderately complex, and examples of such research problems tend to have evidence-based approaches for attaining the knowable outcomes, such as teaching someone to swim. The study might integrate diverse methods and disciplines to reach slightly different, yet recognizable outcomes. In so doing, these procedures could be adapted to compare across different approaches to swimming within similar study populations with somewhat predictable results.

Complex is a term used in the literature to describe conditions characterized by unpredictable outcomes and 'high uncertainty and high social conflict ... so many factors and variables are interacting, many of them are not only unknown but *unknowable*' (Patton, 2010, p. 90; emphasis in original). If a researcher assesses their study as having **high complexity,** several of the following conditions have been met: no assumption of stability and evidence of nonlinear influences; the mixing purposes are yet to be known and the study need for integration may be difficult to pinpoint beyond innovation; the research contexts are yet to be defined and few boundaries describable; the necessary capacities involve yet-to-be-known expertise based on emergent contributions; the research designs are yet-to-be-known integration procedures and implementation plans; and the research outcomes are unknowable and are generated using yet-to-be-known integration strategies. In my experience, few studies have been consistently assessed as high complexity; more commonly there is a mix across levels, yet as our practices become more complexity-sensitive, it is natural (and desirable) for the field to see an increased uptake of studies assessed as highly complex. High-complexity research problems require innovative approaches for tackling understudied yet highly pressing issues such as homelessness because of the many social and health factors that may be interacting with other factors that we have yet to understand. The expertise and procedures will be vastly different each time, with unknowable results.

A highly complex research problem that my colleague Jacqueline Pei and I are pursuing along with members of our Alberta Community and Clinical Research Team (ACCERT) involves examining the contributing factors and lived experiences of complex individuals involved in housing programmes, and specifically for individuals affected with fetal alcohol spectrum disorder (FASD). FASD is an umbrella term used to classify a range of disabilities caused by prenatal alcohol exposure, including physical, cognitive, emotional, and behavioural deficits (Pei, Denys, Hughes, & Rasmussen, 2011; Poth, Pei, Job, & Wyper, 2014). In the literature they are considered a particularly 'difficult-to-house' population because they can be initially 'hard to reach' and also hard to maintain in housing, often described as high risk for losing their housing status. You can imagine that this study requires generating understandings of the social and health needs of this population as well as increasing knowledge regarding the existing health, community social services, and educational (among others!) supports for supporting success with this complex group. Among the challenges for us in beginning this work is how to begin. In the following chapters I will continue to share details about this ongoing work. Consider the challenges experienced by a Commonwealth scholar from the UK and doctoral candidate at Auckland University of Technology (New Zealand) when tackling complex problems requiring drawing upon diverse disciplinary and methodological expertise, described in Researcher Spotlight 1.2.

 **Researcher Spotlight 1.2**

Amrit Dencer-Brown on mitigating the challenges of interdisciplinary mixed methods research under high-complexity conditions

The main challenge for me as a mixed methods researcher is engaging with academics in an inter- or cross-disciplinary fashion at my university. I am part of an Applied Ecology Institute, which generally focuses on pure science. There is not a big working space for mixed methods research, so I need to find ways to present my research in a context that is accessible to people working in quite distinctive and separate areas of research. This year is the first year we have run a social ecology course, and mixed methods fits very well into this research discipline. I hope that we have given our undergraduates a broader perspective on ways to carry out research using a variety of techniques that can span different disciplines. I am also part of two research groups conducting mixed methods research, so I guess we are paving the way for the future of mixed methods research at our university. I think it is very important for scientists to see a more holistic and integrated way of addressing complex problems through mixed methods research and for further validation of this emerging research field.

Niche for Complexity-Sensitive Approach

The limitations of the terms 'simple', 'complicated' and 'complex' become apparent when you consider your own life experiences. I draw upon my diverse teaching and research experiences to recognize that these examples of problems are simply different variations of complex situations. Throughout this book you will see the terms 'low complexity', 'moderate complexity' and 'high complexity' used to describe the varying mixed methods research conditions and my emphasis on the need to initially assess the research conditions before anything else. This initial step is essential for being able to gauge the extent to which the traditional mixed methods research practice tendencies are appropriate for the particular study conditions or whether new, adaptive practices will better position the researcher to respond to the dynamic influences characteristic of more complex study conditions. By recognizing the inherent complexity in our studies and adopting the six adaptive research practice tendencies, I model creative and integrative thinking that creates the potential for enhanced authenticity of research reporting. This is because we tend to report only what happened rather than the thinking and actions involved throughout the research. By documenting the research process and the responses to changing conditions, I am able to be more reflective of the realities in which researchers operate and create accounts that are more authentic and useful for guiding researchers. Furthermore, the principles of complexity science as a theoretical framework guide the researcher to make sense of the dilemmas, conditions, and outcomes related to their experiences, the present opportunities, and the future possibilities.

I define the niche for a complexity-sensitive mixed methods research approach as providing practical guidance for researchers under varying conditions of complexity and supporting **innovation** in mixed methods research in six important ways:

- It promotes innovations in *researcher responsiveness* under varying complexity of mixed methods research conditions.
- It encourages innovations in *mixing purposes* when framing complex mixed methods research problems.
- It boosts innovations in *system considerations* when defining interrelated mixed methods research contexts.
- It inspires innovations in *design creations* when realizing agile mixed methods research procedures.
- It stimulates innovations in *capacity decisions* when developing emergence in mixed methods research interactions.
- It motivates innovations in *quality indicators* when assessing integration of mixed methods research outcomes.

In this first part of the book (Chapters 2 and 3), I recount how I came to identify the adaptive research practice tendencies that comprise a complexity-sensitive approach to mixed methods research through integrative thinking with complexity science. Through describing the theoretical underpinnings of complexity science, I engage in integrative thinking to advance an approach to mixed methods research that goes beyond the usual attempts to reduce, control, or simply ignore the effects of complexity. In Part II (Chapter 4–9), I will guide you in revisiting your underlying assumptions and in turn adapt some mixed methods research practice tendencies to the conditions encountered and thus adopt a more complexity-sensitive approach. Finally in Part III I will provide some closing commentary and ideas for future directions.

Audiences for the Book

This book is written for those with various roles and expertise in mixed methods research. The common element is an interest in adapting practices for mixed methods research under conditions of complexity. It may be that some of you recognize the demand for complexity-sensitive practices from your own experiences. These include (but are not limited to) the following:

- *Graduate (master's and doctoral) students* – the book could be used as a core text for graduate-level classes, mixed methods-focused workshops or independent learning. Examples of courses include introductory research courses focused specifically on mixed methods research or more generally on designs, or advanced research courses focused on mixed methods research, writing proposals, and programme evaluation. Because of its usefulness for guiding the pursuit of more complex mixed methods research problems, the text could be used throughout and beyond a graduate programme.
- *Instructors of mixed methods research courses or workshops* – the book could be used as the organizing framework for intended learning outcomes, as a guide to assessment methods, and as a text that can familiarize participants to the five complexity-sensitive mixed methods research practices.

- *Researchers who are relatively new to mixed methods research* – the book could be used to enhance addressing some of society's puzzling problems after reading an introductory text or participating in an introductory course, workshop or seminar and support planning for next steps.
- *Experienced mixed methods researchers who are familiar with the knowledge and skills required for planning, conducting, and reporting mixed methods research* – the book could be used to identify next steps in their learning progression beyond established practices by those who have already engaged in a study or the planning for one.
- *Mixed methods research team members* – the book could be used by those seeking practical guidance for mixed methods research teams tackling research under conditions of complexity and further developing their integrative capacity.
- *Research associations and communities embracing mixed methods research* – the book could be used to guide training, certificate programmes, and designations by providing members and instructors with a practice framework on which to base their professional learning initiatives.
- *Research managers who commission, supervise, and translate mixed methods research for policy, practitioner, and academic audiences* – the book could be used to guide learning about mixed methods research by organizational and advocacy team members.
- *Researchers who review mixed methods research grants or publications* – the book could be used to introduce the field of mixed methods research and to assess the quality of studies pursuing research under conditions of complexity in mixed methods research plans and reports.

Organization and Learning Features

This book is presented in three parts, to reflect the practical nature of the text. Part I (Chapters 1–3) introduces the essential foundations for this mixed methods research book focused on innovations under conditions of complexity, and begins with this chapter orienting the reader to the book. Chapter 2 familiarizes the reader with the usefulness of and essential characteristics of mixed methods research, phases and practices involved in an organic process, and introduces the dilemmas and demands for innovations and innovators under conditions of complexity. Chapter 3 describes the theoretical underpinnings for a complexity-sensitive mixed methods research approach through examining the opportunities for integrative thinking with complexity and introduces the six adaptive practices for guiding researchers. Each of the six chapters in Part II (Chapters 4–9) then focuses on one of the adaptive mixed methods research practices. For each practice, I provide access to the integrative thinking underpinning the complexity-sensitive approach and then describe the actions for responding with a complexity lens throughout the research process. The adaptive mixed methods research practices involve diagnosing the complexity of research conditions, framing complex research problems, defining interrelated research contexts, developing emergence in research interactions, realizing agile research integrations, and assessing the quality of research outcomes. The book concludes with Part III (Chapter 10) advancing onward considerations for complexity-sensitive mixed methods research focused on its distinctive niche, potential challenges, and final guidance. To optimize the design features in this book, you should not feel restricted to reading the chapters in order, but instead read ahead and return as you are compelled.

The learning features included in this book are intended to describe an approach that is relevant, accessible, and practical. Each chapter begins by outlining the key questions and terms the chapter addresses. The key questions have a practical focus, identifying the skills you need and the knowledge necessary for executing those skills. The end-of-chapter check-in guides you in assessing the extent to which you have developed the intended knowledge and skills. Embedded within each chapter are practice alerts – opportunities for you to apply understandings to your own mixed methods research studies based on key learnings from my own perspective. Researcher spotlights provide you with access to the experiences and viewpoints of several prominent and emerging mixed methods researchers about key pressing and future challenges and possible ways we can better prepare mixed methods researchers for working under conditions of complexity. Guiding tips offer succinct advice from a variety of perspectives for navigating the complexity of mixed methods research. Visual organizers are used throughout the book for two purposes: to provide a 'roadmap' in advance of a written description, and to provide a summary of text. Featured complex mixed methods research studies are introduced later in this first chapter and revisited throughout the book as a means of bridging theory with article examples purposefully selected to represent a range of conditions of complexity. Readers should note that words in bold indicate the first time a key term is used throughout the book. Definitions of the key terms can be accessed through the Glossary (Appendix A). Words in italics indicate either a key term that has already appeared but is also important to the current chapter, or words or phrases highlighted for emphasis.

Each chapter concludes with a summary of key chapter concepts and a compilation of further reading recommendations so that you can access additional information and different perspectives essential for in-depth understanding. In the selections, I try to provide a global and interdisciplinary perspective. It is my intention that this book be as inclusive as possible in terms of language used, study populations, methodological approaches, and modes of inquiry. That said, space and time limitations mean that the breadth of what can be covered has often been limited in this text to those designs and methods that are most frequently used to generate qualitative and quantitative data. Readers, and especially students, should not feel limited by what is included. Rather, I hope this book provides a platform for further reading.

Introducing ways of assessing conditions of complexity and mixed methods research foundations, describing the integrative thinking and actions underpinning six complexity-sensitive practices, and advancing onward considerations for complexity-sensitive mixed methods research are essential in providing a resource that is relevant, accessible, and practical. My aim for this book is that it should support informed use of a complexity-sensitive approach to mixed methods research. The adaptive practices do not prescribe a path, but rather promote understanding that conditions of complexity are unique to each mixed methods study. Generating innovation in the form of mixed insights, integrative interactions, adaptive practices, and novel designs through the use of a complexity-sensitive approach to mixed methods research may help us solve some of society's most pressing problems. Let us get started on the mixed methods research journey together.

Selection of Six Featured Mixed Methods Studies

This book features six mixed methods studies that address the practice gap in many textbooks. These also provide authentic examples of published articles representing a wide variety of research topics, authors, problems, designs, and locales. In all of these studies, the research took place under a continuum of complexity conditions. In varying ways, the need for adaptive mixed methods research practices is reflected in each of the studies and provides a catalyst on which to advocate for complexity-sensitive approaches to mixed methods research. These six studies also represent research topics and problems that draw upon a range of disciplines, including education, justice, psychology, gender, technology, and health. I have deliberately chosen articles not authored by well-known mixed methods researchers. I wanted to feature studies that could be seen as feasible to conceptualize, realize, and publish, rather than ones by the superstars of mixed methods research. The articles represent diverse research locales (studies took place on six continents) and include the gamut of mixed methods research designs and data sources. Four articles appeared in the *Journal of Mixed Methods Research*, which is not a surprising source, given the rigorous peer-review process I know at first hand as an associate editor. None of these featured studies should be considered exemplars of a complexity-sensitive approach to mixed methods research – each one was chosen because it includes some traditional mixed methods research practice tendencies and provides the opportunity to demonstrate how a particular adaptive practice discussed in the book might take place. These articles are readily available on the companion website for this book. Table 1.2 summarizes the diversity of each study's details of research topics, disciplines, locales, and questions. A narrative summary can be read in the further readings section of this chapter, and in-depth discussions are embedded within subsequent chapters of this book.

Table 1.2 Summary of overall details for the six featured mixed methods studies

Study Reference	Research Topics	Research Disciplines	Research Locale	Research Question
Chui, W. H., & Cheng, K. K.-Y. (2017). Perceptions of fairness and satisfaction in lawyer–client interactions among young offenders in Hong Kong.	Law clients	Justice, Psychology	Hong Kong	How do young offenders perceive fairness and satisfaction towards their lawyers in Hong Kong's criminal justice system?
Colditz, J. B., Welling, J., Smith, N. A., James, A. E., & Primack, B. A. (2017). World vaping day: Contextualizing vaping culture in online social media using a mixed methods approach.	Vaping culture	Health, Technology	Global	What can contextualizing vaping culture in social media add to our understanding?
Dickson, V., Lee, C. S., & Riegel, B. (2011). How do cognitive function and knowledge affect heart failure self-care?	Heart care	Health	US	How does cognitive function and knowledge affect heart failure self-care?
Strudsholm, T., Meadows, L. M., Robinson Vollman, A., Thurston, W. E., & Henderson, R. (2016). Using mixed methods to facilitate complex, multiphased health research.	Leadership competencies	Health, Leadership	Canada	What public health leadership competencies could apply to public health practice across the country?

Study Reference	Research Topics	Research Disciplines	Research Locale	Research Question
Taylor, L. K., Merrilees, C. E., Corkalo Biruski, D., Ajdukovic, D., & Cummings, E. M. (2017). Complexity of risk: Mixed-methods approach to understanding youth risk and insecurity in postconflict settings.	Postconflict risk	Psychology, Education	Croatia	How does political violence affect youth, particularly in postconflict settings?
Zea, M. C., Aguilar-Pardo, M., Betancourt, F., Reisen, C. A., & Gonzales, F. (2014). Mixed methods research with internally displaced Colombian gay and bisexual men and transwomen.	Safe places	Gender, Health	Colombia	What does developing safe places involve for internally displaced Colombian gay and bisexual men and transwomen?

CHAPTER CHECK-IN

1   Can you 'see' how this book is distinguished from other books in its focus on adaptive practices associated with a complexity-sensitive approach to mixed methods research?

   • Compare how the purpose for this book differs from at least two other mixed methods resources.
   • Compare how the audience for this book differs from at least two other mixed methods resources.

2   Can you begin to conceptualize the usefulness of a complexity perspective for mixed methods researchers under varying research conditions?

   • Consider research you have done or are planning to do. Would the problem pursued be categorized as simple, complicated, or complex?
   • Consider the extent of your agreement with the author's assertion that 'all research should be considered as undertaken in varying conditions of complexity'.

3   Can you begin to distinguish among the indicators for the continuum of complexity conditions for the six mixed methods practices in Table 1.1?

   • Consider research you have done or are planning to do. Would the research conditions be considered low, moderate, or high complexity?
   • How might your mixed methods research practices be adapted under conditions of higher complexity?

4   Can you identify differences and similarities across the six featured studies in Table 1.2?

   • Compare the studies in terms of research topics, disciplines, and locales.

.... **KEY CHAPTER CONCEPTS**

This chapter orients the reader to this book and introduces the focus on complexity in mixed methods research, positions the need for this book, defines conditions of complexity and innovation, and explains the book organization and learning features. This orientation is foundational for introducing the demand for boosting innovations in mixed methods research discussed in the next chapter.

.... **FURTHER READINGS**

The following are the six featured studies that are readily available on the companion website for the textbook indicated with an asterisk. I strongly suggest you read them now because by referring to this series of six studies throughout the book, I avoid lengthy descriptions of the study details.

*Chui, W. H., & Cheng, K. K.-Y. (2017). Perceptions of fairness and satisfaction in lawyer–client interactions among young offenders in Hong Kong. *Journal of Mixed Methods Research, 11*(2), 266–285. doi: 10.1177/1558689815593834.

Drawing upon procedure justice theory, Wing Hong Chui and Kevin Kwok-Yin Cheng use an explanatory mixed methods design to examine the perceptions of fairness and satisfaction that young offenders have towards their lawyers in the Hong Kong criminal justice system. Particularly noteworthy is the article description of the legal profession and the local study context.

*Colditz, J. B., Welling, J., Smith, N. A., James, A. E., & Primack, B. A. (2017). World vaping day: Contextualizing vaping culture in online social media using a mixed methods approach. *Journal of Mixed Methods Research*. doi: 10.1177/1558689817702753.

The authors use a convergent parallel mixed methods design to contextualize vaping culture in social media. This article capitalized on both the quantitative breadth and qualitative depth of primary Twitter data globally, and used an innovative integration approach.

*Dickson, V., Lee, C. S., & Riegel, B. (2011). How do cognitive function and knowledge affect heart failure self-care? *Journal of Mixed Methods Research, 5*(2), 167–189. doi: 10.1177/1558689811402355.

The authors used a concurrent triangulation mixed methods design to explore how knowledge and cognitive function influence the self-care of 41 adult Colombian heart failure patients. This article is noteworthy for its conceptualization of self-care as a naturalistic decision-making process and for its cross-case integrated findings from in-depth interviews and standardized surveys.

*Strudsholm, T., Meadows, L. M., Robinson Vollman, A., Thurston, W. E., & Henderson, R. (2016). Using mixed methods to facilitate complex, multiphased health research. *International Journal of Qualitative Methods, 15*(1), 1–11. doi: 10.1177/1609406915624579.

The authors illustrate the benefits of using a multiphase mixed methods design to identify public health leadership competencies that could be applied to public health practice across Canada. The article is noteworthy for its discussion of the challenges and opportunities encountered in its use of literature review, online survey, focus group webinars, and modified Delphi.

*Taylor, L. K., Merrilees, C. E., Corkalo Biruski, D., Ajdukovic, D., & Cummings, E. M. (2017). Complexity of risk: Mixed-methods approach to understanding youth risk and insecurity in postconflict settings. *Journal of Adolescent Research, 32*(5), 585–613. doi: 10.1177/0743558416684950.

The authors use an exploratory sequential mixed methods design to identify community-level risk factors and related emotional insecurity responses among youth in Vukovar, Croatia. The article reports how the initial focus group discussions with parents and adolescents were further explained by the quantitative youth surveys.

*Zea, M. C., Aguilar-Pardo, M., Betancourt, F., Reisen, C. A., & Gonzales, F. (2014). Mixed methods research with internally displaced Colombian gay and bisexual men and transwomen. *Journal of Mixed Methods Research, 8*(3), 212–221. doi: 10.1177/1558689814527941.

The multinational, interdisciplinary research team drew upon the framework of communicative action to explore the subjective, objective, and social worlds of displaced Colombian gay and bisexual men and transwomen through life history interviews and surveys. The article is noteworthy for its description of the research team's promotion of social change through egalitarian dialogue.

Apply your mixed methods knowledge with videos, activities, SAGE journal articles and project templates at **https://study.sagepub.com/poth**

2

POSITIONING DEMAND FOR INNOVATION IN MIXED METHODS RESEARCH

.... KEY CHAPTER QUESTIONS

By the end of this chapter, you will be able to answer the following questions:

- Why use mixed methods research?
- What distinguishes mixed methods research?
- What key practice dilemmas emerge under higher-complexity mixed methods research conditions?
- What demands can be met by innovations and innovators in mixed methods research?
- What do we know about the featured mixed methods research studies for this book?

.... NEW CHAPTER TERMS

- Grand challenges
- Quantitative data
- Integrated findings
- Research design
- Integration procedures
- Research outcomes
- Methodological congruence
- Research problem
- Methodological rigour

- Research purpose
- Mixed insights
- Research question
- Mixing purpose
- Research team
- Organic mixed methods research process
- Research topic
- Qualitative data
- Wicked problems

This chapter explores a foundational question for this book: *What practice dilemmas emerge under conditions of increased complexity and what innovations in mixed methods research are recognized and warranted?* Writing this book has been a journey inspired by my desire to help students and colleagues meet emerging demands for innovation by harnessing the potential of mixed methods research under varying conditions of complexity. What I had seen and experienced over a decade as an instructor, researcher, and supervisor was the need to attend to the complexities inherent in the mixed methods research process. All too often, our responses involve attempts to reduce, control, or simply ignore the effects of complexity rather than revisiting our assumptions, adapting our approach, or monitoring our conditions. Reconceptualizing the mixed methods process as organic helps us as researchers to consider the process as more creative, evolving, and emergent than it is sometimes portrayed. This is important as we explore the possibilities for mixed methods research under conditions of complexity and not just its current use in the literature.

Work on this chapter was informed by the dilemmas described to me by students and colleagues as well as my own experiences as a researcher. Considering the key practice dilemmas was essential, because others may only realize the challenges faced under conditions of complexity once they are involved in the mixed methods research. To that end, I have come to consider those effective under conditions of complexity to be 'adaptive mixed methods researchers'. This understanding emerged from having traced many of the challenges the mixed methods researchers experience to a lack of guidance on how to respond appropriately under conditions of complexity. After considering the wide variability and unpredictable nature of research conditions I had experienced, a predetermined response was not possible.

The dilemma I then faced was how to guide others in responding under varying conditions of complex mixed methods research.

What I came to realize was the importance of attending to and recognizing changeable research conditions as the 'new' normal. This represented a clear change from the assumption of stability, and it aligned with many of my recent experiences. In deciding to embrace this new mindset and write this book, I wanted to ensure the book was accessible to all mixed methods researchers – regardless of expertise or experience. To that end, an introductory chapter was necessary to consider the conditions under which our traditional mixed methods research practice tendencies are an appropriate fit and the conditions under which these practices may be limiting and require rethinking and innovation. Before we begin I wish to recognize that mixed methods research is a diverse field whose contributors have generated many definitions, frameworks, and practices for guiding how to think about and conduct mixed methods research; for example, skills training, suitability of problems, fit of designs, and evaluation of quality. As a global mixed methods research community, we continue to benefit from this diversity, yet from a practical viewpoint I am told by novice mixed methods researchers that presenting many diverse perspectives also creates confusion for some. To that end I acknowledge that, by focusing this chapter on particular authors or trends as representative of predominant tendencies in traditional mixed methods research practice, I am bound to overgeneralize and narrow the viewpoint. I strongly recommend this book as a catalyst for further exploration of additional perspectives also valuable to consider. This reference point is necessary to realize the purpose of this book, to advance guiding practices for integrative thinking with complexity, because some common ground in mixed methods research is necessary to build from. As a starting point, let us establish some of the foundational ideas about the field of mixed methods research for this book. For some, this will be new information; for others, it can provide essential review and orientation.

Why Use Mixed Methods Research?

There is little doubt that the use of mixed methods research has increased during the past four decades, and every indicator suggests further increases to come. This global trend is well documented in studies measuring the prevalence of mixed methods research across a variety of disciplines and journals (Molina-Azorin & Fetters, 2016). The recognition of mixed methods research as a field worthy of attention and the acceptance of mixed methods research as a distinct approach is evidenced by its increased global use across disciplines, nations, and in projects funded by diverse sectors (Creswell & Plano Clark, 2018). Many factors contribute to the growing global use of mixed methods research (Creswell & Plano Clark, 2018; Hesse-Biber, 2015; Plano Clark & Ivankova, 2016). Below, I discuss factors that I have witnessed at first hand and considered integral during the writing of this book.

Enhanced Advocacy of the Value and Contributions

While we can confidently state that the use of mixed methods research is well established, ask many researchers, 'Why use mixed methods research?' and you will surely hear different answers. The value and contributions of a mixed methods approach have been variously defined by researchers, diversely associated with design typologies, and differently linked to disciplinary origins. Among the numerous mixed methods research contributions that have been recognized in the literature, those that I consider essential involve the generation of more data evidence, the ability to offset weaknesses in one type of data, and the capacity to tackle problems that were previously inaccessible by either quantitative or qualitative research approaches alone (Creswell & Plano Clark, 2018). For this book, I verify the value and potential of these and other contributions already identified and suggest that we are only just beginning to value and realize the potential of mixed methods research contributions. The rationale underlying my working definition of mixed methods research reflects this thinking and emphasizes the design of research to generate previously inaccessible insights from the integration of qualitative and quantitative data: mixed methods research requires the integration of both **quantitative data** and **qualitative data**, and assumes that their collective contribution mitigates inherent weaknesses in either type of data (Poth, 2018a). I recognize the uniqueness of contributions of qualitative and quantitative outcomes to the integration procedures: whereas qualitative data generates text- and image-based evidence, quantitative data generates numeric-based evidence. Thus, my rationale for using mixed methods is focused on the **mixing purposes** addressing the problem, the **integration procedures** guiding the design, and the **mixed insights** providing access to novel contributions. The requirement to integrate both qualitative and quantitative data differentiates mixed methods research (in my view) from multimethod research. Others use the terms interchangeably – see Greene (2015) for an excellent discussion – whereas I consider multimethod research to include, for example, more than one source of qualitative data.

Like others, I consider the significance of the problem being pursued and intended outcomes of the research from the integration of qualitative and qualitative data when planning mixed methods research (Creswell & Plano Clark, 2018). This is because conveying the unique contributions of the mixed insights generated by a mixed methods research approach plays an essential role in convincing others of its value and advocacy for its use. It is thus important to recognize the potential contributions of a mixed methods research approach and convey the advantages of the mixed insights as the **research outcomes**. As the acceptance and use of mixed methods research have permeated disciplines, awareness of the potential contributions of mixed methods research for addressing more complex research problems has greatly increased. In the third edition of *Designing and Conducting Mixed Methods Research*, the authors, Creswell and Plano Clark (2018, p. xxi), note: 'Today, from our workshops, presentations, and classes, we know that people no longer wonder what this approach is and question whether it is a legitimate model of inquiry. Their interests now have shifted towards the procedures of research – how to conduct a mixed methods study – and to the value mixed methods adds to their knowledge about complex problems.'

Researchers are increasingly being called upon to tackle the **wicked problems** and **grand challenges** that occur in today's complex world (Mertens et al., 2016a). Wicked problems are those that 'involve multiple interacting systems, are replete with social and institutional uncertainties, and for which only imperfect knowledge about their nature and solutions exists' (Mertens, 2015, p. 3). Grand challenges arise from conditions of 'environmental degradation and climate change, poverty, health, social and economic inequality, and geopolitical instability, among many others' (Mertens et al., 2016b, p. 12). In his 2005 book, *The Working Poor: Invisible in America*, David Shipler provides a masterful description of a wicked problem:

Every problem magnifies the impact of the others, and all are so tightly interlocked that one reversal can produce a chain reaction with results far distant from the original causes. A rundown apartment can exacerbate a child's asthma, which leads to a call for an ambulance, which generates a medical bill that cannot be paid, which ruins a credit record, which hikes the interest rate on an auto loan, which forces the purchase of an unreliable used car, which jeopardizes a mother's punctuality at work, which limits her promotions and earning capacity, which confines her to poor housing.

Shipler, like many others, highlights that such problems cannot be solved with traditional responses:

If problems are interlocking then so too solutions must be ...: a job alone is not enough. Medical insurance alone is not enough. Good housing alone is not enough. Reliable transportation, careful family budgeting, effective parenting, effective schooling are not enough when each is achieved in isolation from the rest.

Shipler alludes to the background influences of poverty on financial, psychological, and personal aspects as well as past and present societal contributors. Thus, poverty represents a highly complex research problem, and as our understandings of the interplay of multiple known and unknown dynamic factors naturally evolves, it seems obvious that mixed methods research is well positioned to contribute to the understandings through the integration of qualitative and quantitative data inherent in mixed methods research.

Improved Access to Learning and Mentoring Opportunities

Along with increased interest in mixed methods research, there exists a pressing demand for building mixed methods research capacity. While general consensus exists that adopting mixed methods as a way of thinking about and doing research requires skills beyond those required by qualitative and quantitative research, less agreement and indeed a dearth of evidence-informed practices exist for guiding how we develop our own expertise as mixed methods researchers and create effective learning opportunities for those new to the field. The lack of access to learning and mentoring opportunities is well documented in the literature as a pressing challenge to those wanting to pursue mixed methods research (Creswell & Plano Clark, 2018).

From my own experience, access to opportunities for learning from and being mentored by experts has been foundational to my development as a mixed methods researcher. Indeed, the increasing presence of communities drawing together mixed methods researchers for learning, mentoring, and networking purposes is important for the field. I know of many special or topical interest groups specific to mixed methods that have emerged within diverse professional associations that might already be familiar to you. Examples are the Mixed Methods Special Interest groups of the Australian and New Zealand Academy of Management (https://www.anzam.org/research/special-interest-groups-sigs/) and the International Society for Quality of Life Research (http://www.isoqol.org/special-interest-groups). Other standalone, diverse researcher-based working groups are emerging, such as the Special Education Mixed Methodology Research Consortium. In Practice Alert 2.1, I consider the role of mixed methods researcher communities for providing networking and learning opportunities, and I invite you to do the same. In so doing, I provide a framework for thinking about your individual learning needs and goals and encourage your investigation of the available options.

 Practice Alert 2.1

What learning and mentoring opportunities can communities of mixed methods researchers offer?

Opportunities for interacting with others and engaging in experiential learning are essential activities for developing proficiency as a mixed methods researcher (Guetterman, 2017). One piece of sage advice I heeded early in my career was to join professional associations in my field as an educational evaluator and researcher. I cannot emphasize enough the benefits provided by many associations, ranging from accessing field-specific information (current developments, upcoming jobs, and training opportunities) to networking (in person at conferences and electronically through discussion forums). Some organizations such as the University of Michigan (www.mixedmethods.org) and Research Talk (www.researchtalk.com) in the USA provide week-long workshops for developing mixed methods research skills, whereas others such as the International Insitute of Qualitative Methods (www.ualberta.ca/international-institute-for-qualitative-methodology) at the University of Alberta (Canada) and the Mixed Methods International Research Association (www.mmira.org) offer single-day workshops concurrently with conferences.

Try this now – sketch your ideas about what you want to learn about mixed methods research, and then explore what learning and networking opportunities your professional associations offer and target new ones to consider attending.

As the acceptance and use of mixed methods research has permeated disciplines, awareness of and discussions about the potential contributions of mixed methods research have greatly increased. It has been encouraging in my experience to see how researchers are 'reaching' across previous disciplinary and methodological boundaries. This is certainly the case among the members of the Mixed Methods International Research Association (MMIRA), established in 2013 (for historical descriptions, see Mertens, 2014; Poth et al., 2018). Members of the mixed methods research community (and others) have found themselves interacting for a common reason, such as to advance design typologies, instructional practices, or quality criteria. My own community of researchers was created by participating as a member and then a board member of the MMIRA (www.mmira.org), the mixed methods research special interest group of the American Educational Research Association (http://www.aera.net/SIG158/Mixed-Methods-Research-SIG-158), the Mixed Methods Evaluation topical interest group of the American Evaluation Association (http://comm.eval.org/mixedmethodsevaluation/home) and as a member of the online mixed methods forum Methodspace (http://www.methodspace.com/).

Several researchers highlight recent developments in understandings of the skills required for conducting mixed methods, accessibility of mixed methods research training opportunities, and development of mixed methods-specific communities as important for mitigating concerns with research feasibility and opening up the possibilities for undertaking their own research. Those seeking to learn about mixed methods research have never had so many opportunities. Becoming familiar with the literature and developing competencies specific to mixed methods research is a great way to start. Another way is to seek out learning opportunities with mixed methods research experts, from participating in a workshop or taking a course to attending a webinar. In Chapter 1, I told the story about how I trace my entry into the field of mixed methods through attending a two-day workshop led by John Creswell back in 2005. Despite the ever-broadening means for accessing training opportunities about mixed methods research, it might be surprising that in Guiding Tip 2.1, a doctoral candidate at the Sir Arthur Lewis Institute of Social and Economic Studies at the University of the West Indies (Trinidad and Tobago) advises a workshop as a valuable learning experience. No matter the format, interaction with a prominent researcher remains an impactful experience and an accessible way to tap into the mixed methods research community.

 Guiding Tip 2.1

Bephyer Parey advising a workshop from a mixed methods expert

Take a mixed methods course or workshop from experts in the field! A lot of methodological gaps in my PhD research were filled by information I received at workshops by renowned persons in the field of mixed methods research.

Continuing Advances in Guiding Practices and Techniques

The past 15 years have been particularly eventful for guiding mixed methods research practice and advancing new techniques. This stage of development in the evolution of the field of mixed methods research has been described by Creswell and Plano Clark (2018) as the 'reflection and refinement period'. It is not surprising that as a field develops, controversies and issues of concern emerge, leading to various discussions of the 'current' state of mixed methods (Creswell, 2009; Greene, 2008; Tashakkori & Teddlie, 2003, 2010). Creswell (2011) discussed 11 of these controversies and pointed out lingering aspects for further consideration. I was struck by the focus, across these controversies, on considering the extent to which our current understandings and guiding practices are sufficiently developed to reflect the emerging (and even unknown future) needs of the field. I consider our practices guiding the field of mixed methods research as 'continually under development'. This shift in mindset helps us to reconsider all of our research practices as simply reflective of our current experiences and to recognize that reconsidering practices is necessary for the as yet unknown future.

Preparing for the unknown future requires us to seek and encourage advancements in techniques to continually revisit the suitability and efficiencies of our practices. For example, recent key advances involving technological innovations in data management and integration have vastly increased our research capacity and streamlined some of our roles as researchers. Technological innovations, including software for data generated by social media, greatly reduce the resources necessary for analysing large data sets (Creamer, 2016). Within the field of mixed methods research Creswell and Plano Clark (2018) identify advances in research techniques related to data mining, designs, visual representations, integration strategies, and evaluating quality. These advances can encourage the ongoing development of new practices for consideration by the field. Now one of the challenges faced by mixed methods researchers is to keep pace with the new practices that are continuing to emerge in the field. Consider Researcher Spotlight 2.1 featuring the challenges faced by mixed methods researchers when developing new research guiding practices related to the integration of data sources, from the perspective of a Canadian nurse holding a research-only postdoctoral position as a Canadian Institute for Health research fellow and National Health and Medical Research Council post-doctoral research officer in the College of Nursing and Health Sciences, Flinders University (South Australia).

 Researcher Spotlight 2.1

Mandy Archibald on the need for contributing new research reflectivity practices within the field of mixed methods research

Research methods can be aided by an understanding of complexity science (for a particularly useful resource, see the white paper on complexity science in health care by Braithwaite et al., 2017). In response to these challenges, I have been incorporating various arts-informed and arts-based methods, such as visual elicitation and reflexive art making, with more conventional narrative and statistical approaches. Guidance is generally lacking on integrating arts and mixed methods research (MMR), despite arts-based and MMR approaches having similar ontological and epistemological positioning, such as recognition of intersubjectivity and a dialectical approach to knowledge production. In my current work I am exploring these intersections, creating a framework for arts–MMR applications. Further, because the preferencing of research methods and realities reflects the influence of power and privilege, I believe there is a key (and underdeveloped) role for researcher reflectivity in MMR, specifically one that questions and challenges the positioning of self and method in broader sociopolitical contexts.

From my viewpoint, further innovation in mixed methods research practice will be pervasive as we tackle problems within increasingly complex conditions. Mertens (2015, p. 5) calls for researchers to consider new ways to tackle wicked problems: 'business as usual will not lead to effective use of research to address wicked problems, problems for which time for solutions is running out'. That the field of mixed methods is well positioned to undertake this important work is certain as is the need for thinking complexitively and creatively. Mertens et al. (2016a, p. 222) described the world of mixed methods in their report to the MMIRA as:

> in some ways like a kaleidoscope—an elegantly simple device made of a cylinder, mirrors, and pieces of plastic or glass that produces seemingly unpredictable patterns full of rich possibilities for diversity and potential to provide opportunities to see things that have not yet been seen. But unlike the kaleidoscope, which produces patterns on a random basis, we write to encourage systematic thinking about the rich possibilities and challenges open to the mixed methods research community in the coming years in terms of fresh understandings of methodology, preparation of mixed methods researchers, and advances in our abilities to be responsive to complex societal problems. Within that systematic process, we also believe that encouragement of creativity and openness to new ideas is necessary for the field to progress. Maintaining a spirit of creativity and openness in the context of advancements in the field of mixed methods brings an exciting and challenging tension into our future.

What Distinguishes Mixed Methods Research?

If you ask many researchers, 'What *is* mixed methods research?' I am confident you will hear a range of answers. You are not alone if you have been challenged when distinguishing mixed methods research using a definition. Mixed methods research has come a long way in establishing itself as a distinctive approach, yet the community of researchers continues to struggle to identify common ground and definitions. I think of the mixed methods research field metaphorically as the outcome of interactions among diverse people who have some purpose in common, yet represent various interests and traditions. The group is so diverse that it is hard to describe. Their influences on each other's contributions are often challenging to discern as well.

The description by Pat Bazeley (2003a, p. 117) endures for representing the convoluted nature of current discussions surrounding mixed methods research definitions: 'Most researchers "know" mixed methods when they meet them, but attempts to precisely define the term have been largely unsuccessful.' Consider the challenges experienced by a senior educational scientist at the Royal College of Physicians and Surgeons of Canada when distinguishing among the many definitions associated with mixed methods research, described in Researcher Spotlight 2.2.

 Researcher Spotlight 2.2

Elaine Van Melle on navigating the confusion with terminology and definitions within the field of mixed methods research

In my experience, there can be confusion between using multimethods and actually using a mixed methods approach. I often hear people use the term 'mixed methods' when actually no mixing has taken place, they are just drawing information from different sources. So, we need

(Continued)

(Continued)

to build understanding in the field that multimethods and mixed methods are not one and the same. We also need to build understanding of the benefits of qualitative and quantitative methods and, more importantly, the practices required to mix the two. I deliberately say 'understand the benefits' of the approaches because I do not believe that it is necessary or even feasible for one person to hold all of the expertise required. But there does need to be an appreciation of the strengths and weaknesses and when each is best applied.

My working definition also recognizes that many methods can produce either quantitative or qualitative data. Qualitative data is also referred to as text- and image-based data. A defining characteristic is that it is open-ended; it is generated by recording stories and personal experiences, without specifying categories (such as 'strongly agree'). Qualitative data is often captured orally and transcribed using sound recordings. It could also be visually documented as still images (photos and drawings) and in motion (film). Quantitative data is also referred to as numeric-based data. It is closed-ended; it is generated by using response categories to answer questions related to predetermined constructs (e.g., variables). Quantitative data is most often captured in writing, yet it is possible to also collect the data in conversation and then transcribe the numbers to generate written forms. Note that I am simply distinguishing data types here and not methods. This is an essential distinction, given the notion that methods should no longer be distinguished as either qualitative or quantitative but rather it depends on the approach to data collection and analysis. For example, in observational methods, one may choose to capture the information and generate qualitative, text-based data (such as a narrative description) or generate quantitative, numeric-based data (such as frequency of interactions). In Guiding Tip 2.2, a prominent mixed methods research scholar and adjunct professor at Western Sydney University (Australia) offers advice for simply collecting the data required for a mixed methods research and avoiding the qualitative/quantitative distinction.

 **Guiding Tip 2.2**

Pat Bazeley advising new ways of thinking about qualitative and quantitative data

All phenomena have qualities and quantities, and elements of both are inherent in most methods. Don't get 'hung up' on whether your data are qualitative and quantitative, or on whether your design has the 'right mix', just work out what you need (and what is accessible) for answering your questions.

In my discussions with students and colleagues I have heard a common theme that mixed methods research offers something distinctive from other approaches to research. When I have further probed such responses, I have heard lots of talk of opening possibilities for new insights and understandings. As an instructor and mixed methods research practitioner, while I wholeheartedly agree that the mixed methods literature reflects some shared under-standings of essential characteristics, suitable problems, organic processes, and researcher roles, I believe that readers will benefit from an orientation to my perspective before we discuss key practice dilemmas under highly complex conditions in the following section.

Essential Characteristics

Interestingly, many shifts have been seen in the emphasis of mixed methods research definitions over the last two decades (see Creswell & Plano Clark, 2018, for a detailed description). A notable trend involves describing core characteristics and a move away from a focus on methods, meth-odologies, and philosophies. Yet, providing a basic definition and description of mixed methods research is a common way of familiarizing a reader to your approach in research proposals and reports (Collins & O'Cathain, 2009; Creswell, 2014; DeCuir-Gunby & Schultz, 2017). In Practice Alert 2.2, I consider the usefulness of delineating what is meant by a mixed methods research approach by creating a definition or citing an existing definition or essential characteristics for conveying a mixed methods researcher's position within the diverse literature.

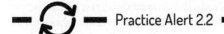 **Practice Alert 2.2**

Why distinguish a mixed methods research approach in proposals and reports?

My approaches to advising how to introduce mixed methods research are informed by my experiences as a member of many review committees of proposals and reports. My advice when preparing a dissertation proposal, funding application or manuscript for publication is that it is in the author's best interest to define mixed methods research. A definition can take many forms, from citing a definition or characteristics advanced by others, to creating an original one. This proactive approach is described by Creswell (2014, p. 217) as being necessary 'because mixed methods research is relatively new in the social and human sciences as a distinct research approach'. Collins and O'Cathain (2009, p. 3) describe providing a definition as being useful 'to facilitate [the reader's] awareness and understanding of mixed methods research as a research paradigm distinct from other monomethod approaches'. The authors of a book about developing a mixed methods research proposal advise selecting a definition that closely aligns with your own perspective. They say 'it is important for you to disclose to the readers how you are conceptualizing mixed methods' (DeCuir-Gunby & Schutz, 2017, p. 53). In my own writing, I like to position my definition as a cohesive approach to ethical and rigor-ous research where qualitative and quantitative data are collected, analysed, and integrated to generate novel inferences that draw on these collective data contributions to address the purpose of the mixed methods study. Then I must make sure that I follow through and present my research in a way that aligns with my stated definition or essential characteristics!

Try this now – select an existing definition, or sketch your ideas representing the distinc-tiveness of mixed methods research into a definition or essential characteristics.

For many mixed methods researchers, a shared understanding of core characteristics brings them together. It is these common characteristics that are essential foundations to this book.

There are five distinctive characteristics of mixed methods research. I have come to these characteristics by studying the evolving definitions and specific core characteristics described by others. Examine Table 2.1 to learn about five introductory mixed methods research books and the characteristics each leading school of thought has advanced during the past decade. These distinctive characteristics are naturally evolving and may not capture all the characteristics that others have noted are important. For example, the unique emphasis of Greene (2007) on mental models and Mertens (2014) on mixed methods research for societal betterment are not captured. You will see emphasis on valid insights, suitable designs, ethical standards, guiding assumptions, and research contexts. These are, in no specific order:

- *Generates mixed insights from the integration of various sources of qualitative and quantitative data.* Mixed insights are generated by integrating various qualitative and quantitative data sources, collection methods, and analysis strategies. In so doing, researchers use rigorous procedures and gather validation evidence specific to mixed methods research, in addition to what is expected from specific qualitative and quantitative procedures. The result is that evidence of validation efforts is represented in many forms throughout a study plan and report.
- *Uses designs to guide the data procedures addressing mixed methods research problems.* Researchers centre their study design on the integration of qualitative and quantitative data to address a research problem suitable for mixed methods. To that end, throughout the process, researchers maintain a focus on why, when, and how to integrate the data. The result is a design guiding the procedures for data collection, analysis, and integration – often represented by an established design or typology.
- *Meets ethical standards for the conduct of qualitative, quantitative, and mixed methods research.* Researchers consider ethical issues throughout initiation, planning, and implementation. To that end, researchers anticipate the ethical issues inherent in mixed methods. They relate and respond to ethical issues as they arise. They gather evidence of meeting the principles that guide the conduct of ethical research. The result is that plans and reports communicate the conduct of ethical mixed methods research.
- *Guides the conduct of mixed methods research using philosophical stances and theoretical frameworks.* Researchers use philosophical or theoretical perspectives to guide the conduct of their mixed methods research. This means that throughout the research, they articulate the philosophical and theoretical perspectives they bring to the study. This helps them better understand their own influence on the study, what they gain from the study, and how they can collaborate with others in a **research team**. The result is that plans and reports convey the researchers' philosophical assumptions. They do this to connect how researchers' backgrounds (e.g., work, cultural, and historical experiences) inform their theoretical approach, their interactions with each other, and their interpretations of the research outcomes.
- *Is situated within and shaped by research conditions.* Mixed methods researchers attend to the interrelated contexts in which research takes place. In so doing, throughout the process, researchers attend to contextual influences. This results in conceptualizing contexts as dynamic. Efforts to identify, monitor, and respond to contextual dynamics are represented in many forms throughout a study plan and report.

Suitable Problems

A necessary consideration when planning mixed methods research is whether the problem warrants the approach (Creswell & Plano Clark, 2018). The question of whether the problem is best addressed by mixed methods research is central to justifying the use of mixed methods research (Creamer, 2018; Creswell, 2015a; Hesse-Biber, 2010). It is thus of primary importance

Table 2.1 Distinctive characteristics of mixed methods research according to five leading schools of thought

Characteristics	Creswell and Plano Clark (2018)	Plano Clark and Ivankova (2016)	Curry and Nunez-Smith (2015)	Teddlie and Tashakkori (2009)	Greene (2007)
Generates mixed insights by integrating various sources of qualitative and quantitative data	Yes	Yes	Yes	Yes	Yes
Uses designs to guide the data procedures addressing mixed methods research problems	Yes	Yes	Yes		Yes
Meets ethical standards for conduct of qualitative, quantitative, and mixed methods research		Yes	Yes	Yes	
Guides the conduct of mixed methods research using philosophical stances and theoretical frameworks	Yes	Yes		Yes	Yes
Is situated within and shaped by research and social contexts.		Yes	Yes		Yes

to recognize the different needs of research problems and assess the suitability of the problems for mixed methods research. Qualitative and quantitative data contribute differently to addressing a research problem; whereas qualitative data provides more detailed understandings, quantitative data provides more generalized understandings. Integrating both types of data has the unique potential to offset the strengths and limitations of one with the other. As a result, in some situations a mixed methods research approach is suitable when integration is needed to generate insights that are inaccessible by either type of data alone. In other situations, either a qualitative or quantitative research approach may be best for addressing the research problem.

Various typologies of study needs for integration and research problems for combining quantitative and qualitative research have been suggested. Key among the typologies generated from completed studies were five justifications from Greene, Caracelli, and Graham (1989) and 16 categories from Bryman (2006). More recently, Creswell and Plano Clark (2018) focused on seven major reasons why research problems require mixed methods. For this book, I identify six distinct types of research needs to represent the scope of mixed methods problems which warrant data mixing. I acknowledge that the study needs for integration are naturally evolving and may not capture all the needs that others have noted are important. These six typologies of mixing purposes are presented in no specific order (see Figure 2.1). There may be some overlap among the five categories I have chosen to focus on. These are the categories I have found most useful for the students and colleagues I work with. I have included additional terms from the literature to demonstrate where I see them fitting. For example, a purpose for integration stated as triangulation, in my view, can serve the purpose of either corroboration or completion. This typology has been under consideration for some time and is intended to reflect the major perspectives about integration rationales for mixed methods research plus an additional research need for integration focused on innovation (Bryman, 2006; Creamer, 2018 Creswell & Plano Clark, 2018; Greene et al., 1989; Mertens, 2003; Plano Clark & Ivankova, 2016; Teddlie & Tashakkori, 2009).

Corroboration among data types addresses a research problem that a single data type is insufficient to answer. An additional data type offers further evidence of divergence or convergence and thus gives the researcher greater confidence in the validity of the study inferences. For example, a study examining the ease of use and readability of internet-based medicine information sites by patients combines quantitative measures of usability with interviews. The qualitative interview data provides the opportunity for researchers to examine issues that were captured quantitatively. This lets them generate evidence-based recommendations for the design of such sites (Nicolson, Knapp, Gardner, & Raynor, 2011).

We conduct mixed methods research when there is a need for *completion,* because an additional data type helps complete evidence. For example, Pincus, Vogel, Breen, Foster, and Underwood (2006) used semi-structured interviews to better understand findings established quantitatively via survey questionnaire. The initial quantitative findings pointed to the practice of providing long-term treatment of low back pain in the absence of improvement. While they found low prevalence of such practice, it emerged during interviews that the reasons were attributed to a broader view of the limited role of a problem-solver. Instead of merely comparing response frequency between social groups or national samples, a qualitative research component may further explore meanings of the constructs measured by the survey questions.

We also use mixed methods research when there is a need for *explanation* of initial findings using additional data types and sources. A research problem using qualitative data can expand initial findings from experimental trials. For example, Plano Clark et al. (2013)

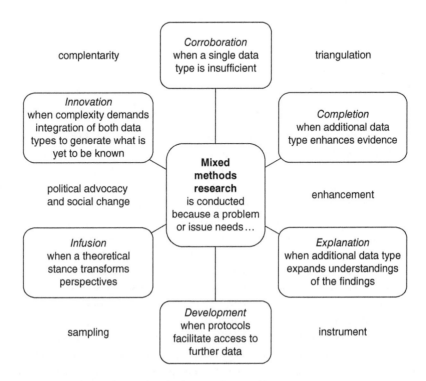

Figure 2.1 Problems for which mixed methods research is suitable

describe their experiences of embedding interpretive qualitative methods within the context of a randomized clinical trial study. That study compared two doses of an intervention to help oncology outpatients manage cancer pain.

We employ mixed methods research for *development* purposes when its protocols facilitate access to further data or populations. Instruments and sampling means are among the common protocols whose development are informed by mixed methods research. To address some research problems, it is necessary to develop an instrument or, in some cases, to adapt and revalidate an existing one. For example, Enosh, Tzafrir, and Stolovy (2014) developed a questionnaire for assessing social workers' exposure to client violence. They used qualitative semi-structured, in-depth interviews to map the forms of client violence experienced by social workers, then quantitatively tested and validated the questionnaire. For some research problems, the target population can be difficult to access. Use of a data source as a sampling mechanism can provide access. For example, researchers could use a quantitative survey to access a population that is then invited to focus groups organized by particular traits. Poth, McCallum, and Atkinson (2014) used a quantitative survey to access a population of preservice teachers who perceived maintaining e-professionalism at all times to be impossible (i.e., always conducting oneself in a professional manner when interacting online). Subjects then participated in a focus group to further explore differences in perspectives among those who perceived they could maintain e-professionalism and those who could not.

We use mixed methods research for *infusion* when a theoretical stance transforms perspectives for political advocacy and social change. Research problems seeking to advocate for the needs of a particular population can, for example, use participatory approaches to research integrating both qualitative and quantitative data. For example, Wilson and Winiarczyk's (2014) case study evaluation of a software tool to support and improve deaf children's literacy in South America empowered a marginalized population. The researchers sought to involve the creators of the software tool, deaf adults and children, teachers of deaf children, and parents of deaf children in the development of instruments to advocate for the needs of this population. The researchers combined findings from interviews to understand the impact on language skills. They used quantitative language measures and gained contextual information through focus groups and a document review. As the demand for mixed methods research becomes ever more widespread, so too are the threats to the appropriate use of mixed methods research warranting attention.

Finally, we use mixed methods to meet the demands of research under some conditions of complexity for *innovations* that are generated by integrating both qualitative and quantitative data. Because of the uncertainty related to the conditions, the mixing purposes for innovation have yet to be specified. As understandings emerge about the conditions, so too can the focus of the innovation. For example, a focus on generating new understandings from integrating data in new ways is the mixing purpose for the featured study on postconflict risk. In this study the authors drew upon data from parents and youth to identify salient community-level risk factors and responses to these risks for adolescents in Vukovar, Croatia (Taylor et al., 2017). In so doing, the authors integrated focus groups and questionnaires administered within the research context of a city devastated during the war in the former Yugoslavia. Ensuring the appropriate use of a mixed methods research approach for problems warranting integration is highlighted in Researcher Spotlight 2.3, from the perspective of a professor in the Department of Curriculum and Instruction in the College of Education & Health Professions at the University of Arkansas – Fayetteville (USA).

Researcher Spotlight 2.3

Kathleen Collins on ensuring the appropriate use of mixed methods research under increasingly complex research conditions

As the field of mixed methods research continues to evolve, I believe a key current and future challenge is to avoid envisioning a mixed methods research approach as a panacea that can be applied to every type of research question. Application of only a quantitative approach or only a qualitative approach might be the 'best' way to address the research question. However, I also believe that a mixed methods research approach is likely to be the 'best' approach to address questions that are complex in terms of exploring a phenomenon of interest. I believe it is important that researchers continue to advance their technical skills and/or work within interdisciplinary teams, so that the expertise is available to select the appropriate approach given the question and the phenomenon to be addressed.

Organic Processes

Another question that has been asked by many is how to conduct mixed methods research. Again, ask many researchers and you may hear as many different answers. My characterization of the mixed methods research process as organic represents a departure from how others may have represented the procedures involved in mixed methods research. Previously, researchers (including myself) have presented the process as more linear or stepwise, even when it was assumed to be also iterative (Onwuegbuzie & Leech, 2006; Poth, 2010). Calling it an organic process explicitly depicts the research process as more creative, evolving, and emergent than might be assumed. The practices may be revisited and outcomes revised at any time in the process. There is no assumption of linearity or of rigidly following a preconceived plan. At no time should the researcher consider that they are going 'backwards'. The process is emergent and ever deepening in focus and detail. Examine Figure 2.2 for a visual representation of the six overlapping research practices involved in the development and unfolding of the mixed methods research process.

This characterization of the mixed methods research process as organic was inspired by my collaborative work with my colleague Dr. Elaine Van Melle. Specifically, it was inspired by our discussions about the influence of methodological stance on research approach decision-making. That catalysed my application of this thinking to represent the mixed methods research practices I engaged in as an organic process. The six practices for mixed methods research, the research tasks involved, and desirable outcomes are described below and summarized in Table 2.2:

- *Determine if the study need or research problem is suitable for mixed methods research.* By definition, mixed methods research involves the integration of qualitative and quantitative data and assumes that their collective contribution mitigates inherent weaknesses in either type of data. A mixed methods research approach is suitable when the research problem warrants insights that are inaccessible by either qualitative or quantitative research alone. When creating a justification for the use of a mixed methods research approach and specifying the research problem, the researcher considers the reasons and significance for

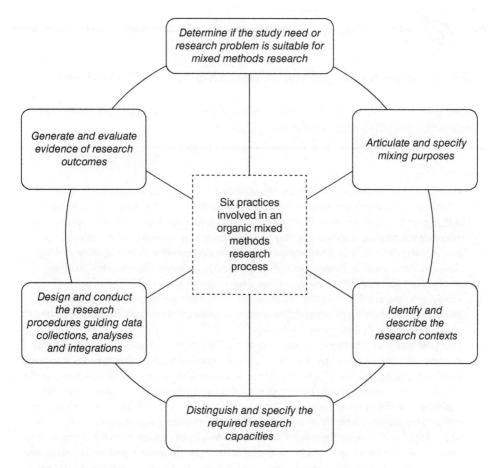

Figure 2.2   Six practices involved in an organic mixed methods research process

pursuing the study and research problem – that is, the *what* and the *for whom* of the research is conveyed. These initial study considerations under varying conditions of complexity may involve the researcher drawing upon their own experiences as well as experiences of others, their motivations, or relevant literature, including media reports, to discover an issue that is of interest to them. Depending on the topic or problem, this may also involve consideration of the intended audience, theoretical framework, and acknowledgement of the broad assumptions the researcher brings to the study. Specifying a **research problem** describes an issue that leads to a need to conduct a study within a broad subject area known as a **research topic**. Defining the research problem is central to identifying the **research purpose** and **research questions.**

- *Articulate and specify the mixing purposes.* A mixing purpose conveys the rationale for integrating qualitative and quantitative research. When creating a description of the mixed methods research problem, the researcher considers the topical and methodological gaps in the existing literature related to the research problem and specifies the mixing purposes and research questions – that is, the *why* and the *for what* of the research is conveyed. These study considerations under varying conditions of complexity may involve the researcher selecting among existing typologies of mixing purposes or describing a mixing purpose focused on innovation that has yet to be fully understood. Specifying a mixing purpose is central to identifying the research questions, which in turn guides the design of the study. In Guiding Tip 2.3 a well-known mixed methods researcher and Professor of Health Services Research at the School of Health and Related Research at the University of Sheffield (UK) reminds us of the central importance of the research question.

 Guiding Tip 2.3

Alicia O'Cathain advising keeping the research question as the focal point

Keep your eye on the research questions you are addressing. Methods are there to help address the research questions rather than be the star of the show.

- *Identify and describe the research contexts.* By definition, the research contexts situate the reader with respect to the people and environments involved in the research. When creating an explanation of the research contexts, the researcher considers the feasibilities and environmental influences when describing the sampling of participants, sites, and organizations for addressing the mixing purposes and research questions – that is, the *where* and the *who is involved* in the research is conveyed. These study considerations under varying conditions of complexity may involve the researcher identifying study features about participants, sites, and their environments that have yet to be fully defined. Specifying research contexts is central to a study and in turn influences research decisions related to designs, implementations, and interpretations such as inclusion criteria for participants, appropriate data procedures, and validity evidence for insights.
- *Distinguish and specify the required research capacities.* The availability of qualitative and quantitative skills and experiences to draw upon in addition to specific mixed methods research expertise is central to mixed methods research. Thus, it is important to be able to recognize the researcher capacities necessary for undertaking a mixed methods research approach and plan for developing or accessing them. When establishing the diverse disciplinary and methodological backgrounds of study members, the researcher considers the necessary expertise and roles for pursuing the study and research problem – that is, the *who* and the *for what roles* of the research is conveyed. These initial study considerations under varying conditions of complexity may involve the researcher drawing upon their own experiences as a research team member and relevant literature. Specifying research capacity is central to ensuring the research feasibility of the study.
- *Design and conduct the research procedures guiding data collections, analyses, and integrations.* By definition, a design guides the planning and implementation of study procedures for addressing the research question – that is, the *how* and the *where integration takes place* in the research is conveyed. Decisions about the mixed methods research procedures must also maintain **methodological congruence** and consider issues such as the appropriateness of the research methods for the participants and for generating the desired data. When we discuss designing, we adapt ideas on methodological congruence advanced by Morse and Richards (2002) and revisited in Richards and Morse (2013), and the interactive approach to research advanced by Maxwell (2013) within qualitative research. In this way, methodological congruence under varying conditions of complexity requires deliberate strategies for maintaining fit among the tasks involved in the mixed methods research phases. The research questions, sampling, recruitment, data collection, data analysis, and integration are all interconnected and interrelated so that the study appears as a cohesive whole rather than as fragmented, isolated parts. All the while, the researcher promotes rigorous strategies and ethical research. Such a description results in articulation of a **research design** that provides specific directions for study procedures. These initial study considerations under varying conditions of complexity may involve the researcher selecting among existing mixed methods research design typologies. For example, a typology often cited is the six major designs described by Creswell and Plano Clark (2011): convergent parallel, explanatory sequential, exploratory sequential, embedded, transformative, and multiphase. A more recent typology by Creswell and Plano Clark (2018) categorizes designs as core or complex. In such cases, a researcher may approach the design by describing

particular features of the study procedures. Describing the design is central to identifying procedures that address the research question, which in turn, guide the conduct of the study.

- *Generate and evaluate evidence of research outcomes.* Representing evidence of the integration and interpretation processes is essential for evaluating the research outcomes. By definition, mixed methods research involves generating mixed insights from the interpretations of the **integrated findings**. From the mixed insights, we generate the *so what* of the research often conveyed as the theoretical, methodological, and practical implications. These initial study considerations under varying conditions of complexity may involve the researcher adapting data procedures so it is also important that our research reports are not written simply through the lens of what *should have happened* but rather *what did happen.* In so doing, researchers create more authentic reports of our responses to changing circumstances so that others can also learn from our experiences. Authentic dissemination of research processes and outcomes, in turn, leads to informed advancement in methodology and in society at large. What is becoming increasingly apparent is the essential role that experience and skills play in conducing rigorous mixed methods research (Guetterman, 2017). In Practice Alert 2.3, I consider some of the shortcomings of many mixed methods research reports to provide authentic accounts, and I invite you to do the same. In so doing, I have enhanced my understandings of the need for these accounts for others to learn from.

 Practice Alert 2.3

To what extent do you provide authentic research accounts?

In my own research as well as the research undertaken by students and colleagues, I have become aware of the challenges we experience when research takes an unexpected turn.

Examples I know of personally have involved aspects of the research process from recruitment difficulties in hard-to-reach populations and study site access being suddenly restricted to problems with data collection and gaining approval to publish. Reading a compilation of cross-disciplinary stories in the aptly-named book, *When research goes off the rails: Why it happens and what you can do about it* (Streiner & Sidani, 2010), helped me to realize others were also experiencing similar trials and to normalize these challenges for others. What I have come to appreciate is the need for authentic reporting in our studies of the challenges we experience, our responses to the challenges, and the consequences of our responses. Together these accounts can help researchers anticipate potential challenges and be better prepared to respond. Such understandings have helped me to move beyond being fearful of challenges and instead to be more comfortable with unexpected events and with working under changeable research conditions.

Try this now – sketch your ideas about what you want to learn from mixed methods research accounts and then explore how this can be conveyed.

Researcher Roles

The answer to the question 'what knowledge do I need to conduct mixed methods research' is not straightforward and is a topic that remains underdeveloped (Guetterman, 2017; Poth, 2014).

Table 2.2 Summary of mixed methods research practices, key researcher tasks, and desirable outcomes

Mixed methods research practices	Key researcher tasks	Desirable outcomes
Determine if the study need or research problem is suitable for mixed methods research	Consider reasons and significance for pursuing the study and research problem	Justification for the use of a mixed methods research approach and specifying the research problem
Articulate and specify mixing purposes	Consider mixing purposes and questions for addressing topical and methodological literature gaps about the research problem	Description of research problem in relation to gaps in the existing literature and specifying the mixing purpose and research questions
Identify and describe the research contexts	Consider feasibilities and environmental influences when describing participants, sites, and organizations surrounding the research contexts	Explanation of research contexts in relation to target study sample and sites for addressing the research questions
Distinguish and specify the required research capacities	Consider the expertise and roles when describing disciplinary and methodological needs for the study	Establishment of research members in relation to necessary capacity for addressing the research questions
Design and conduct the research procedures guiding data collections, analyses, and integrations	Consider needs of participants, research methods, and points of integration for the study conditions	Design of research procedures in relation to integrations necessary for addressing the research questions
Generate and evaluate evidence of research outcomes	Consider standards of rigour during interpretation and representations of integrated findings and mixed insights	Generate authentic evidence of integration and insights for addressing the research problem

I identified five roles that researchers assume when engaging in the six mixed methods research practices and realizing the organic research process. Research is by nature a social process involving people undertaking practices and negotiating processes. How we go about research is naturally influenced by many factors, key among them whom the research involves, where the research is situated, and why the research is pursued. These roles provide the organizing structure for a list of competencies I sketched. I am currently working on a validation study of these competencies as part of a competency-based framework for guiding mixed methods education. To that end, I share the roles and their definitions here and situate them within the research practices (see Figure 2.3):

- A *practitioner* develops a distinct ethos for and promotes the field of mixed methods research. Key among the many practitioner tasks are professional learning about qualitative, quantitative, and mixed methods research and engaging as a member of mixed methods research communities.
- An *architect* formulates the research problems and aligns the plans guiding a mixed methods study. Key among the many architect tasks is designing procedures that are appropriate for the mixed methods study conditions.
- An *engineer* conducts the procedures and guides the technical aspects of a mixed methods study. Key among the many engineer tasks are negotiating and adapting the mixed methods study implementation.
- A *collaborator* facilitates the social interactions and develops capacity for a mixed methods study. Key among the many collaborator tasks are monitoring and mitigating issues as they arise in a mixed methods study.
- A *manager* coordinates data management and oversees logistics in a mixed methods study. Key among the many manager tasks are organizing and maintaining records for a mixed methods study.

These roles become more apparent as a mixed methods researcher gains knowledge and experience. The question remains, how does one know when one is ready to engage in mixed

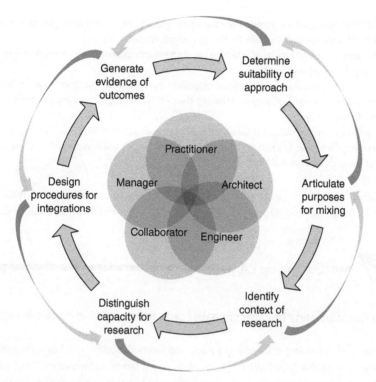

Figure 2.3 Visual representation of the mixed methods researcher roles for realizing the six practices involved in an organic research process

methods research? I am often asked if expertise and experience in qualitative and quantitative research are sufficient preparation for a mixed methods researcher. Some noteworthy contributors have included suggestions for teaching mixed methods research, largely based on their own experiences (Bazeley, 2003a; Christ, 2009; Hesse-Biber, 2015; Mertens, 2015). In my view, qualitative and quantitative researchers contribute different yet necessary expertise to conducting rigorous mixed methods research. The outcomes of previous work to investigate what novices gained from an introductory mixed methods course identified the need for learning specifically about mixed methods research as well as the usefulness of the course for enhancing skills in both qualitative and quantitative research (Poth, 2014). What interests me now is the lack of availability of more advanced guidance for teaching mixed methods research under varying conditions of complexity. Hence one of the reasons for writing this book is to provide such a mixed methods research resource for supporting ongoing professional development and learning! Experience tells me that among the most important indicators of readiness is that the mixed methods researcher is willing to do the following:

- *Adopt a worldview that is philosophically open to mixed methods research.* Demonstrate tolerance of methodological and disciplinary differences to draw from diverse expertise as needed.
- *Embrace learning specific to the field of mixed methods research.* Become familiar with practices and literature relevant to initiating, planning, and implementing mixed methods research and perhaps assume an advocacy role.
- *Adapt to dynamic mixed methods research conditions.* Situate the research within its problems, members, contexts, and procedures. Adapt to dynamic influences surrounding the research.

- *Commit to extensive data and resource management.* Spend plenty of time managing data collection, budget, and human resources involved in mixed methods research.
- *Attend to anticipated and emergent ethical issues.* Address anticipated ethical issues as well as those that arise during the mixed methods study.
- *Engage in the complex task of data analysis, integration, interpretation, and representation.* Dedicate extensive effort to generating integrated findings through individual data type analysis, mixed analysis, and creation of joint displays.
- *Create authentic research accounts for dissemination.* Provide accurate portrayals of research processes and outcomes. This requires a variety of communication strategies and is important for others to learn from our research experiences.

In Guiding Tip 2.4, a professor of international communication at Aoyama Gakuin University in Tokyo (Japan) offers advice for preparing to undertake mixed methods research.

 **Guiding Tip 2.4**

Hisako Kakai advising how to navigate the waters of mixed methods research

Be creative and innovative in designing your mixed methods study. First, however, make sure to acquire the essential foundations of qualitative, quantitative, and mixed methods research. Without such foundations, you will be a boat drifting on the ocean without an anchor.

Key Practice Dilemmas under Highly Complex Conditions

After hearing many accounts reflective of what initially appeared to be diverse challenges, I mapped the similarities among these accounts onto my own experiences as a researcher, thesis supervisor, and research team methodologist. From this work emerged patterns of dilemmas attributable to a previously unknown source of influence in the literature. It affected the research conditions in such a way that the viability of the study was threatened and the outcomes of the dilemma depended upon the researcher's response. These key dilemmas are as follows:

- *Traditional practices for justifying a mixed methods approach are based on assumptions of stable research conditions.* I consider those effective under conditions of complexity to be 'adaptive mixed methods researchers'. This understanding emerged from having traced many of the challenges experienced by mixed methods researchers to a lack of guidance on how to respond appropriately under conditions of complexity. When researchers attend to changing conditions, they are more able to respond appropriately.
- *Traditional practices for articulating mixing purpose based on existing literature gaps.* I consider a necessary mixing purpose typology to be focused on innovation. This understanding emerged from situations where the background influences on the research problem were not well understood, and literature guidance and fit within established design typologies were lacking. When researchers consider possibilities that are yet to be known for mixing purposes, they are better positioned to realize innovations in mixed methods research outcomes.

- *Traditional practices for situating of research contexts are based on predetermined boundaries.* I consider a systems perspective as necessary for defining the interrelatedness of contexts. This understanding emerged from studies where the contexts and environmental influences had yet to be defined, and literature guidance and fit within established contexts were lacking. When researchers adopt a systems perspective for identifying research systems that are yet to be known, they are more able to accurately represent the sources for changing conditions.
- *Traditional practices for establishing necessary research capacities are based on known contributions.* I consider an emergent approach as necessary for identifying research members based on emerging understandings of the disciplinary and methodological needs of the study. This understanding emerged from studies where the necessary expertise and social influences had yet to be defined, and literature guidance was lacking. When researchers consider the nature of the interactions required by the research problem, they can make more informed choices about whom to involve in the study.
- *Traditional practices for communicating research designs are based on knowing the procedures for integration.* I consider a descriptive design approach as necessary for planning based on emerging understandings of the procedures for integration. This understanding emerged from studies where literature guidance and fit of the desired procedures within established designs were lacking. When researchers consider possibilities that are yet to be known for designs, they are better positioned to realize the intended research outcomes.
- *Traditional practices for assessing evidence of research outcomes are based on expectations of methodological rigour.* I consider the assessment processes associated with setting standards for integration evidence to be responsive to the research conditions. This understanding emerged from studies where the practical influences on the integration procedures were not well understood and where the expectations of **methodological rigour** were constraining. When researchers consider possibilities that are yet to be known for evidence of methodological rigour, they are better positioned to realize the research outcomes.

Demand for Innovations and Innovators in Mixed Methods Research

It may not be surprising that the dilemmas researchers face centre on how to go about the mixed methods research process and practices when the way we have been trained no longer works for the surrounding research conditions. Reports of such dilemmas are ever increasing in cases where researchers are working under conditions of complexity, such as tackling wicked problems and grand challenges (Mertens et al., 2016a). Common to wicked problems and grand challenges is the idea that these societal issues are interdependent, with no known solution or established methods and expertise for studying the dynamic societal contexts in which they take place. When thinking about the **organic mixed methods research process**, especially under conditions of complexity, I re-emphasize here the need to keep in mind the interconnected, nonlinear, and iterative nature of the practices. Further, I restate the researcher's need to respond appropriately to emergent and dynamic influences inherent in conditions of complexity.

We need to transform our approach to mixed methods research practices. This way, we can be more reflective of the necessity to be responsive to dynamic conditions. Over the last decade, I have sought to optimize the researcher response to dynamic conditions. This quandary has led me to examine the extent to which the assumptions underlying mixed methods research practice fit the realities faced by researchers under conditions of complexity. It is this practice gap that has become the focus of my efforts, because of the harmful effects I see on the research outcomes and those involved in the research when the researcher's response is less than ideal. Numerous resources exist to guide mixed methods research under assumptions of stability; however, an opportunity exists for a resource that transforms these practices under conditions of complexity. Responding appropriately requires new sensitivities in our approach; recognizing that is another challenge. So far, I see that sensitivities are important in order to differentiate levels of complexity among the research conditions related to problems, contexts, integrations, interactions, and outcomes that may appear similar at first glance, thus allowing a tailored approach. These are the five areas where I have seen the impacts of uncertainty on mixed methods researchers, so this provides a place to start. Specific to the focus of this book, as the variability of conditions in which mixed methods research is applied increases, so does the need for a customized researcher response.

As I introduced in Chapter 1, a research problem under conditions of high complexity that my colleague and I are currently pursuing with our ACCERT team relates to the types of systemic problems and grand challenges associated with equitable access to housing. Much of our work focuses on populations who are considered 'difficult to house', and specifically people affected with fetal alcohol spectrum disorder. The six traditional mixed methods research practices within an organic process would have us predetermine the suitability of the research problem for mixed methods research, identify a mixing purpose typology, situate the research contexts, establish the necessary capacities, select a design typology for guiding data procedures, and assess evidence of research integrations. We would experience lots of dilemmas because we do not yet understand the conditions under which this research takes place but we do know it is dynamic and the people, programme, and needs are ever changing. We recognize that the solutions and methods are indeed complex in nature, yet the extent to which the research conditions can be considered complex are not yet known. We suspect we are working under conditions of higher complexity and our mixed methods research practices are in need of transformations to be more complexity-sensitive simply because the traditional practices are not feasible to implement.

Common to conditions of higher complexity is the lack of known solution and established methods and expertise for the research. I wholeheartedly agree with Pat Bazeley's (2018, p. 4) statement that 'This complexity, evident across many fields of action and inquiry, demands methods able to investigate a problem from multiple viewpoints, with flexibility to adapt to changing situations, yet able to produce credible results convincing to diverse audiences'. To that end, this book guides the implementation of six adaptive mixed methods practices as part of a complexity-sensitive approach when tackling a study under varying conditions of complexity:

1   Complexity of *research conditions* through ongoing integrative thinking about diagnosing the five dimensions of complexity in mixed methods research: problems, contexts, integrations, interactions, and outcomes
2   Complexity of *research problems* through ongoing integrative thinking about framing literature gaps and background influences
3   Complexity of *research contexts* through ongoing integrative thinking about defining interrelated systems and environmental influences
4   Complexity of *research integrations* through integrative thinking about describing agile designs and feasibility influences
5   Complexity of *research interactions* through ongoing integrative thinking about developing emergence capacity and social influences
6   Complexity of *research outcomes* through integrative thinking about generating integration evidence and practical influences.

Individually these adaptive practices guide new ways of diagnosing research conditions, framing research problems, defining research contexts, describing research integrations, developing research interactions, and assessing research outcomes. Together these adaptive practices guide a complexity-sensitive approach useful for mitigating the dilemmas experienced with traditional mixed methods research tendencies under conditions of complexity, and in so doing generate opportunities for innovations within mixed methods research.

Survey of Six Featured Mixed Methods Studies

These six featured studies represent diverse research problems, designs, and data sources. These articles are readily available on the companion website for this book. Table 2.3 summarizes the diversity of each study's details of problems, designs, and members – in no particular order. You can also read further details in subsequent chapters of this book.

Table 2.3 Summary of research questions, designs, and members for the six featured mixed methods studies

Research Topics	Research questions	Research designs	Research members
Law Client (Chui & Cheng, 2017)	How do young offenders perceive fairness and satisfaction towards their lawyers in Hong Kong's criminal justice system?	Explanatory sequential design with quantitative questionnaire with follow-up qualitative interviews	Two researchers affiliated with different Hong Kong universities
Postconflict Risk (Taylor et al., 2017)	How does political violence affect youth, particularly in postconflict settings?	Exploratory sequential design with qualitative focus groups with youth, mothers, and fathers with follow-up youth quantitative questionnaire	Five researchers affiliated with UK, Croatia, and USA universities in addition to undergraduate and graduate researchers
Heart Care (Dickson et al., 2011)	How does cognitive function and knowledge affect heart failure self-care?	Concurrent triangulation design with qualitative interviews and quantitative standardized measures (self-care heart failure index)	Three researchers affiliated with different US universities
Safe Places (Zea et al., 2014)	What does developing safe places involve for internally displaced Colombian gay and bisexual men and transwomen?	Transformative design with qualitative life history interviews and focus groups with follow-up respondent-driven online quantitative surveys	Five researchers affiliated with three US universities and two with Colombian community organizations
Leadership Competencies (Strudsholm et., 2016)	What public health leadership competencies could apply to public health practice across the country?	Multiphase with literature review, online survey, online focus groups, and modified Delphi	Five researchers affiliated with two Canadian universities
Vaping Culture (Colditz et al., 2017)	What can contextualizing vaping culture in social media add to our understanding?	Convergent parallel with Twitter	Five researchers affiliated with three US universities

Note. A summary of these studies can be read in the Further Readings section of Chapter 1.

.... CHAPTER CHECK-IN

1   Can you identify the differences and similarities in foundational concepts across the five introductory mixed methods research books in Table 2.1?

- Compare how at least two authors define the distinctive characteristics of mixed methods research. Note the wording they use and relate your analysis to characteristics presented in Table 2.1.
- Compare how at least two authors categorize the problems for which mixed methods research is suitable. Note the wording they use and relate your analysis to the categories presented in Figure 2.1.
- Compare how at least two authors describe the mixed methods research process. Note the wording they use and relate your analysis to the organic process presented in Figure 2.2.

2   Can you see how authors incorporate the characteristics of mixed methods research into their published studies? Read mixed methods papers that address different needs for integrating qualitative and quantitative data types. For example: Nicolson et al. (2011) for corroboration, Enosh et al. (2014) for development, Pincus et al. (2006) for completion, Plano Clark et al. (2013) for explanation, Wilson and Winiarczyk (2014) for infusion, and Taylor et al. (2017) for innovation.

- Begin by identifying how the five distinctive characteristics have been applied (see Table 2.1). Note which characteristics are easy to identify and which are more difficult.
- Then find the authors' definition of mixed methods. Note what (if any) description is provided and what (if any) information is provided about a definition.

3   Can you identify differences and similarities across the six featured studies in Table 2.3?

- Compare authors' definitions and distinctive characteristics of mixed methods research. Note the wording they use and relate your analysis to characteristics presented in Table 2.1.
- Compare how the authors of at least two studies categorize the problems for which mixed methods research is suitable. Note the wording they use and relate your analysis to the categories presented in Figure 2.1.
- Compare how the authors of at least two studies describe the organic mixed methods research process. Note the wording they use and relate your analysis to the six practices presented in Figure 2.2.

4   Can you identify any dilemmas that conditions of complexity pose for researchers? Consider research you have undertaken and any dilemmas you, or someone familiar to you, has experienced.

- During which practices within the research process did each dilemma became apparent? Relate your analysis to the research practices and researcher tasks presented in Table 2.2.
- How do the dilemmas map onto the dilemmas discussed in this chapter?

.... KEY CHAPTER CONCEPTS

This chapter explored a foundational question for this book: What practice dilemmas emerge under conditions of increased complexity and what innovations in mixed methods research are recognized and warranted? The use of mixed methods research is described by three trends: enhanced advocacy of the value and contribution, improved access to learning and networking opportunities, and continuing advances in guiding practices and techniques. Mixed methods research is distinguished by the following features: essential characteristics, suitable problems, organic processes, and researcher roles. The working definition of mixed methods research is expanded to five essential characteristics: the generation of valid insights from the collection, analysis, and integration of qualitative and quantitative data using rigorous procedures; the central positioning of the fixed or emergent research design on the mixed methods research procedures; the use of ethical research procedures; the framing of the research guided by philosophical or theoretical perspectives; and the research as situated within and shaped by its contexts.

A mixed methods approach is appropriate for generating mixed insights for a research problem when it is needed to: corroborate among data types, enhance the completeness of the evidence, explain initial findings, develop protocols, infuse a theoretical stance, and integrate both types of data to generate what is yet to be known. An organic mixed methods research process involves six iterative practices: determine if the study need or research problem is suitable for mixed methods research; articulate and specify mixing purposes; identify and describe the research contexts; distinguish and specify the required research capacities; design and conduct the research procedures guiding data collections, analyses, and integrations; and generate and evaluate evidence of research outcomes. The five roles researchers assume when engaging in the six mixed methods research practices and realizing the organic research process are those of practitioner, architect, engineer, collaborator, and manager. Furthermore, a researcher must be willing to adopt an open worldview, embrace specific learning, adapt to conditions, commit to extensive management, attend to ethical issues, and engage in complex tasks.

The demands for innovations using mixed methods research and explanations of the featured studies are further described in subsequent chapters – specifically, how conditions of complexity can be recognized and how mixed methods research can be transformed into a more complexity-sensitive approach.

FURTHER READINGS

The following resources are offered as introductory references for mixed methods research. The list should not be considered exhaustive. Readers are encouraged to seek out additional readings in the end-of-book reference list. Readings denoted with an asterisk are available on the online resources website for this book.

Creswell, J., & Plano Clark, V. (2018). *Designing and conducting mixed methods research* (3rd ed.). Thousand Oaks, CA: Sage.

In this third edition, John Creswell and Vicki Plano Clark provide an accessible introduction to the field of mixed methods research. Particularly noteworthy is the focus on the nature (Chapter 1), foundations (Chapter 2), and complex designs (Chapter 4) of mixed methods research.

Curry, L. A., & Nunez-Smith, M. (2015). *Mixed methods in health sciences research*. Thousand Oaks, CA: Sage.

Lesley Curry and Marcella Nunez-Smith provide a pioneering resource focusing on applications of mixed methods specific to health science research (Chapter 2), proposal writing (Chapter 4), and grant applications (Chapter 5).

Greene, J. (2007). *Mixed methods in social inquiry*. San Francisco: Jossey-Bass.

Jennifer Greene weaves multiple perspectives into her descriptions of mixed methods research practice. Of particular note are the discussions of mental models (Chapter 1) and illustrations of a mixed way of thinking (Interlude 1).

*Molina-Azorin, J. F., & Fetters, M. (2016). Mixed methods research prevalence studies: Field-specific studies on the state of the art of mixed methods research. *Journal of Mixed Methods Research, 10*(2), 123–128. doi: 10.1177/1558689816636707.

This editorial highlights four essential elements involved in reporting a mixed methods research prevalence study. These insights guide a type of research often undertaken by those wanting to advance understanding specific to mixed methods research within their own disciplines.

Plano Clark, V. L., & Ivankova, N. V. (2016). *Mixed methods research: A guide to the field*. Thousand Oaks, CA: Sage.

Vicki Plano Clark and Nataliya Ivankova provide a user-friendly introduction to mixed methods research. Their unique approach to guiding mixed methods research practice using a socio-ecological conceptual framework is explained in the first two chapters.

Teddlie, C., & Tashakkori, A. (2009). *Foundations of mixed methods research: Integrating quantitative and qualitative approaches in the social and behavioral sciences*. Thousand Oaks, CA: Sage.

Charles Teddlie and Abbas Tashakkori present a comprehensive description of the historical foundations and essential concepts of mixed methods research in the first half of this book. The second half is focused on the methods and strategies of mixed methods research.

Website for Methodspace (http://www.methodspace.com/)

Connecting the research community is the purpose of this SAGE Publishing-sponsored online forum that provides access to blogs, videos, discussion threads, and events. Mixed methods researchers may find specific groups useful for posting questions.

Apply your mixed methods knowledge with videos, activities, SAGE journal articles and project templates at **https://study.sagepub.com/poth**

3

ADVANCING INTEGRATIVE THINKING WITH COMPLEXITY IN MIXED METHODS RESEARCH

.... KEY CHAPTER QUESTIONS

By the end of this chapter, you will be able to answer the following questions:

- Why integrative thinking with complexity in mixed methods research?
- What are some examples of complex adaptive systems under study?
- What do the principles of complexity science offer to mixed methods research(ers)?
- What are the indicators of integrative thinking with complexity in mixed methods research?
- What evidence of integrative thinking with complexity is found in the featured mixed methods research studies?
- What are the guiding practices for integrative thinking with complexity in mixed methods research?

.... NEW CHAPTER TERMS

- Complex adaptive system
- Self-organization

- Emergence
- Adaptive mixed methods research practices

This chapter positions the foundational theoretical underpinnings for this book: *What does adopting a complexity-sensitive approach to mixed methods involve, and how can integrative thinking with complexity transform mixed methods research practices?* The focus of this chapter is on positioning a complexity-sensitive approach as occupying a distinct niche, especially useful under conditions of complexity, and whose theoretical foundation is provided by the principles of complexity science. In adopting a complexity-sensitive approach, a researcher mitigates some of the dilemmas with traditional mixed methods research practices through the use of adaptive practices and expands what they previously imagined as possible.

Over the last decade, I have sought to describe the opportunities that complexity science affords to mixed methods researchers, and to identify the adaptive practices guiding a complexity-sensitive mixed methods research approach. Work on this chapter was informed by extensive readings in the field of complexity science and feedback from students and colleagues on earlier versions. My intent is not for us to get lost in the theory that underpins complexity science, but rather to apply foundational understandings to the transformation of mixed methods research practices so they can become more complexity-sensitive. Considering the theoretical and practical niche for a complexity-sensitive approach to mixed methods was essential, because only by describing the theoretical underpinnings can we understand the opportunities afforded by complexity science. From there we can apply the understandings related to integrative thinking with complexity across the six featured studies and advance six guiding practices for a complexity-sensitive approach to mixed methods research. To start, let us position the need for integrative thinking with complexity related to current practices in mixed methods research.

Why Integrative Thinking with Complexity in Mixed Methods Research Approach?

Integrative thinking with complexity has emerged as a practical approach to addressing many of the dilemmas described to me by researchers. As discussed in Chapter 1, a complexity perspective recognizes that research conditions call into question six traditional mainstays of mixed methods research practice tendencies:

- stability of the research conditions can be assumed;
- mixing purposes can be identified;
- contextual study boundaries can be defined;
- expertise for necessary capacities can be predetermined;
- integration procedures can be fixed;
- and indicators of outcome legitimacy can be anticipated.

Complexity-sensitive practices are well established across diverse disciplines (e.g., business, evaluation, and health) and without exception require rethinking and indeed transforming traditional practices. Among the key benefits of complexity-sensitive approaches is the capacity to respond and adapt to evolving conditions.

A complexity-sensitive approach has emerged as guiding my own mixed methods research practices because it affords new opportunities for me to be creative in my work on challenging and pressing societal issues. Integrative thinking with complexity has supported innovations in my own mixed methods research experiences. Mixed methods research innovations can take many forms, including novel insights, integrative interactions, dynamic responses, and new designs. A complexity-sensitive mixed methods approach occupies a niche that supports a study's needs for innovation under conditions of complexity in six important ways:

- It promotes innovations in *researcher responsiveness* under varying complexity of mixed methods research conditions.
- It encourages innovations in *integration rationales* when framing complex mixed methods research problems.
- It promotes innovations in *system considerations* when defining interrelated mixed methods research contexts.
- It stimulates innovations in *capacity decisions* when developing emergence in mixed methods research interactions.
- It inspires innovations in *design creations* when realizing agile mixed methods research procedures.
- It supports innovations in *quality indicators* when generating evidence of mixed methods research outcomes.

By detailing our responses to the inherent complexity in our studies through adaptive practices, we offer a more authentic account of the realities in which researchers operate. The principles of complexity science as a theoretical framework guide the researcher to make sense of the dilemmas, conditions, and outcomes related to experiences, the present, and the future. In so doing, complexity science offers a new way of interpreting the world around us. It does this because it 'offers a way of going beyond the limits of reductionism, because it understands that much of the world is not machine-like and comprehensible through a cataloguing of its parts[,] but consists instead of organic and holistic systems that are difficult to comprehend by traditional scientific analysis' (Lewin, 1993, p. 10). Thus, complexity provides a new perspective to inform integrative thinking about our work as mixed methods researchers, as described by Eve Mitleton-Kelly (2003, p. 25): 'Complexity is not a methodology or a set of tools (although it does provide both). It certainly is not a management fad. The Science of Complexity provides a conceptual framework, a way of thinking, a way of seeing the world.'

A complexity lens is useful in highlighting the limitations inherent in many of our current mixed methods research practices under conditions of complexity. These mixed methods research practices, based on linear, mechanical principles where there are assumptions of stability in the environment, mean the adopted role of the researcher is that of the producer of information and knowledge. Such a lens is particularly germane when emphasizing the shortcomings of an iterative stepwise approach as an effective way to manage mixed methods research under dynamic conditions. Thus, an organic mixed methods research process should be considered more creative, evolving, and emergent than might be initially assumed (see also Chapter 2).

Together, the interacting and interdependent influences exert pressure in ways that are often unpredictable and, in turn, contribute to the dynamic mixed methods conditions. Mixed methods research can be considered to represent a nonlinear and **complex adaptive system** because it is influenced by a large number of interacting and interrelated contextual components for which there is no central control while researchers adapt to new conditions. Phenomena that defy simplistic analyses of cause and effect and that have the capacity to adapt to contextual changes are known as complex adaptive systems (Weaver, 1948):

- *complex* means composed of many parts which are entwined;
- *adaptive* refers to the fact that all living systems dynamically adapt to their constantly changing environments as they strive to survive and thrive; and
- *system* denotes that everything is interconnected and interdependent.

John H. Holland, in his book, *Emergence* (1999, p.5) goes on to explain that 'The task of formulating theory for [complex adaptive systems (CASs)] is more than usually difficult because the behaviour of a whole CAS is more than a simple sum of the behaviours of its parts; CAS[s] abound in nonlinearities'. In so doing, Holland highlights the usefulness of a systems perspective for understanding outcomes that are greater than their components.

Examples of Complex Adaptive Systems under Study

My research has focused on enhancing the learning environments within and across three contexts: organizations, classrooms, and clinical settings. My projects examine a range of issues concerned with developing and implementing innovative programmes within dynamic situations. These issues include how to facilitate organizational evidence-based programme development (e.g., in professional associations, government ministries, school boards), how to provide learners (e.g., graduate students and faculty, pre-service and practising teachers, medical students and residents) with timely access to feedback, and how to engage instructors in innovative instructional developments across diverse instructional media (e.g., virtual and face-to-face learning environments and clinical settings). This work has helped me to understand both the challenges and opportunities afforded by complex adaptive systems. This is because many people believe the complexities of health care and learning provide illustrative examples of familiar complex adaptive systems for discussion (Braithwaite et al., 2017; Davis, Sumara, & Luce-Kapler, 2000).

Common to both health care and learning is the involvement of a daunting diversity of stakeholders across the systems – from children and caregivers to professionals and politicians, and in many countries education and health services span the public and private sectors and are delivered across many settings and through various organizations. The individuals provide the services through groups, networks, and associations that interact and influence once another. In so doing, the systems providing the services will naturally adapt to the dynamic conditions in ways that are unpredictable. This is certainly what I am learning about the conditions surrounding the current research focused on populations who are considered 'difficult to house', and specifically people affected with fetal alcohol spectrum disorder, that I introduced in Chapters 1 and 2. Let me now expand this description to the present context and examine how housing programmes can be considered complex adaptive systems. Housing initiatives in Alberta span many provincial ministries (Children's Services, Community and Social Services, Seniors and Housing, Alberta Health Services, and Indigenous Relations) which offer housing programmes through a variety of providers (e.g., housing and rent assistance programmes, models guiding programme implementations) affected by environmental influences such as funding, demand for services, and societal priorities. In response to the emergent influences, the systems providing the services adapt in unpredictable ways yet generate patterns that can only be captured retrospectively. Over the years I have learned to work within the changing conditions, to pay attention to individuals, their interactions, and system-level influences, and to adapt my research approaches. The interconnectedness of these systems for housing or education or health is why one person, one programme or one government ministry working alone is unlikely to make sustainable progress. Instead, greater integration across sectors, service providers, and ministries, as well as those researchers seeking to monitor effective practices, is needed to adopt a systems approach and integrative thinking with complexity. In so doing, our ACCERT team advance a complexity-sensitive approach to housing initiatives that goes beyond the usual attempts to reduce, control, or simply ignore the effects of complexity. Germane to an understanding of complexity in housing, learning, and health care is not only recognizing the dynamic system conditions but also beginning to transform my mixed methods research practices. How we do this exactly is still to emerge, but adopting a mindset that is open to possibilities is a good place to start.

On a much smaller scale but perhaps more relatable, my recent contributions as a member of an interdisciplinary team highlighted to me how a complexity lens has impacted my approach to planning a mixed methods study. The three-member research team included a social psychologist, a classroom teacher, and a doctoral student. The social psychologist had extensive expertise in motivational and quantitative research, as well as familiarity with qualitative research. The classroom teacher had extensive expertise in assessment, mixed methods and qualitative research, as well as familiarity with quantitative research. The doctoral student was actively acquiring diverse experiences across both the content area of motivation and that of diverse research methodologies.

Our team was formed based on our assumptions of the methodologically diverse expertise the study required. Yet the differences among our approaches to planning remained striking. During our initial discussions based on the limitations we were finding in our initial literature review, the suitability of a mixed methods approach became apparent to me because of the need to generate innovative insights concerning how teachers perceive their responsibility for student motivation.

This study rationale emerged from the almost exclusive use of quantitative research approaches and the use of existing scales across diverse contexts and populations, with little evidence of validation beyond the scales' initial development.

Whereas the social psychologist on the team wanted to begin by identifying the mixed methods design typology, I wanted to begin by identifying the study's purpose for integration and the potential audiences for the mixed insights. By first describing the desired design features related to the points of interface (i.e., sampling, data collection procedures) that would allow us generate insights that address the purpose and our audiences, we were able to talk through the numerous interacting contexts and potential dynamic influences that could affect our study. Thus, we were able to develop a shared initial understanding of the conditions of complexity under which the study was situated. In so doing, I was able to bring a systems perspective to bear to bound this particular research study and inform the data collection in a mindful and complex way. If we scale up this example, it is no wonder that societies and researchers around the world are struggling to address issues under conditions of high research complexity. By discussing and applying the ideas from complexity science to our traditional mixed methods research practice tendencies, we are better able to move forward despite the uncertainties we experience in terms of defining a mixing purpose, dynamic contexts, necessary expertise, integration procedures, and mixed insights. The challenge of course, as I continue to experience and as others have also recounted, is that researchers, as a group, remain ill-equipped for adopting complexity-sensitive approaches. Some blame the lack of focus on complexity science in educational programmes. For example, Castellani (2014, p. 14) says: 'if you – like me – received a social science education in conventional statistics alone, your professors failed you. And, they failed you because they should have taught you five additional things' related to complexity. Consider the challenges experienced by a Commonwealth scholar from the UK and doctoral candidate at Auckland University of Technology (New Zealand) with mixed methods research problems under conditions of complexity described in Researcher Spotlight 3.1.

 Researcher Spotlight 3.1

Amrit Dencer-Brown on predicting the future challenges for mixed methods researchers under high complexity conditions

The key challenges are linked directly to our ever changing biosphere, and the challenges we face as humans and nature are increasingly opposed due to anthropogenic pressures. The 'wicked' and 'creeping' problems we have contributed to require us as mixed methods researchers to think innovatively, outside of the box, for long-term sustainable solutions which support life as a whole. We need to find ways to understand complexity as it evolves and changes. This can be achieved through adaptive management and governance of our environment. It is not enough just to research our biosphere; we have the responsibility to protect and improve the current state of affairs, and mixed methods can help provide effective and flexible frameworks to do this. What we need to do is embrace the complexity of our living world and accept that we cannot simplify our actions to achieve our goals. We need theories of change to put our ideas into action and learn from our mistakes in order to ensure that life on Earth is resilient and sustainable.

Opportunities Afforded by Complexity Science for Mixed Methods Researchers

My research experiences, readings of the principles of complexity, and applications of a complexity lens have shaped how I think about my actions and reactions as a researcher. They also shape how I consider and explain potential research problems to pursue, how I create and manage contextual boundaries in my research, how I seek and describe desirable interactions among my research team members, how I monitor and adapt research procedures to emerging conditions, and how I generate and assess evidence of research quality. I first began exploring the connections between the principles of complexity science and research systems because of my interest and undergraduate studies in the natural sciences. As I became immersed in reading about the roots of complexity science relevant to the areas of chaos theory, cybernetics, thermodynamics, and ecology (see Kauffman, 1995; Prigogine & Stengers, 1984; Waldrop, 1992), I came to realize how examples in the natural world helped me to understand my own actions and interactions as a researcher. I also recognized that I was not alone in my thinking because complexity science had already arisen as a disciplined and demanding approach to the study of complex phenomena in subjects as diverse as cognition, biology, business, and education (e.g., Capra, 2002; Davis & Sumara, 2006; Johnson, 2001; Lewin & Regine, 2001).

My thinking continues to be influenced by research approaches informed by complexity – such as narratives by Emma Uprichard (2012) – and by the promising transdisciplinary role for complexity theory in the social sciences – emphasized by David Byrne and Gill Callaghan (2014). 'Complexity theory represents an important challenge to the silos of the twentieth-first-century academy' (Byrne & Callaghan, 2014, p. 3). It is important to remember that complexity science is not new, rather that its applications have long been described across many fields of study beyond the natural sciences – for example, Manson (2001) in human geography and related fields and Anderson (1999) in strategy, management, and organization theory. Some familiarity with complexity science is useful in understanding the lens that researchers adopt and lessons that are derived from (or inform) responses of mixed methods researchers operating under conditions of complexity.

We now recognize that nonlinear and complex adaptive systems offer an authentic way to understand systems involving people working under conditions of varying complexity. This arises because people have the capacity to emerge, evolve, and thrive (Lewin, 1999). Mixed methods research practices predicated on linear thinking, control, predictability, and stability are limited in their usefulness because the world in which we operate as researchers is simply too complex. The work of organizational theorists (e.g., Stacey, Griffin, & Shaw, 2000) helps us understand changeable research conditions as involving people. People are key among the many interactions that occur as part of our research. I apply these understandings of complexity science principles and complexity lens assumptions to make sense of what I have experienced as a researcher. In Guiding Tip 3.1, an emerging scholar from South Africa echoes advice for engaging in learning and reflecting as a means for navigating the complexities of mixed methods research.

 Guiding Tip 3.1

Christo Ackermann advising how to navigate the complexity of mixed methods research

Embrace it, be willing to learn and take responsibility for knowing – the rest will then flow naturally.

There are two key contributors to conditions of research complexity that can be attributed to interactions between people:

- The distinct human ability to think and intentionally influence behaviour
- The ability for people to participate simultaneously across research systems.

I am guided by the four principles of complexity in my interactions as a researcher with others under conditions of varying complexity. Figure 3.1 shows the theoretical connections among the opportunities afforded by each of the four complexity science principles and the assumptions of a complexity lens that are further explained in the sections that follow. These come from lessons I have learned as a researcher working under conditions of complexity and from discussions of the featured studies in this book.

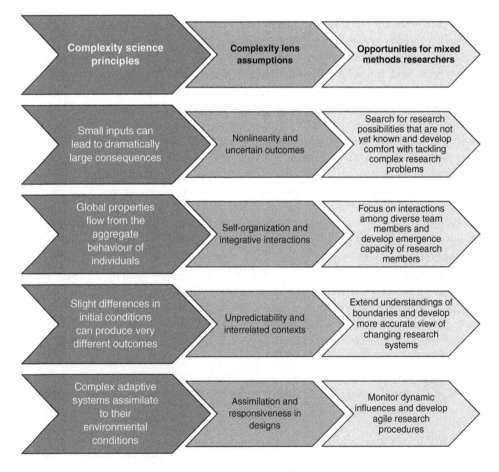

Figure 3.1 Opportunities for mixed methods research afforded by the theoretical underpinnings of complexity science

Adapted from Poth (2018a). Copyright © 2018 by Dialectical Publishing. Reprinted with permission.

Small Inputs Can Lead to Dramatically Large Consequences

As a researcher, you may have observed surprisingly large effects from what was initially perceived as an insignificant influence during a study, and struggled to make sense (as I have) of how to recognize such processes earlier. An illustrative example from my own research experience involved one person on a research team challenging the members to think beyond what we knew were possible outcomes during the planning stage of a project. This unique perspective shifted some decisions about how we collected data and opened up new opportunities during the analysis that we could not have imagined. In retrospect, I had erroneously anticipated only small contributions to the research by this person. In the end, their influence on our mixed insights had been large. Since then, similar experiences have reminded me of the need to assume nonlinear and uncertain mixed methods research outcomes.

As I have searched for research possibilities that are not yet known, I have embraced one of the key characteristics of complex adaptive systems: 'small changes can lead to large effects' (Lewin, 1999, p. 203). Indeed, nonlinear relationships are known to be distinctive, and changes are disproportionate between source and consequence (Byrne & Callaghan, 2014). Thus, researchers are said to develop greater comfort with tackling complex mixed methods research problems because of an increased understanding that from the edge of chaos and the unknown come new possibilities for innovations. We are beginning to see evidence in published accounts that researchers perceive mixed methods as uniquely positioned to address complex research problems where the outcomes are nonlinear and uncertain. For example, in the introductory sentence of the featured study on safe places, the authors state: 'Mixed methods studies can contribute to a reduction in inequalities and provide solutions for pressing problems of society' (Zea et al., 2014, p. 212). The authors then describe their article as 'an international study of HIV prevalence, sexual risk, and attitudes towards circumcision among Colombian gay and bisexual men and transwomen' (p. 212) and specify two study aims. The second aim involves integrating the information generated by the study to draw conclusions and ultimately inform the design of policies and interventions even though the specific insights were yet to be known. Similarly, the authors of the featured study on vaping culture position mixed methods as facilitating their investigation of a large sample in order to generate broad understandings of vaping culture to 'ultimately gain better understandings of health beliefs, policy attitudes, and other potentially salient aspects of this phenomenon' (Colditz et al., 2017, p. 3). Common to both studies is that the authors present logical lines of argument that undertaking these studies will contribute to tackling a larger societal issue, even though the specific study outcomes are yet uncertain.

Global Properties Flow from the Aggregate Behaviour of Individuals

As a researcher, you may have realized the capacity that more than one research member, as part of a team, can generate outcomes that are greater than the sum of individual contributions. You may also have struggled (as I have) to make sense of how to optimize such individual and team potential. An illustrative example from my own research experiences involved a team who developed the capacity to integrate their contributions following a period of conflict in ideas and negotiation of roles. Their collaborative work drawing on their unique expertise and experiences generated understandings that (I genuinely believe) would not have been otherwise accessible. In retrospect, I had mistakenly interpreted the conflict and negotiation as negative. I had not anticipated the need for members to manage their own team development. Since then, similar experiences have reminded me of the need to create conditions for **self-organization** (also known as **emergence**) that describe the capacity of members and teams to accommodate the products of their integrative interactions. Indeed, emergence means the properties of the whole cannot be accounted for by its components (Byrne & Callaghan, 2014).

As I engage members in interactions that are integrative, I have incorporated one of the key characteristics of complex adaptive systems: that 'the source of emergence is the interaction among agents who mutually affect one another' (Lewin, 1999, p. 202). Thus, researchers are said to develop greater capacity for emergence because of an increased understanding that from the development of mutual relations come new possibilities for innovation. We are beginning to see evidence in published accounts of concerted development of mixed methods research teams involving integrative interactions creating conditions for emergence. This was almost certainly the case, although not explicitly explained using such terms, in the featured study on safe places. Zea et al. (2014) provide a detailed description of team development and the interactions among the transdisciplinary and culturally diverse members in order to develop egalitarian relationships that enable intensive collaborations that were detailed throughout the study. One such example involved a description of how different team members contributed to the generation and validation of the mixed insights that would have been otherwise inaccessible. Similarly, the authors of the featured study on leadership competencies (Strudsholm et al., 2016) position their interactions among diverse team members as essential for interpreting their findings. This provided evidence of the validity of their insights as well. Common to both studies is that the authors present evidence focused on the development of diverse research teams and the collaborative interactions among members which generated evidence of integrative capacity. Otherwise, they may not have produced validation evidence for the study outcomes.

Slight Differences in Initial Conditions Can Produce Very Different Outcomes

As a researcher, you may have experienced unusual results from what were initially perceived as similar research conditions, and struggled (as I have) with how to distinguish interrelated contexts. An illustrative example from my own research experiences involved the comparison of two sample populations in an intervention study where the differing results could not be accounted for by the intervention. This finding led me to reconsider how we developed our initial understandings of the research conditions. In retrospect, I had not taken into account the dynamic influences including the interrelatedness of the personal differences on the local study context. Since then, similar experiences have reminded me of the need to assume unpredictable and varying mixed methods research contexts.

As I have extended my understandings of the boundaries surrounding mixed methods research, I have come to appreciate one of the key characteristics of complex adaptive systems: that 'greater diversity of agents in a system leads to richer emergent patterns' (Lewin, 1999, p. 203). Thus, researchers are said to develop a more accurate view of the mixed methods research contexts, because from an increased understanding of the changeable nature of the interrelated research systems come new possibilities for innovations. We are beginning to see evidence in published accounts that researchers are adopting a system perspective in order to diagnose research conditions that are unpredictable and involve interrelated contexts. For example, in the featured study on safe places, Zea et al. (2014) provide details of the societal, local, and personal contexts involved in the study. They do this through descriptions of political, economic, and social influences on Colombian society, the specific influences on the displaced gay and bisexual men and transwomen who are the study population, and the relevant training and experiential backgrounds of those involved in the research. Similarly, yet to a lesser degree of detail, the authors of the featured study on law clients (Chui & Cheng, 2017) also describe the interrelated contexts of their research as involving the societal judicial system within Hong Kong, individual lawyer differences in their approaches as either publicly or privately hired, and the variability among young offenders who were the study population. Common to both studies is that the author descriptions of the interrelated contexts and descriptions of dynamic influences present a more accurate view of the research systems as unpredictable and interrelated.

Complex Adaptive Systems Assimilate to their Environmental Interactions

As a researcher, you may have seen how adaptations have occurred in response to dynamic influences and struggled to make sense (as I have) of how to predict such occurrences. An illustrative example from my own research experiences involved a gatekeeper to a research site who, as the study was about to begin, blocked access to the site in response to a policy shift in government. In retrospect, I had incorrectly assumed that the research would be buffered from societal-level influences and had not anticipated the need to attend to these influences. Since then, similar experiences have reminded me of the need to assume the need for responsive designs and agile procedures within the mixed methods research process.

As I have accommodated dynamic influences, I have adapted to one of the key characteristics of complex adaptive systems: 'emergence is certain, but there is no certainty in what it will be' (Lewin, 1999, p. 203). Thus, researchers are said to develop more appropriate mixed methods research procedures because of their increased understanding that from assimilation come new possibilities for innovations. We are beginning to see evidence in published accounts, albeit infrequent, of researchers adapting their procedures in response to emerging understandings of study environments under conditions of complexity. For example, in the featured study on safe places, Zea et al. (2014) describe adaptations to the original larger study design to include more interviews in response to low rates of HIV testing among participants. Similarly, in the featured study on leadership competencies, Strudsholm et al. (2016) refer to feasibility issues attributable to time zones. This led to a change in focus group planning and implementation. Common to both studies are that the authors provide a rationale for their procedural adaptations.

Indicators of Integrative Thinking with Complexity in Mixed Methods Research

As with all research, individuals (e.g., supervisors, grant reviewers, journal editors) are tasked with applying criteria to evaluate mixed methods studies. Like others, I apply criteria in my appraisal of the quality of mixed methods research proposals and completed studies I read across my various roles. When I do so, I transform the available standards for assessing the evidence of mixed methods research quality (Collins, 2015; O'Cathain, 2010; Onwuegbuzie & Poth, 2016) into a more complexity-sensitive mixed methods research approach. A sensitivity to complexity requires incorporating criteria for feasibility and authenticity in assessing quality of complexity-sensitive mixed methods research. Examine Figure 3.2 for a visual representation of indicators of integrative thinking with complexity in mixed methods research. During proposal writing, researchers make explicit their initial understandings of potential influences, and in so doing make the case for feasibility by describing how they will manage the tasks under conditions of complexity. Throughout the study, researchers create strategies for monitoring and tracking responses, and in so doing document adaptations to changing research conditions. During report writing, researchers make explicit their evolved understandings of dynamic influences and impacts on tasks based on study processes and outcomes, and in so doing create an authentic report of the study conditions of complexity inherent in the particular complex mixed methods research. Examine Table 3.1 to learn about the indicators of integrative thinking with complexity that are explained in this section, which includes my short list summarizing what I look for and where I look for the evidence within a study proposal and report.

Need for Approach

Researchers are tasked with the responsibility of justifying the research approach – in this case, for applying integrative thinking with complexity to the use of a complexity-sensitive approach to mixed methods research for their study. To mitigate concerns with recognizing today's pluralist social inquiry field, I conceptualize qualitative, quantitative, and mixed

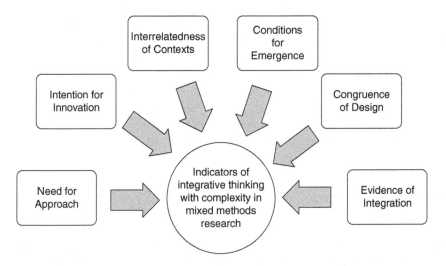

Figure 3.2   Indicators of integrative thinking with complexity in mixed methods research

methods approaches as representing a narrow definition of research approaches and that many others also exist (e.g., action research, critical social science, critical race theory), each with their own history and procedures. Typical practice for many researchers explaining their selection of a mixed methods approach involves defining the unique contributions of mixed methods research for addressing the study needs for integration of qualitative and quantitative data. For those explicitly adopting a complexity-sensitive approach, this task also involves assessing the conditions of complexity under which the mixed methods study will be or was pursued: in a study proposal by describing initial understandings of the conditions of complexity across the five dimensions of complexity, or in a completed research report by presenting evolved understandings of the conditions of complexity.

To assess the indicators of integrative thinking with complexity related to the need for a complexity-sensitive mixed methods research approach I look for evidence of the following in a study introduction (they might also be found within the descriptions of methods):

- Positioning of the mixed methods research approach as a distinct approach
- Definition of mixed methods research as involving integration of qualitative and quantitative data
- Descriptions of research conditions as being influenced by dynamic effects or recognizing changeability of the study environment.

Intention for Innovation

Researchers are tasked with the responsibility of introducing the study need for integration – in this case, for rationalizing integrative thinking with complexity to the integration intention for innovation. To provide a definition, I conceptualize complex research problems as those involving interdependent societal issues with no known solution or established methods and expertise for studying the dynamic societal contexts in which they take place. Typical practices for many researchers narrowing the focus of their mixed methods study involve exploring research topics of interest to the study, identifying particular issues related to a research problem in need of investigation, and advancing the integration purpose informing the drafting of research questions. For those explicitly adopting a complexity-sensitive approach this task also involves conveying the significance of the mixed methods research problems by framing what is initially or eventually known about the relevant integration purposes focused on innovation and dynamic background influences: in a study proposal by describing initial understandings of the integration purposes and potential background influences related to existing literature, or in a completed research report by presenting evolved understandings of the integration purposes and background influences in light of the study implementation.

To assess the indicators of integrative thinking with complexity related to the intention for innovation for a complexity-sensitive mixed methods research approach I look for evidence of the following in a study introduction (they might also be found within the reviews of literature):

- Positioning of the significance of the mixed methods research problems
- Relating the mixed methods research problems to relevant topics and issues
- Descriptions of integration intention as focused on innovation and dynamic background influences for the complex problems and grounded in existing literature and (if applicable) previous experiences.

Interrelatedness of Contexts

Researchers are tasked with the responsibility of defining the mixed methods research contexts – in this case, using integrative thinking about the surrounding systems to the use of a complexity-sensitive approach to mixed methods research for their study. In response to the need for expanding the boundaries beyond the local mixed methods study context, I conceptualize mixed methods research systems as involving three interdependent contexts, described as proximal, communal, and global. Typical practice for many researchers bounding their mixed methods study involves exploring the people and places involved in the local context. For those explicitly adopting a complexity-sensitive approach this task also involves conveying what is initially or eventually known about the relevant communal and global contexts as well as the dynamic environmental influences: in a study proposal by describing initial understandings of the relevant systems and potential environmental influences within and across the interrelated systems related to existing literature, or in a completed research report by presenting evolved understandings of the relevant interrelated systems and environmental influences in light of the study implementation.

To assess the indicators of integrative thinking with complexity about the interrelatedness of contexts for a complexity-sensitive mixed methods research approach I look for evidence of the following in a study introduction (they might also be found within the reviews of literature and descriptions of methods):

- Identification of the multiple contexts of the mixed methods research systems
- Positioning of mixed methods research systems as being situated within interrelated and dynamic contexts
- Descriptions of research systems as having interrelated proximal, communal, and global systems and dynamic environmental influences.

Conditions for Emergence

Researchers are tasked with the responsibility of facilitating mixed methods research interactions – in this case, for applying integrative thinking with complexity related to developing conditions for emergence. In recognition of the various possible intensities of collaborations, I conceptualize mixed methods research interactions as drawing upon members' collective experiences, expertise and intuition to generate outcomes that are otherwise inaccessible. Typical practice for many researchers developing mixed methods research interactions involves bringing together diverse and willing individuals to work as members of a research team. For those explicitly adopting a complexity-sensitive approach this task also involves committing to diverse roles that have yet to be defined, creating a team identity in which individuals consider themselves part of an entity, and offering individual contributions that others can draw upon and integrate with their own: in a study proposal by describing initial understandings of the relevant methodological and disciplinary diversity of individual members and potential social influences, or in a completed research report by presenting evolved understandings of the relevant methodological and disciplinary diversity of individual members and social influences in light of the study implementation.

To assess the indicators of integrative thinking with complexity related to the conditions for emergence for a complexity-sensitive mixed methods research approach I look for evidence of the following in the study methods (they might also be found within the introduction):

- Identification of the individual contributions of mixed methods researchers
- Descriptions of the methodological and disciplinary diversity of mixed methods teams and the nature of intended outcomes from interactions
- Descriptions of relevant team development efforts and dynamic social influences and (if applicable) previous experiences.

Congruence of Design

Researchers are tasked with the responsibility of reporting details about the compatibility among elements of the mixed methods research procedures – in this case, for promoting integrative thinking with complexity related to the congruence within the mixed methods research designs. In recognition of the various approaches to establishing methodological congruence (see Chapter 2), I conceptualize congruent mixed methods research designs as involving deliberate strategies for maintaining fit among the tasks involved in conducting the research; for example, the research questions, along with sampling, recruitment, data collection, data analysis, and integration are all compatible and interrelated. In so doing, the study features appear as a cohesive whole rather than as fragmented and isolated parts. Typical practice for many researchers establishing methodological congruence involves selecting a mixed methods research design from existing typologies. For those explicitly adopting a complexity-sensitive approach this task also involves embedding agility in study procedures to respond to changing conditions: in a study proposal by describing initial understandings of the relevant features for each of the points of interface and practical influences, or in a completed research report by presenting evolved understandings of the relevant features for each of the points of interface and dynamic feasibility influences in light of the study implementation.

To assess the indicators of integrative thinking with complexity related to the congruence of design for a complexity-sensitive mixed methods research approach I look for evidence of the following in the study methods (they might also be found within the introduction):

- Positioning of the compatibility of the tasks involved in the mixed methods designs
- Descriptions of integration procedures related to points of data interface and (if applicable) identification of design typology
- Descriptions of embedded agility in the procedures and dynamic feasibility influences related to existing literature and (if applicable) previous experiences.

Evidence of Integration

Researchers are tasked with the responsibility of generating evidence of methodological rigour within mixed methods integrations – in this case, for enhancing integrative thinking with complexity to the appraisal of mixed methods research insights. With various strategies for demonstrating evidence of qualitative, quantitative, and mixed methods research rigour, I conceptualize appraisal of mixed methods research as an ongoing, adaptive, and embedded process. Typical practice for many researchers appraising mixed methods research involves drawing upon the established standards of rigour in qualitative and quantitative research as well as those specific to legitimacy in mixed methods research. For those explicitly adopting a complexity-sensitive approach this task also involves adapting and creating innovative ways of doing and representing integration that have yet to be established in the literature: in a study proposal by describing initial understandings of the relevant strategies for generating integration evidence and dynamic practical influences, or in a completed research report by presenting evolved understandings of the relevant strategies for generating evidence of integration in light of the study implementation.

To assess the indicators of integrative thinking with complexity related to the evidence of integration for a complexity-sensitive mixed methods research approach I look for the following in the study methods (they might also be found within the findings, discussion and conclusion):

- Positioning of the interpretations of the mixed methods research integrations as legitimate and addressing the integration intentions of the study problems
- Justification of strategies used for generating evidence of rigour and grounding of mixing strategy in existing literature (if applicable)
- Descriptions of appraisals of evidence from relevant integration processes and adaptations made in response to dynamic practical influences.

Table 3.1 Summary of descriptions of complexity-sensitive mixed methods research indicators, tasks, evidence, and study locations

Indicators	Tasked with responsibility of	Evidence sought	Typical study location for evidence
Need for approach	Justifying the complexity-sensitive mixed methods research approach	Positioning of the mixed methods research approach as a distinct approach	Introduction (might also be found within the descriptions of methods)
		Definition of mixed methods research as involving integration of qualitative and quantitative data	
		Descriptions of research conditions as being influenced by dynamic effects or recognizing changeability of the study environment	
Intention for innovation	Rationalizing the intention for innovation of the study	Positioning of the significance of the mixed methods research problems	Introduction (might also be found within the reviews of literature)
		Relating the mixed methods research problems to relevant topics and issues	
		Descriptions of integration intention as focused on innovation and dynamic background influences for the complex problems and grounded in existing literature and (if applicable) previous experiences	
Interrelatedness of contexts	Defining the mixed methods research systems	Identification of the multiple contexts of the mixed methods research systems	Introduction (might also be found within the reviews of literature and descriptions of methods)
		Positioning of mixed methods research systems as being situated within interrelated and dynamic contexts	
		Descriptions of research systems as having interrelated proximal, communal, and global systems and dynamic environmental influences	

Indicators	Tasked with responsibility of	Evidence sought	Typical study location for evidence
Conditions for emergence	Facilitating the mixed methods research interactions	Identification of the individual contributions of mixed methods researchers Descriptions of the methodological and disciplinary diversity of mixed methods teams and the nature of intended outcomes from interactions Descriptions of relevant team development efforts and dynamic social influences and (if applicable) previous experiences	Methods (might also be found within the introduction)
Congruence of design	Promoting congruence within the mixed methods research designs	Positioning of the compatibility of the tasks involved in the mixed methods designs Descriptions of integration procedures related to points of data interface and (if applicable) identification of design typology Descriptions of embedded agility in the procedures and dynamic feasibility influences related to existing literature and (if applicable) previous experiences	Methods
Evidence of integration	Enhancing the rigour within mixed methods research integrations	Positioning of the interpretations of the mixed methods research integrations as legitimate and addressing the integration intentions of the study problems Justification of strategies used for generating evidence of rigour and grounding of mixing strategy in existing literature (if applicable) Descriptions of appraisals of evidence from relevant integration processes and adaptations made in response to dynamic practical influences	Methods (might also found within the findings, discussion, and conclusions)

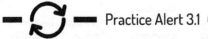 Practice Alert 3.1

How do you incorporate complexity-sensitive quality criteria in a mixed methods study proposal?

When preparing a study proposal for a dissertation or funding application, it is in the author's best interest to consider expectations of others and criteria used for assessing quality mixed methods research (DeCuir-Gunby & Schultz, 2017). Quality criteria can take many forms (Fàbregues & Molina-Azorin, 2017), but I find the six complexity-sensitive quality indicators to be helpful in guiding my thinking about what I have considered in my study proposal and identifying areas for greater description. For example, am I clearly justifying the need for a mixed methods approach and the focus of innovation of my study purpose? Have I described the boundaries and influences of the interrelated personal, interpersonal, and societal systems involved in the study? Have I described the diversity among research members and efforts for developing their capacity for emergence? Have I explained the congruency of my design so

(Continued)

(Continued)

that the outcomes clearly address the problem? Do my procedures include generating evidence of validity for the insights I will generate?

Try this now – use the questions listed above to review a study proposal that you wish to undertake, focusing on what areas were well developed and what areas required further development.

Indicators of the Six Featured Mixed Methods Studies

I have always found that the best way to learn about how to assess is to view the indicators applied across a number of published mixed methods journal articles. By looking closely at what was made explicit by the researchers, we can also note what indicators are less obvious or missing in their study accounts. My appraisal was based on the evidence found in the featured studies, as shown in Table 3.2.

Here 'fully' means evidence for all three features of the indicator was present, 'partially' means evidence for at least one of the three features of the indicator was present, and 'no evidence' means there was a lack of evidence for all the three features. To convey my appraisal of each of the indicators of integrative thinking with complexity, I describe the patterns for each indicator across the six studies in this section. Note that all the featured studies met, at least partially, all of the indicators of integrative thinking – the sole exception was the conditions for emergence indicator for the featured study on law

Table 3.2 Appraisal of indicators for integrative thinking with complexity across the six featured mixed methods studies

Featured study	Need for approach	Intention for innovation	Interrelatedness of contexts	Conditions for emergence	Congruence of design	Evidence of integration
Law clients (Chui & Cheng, 2017)	P	P	P	–	P	P
Postconflict risk (Taylor et al., 2017)	P	F	F	P	P	P
Heart care (Dickson et al., 2011)	P	F	P	P	P	P
Safe places (Zea et al., 2014)	P	F	F	F	F	P
Leadership competencies (Strudsholm et al., 2016)	P	F	F	F	F	P
Vaping culture (Colditz et al., 2017)	P	F	F	P	P	P

Note. F = Fully, P = Partially.

clients. As you examine the descriptions and summary presented in Table 3.2, notice both the similarities and differences among the indicators of integrative thinking across the featured mixed methods studies. The following descriptions are not intended to be comprehensive, as more comprehensive discussions of these patterns across the featured studies are embedded in Part II of this book where each of the six complexity-sensitive guiding practices is described in detail. Among the many challenges faced by those new to mixed methods research is the lack of capacity for guiding mixed methods research. Examine Researcher Spotlight 3.2, from the perspective of an emerging scholar from South Africa, on the need for researchers to explore new approaches to complex mixed methods research problems.

 Researcher Spotlight 3.2

Christo Ackermann on the need for exploring new approaches to complex mixed methods research problems

In my limited experience as an emerging mixed methods scholar, a pressing challenge is not knowing about mixed methods as a logical map to best approach complexities. The challenge here is twofold: students not knowing or understanding mixed methods, and supervisors experiencing the same challenge. As a result, most students approach complexities by employing the same type of designs (either quantitative or qualitative approaches) and methods in conducting research as their supervisors. When students do pursue mixed methods as part of their (especially doctoral) studies, supervisors not schooled in these approaches push back, and this in itself may create student and supervisor challenges. In the end, the research problem does not get justice. As a start, I think we need even more awareness of mixed methods and a willingness to expose yourself to these approaches. Then we start learning and applying.

High consistency was found within the first three indicators and across all the featured studies. Common across all the featured studies was the appraisal of having partially met the quality indicator of need for approach. This is not surprising because none of the featured studies explicitly adopt a complexity-sensitive approach to mixed methods research, yet there exists evidence for the need for a mixed methods approach. This evidence differed in content and details: whereas many studies referred to the unique contributions of a mixed methods research approach, only the featured study on leadership competencies (Strudsholm et al., 2016) provided a definition specific to mixed methods. In contrast, the majority of studies mentioned integration of qualitative and quantitative data in their definitions of a specific mixed methods research design. Also consistent across all the featured studies was evidence of study intentions for innovation and the interrelatedness of study contexts. Evidence of a focus of innovation was reflected in well-developed descriptions of the significance of the problems being pursued: many studies provided a grounding in related literature and alluded to the need for new understandings of pressing societal issues. Each study also provided some evidence of the interrelatedness of contexts in their descriptions of more than one system in which the study was situated.

In contrast, greater variability was found within the second group of three indicators across the featured studies. For these three indicators, none of the studies fully met all of them. Interestingly, the same featured studies on safe places (Zea et al., 2014) and leadership competencies (Strudsholm et al., 2016) fully met the indicators of conditions for emergence and congruence of design by providing detailed descriptions of their team members and development and how their data procedures responded to study conditions. For the final indicator, none of the featured studies fully met the indicators for evidence of integration.

Guiding Practices for Integrative Thinking with Complexity in Mixed Methods Research

A complexity-sensitive approach to mixed methods research cannot be thought of as a set of steps to be followed. Rather, think of it as a mindset shift that optimizes the efforts of researchers working in complex conditions. This means embracing change. To guide researchers in what I consider more authentic mixed methods research under varying conditions of complexity, I advance six **adaptive mixed methods research practices**. A practices-based approach is intentional because it implies the need to adapt to the unique research conditions each study presents. Researchers may find that they focus on particular practices more often than others. This is to be expected. A practices-based approach is contrasted with prescriptive and progressive frameworks which assume each research phase is completed before going onto the next. Instead, complexity-sensitive practices assume our research process will be iterative and phases revisited throughout the study. Each of the practices must be interpreted and adapted to the unique needs of the researcher. How you use the practices will depend on a variety of factors including the tasks within particular phases of the research and the specific contexts of the study. Of key importance is that study proposals make explicit our initial understandings of the conditions of complexity specific to our study and that we describe in our study reports the consequences of our responses to the dynamic influences on the research conditions.

I present six interrelated complexity-sensitive guiding practices here because each contributes to the structural organization of the next part in this book. Taken together, these complexity-sensitive practices can guide researchers to identify, monitor, and respond to conditions of complexity. Because of the close interrelatedness of these practices, it is likely that a researcher will be engaged in several of them concomitantly. Examine Table 3.3 to trace how the traditional mixed methods research practice tendencies are transformed by a complexity lens to create the six adaptive mixed methods research practice tendencies described in the forthcoming six chapters.

Table 3.3   Six adaptive practices for guiding complexity-sensitive mixed methods research

Traditional mixed methods research practice tendencies	Adaptive mixed methods research practice tendencies	Key researcher tasks for adaptive practices	Chapter reference
Assess approach suitability based on assumptions of stability in the surrounding study conditions	Diagnosing of complexity of conditions through ongoing integrative thinking about the stability of five dimensions of complexity	Monitor study conditions for evidence of nonlinear influences, and adjust study conditions in light of emerging patterns in complexity dimensions	4
Articulate research purpose based on identifications of gaps in the existing study literature	Framing of complex problems through ongoing integrative thinking about relevant literature and background influences	Consider experiences, motivations, and literature relevant to the research problem being pursued and adjust study purpose to emerging understandings of problem background	5
Situate research contexts based on definitions of target study participants, sites, and organizations	Defining of interrelated contexts through ongoing integrative thinking about potential systems and environmental influences	Consider proximal, communal, and global systems relevant to the research context and adjust study systems to emerging understandings of interrelated systems	6
Establish research capacity based upon predeterminations of required study expertise and roles	Developing emergence in interactions through ongoing integrative thinking about member diversity and social influences	Consider experiences, intuition, and expertise relevant to the research members and adjust study interactions to emerging understandings of social interactions	7
Design research integrations based on selections of study procedures	Realizing agile integrations through integrative thinking about data procedures and feasibility influences	Consider design considerations and adjust study procedures to emerging understandings of feasible integrations	8
Evaluate research outcomes based on expectations of methodological rigour	Generating evidence of outcomes through integrative thinking with complexity about existing criteria and practical influences	Consider quality indicators relevant to the research outcomes and adjust study processes to emerging understandings of evidence of rigour	9

.... **CHAPTER CHECK-IN**

1   Can you begin to conceptualize the usefulness of a complexity perspective for mixed methods researchers under varying research conditions?

- Consider research you have done or are planning to do. Would any of the studies be considered an example of a complex adaptive system? Why or why not?
- Consider the extent of your agreement with the author's assertion that 'Mixed methods research can be considered to represent a nonlinear and complex adaptive system because it is influenced by a large number of interacting and interrelated contextual components for which there is no central control while researchers adapt to new conditions.'

2   Can you apply integrative thinking with complexity in mixed methods research?

- Begin by considering how a complexity lens might provide an effective way to manage mixed methods research under dynamic conditions.

- Then, using a mixed methods study that you have experienced or want to pursue, consider which (one or more) of the opportunities afforded by the theoretical underpinnings of complexity science might be useful in guiding your study (see Figure 3.1).
- Finally, imagine you incorporate some of the principles of complexity science. What key transformations would inform your adaptive practices to mixed methods research?

3   Can you recognize evidence of integrative thinking with complexity in mixed methods research?

- Begin by identifying which of the indicators are familiar and how each has been transformed by a complexity-sensitive approach (see Figure 3.2).
- Then consider how incorporating the indicators differs between a proposal and a report, and where evidence is located in a study.

4   Can you identify indicators of integrative thinking with complexity across the six featured studies?

- Compare how the authors of at least two of these studies describe the need for a mixed methods approach, the intention for integration, the interrelatedness of contexts, the conditions for emergence, the congruence of design, and evidence of integration (see Table 3.1). Note the wording they use.
- Then check your work with the appraisal presented in Table 3.2.
- Discuss the extent to which the researcher tasks contribute to adaptive practices described in Table 3.3.

KEY CHAPTER CONCEPTS

This chapter positioned the foundational theoretical underpinnings for this book: what does adopting a complexity-sensitive approach to mixed methods involve, and how can integrative thinking with complexity transform mixed methods research practices? There is a need for complexity-sensitive mixed methods research to support innovations and to be adaptive to address the dilemmas experienced under conditions of complexity. Among the opportunities for researchers afforded by a complexity lens are providing new perspectives to inform our work as well as more authentic accounts of the realities in which we undertake our studies.

Six criteria for assessing indicators of integrative thinking with complexity are: need for approach, intention for innovation, interrelatedness of contexts, conditions for emergence, congruence of design, and evidence of integration. Finally, the integrative thinking with complexity criteria are applied to the six featured mixed methods studies, and six guiding practices for complexity-sensitive mixed methods research are advanced. Each of the following chapters describes one of the guiding practices.

FURTHER READINGS

The following resources are offered as introductory references for complexity theory and a complexity-sensitive approach to mixed methods research. The list should not be considered exhaustive. Readers are encouraged to seek out additional readings in the end-of-book reference list. Readings denoted with an asterisk are available on the companion website for this book.

Braithwaite, J., Churruca, K., Ellis, L. A., Long, J., Clay-Williams, R., Damen N, ..., Ludlow, K. (2017). *Complexity science in healthcare – Aspirations, approaches, applications and accomplishments: A white paper.* Sydney: Australian Institute of Health Innovation, Macquarie University. Retrieved from http://bit.ly/2If4KMG

The founding director of the Australian Institute of Health Innovation, Jeffrey Braithwaite, and the Complexity Science Team in the Centre for Healthcare Resilience and Implementation Science offer applications of complex systems in health care.

Byrne, D., & Callaghan, G. (2014). *Complexity theory and the social sciences: The state of the art.* New York: Routledge.

David Byrne and Gill Callaghan provide a much needed introduction to the implications of complexity within the social sciences. Particularly noteworthy for mixed methods researchers is Chapter 9, which focuses on researching the complex social world, as well as the concluding chapter, which proposes the way forward for social science researchers.

Castellani, B. (2014). Complexity and the failure of quantitative social science. *Focus, 14.* http://discoversociety.org/2014/11/04/focus-complexity-and-the-failure-of-quantitative-social-science/.

Brian Castellani reflects on his training as a psychology undergraduate in the USA over three decades ago to argue the pressing need for methods beyond statistics to explore and inform the social realities that are studied. An interesting read providing a noteworthy introduction to the complexity literature.

*Koopmans, M. (2016). Mixed methods in search of a problem: Perspectives from complexity theory. *Journal of Mixed Methods Research, 11*(1), 16–18. doi: 10.1177/1558689816676662.

Matthijs Koopmans advances complexity theory as a useful framework for mixed methods research in describing the behaviour of individuals within interrelated systems. In so doing, he provides a concise introduction for those new to complexity theory.

Lewin, R. (1999). *Complexity: Life at the edge of chaos* (2nd ed.). Chicago: University of Chicago Press.

Roger Lewin builds on his highly accessible approach to introducing readers to the field of complexity science by giving examples drawn from diverse disciplines.

Williams, M., & Vogt, W. P. (Eds.) (2012). *The SAGE handbook of innovation in social research methods.* Thousand Oaks, CA: Sage.

Handbooks are often a logical starting point for emerging research, and in this one Malcolm Williams and W. Paul Vogt provide access to innovative research designs and data collection. Noteworthy is Emma Uprichard's description of narratives of the future which involves complexity, time, and temporality.

Warwick Centre for Interdisciplinary Methodologies (http://www2.warwick.ac.uk/fac/cross_fac/cim/)

This website has the overall aim of creating interdisciplinary networks of scholars applying complexity to social science research problems. Some of the work focuses specifically on addressing methodological challenges by developing mixed methods approaches.

Apply your mixed methods knowledge with videos, activities, SAGE journal articles and project templates at **https://study.sagepub.com/poth**

PART II

In the next six chapters I describe guiding practices initially developed to help my students and colleagues move their mixed methods studies forward. What I did not have at the time was the capacity to articulate why these practices helped when tackling more complex research. The goal is not simply to advance new practices under conditions of complexity. Rather, I describe how adapting traditional mixed methods research practices mitigates the dilemmas experienced under conditions of complexity. In so doing, I aim to recognize and build upon the solutions offered by others and provide practical guidance for heeding the call for innovation in mixed methods research.

The field of mixed methods research is well established in the literature, yet practical guidance for implementing a mixed methods research study under conditions of complexity continues to emerge. Among the qualities I appreciate most about the field of mixed methods research is that promising practices continue to emerge from both planned and fortuitous efforts. While these developments might make some readers nervous because of the desire for established best practices to follow, I am excited by the opportunity to contribute new ideas as well as to build upon existing practices.

My intention in advancing six adaptive practices is to help researchers harness the complexity inherent in their mixed methods research studies. The practices described in this book have emerged and evolved over the past decade as I responded to dynamic influences I was experiencing as a mixed methods researcher as well as to those around me. These practices continue to emerge and evolve. I have organized the chapters in this part by practice, and for each practice I begin with describing the function by relating the practice to current research and dilemmas, the opportunities by exploring possibilities the adaptive practice offers, and the hazards researchers would be well served to be aware of. Then I describe strategies for planning and implementing each practice, followed by features for engaging readers. Finally, I offer writing and diagramming structures for conveying the practice in proposals and reports.

REALIZING INNOVATION IN GUIDING PRACTICES

The six chapters in Part II are as follows:

4

DIAGNOSING COMPLEXITY OF MIXED METHODS RESEARCH CONDITIONS

.... **KEY CHAPTER QUESTIONS**

By the end of this chapter, you will be able to answer the following questions:

- Why diagnose the complexity of mixed methods research conditions?
- What opportunities exist to diagnose complex mixed methods research conditions?
- Why can assumptions of stability become hazardous for mixed methods researchers?
- What procedures guide the diagnosis of complex mixed methods research conditions?
- What features engage readers with complex mixed methods research conditions?
- What writing and diagram innovations are useful for conveying the complexity of mixed methods research conditions?

.... **NEW CHAPTER TERMS**

- Complexity effects
- Complexity study profile

- Dimensions of complexity
- Messiness

This chapter advances the adaptive practice for guiding a complexity-sensitive approach to mixed methods research. It addresses the question: *What does diagnosing the complexity of mixed methods research conditions involve, and how can the suitability of a complexity-sensitive approach be recognized, promoted, and conveyed?* Consider a recent research study that you read. Did you become aware of any conditions under which the study was undertaken and, if so, what conditions were emphasized? Were there any indications of changeability in the conditions during the study? If so, what details were provided? Great variability exists with regard to the details researchers convey about the conditions surrounding their mixed methods research studies. This variability in details we see in study proposals and published reports indicates a lack of attention to and guiding examples of diagnosing research conditions. The significance of information gleaned from diagnosing research conditions becomes more important under conditions of high complexity.

Being able to recognize sources of complexity and apply these understandings in a way that can inform their approach constitutes one of the dilemmas experienced by mixed methods researchers. If researchers are unable to diagnose the specific conditions involved in the study problems, contexts, integrations, interactions, and outcomes, then they are not able to adapt their practices within a suitable approach. Assumptions of stability have emerged as key dilemmas experienced by researchers under conditions of complexity. Traditional practices described in the literature work well under many conditions, but under more complex conditions they can create unintended constraints on innovation possibilities. A focus on integrative thinking with complexity advances the possibility of adaptive practices and creating yet-to-be-known framing of problems, definitions of contexts, descriptions of integrations, developments of interactions, and generation of outcomes.

Work on this chapter is informed by my experiences as a learner, researcher, and instructor and informed by my readings in the fields of complexity science and mixed methods research too numerous to list here. Specifically, in seeking to guide others to diagnose the complexity of conditions involved in some mixed methods research, I draw upon my research, evaluation, and life experiences where I have adapted to evolving conditions and gained comfort with uncertainty. I have always felt that the best way to learn how to do something is first to be guided and then to be asked to apply my understandings. Thus, the focus of this chapter is to introduce and then demonstrate the application of the five dimensions for diagnosing the complexity of mixed methods research conditions: intentions of research problems, systems of research contexts, designs of research integrations, capacity of research interactions, and evidence of research outcomes. Embedding the featured mixed methods studies in this chapter reflects a continued effort to address the practice gap in many textbooks and to provide authentic examples of published articles that represent varying conditions of complexity. The current chapter builds upon the aspects of the featured complex mixed methods research studies already introduced in Chapters 1–3 as a means of bridging theory with article examples and avoiding repetition. Chapter 1 described the purposeful selection of these studies by highlighting the range of research topics, problems, designs, and locales represented. Chapter 2 summarized the initial survey of these studies, revealing the commonalities and differences across the research problems, designs, and members. Chapter 3 provided further details of integrative thinking with complexity across the studies. This chapter compares the complexity assessments of the conditions across the featured studies to demonstrate the usefulness of a **complexity study profile** for mixed methods researchers adopting a complexity-sensitive approach. Additionally, by providing accessing to the thinking behind the early formulations of the housing research example, it is my hope that this chapter helps you gain understandings of **complexity effects** and to apply the understandings of the five **dimensions of complexity** to real-world studies beyond those featured. Let us now consider how the opportunities, hazards, and procedures involved in diagnosing the complexity of mixed methods research conditions are distinctive for a study that is incorporating complexity-sensitive practices.

Why Diagnose Complexity of Mixed Methods Research Conditions?

Researchers are tasked with the responsibility of justifying the suitability of the research approach for the problem being pursued. For a mixed methods study, this involves making the case for why a mixed methods research approach is necessary. Specific to a complexity-sensitive approach to mixed methods research, this also involves assessing the extent of complexity in the conditions. The purpose for diagnosing the conditions is to justify the need for complexity sensitivities in the mixed methods research approach and adaptive mixed methods research practices. Mixed methods researchers are well served by assessing the complexity within their research. This is because when recognizing potential sources of complexity, researchers are more likely to respond appropriately to changes in surrounding conditions as the research unfolds. Diagnosing research conditions is realized through ongoing integrative thinking with complexity about the stability (or lack thereof!) across five dimensions of complexity. In so doing, researchers are better positioned to assimilate and respond to emerging understandings of research conditions in a way that both influences and is influenced by the changing conditions surrounding the mixed methods research.

What is becoming increasingly evident is that, although few research conditions can be conceived of as stable, many of our guiding practices as researchers are based on assumptions of stability. This means that efforts are often focused on reducing the complexity inherent in research conditions. It has become apparent that researchers working under conditions of complexity are ill-equipped to diagnose and report the conditions as they relate to evolving understandings of the intentions of the research problems, contexts, integrations, interactions, and outcomes. My thinking is guided by the realization that few published research projects have yet to capture such details of research conditions in their reports. The lack of authenticity in our reporting has become a practice concern because of the lost opportunity for researchers to reflect upon and learn from research that has been completed under varying conditions of complexity. It is this communication gap that has become the focus of my efforts to transform some of our mixed methods research practices to be more complexity-sensitive and our reporting to be more authentic. Consider Researcher Spotlight 4.1 describing the pressing challenge of responding to dynamic conditions, from the perspective of a professor of educational psychology and a university faculty scholar in the Department of Teacher Education and Learning Sciences at North Carolina State University in Raleigh (USA).

 Researcher Spotlight 4.1

Jessica DeCuir-Gunby on authentic reporting of research under conditions of high complexity

Real-world research can get complicated, especially research conducted in schools. I learned this lesson when I was co-principal investigator on a National Science Foundation grant-funded project, Nurturing Mathematics Dreamkeepers (with Patricia Marshall and Allison McCulloch). This mixed methods, multi-year study proved to be methodologically challenging in a few distinct areas. First, the research team utilized a complex mixed methods design. The study initially started as an embedded design; however, over time, it began to take on elements of other designs. We also had a large research team consisting of professors, graduate students, and undergraduate students. Training all team members in data collection and analysis was time-consuming because not everyone had the same methodological background knowledge. Next, we encountered problems with how best to address data collection (coordinating the schedules of multiple teachers from multiple schools, etc.) and data analysis (making sense of the data sources, including interviews, video-taped mathematics lessons, and student mathematics assessments, etc.). Also, we struggled with how to integrate the quantitative and qualitative data from the various years of the study. Overall, we learned that conducting mixed methods research requires having flexibility and being open to making changes based upon what is happening in real time. We documented all of our challenges in our book, *When Critical Multiculturalism Meets Mathematics: A Mixed Methods Study of Professional Development and Teacher Identity* (Marshall et al., 2015). The book illustrates the methodological complexities of conducting mixed methods research in schools as well as how we attempted to address the challenges we faced within our study.

Taking the time to assess a study's initial conditions of complexity is essential so that researchers can respond to changing conditions as they occur. Thus, it is important that we consider our understandings of the conditions of complexity as incomplete and make this understanding explicit. In fact, knowing that conditions are under development is critical for a complexity-sensitive approach. Adopting such an approach during proposal writing involves exploring and generating initial understandings of conditions of complexity. Then, throughout the study implementation, monitoring and tracking emerging understandings. During report writing, finally, revising and describing evolved understandings of conditions of complexity. In so doing, complexity-sensitive mixed methods researchers are tasked with recognizing, assessing, and ultimately communicating the complexity inherent in their study conditions. Communicating assessments of the complexity of research conditions in both proposals and reports is useful in enhancing authenticity in our work. The pioneering opportunities afforded by assessing and describing the complexity inherent in our research conditions can be useful for researchers, yet it is not yet a common feature of mixed methods research proposals or reports. In Guiding Tip 4.1, a professor of empirical pedagogy from the University of Vienna (Austria) whose work emphasizes mixed methods offers advice for navigating the complexity of mixed methods research.

 Guiding Tip 4.1

Judith Schoonenboom advising how to deal with complexity in mixed methods research

Get a grip on complexity in your mixed methods research project without resorting to simplification.

Making the case for the research approach used in the study is necessary in mixed methods research (see Chapter 2 for the initial introduction of the organic mixed methods research process). The need for complexity-sensitive research practices creating opportunities for innovation is a timely and well-established pursuit that also resonates with my own experiences. In an effort to capture the present status of the field of mixed methods research, I concur that we are currently in an era focused on reflection and refinement (for historical descriptions, see Creswell & Plano Clark, 2007, 2011, 2018; Johnson & Onwuegbuzie, 2004). In addition to reflecting on and refining our practices, I propose that our tasks also involve advancing new practices for expanding the contexts in which mixed methods research is currently applied. Indeed, work is already under way to expand the scope of purposes for integration, interrelatedness of contexts, interactions of research teams, and predetermination of designs for mixed methods research under varying conditions of complexity. The concept of the 'messiness' of mixed methods research found in the literature reflects efforts to work within such research conditions. This concept is defined by Plano Clark and Ivankova (2016, p. 277) as 'recogniz[ing] the inherent complex, dynamic, and undetermined nature of mixed methods research practice'. The challenge for researchers, then, is to describe complexity-sensitive practices that are useful in diagnosing the complexity of conditions inherent in their studies, and to report with greater authenticity on how they responded to changing conditions.

Diagnosing Opportunities and Hazards for Mixed Methods Researchers

Identifying Dimensions for Complexity Opportunities

If innovations in mixed methods research are the desired outcome, then we must consider the conditions under which research takes place. The analysis of dilemmas described to me by researchers revealed five categories of conditions that researchers find puzzling. When I examined these categories alongside my own experiences and my reading of the literature, I realized that the categories provided a useful framework for understanding the variations among conditions of complexity. Thus, I advance these five categories as dimensions for diagnosing conditions of complexity: intentions of research problems, systems of research contexts, designs of research integrations, capacity of research interactions, and evidence of research outcomes (Figure 4.1). In this section I describe these dimensions and highlight the key challenges and opportunities of a complexity-sensitive approach (see also Table 4.1).

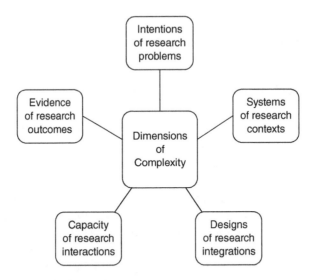

Figure 4.1 Five dimensions of complexity for diagnosing research conditions

Complexity Dimension 1: Intentions of Mixed Methods Research Problems

A research problem describes what the study intends to address (see also Chapter 2 for initial discussion). As the potential of mixed methods research continues to be realized, researchers are being asked to pursue increasingly complex research problems. Among the key challenges for mixed methods researchers is categorizing an innovation-focused study need for integration among the current typologies of mixing purposes. For example, the integration purpose of the featured study on postconflict risk (Taylor et al., 2017) focused on identifying new understandings of the community-level risk factors and related emotional insecurity responses among youth in Vukovar, Croatia. This purpose reflected the need for innovative insights from the integration of qualitative and quantitative data – a departure from the existing mixing purposes focused on corroboration, completion, explanation, development, and infusion. A complexity-sensitive approach that recognizes innovation as a mixing purpose, and thus a desirable study outcome, is necessary to address more complex mixed methods research problems.

Complexity Dimension 2: Systems of Mixed Methods Research Contexts

A research context describes the setting for the study (see also Chapter 2 for initial discussion). This can include information about the physical location, historical, political, economic, and social influences. In the past, we might have limited our description of the research context to the immediate surroundings at the start of the study. While the local environment remains an important consideration, we now recognize the contributions of the interconnected personal, social, and societal systems (Plano Clark & Ivankova, 2016). There is also a recognized need for monitoring and describing the environmental influences on and effects within as well as between the systems over time. Among the key challenges for researchers is identifying the interrelated contexts in which research takes place and the inherent dynamic influences that create complex mixed methods research systems. For example, Vukovar is described by Taylor et al. (2017) as having been affected by the ethnic violence following Croatia's declaration of independence in 1991. These represent the social, geographical, and historical contexts for the featured study on postconflict risk. The authors also describe the societal context of the postconflict risks for individuals and communities from a global perspective and selection criteria for the study population (e.g., balanced ethnicity among Croats and Serbs and gender among the youth in each target age group in the focus groups). This description reflects the need to document the evolving environmental influences (i.e., political, economic, and social) on the three interrelated study contexts in this case (country, community, and individuals) – a departure from simply describing the immediate physical locale and social interactions at the beginning of the study. A complexity-sensitive approach that promotes definition of mixed methods research system as interrelated and monitoring the systems for dynamic influences and effects puts the researcher in a good position to adapt to new conditions.

Complexity Dimension 3: Designs of Mixed Methods Research Integrations

Research integrations describe the data procedures for guiding the study (see also Chapter 2 for initial discussion). As the mixed methods research problems become more complex, so does the logistics of addressing them. The limitations of existing mixed methods design typologies to represent complex designs also become more pronounced (Guest, 2013). Among the key challenges for researchers is to embed agility in the procedures for responding to dynamic influences and emergent conditions while also maintaining methodological congruence. For example, the research procedures for the featured study on safe places (Zea et al., 2014) apply the theory of communicative action to the research process. The researchers pursued increased knowledge about internally displaced gay and bisexual men and transwomen (GBT) in Colombia, whom the researchers describe as a 'more vulnerable and marginalized subset of the Colombian GBT population, and [for whom] displacement has engendered extreme poverty among many' (2014, p. 213). The original design of the larger study, as described by the authors, included 19 key informant interviews, 11 focus groups, 42 life history interviews, 100 pilot surveys, and 1000 audio computer-assisted surveys. Additional qualitative data was collected (20 qualitative interviews and 13 key informant interviews) when the preliminary results indicated low rates of HIV testing. The resulting research procedures were necessarily emergent. The team responded as the researchers engaged in non-coercive dialogue as a key aspect of the guiding theoretical framework of the theory of communicative action. This description reflects the need for procedural adaptations as the study unfolded – a departure from predetermined designs. A complexity-sensitive approach that supports responsive procedures and thinking beyond existing research designs is necessary to address more complex mixed methods research problems.

Complexity Dimension 4: Capacity of Mixed Methods Research Interactions

Research capacity describes the necessary skills and experiences for undertaking a study (see also Chapter 2 for initial discussion). Research is a social activity and can be undertaken by independent researchers or a research team. Completing mixed methods research as an independent researcher remains viable. Teams are increasingly recognized as an optimal configuration for addressing more complex mixed methods research problems. This can be attributed to the limitless possibilities for generating innovations that come from interactions among researchers with diverse methodological and disciplinary expertise. Yet there exist inherent challenges when bringing together a team with differing perspectives, experiences, and assumptions (Bryman, 2006; Curry et al., 2013). Among the key challenges for mixed methods researchers are assessing the necessary expertise and roles required to carry out the study and developing the capacity for the desired intensity of research collaborations among members. For example, in the featured study on safe places, Zea et al. (2014) provide a detailed description of the transdisciplinary and transcultural composition of the research team. In so doing they make explicit (to some degree) the philosophical assumptions, methodological training, and disciplinary backgrounds of each member. In addition, the authors detail their development as a team and the interactions they undertook in this process: 'Many hours of planning, developing mutual trust, establishing different means of communication across countries (e.g., face-to-face meetings, e-mails, Skype meetings), as well as honoring diverse styles of communication (e.g., more or less philosophical, analytic, political, direct) were needed to develop an egalitarian relationship among team members' (2014, p. 215). This description reflects the usefulness of documenting the backgrounds of individual members and their development of their capacities for interactions – a departure from simply stating that a team approach was used and interactions occurred. A complexity-sensitive approach that develops the necessary capacity for interactions among researchers puts those involved in a study in a good in a good position to generate insights greater than the sum of the individual efforts.

Complexity Dimension 5: Evidence of Mixed Methods Research Outcomes

Research outcomes describe what is generated by the processes involved in the study (see Chapter 2 for initial discussion). This can include information about the analysis, findings, interpretations, and implications. In the past, we might have limited our description of the research outcomes to the validation evidence of qualitative and quantitative research. While the contributions of qualitative and quantitative evidence of validation remain an important consideration, we now recognize the need for evidence specific to the integration processes and products.

Among the key challenges for researchers is describing the procedures and evidence that achieve the standards of quality for qualitative and quantitative research in addition to those specific to mixed methods research because of the inherent dynamic influences that create complex mixed methods research outcomes. For example, the evidence of mixed methods research outcomes for the featured study on heart care (Dickson et al., 2011) are detailed in several ways. Where, when, and how integration was undertaken during the concurrent triangulation mixed methods design is visually represented in a diagram complemented by narrative description. In this way, the authors clearly indicate how the quantitative and qualitative results were independently generated and then integrated for three constructs: self-care, knowledge, and cognition. It is apparent that the mixed analysis strategy involved comparing and contrasting quantitative and qualitative results related to each of the constructs, thus fulfilling the mixing purpose of triangulation. Information enhancing the validity of the research outcomes was provided in the form of reliability coefficients, and an interpretation framework for each of the quantitative standardized instruments is also provided by a

Table 4.1 Key challenges and opportunities related to five dimensions for diagnosing conditions of research complexity

Dimensions of complexity	Key challenges related to conditions under varying complexity	Opportunities offered by a complexity-sensitive approach
Intentions of research problems	Categorizing an innovation-focused study need for integration among the current typologies of mixing purposes	Recognize innovation as a mixing purpose and thus a desirable mixed methods study outcome
Systems of research contexts	Identifying the interrelated contexts in which research takes place and the inherent dynamic influences	Promote definition of mixed methods research system as interrelated and monitoring for system influences and effects
Designs of research integrations	Embedding agility within the procedures for responding to dynamic influences and emergent conditions	Support responsive procedures to conditions and thinking beyond existing mixed methods research designs
Capacity of research interactions	Assessing the necessary expertise and roles to carry out the study, and developing the capacity for the desired intensity of research collaborations	Develop the necessary mixed methods research capacity for interactions for generating insights greater than the sum of the individual efforts
Evidence of research outcomes	Describing the procedures and evidence that achieves the standards of quality for qualitative, quantitative, and mixed methods research	Generate the necessary indicators of integration and embed processes and products for meeting the standards of methodological rigour

table with a narrative description. Information related to the development of the interview protocol, procedures, and interpretations is given along with typical strategies to enhance the methodological rigour of qualitative research. These included audit trails, inter-coder reliability, and member checking. The integrated cross-case findings for three participants are represented using an informational matrix. The quantitative and qualitative findings are also reported and, lastly, the mixed insights are discussed. This description of the processes and products of the research outcomes represents a departure from simply stating that integration happened and the mixed insights were generated.

Complexity-Effect Diagnosing Hazards

The extent to which the complexity of mixed methods research conditions is conveyed can have considerable consequences for the study's feasibilities. This can be attributed to what I am calling the complexity effect. I propose peeling an onion as a metaphor for introducing the complexity effect when assessing mixed methods conditions. The onion is used metaphorically to describe sequentially removable layers that conceal something important. One progresses inward in understanding from superficial understandings to increasing awareness of issues and considerations. With every layer, the researchers' understanding of the conditions under which they perform the research is deepened. This is a progressive learning experience, as we begin to recognize the complexities. As researchers, we can no longer accept the conditions at face value, as we know there are complexities that are shielded from the initial view. Each time a layer is removed, there is another, and another, yet to understand. Getting to know the onion means taking the time to assess the complexities of the conditions across the five dimensions before beginning the study and then paying attention to the changes in conditions over time.

Diagnosing plays an essential, continuing function in guiding the researchers' perceptions and understandings of the study conditions. This task has no end and so it is important to begin the study even when understandings are incomplete, and we need to represent these understandings as so. In our researcher roles, we tend to present research conditions in their most stable form. Once we begin to recognize sources of complexity there is an obligation to present the conditions as authentically and incompletely as we can. By adopting an enlightened approach to mixed methods research that is more complexity-sensitive, we become more prepared for whatever unfolds during the study. The reality is that mixed methods research is a messy endeavour that occurs under unique and changeable conditions each time. Throughout the initiating, designing, implementing, and communicating processes involved in a mixed methods study, researchers need to respond to the complexity inherent in their research. To be able to respond to changes in conditions, researchers need to consider what dilemmas might arise during the study and consider how these issues might be addressed. A common misconception is that these dilemmas only surface during study implementation. They can arise throughout the research phases, and because these phases are interrelated, if the dilemmas are not addressed, the consequences are disruptive to those involved in the study and the study outcomes. In Practice Alert 4.1, I consider some of the indicators of complexity I have observed in my own experiences as a supervisor and researcher that justify the need for complexity sensitivities in my mixed methods research approach. I invite you to do the same. In so doing, I am enhancing my understandings of what the sources of complexity might look like when generating an initial understanding of the research conditions.

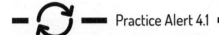 **Practice Alert 4.1**

What might be indicators of the need for a complexity-sensitive approach?

There are many ways conditions of complexity can be recognized. When conducting a literature review, you may notice a gap in the literature or a media report that leads you to formulate a problem you deem worthy of pursuit. If your further review of the literature cannot locate material to guide you in describing the background influences to the problem, this may indicate that the problem should be considered to have some level of complexity. The characteristics to help you assess the degree to which the problem might be complex will be further discussed in this chapter. For some researchers a lack of guiding literature will be a deterrent, but others, like myself (and perhaps you!), might see opportunity. This is because the reasons why some problems have yet to be pursued can often be attributed to their inherent complexity – it might be that the population who would best inform the problem is either hard to reach or yet unknown, or perhaps because the most appropriate procedures for addressing the problem require considerable resources and time or have yet to be developed. I know this first-hand, as my colleague and I pursue what we now recognize as being complex problems related to housing of populations who are considered 'difficult to house'. When we first began to recognize both the opportunities and challenges presented by this problem, we sought to understand the initial conditions surrounding the problem by sketching what we knew about the problems we were pursuing and the contexts in which the problems are situated. Our complexity-sensitive approaches to framing the problems and defining the contexts are, in turn, influencing our approaches to describing research designs, developing research capacities, and generating research outcomes. That is how we realized the need for embedding more complexity-sensitive mixed methods research practices.

Try this now – sketch your ideas about a potential research problem to pursue. To what extent can your problem be considered complex? Then consider the effects of a more complexity-sensitive approach to your problem. Would a complexity-sensitive approach be suitable for pursuing your mixed methods research problem?

Guiding Procedures for Diagnosing Five Complexity Dimensions of Research Conditions

Now that you may be convinced (or at least open to) diagnosing research conditions, I hope you are inspired to give it a try. I should mention upfront that no agreed-upon approach exists for diagnosing complexity of conditions. Indeed, this line of thinking and practice may be considered nascent. A logical place to begin diagnosing the complexity of mixed methods research conditions is attending to the five dimensions of complexity for the study. Each of the dimensions includes a number of characteristics where the level of complexity can be assessed. My approach continues to evolve, but I share how I approach diagnosing conditions of complexity using guiding questions across the five dimensions: intentions of research problems, systems of research contexts, designs of research integrations, capacity of research interactions, and evidence of research outcomes. Examine Table 4.2 ... for descriptions of the relationships among the guiding questions for researchers for each of the dimensions, the indicators of complexity, and the interpretation rationale. This section describes the relationship in greater detail for each dimension. After you have read the procedures for diagnosing each of the complexity dimensions, examine Table 4.3 (p. 99) for descriptions of low, moderate, and high levels of complexity for each characteristic across the five dimensions of complexity. Remember that variability is to be expected and a research study may be assessed as having a high degree of complexity on some characteristics but a low degree on others even within the same dimension. These descriptions in Table 4.3 are useful for assessing the levels of complexity for individual characteristics as well as for the overall dimension and study. You can imagine that, as a study proceeds, the understandings of the dimensions of complexity will develop. It would be erroneous to assume that just because something is missing in a study proposal or report, it is not relevant. In addition to some overlap being implied, these dimensions should not be considered static but rather influenced by new research and evolving circumstances. Researchers are tasked with recognizing, assessing, and ultimately communicating the complexity inherent in their study conditions. To see the guide to assessing the levels of complexity in Table 4.3 applied in practice, examine Table 4.4 (p. 100) for ratings of complexity for each characteristic and then overall for each dimension among the six featured studies.

Intentions of Mixed Methods Research Problems

Several features should be considered when assessing the extent to which mixed methods research problems are complex. It should be noted that research problems cannot easily be categorized as low, moderate, or high complexity (see also Chapter 1 for initial discussion). Most problems represent some mixing of characteristics. However, identifying the unique mix of problem features can be helpful in mitigating the challenges encountered by researchers. The following questions can help assess the level of complexity for the dimension related to mixed methods research problems (see also Table 4.2):

- What is known about the dynamic background influences (i.e., motivations, issues, and topics) on the mixed methods research problem? Research problems involving backgrounds that are well established and considered stable in the literature are considered less complex.
- What is the study's purpose for integration to address the mixed methods research problem? Research problems where the mixing purpose(s) are focused on a need for innovation (and cannot be easily categorized within the existing typologies) are considered to be more complex.
- What is known about the intended mixed methods study outcomes addressing the mixed methods research problem? Research problems that can be addressed by drawing upon identifiable expertise and established research practices are considered to be less complex.

Highly complex problems are often characterized by less-established background influences and yet-to-be-determined study needs to integrate, or not easily categorized within

Table 4.2 Relationships among the guiding questions for researchers for each of the dimensions, the indicators of complexity, and the interpretation rationale

Dimensions of complexity	Guiding questions for researchers	Indicators of complexity for consideration	Interpretation rationale which assumes greater complexity
Intentions of research problems	What is known about the background dynamics for the problem?	When background influences are not well understood by researchers or established in the literature	Less stability in background influences
	What is the study's purpose for integration?	When needs for integration are yet to be determined or not easily categorized within existing typologies for mixing purpose	Less clarity in study's purpose for integration
	What is known about the intended outcomes?	When outcomes are uncertain for solving the research problem	Less certainty in intended study outcomes
Systems of research contexts	What is known about the environmental dynamics acting on the systems?	When environmental influences are not well understood by researchers or established in the literature	More sources of environmental influences
	What is the geographical range and dispersion of the research systems?	When range and dispersion characteristics are not easily described or known	More range and dispersion in research systems
	What is known about the diversity in participants' characteristics?	When differences within and across the study population are not well understood or established in the literature	More diversity in participant characteristics
Designs of research integrations	What is known about the feasibility dynamics acting on the research design?	When feasibility influences are not well understood by researchers and unpredictable in nature	Less predictability in feasibility influences
	What are the procedural needs for integration according to the designs?	When procedural needs are not easily categorized into existing design typologies	Less agreement for procedures and use of emergent designs
	What is known about the timeframe and resource allocations of the integrations?	When timeframes and resources for data procedures in designs cannot be predetermined and are uncertain	Less timeframe and resource definition
Capacity of research interactions	What is known about the social dynamics on the research interactions?	When social influences are not well understood by researchers and unpredictable in nature	Greater social influences
	What is the extent of capacity and role predetermination for research interactions?	When capacity and roles are not easily predetermined or known	Less role definition
	What is known about the expected nature of the outcomes generated by research member interactions?	When nature of outcomes from research member interactions are uncertain	More intensive collaborations
Evidence of research outcomes	What is known about the practical dynamics for the research outcomes?	When practical influences are not well understood by researchers or established in the literature	Less predictability in practical influences
	What is the expected evidence for representing the mixed insights?	When expected evidence for mixed insights is not easily categorized within existing mixed analysis typologies	Less established integration evidence
	What is known about the predictability of the study's impacts?	When impacts are uncertain	Less predictability in study impacts

existing typologies for mixing purposes. The lack of clarity in mixing purposes is often attributable to a dearth of guiding literature and uncertain intended outcomes (see also Table 4.3). Of the six featured studies, three research problems were rated as highly complex and three as moderately complex (see also Table 4.4). For example, a high rating of complexity is assigned to the research problem of the featured study on safe places (Zea et al., 2014) exploring the subjective, objective, and social worlds of internally displaced Colombian gay and bisexual men and transwomen. Minimal literature was referenced in areas such as displacement of GBT populations, with the exception of the guiding framework of the theory of communicative action for supporting egalitarian dialogue among researchers and participants. Along with a low degree of certainty in the outcomes, researchers identified an innovation-focused mixing purpose. The safe places study was to contribute new understandings of social change, to inform the design of policies and innovative interventions. In contrast, the conditions surrounding low-complexity mixed methods research problems may be multifaceted and important, yet they are also characterized as having a clearly defined mixing purpose and known intended outcomes because of the high degree of consensus related to the issue being explored and the approach to its study. Perhaps given the focus of this book on adaptive practices as part of justifying a complexity-sensitive approach, it is not surprising that none of the research problems of the featured studies are rated as having low complexity.

Systems of Mixed Methods Research Contexts

Several features should be considered when assessing the extent to which mixed methods research contexts are complex. It should be noted that research contexts cannot easily be categorized as low, moderate, or high complexity (see also Chapter 1 for initial discussion). Most problems represent some mixing of characteristics. However, identifying the unique mix of system features can be helpful in mitigating the challenges encountered by researchers. The following questions can help researchers assess the level of complexity for the dimension related to mixed methods research systems (see also Table 4.2):

- What is known about the dynamic environmental influences (i.e., physical location, history, political, economic, and social aspects) on the mixed methods research systems? Research systems involving few environmental influences that are well defined and outcomes that are familiar are considered less complex.
- What is the geographical range and dispersion of the mixed methods research systems? Research systems involving a larger number of sites that are geographically dispersed tend to be more complex.
- What is known about the scope of differences among participant characteristics? Research systems involving a larger number of participants with diverse characteristics tend to be more complex.

Highly complex mixed methods research systems may involve many sources of environmental influences that are not well understood, geographically disperse or yet unknown research sites, and yet-to-be-known participant characteristics (see also Table 4.3). Of the six featured studies, three research contexts were rated as highly complex and three as moderately complex (see also Table 4.4). For example, the high rating of complexity assigned to the research contexts of the featured study on vaping culture (Colditz et al., 2017) is attributed to the detailed descriptions of the dynamic historical and current influences on the global use of Twitter and the increasing use of vaping. The large range of dispersion across the global context assumes great diversity among the Twitter users. We can also assume a high level of diversity from the random selection of global electronic nicotine delivery system users on the social media platform Twitter. In contrast, low complex research contexts may involve multiple research sites, yet they may also be characterized as having similar geographical locations and participant characteristics. Perhaps given the focus of this book on adaptive practices as part of justifying a complexity-sensitive approach, it is not surprising that none of the research contexts of the featured studies are rated as having low complexity.

Designs of Mixed Methods Research Integrations

Several features should be considered when assessing the extent to which mixed methods research integrations are complex. It should be noted that research integrations cannot easily be categorized as low, moderate, or high complexity (see also Chapter 1 for initial discussion). Most integrations represent some mixing of characteristics. However, identifying the unique mix of integration features can be helpful in mitigating the challenges encountered by researchers. The following questions can help assess the level of complexity for the dimension related to mixed methods research integrations (see also Table 4.2):

- What is known about the dynamic feasibility influences (i.e., potential for issues of resources and time, conduct of ethical research, and rigour) on the research integrations? Research integrations involving intensive participation and innovative (i.e., less established or familiar) procedures with less-studied populations are considered more complex because the feasibilities are less predictable under dynamic conditions.
- What are the procedural needs for integration according to the mixed methods designs? Research integrations are considered to be less complex when they can be addressed by drawing on predetermined mixed methods design typologies and established data collection and analysis methods.
- What is known about the timeframe and resource allocations for the mixed methods research integrations? Research designs without clear start and end dates, and with rigid resource allocations, tend to be more complex than those with clear study durations and require adaptable resources.

Highly complex integrations are often characterized by feasibility influences that are not well understood, a lack of fit with predetermined designs and methods, as well as less-defined timeframes and adaptable resources – often because procedures tend to evolve because of evolving understandings of how to proceed (see also Table 4.3). Of the six featured studies, one research integration is rated as highly complex, one as moderately complex, and four as having low complexity (see also Table 4.4). For example, a high rating of complexity assigned to the research integrations of the featured study on safe places (Zea et al., 2014) is supported by what was reported in the article. Many adaptions were made to procedures, and the transformative design was responsive to study findings and to upholding the desire to create non-coercive dialogue between researchers and participants (42 completed semi-structured life history interviews and 113 responded to surveys). In contrast, low complexity in research procedures reflects use of an existing design typology and well-established procedures, timeframes, and resources. Thus, research integrations are considered to be more complex for topics and problems that we know little about and when we do not know how to study them. For example, a low rating of complexity for the research procedures for the featured study on heart care (Dickson et al., 2011) is supported by what was reported in the article. No adaptions were required to procedures, and the concurrent triangulation design was assumed to be conducted as predetermined. That involved questionnaires and semi-structured interviews with 42 purposefully sampled adults with heart failure. It is curious that no information related to resources and time-frames was provided. This leads me to consider whether this article, like others, simply did not report adjustments to the procedures.

Capacities of Mixed Methods Research Interactions

Several features should be considered when assessing the extent to which mixed methods research interactions are complex. It should be noted that research interactions cannot easily be categorized as low, moderate, or high complexity (see also Chapter 1 for initial discussion). Most interactions represent some mixing of characteristics. However, identifying the unique mix of capacity features can be helpful in mitigating the challenges encountered by research-ers. The following questions can help assess the level of complexity for the dimension related to research interactions (see also Table 4.2):

- What is known about the dynamic social influences on research interactions? More complex interactions among research members tend to be required when research involves less-established teams with a great diversity of background experiences, disciplinary and methodological expertise.
- What is the extent of capacity and role predetermination for research interactions? Research involving low degrees of role predetermination tends to require more complex interactions among research members.
- What is known about the expected nature of the members' outcomes generated by research interactions? Research requiring insights beyond the sum of individual contributions and involving intensive collaborations tends to require more complex interactions among research members.

Highly complex mixed methods research interactions are often characterized by social influences that are not well understood, a lack of predetermined roles, and potential for generating insights that are greater than the sum of what would have been individually accessible. The nature of the outcomes of the research is thus dependent on how team member interactions are developed (see also Table 4.3). Of the six featured studies, two research interactions are rated as highly complex, three as moderately complex, and one as lacking information and thus unknown (see also Table 4.4). For example, a large research team involving collaborations among a dozen geographically, disciplinarily, and method-ologically diverse members requires more complex interactions than a doctoral research committee involving the student, a supervisor, and two committee members. The high rating of complexity for research interactions of the featured study on safe places (Zea et al., 2014) is attributed to the detailed descriptions of the dynamic historical and social influences on the research context and Colombian participants, and the guiding theoretical framework. Even though the range of dispersion might be considered small within a single country, the existing relationships between researchers and members of the vulnerable population and description of the development of integrative interactions among the researchers provided evidence of highly collaborative interactions. In contrast, low complexity research interac-tions may have a high degree of role definition and only require low levels of collaboration. Perhaps given the focus of this book on adaptive practices as part of justifying a complexity-sensitive approach, it is not surprising that none of the research interactions of the featured studies are rated as having low complexity.

Evidence of Mixed Methods Research Outcomes

Several features should be considered when assessing the extent to which mixed methods research outcomes are complex. It should be noted that research outcomes cannot easily be categorized as low, moderate, or high complexity (see Chapter 1 for initial discussion). Most outcomes represent some mixing of characteristics. However, identifying the unique mix of outcome features can be helpful in mitigating the challenges encountered by researchers. The following questions can help assess the level of complexity for the dimension related to mixed methods research outcomes (see also Table 4.2):

- What is known about the dynamic practical influences (i.e., issues of validity, reliability, trustworthiness, confidence, and legitimacy) on the research outcomes? Research outcomes drawing upon many different data sources and designs with less established validation processes are considered more complex.
- What is the integration evidence for representing the mixed insights? Research outcomes involving several points of integration, high intensity of mixing, and innovative (i.e., less established or familiar) mixing strategies with less-studied procedures are considered more complex.
- What is known about the intended mixed methods study impacts? Research outcomes that transcend diverse disciplinary and methodological boundaries in yet unknown ways tend to be more complex than when those impacts can be known.

Highly complex outcomes are often characterized by practical influences that are not well understood and yet-to-be-known impacts. The lack of established integration evidence is often attributable to still emerging guiding literature and unpredictable outcomes (see also Table 4.3). Of the six featured studies, only one research outcome is rated as highly complex, three as moderately complex, and two as having low complexity (see also Table 4.4). For example, a high rating of complexity for the research integrations for the featured study on vaping culture (Colditz et al., 2017) is supported by the descriptions of mixing influences, integration needs, and generating validation evidence that combined both more established procedures (i.e., inter-coder reliability) along with new processes of synthesizing a subsample of tweets and comparing that to a full data set and keyword prevalence. The conditions surrounding low-complexity mixed methods research outcomes are characterized as having established integration evidence and known intended impacts because of the high degree of certainty with regard to the procedures and integrations involved in the predetermined designs. For example, the low rating of complexity for research outcomes for the featured study on safe places (Zea et al., 2014) is evidenced by the well-established need to integrate the qualitative findings to inform instrument development and the lack of any integrated findings or information about the practical influences. The lack of information about some characteristics may mean that the ratings of the study conditions appear less complex than the reality faced by researchers.

Features that Engage Readers with Research Conditions

It is often advantageous for research to be distinctive. Research conditions are a great place to start distinguishing your study. The following list provides some ideas from my own experiences as a researcher, as a reviewer of mixed methods research proposals for funding and of manuscripts for publication, and from working with graduate students as an instructor, supervisor, and examiner. See also the featured studies for illustrative examples of some of these engaging features.

- *Seek significant conditions in which to situate your mixed methods research.* Read current literature and media reports to identify noteworthy dimensions of complexity on which to situate your study. Confirm your ideas by going to conferences and talking to researchers. This will help you situate your study within conditions that align with research and funding priorities.
- *Focus on some highly complex mixed methods research conditions.* There are varying possible combinations of complexity across the five dimensions where studies can be situated. Consider the desired dimensions that are highly complex in light of available expertise and resources. This will help ensure the feasibility of your study.
- *Introduce your diagnosis of the mixed methods research conditions uniquely.* Catch readers' attention with a statistic, quote, or personal narrative relevant to your conditions of complexity. This will help you create reader interest in your study right from the start.
- *Assume unconventional conditions in which to situate your mixed methods study.* Consider new contributions for integration or procedures. Involve research team members from disciplines not yet reflected in studies. Or assume research conditions that are not yet reflected in the literature. This will help you to persuade your reader of the need for your study.

Innovations in Diagnosing Complexity of Mixed Methods Research Conditions

Researchers working under conditions of complexity are tasked with recognizing the dimensions of complexity within their studies and adjusting their responses as the study unfolds. Also important, not yet widely considered in our practices, involves thinking about our understandings of research conditions as under development. Adopting such an approach during proposal writing involves exploring and generating initial understandings of conditions of complexity across the five dimensions. Then, throughout the study implementation, monitoring and tracking emerging understandings. During report writing, finally, revising and describing evolved understandings of conditions of complexity across the five dimensions. In so doing, complexity-sensitive mixed methods researchers are tasked with recognizing, assessing, and ultimately communicating the complexity inherent in their study conditions. Communicating assessments of the complexity of research conditions in both proposals or reports is useful in enhancing authenticity in our work. The pioneering opportunities afforded by assessing and describing the complexity inherent in our research conditions can be useful for researchers, but it is not yet a common feature of mixed methods research proposals or reports.

We have long recognized the complexity inherent in research as a pursuit – the processes involved draw upon expertise across many areas of competency. Yet we are only beginning to realize the need for authentic descriptions of the conditions and of our responses to changing conditions as well as the consequences of those responses. This is essential for addressing the practice gap under conditions of complexity, because the lack of authentic reporting of researchers' responses to varying conditions of complexity means that others cannot learn from them. Indeed, how do we mitigate the consequences of mismatches between the assumptions underlying our practices and the realities we face if we do not understand the nature of the complex conditions in which we work? In this section I describe two innovations for communicating and tracking the complexity diagnosis of mixed methods research conditions.

Table 4.3 Guide to diagnosing levels of complexity across five dimensions of mixed methods research conditions

Dimension of complexity	Dimension characteristics	Level of complexity		
		Low	Moderate	High
Intentions of research problems	Background influences	High degree of stability and established literature	Some degree of stability and established literature	Low degree of stability and lack of guiding literature
	Mixing purposes	Singular and clearly defined need for mixing	Few and somewhat defined need for mixing	Multiple and innovation-focused need for mixing
	Study outcomes	High degree of certainty of insights	Some degree of certainty of intended insights	Low degree of certainty of insights
Systems of research contexts	Environmental influences	Few sources of dynamics that are well defined and outcomes that are familiar	Some sources of dynamics and familiarity	Many sources of dynamics that are ill-defined and unknown outcomes
	Geographical range	Low degree of potential geographical dispersion	Some degree of potential geographical dispersion	High degree of potential geographical dispersion
	Participant diversity	Low degree of differences among characteristics	Some degree of differences among characteristics	High degree of differences among characteristics
Designs of research integrations	Feasibility influences	Few sources of dynamics from well-defined procedures with familiar populations	Some sources of dynamics and familiarity	Many sources of dynamics from yet-to-be-known procedures and less familiar populations
	Design approaches	Much agreement on procedures, and predetermined designs	Some agreement on procedures, and defined designs	Little agreement on procedures, and evolving designs
	Timeframe and resource definitions	Clear start and end dates and fixed resourcing	Some clarity in dates and resource needs	No clear start or end date and adaptive resourcing
Capacities of research interactions	Social influences	Few sources of diversity with familiar social dynamics	Some sources of diversity and familiarity	Many sources of diversity and yet-to-be-known social dynamics
	Role definitions	High degree of role predetermination	Some degree of role predetermination	Low degree of role predetermination
	Member contributions	Collective of individual contributions resulting from low level of collaboration	Some collective and some collaboration	Integrative beyond sum of individual contributions, resulting from intensive collaborations
Evidence of research outcomes	Practical influences	Few sources of dynamics that are well defined and outcomes that are familiar	Some sources of dynamics and familiar outcomes	Many sources of dynamics and outcomes that are unknown
	Integration strategy	Familiar strategies and collective outcomes from low level of integration	Some collective and some integration from mixing strategies	Less established and more intensive mixing strategies generating integrative outcomes
	Study impacts	High predictability of study's impacts	Some predictability of study's impacts	Low predictability of study's impacts

Table 4.4 Diagnosis of conditions of complexity across the six featured studies

Dimension of complexity	Dimension characteristics	Complexity assessments of featured studies					
		Law clients (Chui & Cheng, 2017)	Postconflict risk (Taylor et al., 2017)	Heart care (Dickson et al., 2011)	Safe places (Zea et al., 2014)	Leadership competencies (Strudsholm et al., 2016)	Vaping culture Colditz et al., 2017).
	Overall assessment of study's complexity	*M*	*M*	*M*	*H*	*M*	*M*
Features of research problems	*Overall problem complexity*	M	M	M	H	H	H
	Stability of background influences	M	M	M	H	H	H
	Clarity of mixing purpose	M	M	M	H	H	H
	Certainty of study outcomes	M	M	H	H	H	H
Contexts of research systems	*Overall systems complexity*	H	M	M	H	M	H
	Dynamics of environmental influences	H	M	M	H	M	H
	Range of geographical dispersion	M	M	M	H	H	H
	Diversity of participants	H	H	M	H	M	H
Capacity of research interactions	*Overall procedural complexity*	L	L	L	H	M	L
	Predictability of practical influences	L	M	L	H	M	M
	Nature of design approach	L	L	L	H	M	L
	Definition of timeframes and resources	L	L	—	M	M	L

Complexity assessments of featured studies

Dimension of complexity	Dimension characteristics	Law clients (Chui & Cheng, 2017)	Postconflict risk (Taylor et al., 2017)	Heart care (Dickson et al., 2011)	Safe places (Zea et al., 2014)	Leadership competencies (Strudsholm et al., 2016)	Vaping culture Colditz et al., 2017.
Designs of research integrations	*Overall relational complexity*	–	M	M	H	H	M
	Diversity of social influences	–	–	–	H	H	–
	Extent of role definition	–	H	M	H	H	M
	Nature of member contributions	–	M	M	H	H	M
Evidence of research outcomes	*Overall integration complexity*	L	L	M	M	M	H
	Familiarity of practical influences	L	–	–	–	–	M
	Transparency of integration strategy	L	L	M	M	M	H
	Nature of study impacts	M	L	H	M	H	H

Complexity Study Profiles Representing Research Conditions

It is not yet an established practice to create a complexity study profile. In addition to conveying information, diagrams have proven to be an effective format for documenting evolutions in my understandings of the research conditions over time. It may not surprise many researchers that great variability exists with regard to the details conveyed about the conditions surrounding mixed methods research studies. Key among the contributing factors to variability in details are logistical constraints such as page limits in publications and lack of examples beyond established practices for describing research conditions. There exists a dearth of illustrative examples specific to complexity-sensitive mixed methods research. Here, I demonstrate the creation of a unique profile for two uses; the first use is for conveying initial understandings of the study conditions in a proposal. Examine Table 4.5 for a complexity study profile related to housing that is under formulation. The second use is for conveying understandings at the completion stage of a study in a research report. Examine Tables 4.6–4.11 for complexity study profiles of the six featured studies. Note the differences and similarities across the featured study profiles. When diagnosing characteristics that are not obvious, I have indicated that they are 'unknown' using a dash. See also Table B.1 in Appendix B, an editable version of which is also available on the companion website for the book.

Analysis Ideas for Diagnosing Influences on Research Conditions

It is uncommon to see a researcher explicitly diagnose the conditions of research along the complexity continuum. This may change as the conditions of complexity under which mixed methods research is pursued become more diverse. One of the risks for researchers proposing research under conditions of high complexity is conveying the study as feasible within the conditions. To that end, while much of the research detail may be yet to be determined, it is important to convey what is known about the influences on the conditions and to advance initial understandings of the conditions as a means of establishing confidence in tackling the problem. This is important to satisfy the expectations of funding agencies and supervisory committees; at the same time, acknowledging a degree of uncertainty positions the researchers' mindset as open to new possibilities of understandings for research problems, contexts, integrations, interactions, and outcomes. This may also, over time, be more welcomed by funding agencies as they recognize the need for responsive researchers to tackle research under conditions of complexity. As we work towards a yet unrealized future, we must also be aware of and work within the current structures. Because under conditions of complexity, understandings of the considerations for the complex conditions and their surrounding influences are considered to be evolving, researchers are faced with the following question: How can a complexity-sensitive research approach contribute to realizing the necessary adaptations under conditions of increasingly complex conditions? One way is to pay attention to and analyse the potential influences on each of the dimensions.

Table 4.5 Complexity study profile for housing project under formulation

Dimension of complexity	Dimension characteristics	Level of complexity			Rationale/description
		Low	Moderate	High	
Intentions of research problems (overall **high** problem complexity)	Stability of background influences			*	There exists some housing literature but not specific to the target population, and problem is likely changeable
	Clarity of mixing purpose			*	Multiple needs for innovation, but focus yet to be known
	Certainty of study outcomes			*	Low certainty of insights
Systems of research contexts (overall **high** system complexity)	Dynamics of environmental influences			*	Many sources of dynamics that remain unknown
	Range of geographical dispersion			*	High degree of potential dispersion
	Diversity of participants			*	High degree of potential differences in characteristics
Designs of research integrations (overall **high** procedural complexity)	Predictability of practical influences			*	Low predictability of dynamics as population is relatively unknown
	Nature of design approach			*	Little agreement about procedures leads to evolving designs
	Definition of timeframes and resources			*	No clear start date or resource allocations
Capacities of research interactions (overall **high** relational complexity)	Diversity of social influences			*	Relatively unknown social dynamics
	Extent of role definition			*	Low degree of role predetermination
	Nature of member contributions			*	Yet to be known
Evidence of research outcomes (overall **high** integration complexity)	Familiarity of practical influences			*	Sources of dynamics are unknown
	Transparency of integration strategy			*	Strategies are yet to be determined, but are thought to be intensive
	Nature of study impacts			*	Low predictability of impacts
Overall study complexity rating		High			
Summary description of study's complexity		This is based on consistent assessments of high complexity across all the dimensions			

Table 4.6 Complexity study profile for the featured study on law clients

Dimension of complexity	Dimension characteristics	Level of complexity			Rationale/description
		Low	Moderate	High	
Intentions of research problems (overall **moderate** problem complexity)	Stability of background influences		*		Some relevant, quantitative-focused literature about perceptions of fairness and satisfaction exists
	Clarity of mixing purpose		*		Study's need for more comprehensive understanding of fairness and purpose of interviews to explain the statistical findings
	Certainty of study outcomes		*		Aims to uncover new areas of unfairness to inform policy, yet uncertain about what those areas are
Systems of research contexts (overall **high** system complexity)	Dynamics of environmental influences			*	Potential for many, including variations in individual lawyer practices and youth experiences from implementation of advocacy policies
	Range of geographical dispersion		*		Recruitment from various youth outreach teams and transitional housing facilities across small geographical area of Hong Kong
	Diversity of participants			*	Young offenders assumed to be diverse
Designs of research integrations (overall **low** procedural complexity)	Predictability of feasibility influences	*			Potential for some intensity, yet no indication of issues and population seemed familiar
	Nature of design approach	*			Literature cited agreement to measures and use of interviews, and design proceeded as predetermined
	Definition of timeframes and resources	*			No indication of any adaptations to timeframes, ethics or resources
Capacity of research interactions (overall **unknown** relational complexity)	Diversity of social influences		—		Potential for team diversity, but lack of description of researcher backgrounds
	Extent of role definition		—		Potential for role distinction, but lack of description of researcher roles
	Nature of member contributions		—		Potential for individual focus, but lack of description of interactions
Evidence of research outcomes (overall **low** integration complexity)	Familiarity of practical influences	*			Potential for some dynamics, yet no indication of any validity issues and reliability scales only provided for quantitative measures
	Transparency of integration strategy	*			Separate findings with qualitative linked to quantitative to explain differing perceptions of private and public lawyers
	Nature of study impacts		*		Importance of procedural fairness and some certainty of impacts of emergent elements
Overall study complexity rating			Moderate		
Rationale for study's complexity rating					This is based on varying assessments from low to high across four of the complexity dimensions, and a lack of information about the fifth

Note. A dash indicates that data was not reported.

Source: Author generated from narrative information provided by Chui and Cheng (2017).

Table 4.7 Complexity study profile for the featured study on postconflict risk

Dimension of complexity	Dimension characteristics	Level of complexity			Rationale/description
		Low	Moderate	High	
Intentions of research problems (overall **moderate** problem complexity)	Stability of background influences		*		Some literature relevant to political violence affecting youth, yet community-level effects not well understood; construct of fairness might be more complex
	Clarity of mixing purpose		*		Study's need to identify salient community-level risk factors and responses to these risks for adolescents, yet mixing purpose stated to deepen understanding about and develop survey instruments
	Certainty of study outcomes		*		Aims to identify contextually relevant risk factors to inform survey development, yet uncertain about what those are
Systems of research contexts (overall **moderate** system complexity)	Dynamics of environmental influences		*		Potential for many is attributable to variations in individual experiences in postconflict settings, yet limited description
	Range of geographical dispersion		*		Recruitment from small geographical area of Vukovar, yet great potential for diversity in individuals, though limited description provided
	Diversity of participants			*	Participants are diverse in terms of their family and community relations and experiences
Designs of research integrations (overall **low** procedural complexity)	Predictability of feasibility influences		*		Potential for some intensity, yet no indication of any challenges and population understudied
	Nature of design approach	*			Literature cited agreement for focus group approach and assumes use of surveys and interviews to be appropriate; design seemed to proceed as predetermined
	Definition of timeframes and resources	*			No indication of any adaptations to timeframe or resources
Capacity of research interactions (overall **moderate** relational complexity)	Diversity of social influences		—		Potential for team diversity, but no description of researcher backgrounds provided
	Extent of role definition			*	Researcher roles described as having conducted focus groups and analysis and developed quantitative scales
	Nature of member contributions				Limited description, but can assume some collaborative interactions as well as some individual contributions
Evidence of research outcomes (overall **low** integration complexity)	Familiarity of practical influences		unknown		—
	Transparency of integration strategy	*			Qualitative results linked to quantitative data collection for instrument development – findings presented separately
	Nature of study impacts	*			Highlights importance of insecurity, yet uncertain impacts of two emergent types of community-level emotional insecurity
Overall study complexity rating	Moderate				
Rationale for study's complexity rating	This rating is based on the moderate ratings of many individual characteristics, even though two of the dimensions were rated overall low				

Note. Dash indicates that no data was provided.

Source: Author generated from narrative information provided by Taylor et al. (2017).

Table 4.8 Complexity study profile for the featured study on heart care

Dimension of complexity	Dimension characteristics	Level of complexity			Rationale/description
		Low	Moderate	High	
Intentions of research problems (overall **moderate** problem complexity)	Stability of background influences		*		Some relevant but quantitative-focused literature about self-care management and knowledge, yet only focused on decision-making process requiring cognitive functioning, and so relationship between knowledge and cognitive function might be more complex
	Clarity of mixing purpose		*		Study's need to determine contributing facets of knowledge and cognitive function to heart failure self-care towards a more in-depth understanding of the phenomenon of self-care
	Certainty of study outcomes			*	Aims to explore how knowledge and cognitive function contribute to heart failure self-care, yet uncertain about what this means for interventions
Systems of research contexts (overall **moderate** system complexity)	Dynamics of environmental influences		*		Potential for many, including variations in individual patients, hospital and doctor experiences, and implementation of interventions and recommendations, yet description is limited
	Range of geographical dispersion		*		Recruitment from small geographical area, yet draws on two outpatient heart failure specialty clinics associated with a large urban medical centre
	Diversity of participants		*		Some diversity assumed, yet all patients diagnosed with heart failure and meet inclusion criteria
Designs of research integrations (overall **low** procedural complexity)	Predictability of feasibility influences	*			Potential for some intensity, yet no indication of any challenges, and population seemed to be familiar
	Nature of design approach	*			Literature cited agreement with survey and interview approaches, and design seemed to proceed as predetermined
	Definition of timeframes and resources	unknown			No indication of any adaptations to resources or description of timeframe
Capacity of research interactions (overall **moderate** relational complexity)	Diversity of social influences	unknown			Potential for team diversity, but no description of researcher backgrounds provided other than the qualitative expertise of one
	Extent of role definition		*		Potential for role distinction, but no description of researcher roles provided other than the qualitative role of one
	Nature of member contributions		*		Limited description, but can assume some collaborative interactions as well as the individual contribution of the qualitative researcher
Evidence of research outcomes (overall **moderate** integration complexity)	Familiarity of practical influences	unknown			No information provided
	Transparency of integration strategy		*		Convergence on three constructs that are well established
	Nature of study impacts			*	Extensive evidence for outcomes informing self-care interventions for heart failure patients
Overall study complexity rating			Moderate		
Rationale for study's complexity rating					This rating is based on the many moderate ratings of individual characteristic assessments as well as four of the overall dimensions

Note. Dash indicates no data provided.

Source. Author generated from narrative information provided by Dickson et al. (2011).

Table 4.9 Complexity study profile for the featured study on safe places

Dimension of complexity	Dimension characteristics	Level of complexity			Rationale/description
		Low	Moderate	High	
Intentions of research problems (overall **high** problem complexity)	Stability of background influences			*	Some relevant literature about safe places, HIV prevalence, challenges for population; many contributors are yet unknown
	Clarity of mixing purpose			*	Study's need to develop safe places for internally displaced Colombian gay and bisexual men and transwomen; mixing purpose contributes new understandings to social change
	Certainty of study outcomes			*	Aims to identify contextually relevant risk factors to inform survey development, yet uncertain about what those are
Systems of research contexts (overall **high** system complexity)	Dynamics of environmental influences			*	Many details of relevant historical and current influences on the study's context, population is understudied, and variations in individual experiences
	Range of geographical dispersion			*	Recruitment from small geographical area, yet specific vulnerable population from across the Colombian city of Bogotá results in great potential for diversity in participants
	Diversity of participants			*	Great diversity assumed
Designs of research integrations (overall **high** procedural complexity)	Predictability of feasibility influences			*	Literature cited agreement with creation of a non-coercive dialogue which required adapting procedures
	Nature of design approach			*	Adaptations were made to the larger study to include more interviews
	Definition of timeframes and resources		*		No indication of any adaptations to timeframe, but resources are assumed to have been adapted
Capacity of research interactions (overall **high** relational complexity)	Diversity of social influences			*	Detailed description of composition of the research team in terms of philosophical assumptions, methodological training, and disciplinary backgrounds of each member
	Extent of role definition			*	A focus on safe environment in which a non-coercive dialogue could take place necessitated roles to emerge
	Nature of member contributions			*	Detailed description of team development and interactions to develop egalitarian relationship detailed throughout
Evidence of research outcomes (overall **moderate** integration complexity)	Familiarity of practical influences	unknown			No information provided
	Transparency of integration strategy		*		Some familiarity with linking qualitative data to inform instrument refinement; no validity evidence for quantitative data, yet details given about coding and memo use for qualitative data
	Nature of study impacts		*		Highlights importance of safe spaces, yet uncertain impacts of understandings and process
Overall study complexity rating		High			
Rationale for study's complexity rating					This rating is based on the consistent high rating of complexity across the dimensions, with the exception of one as moderate

Note. Dash indicates no data provided.

Source. Author generated from narrative information provided by Zea et al. (2014).

Table 4.10 Complexity study profile for the featured study on leadership competencies

Dimension of complexity	Dimension characteristics	Level of complexity			Rationale/description
		Low	Moderate	High	
Intentions of research problems (overall **high** problem complexity)	Stability of background influences			*	Some relevant literature about leadership competencies for this population, but many contributors are yet unknown
	Clarity of mixing purpose			*	Study goal of the larger project was to identify public health leadership competencies, yet multiple mixing purposes contributed to development
	Certainty of study outcomes			*	Aims to identify public health leadership competencies that could apply to public health practice across Canada, yet uncertain about what those are
Systems of research contexts (overall **moderate** system complexity)	Dynamics of environmental influences		*		Some details of relevant historical and current influences on study context and variations in public health workforce and leader population experiences
	Range of geographical dispersion			*	Recruitment from large cross-Canadian geographical area, yet specific inclusion criteria result in good potential for diversity in participants
	Diversity of participants		*		Some diversity, yet all workforce and leadership in public health
Designs of research integrations (overall **moderate** procedural complexity)	Predictability of feasibility influences		*		Agreement on the need of a literature review, followed by a national survey of public health workforce, followed by a focus group with leaders, yet the description of many sources of diversity was limited
	Nature of design approach			*	Adaptations were made to the design in response to participant needs
	Definition of timeframes and resources			*	No indication of any adaptations to timeframe, but resources are assumed to have been adapted
Capacity of research interactions (overall **high** relational complexity)	Diversity of social influences			*	Detailed description of team member backgrounds in terms of training, research, and practice expertise
	Extent of role definition			*	Detailed description of efforts to maintain methodological congruence, including use of software across the team, and active engagement
	Nature of member contributions			*	Detailed description of team development and interactions to develop collaborative relationships to enable interactions that are detailed, especially in the analysis
Evidence of research outcomes (overall **moderate** integration complexity)	Familiarity of practical influences	unknown			No information provided
	Transparency of integration strategy		*		Some integration was straightforward linking of developing items, whereas the survey linked with focus groups for clarification was not as well established
	Nature of study impacts			*	Highlights importance of leadership competencies, yet uncertain impacts of understandings and process
Overall study complexity rating			Moderate to high		
Rationale for study's complexity rating					This is based on the assessments of complexity across the dimensions at least moderate, with two high.

Note. Dash indicates no data provided.

Source: Author generated from narrative information provided by Strudsholm et al. (2016).

Table 4.11 Complexity study profile for the featured study on vaping culture

Dimension of complexity	Dimension characteristics	Level of complexity			Rationale/description
		Low	Moderate	High	
Intentions of research problems (overall **high** problem complexity)	Stability of background influences			*	Some relevant literature about use of Twitter in health research and vaping culture, but many contributors are yet unknown
	Clarity of mixing purpose			*	Mixing purpose does not fit an existing typology as it is stated to contextualize vaping culture in social media
	Certainty of study outcomes			*	Aims to contextualize vaping culture that could apply to health promotion policy and practice around the globe, yet uncertain about what those are
Systems of research contexts (overall **high** system complexity)	Dynamics of environmental influences			*	Some details of relevant historical and current influences to social media, little is known about vaping culture, and variations in electronic nicotine delivery system users' experiences
	Range of geographical dispersion			*	Recruitment from across the globe results in great diversity of participants
	Diversity of participants			*	Assumed to be high because of random global sampling, yet all electronic nicotine delivery system users of Twitter
Designs of research integrations (overall **low** procedural complexity)	Predictability of feasibility influences		*		Agreement with the use of Twitter and no indication of any challenges, yet population unfamiliar
	Nature of design approach	*			Design seemed to proceed as predetermined
	Definition of timeframes and resources	*			No adaptations to timeframe or resources indicated
Capacity of research interactions (overall **moderate** relational complexity)	Diversity of social influences	unknown			Potential for team diversity, but no description of researcher backgrounds provided other than they were health researchers and some were 'supervising'
	Extent of role definition		*		Some description of efforts to maintain methodological congruence involved in coding and some details about 'supervising' researcher
	Nature of member contributions		*		Limited description, but can assume some collaborative interactions as well as the individual contribution of the supervising researcher
Evidence of research outcomes (overall **high** integration complexity)	Familiarity of practical influences		*		Some descriptions of influences on integration informing data decisions
	Transparency of integration strategy			*	Contextualizing is not well established in MMR, yet provided embedded descriptions and separate section summarizing how validity evidence was generated by coding and synthesizing subsample of tweets and comparing that to the full data set and keyword prevalence
	Nature of study impacts			*	Highlights importance of understanding vaping, yet uncertain impacts of understandings and process
Overall study complexity rating		Moderate to high			
Rationale for study's complexity rating		This rating is based on the varying complexity across the dimensions: mostly high, some moderate, and one low			

Note. Dash indicates no data provided.

Source: Author generated from narrative information provided by Colditz et al. (2017).

Consider common structures for organizing the descriptions related to research problems, contexts, integrations, interactions, and outcomes. Now consider how these descriptions might be adapted to include a diagnosis of the influences on research conditions. First examine the information about the conditions described for the featured study on law clients (Chui & Cheng, 2017). I present the narrative to give access to my thinking behind developing the individual complexity study profile. In Figure 4.2, I advance four types of influences to consider in the descriptions of research conditions for each of the five dimensions which can be used to complement the visual presentation of the complexity study profile.

- *Diagnose the complexity of the research problem and potential background influences.* A moderate rating of complexity is assigned to the research problem of how young offenders perceive fairness and satisfaction towards their lawyers in the Hong Kong criminal justice system. Established literature was referenced in some relevant areas (such as procedural justice and fairness) along with a low degree of certainty in the outcomes. A strong potential exists for high influence and changeability of dynamic background influences because while researchers identify a mixing purpose to explain the initial quantitative findings, they also allude to the fact that fairness may not yet be well understood.
- *Diagnose the complexity of the research contexts.* A high rating of complexity for the research context is attributed to the detailed description of the Hong Kong location and justice systems. This is because, although the study context was Hong Kong, much of the British justice system remains intact at the time of the study, which was 17 years after the handover of Hong Kong to China. A strong potential exists for high influence and changeability of environment influences because lawyers may practice differently and individual characteristics of the young offenders might influence their lawyer interactions.

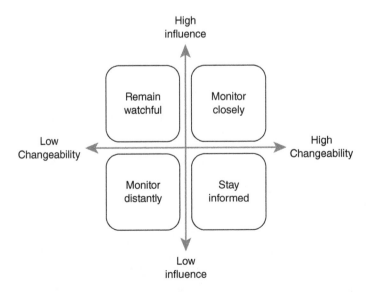

Figure 4.2 Analysing ideas for diagnosing influences on complex mixed methods research conditions

- *Diagnose the complexity of the research integrations.* A low rating of complexity for the research procedures is supported by the description of the research procedures as implemented as planned. Few details of feasibility influences are described, and it seems that an explanatory sequential design was conducted as predetermined, using a questionnaire with 168 young offenders and follow-up interviews with 30 participants. Intended timeframes were met.
- *Diagnose the complexity of the research interactions.* A rating of unknown for the research interactions is simply due to a lack of available information, yet I would hazard a guess that the social influences would potentially be low influence, high changeability because a preliminary search of the two authors' backgrounds revealed similarities.
- *Diagnose the complexity of the research outcomes.* A low rating for the research integrations is supported by the well-established integration need for sampling of quantitative data and for follow-up qualitative data, and a lack of evidence of integrated findings. The lack of information related to practical influences may mean that the interpretations of the study conditions are less dynamic than the reality faced by researchers.

CHAPTER CHECK-IN

1 Can you discern the differences and similarities in the descriptions of conditions of complexity across the authors of the six featured mixed methods studies? (See the further readings in Chapter 2.) Compare how the authors of at least two of these articles describe any key challenges related to conditions under varying complexity according to the following five dimensions (use Table 4.1 as a guide).

- Intentions of their research problems
- Systems of their research contexts
- Designs of their research integrations
- Capacity of their research interactions
- Evidence of their research outcomes.

Consider what your analysis tells you (or does not tell you) about the opportunities offered by a complexity-sensitive approach.

2 Can you diagnose the complexity of mixed methods research conditions for a study that is of interest to you?

- Apply the guiding questions for researchers from Table 4.2 to diagnose indicators of complexity for consideration.
- Diagnose the levels of complexity across five dimensions using Table 4.3 and look at the differences and similarities among ratings of complexity to generate an overall complexity rating.
- Which dimensions were easy to assess and which ones were more difficult?
- Create a study complexity profile (see Table B.1 in Appendix B).

3 What features that engage readers can you use to begin creating your complexity-sensitive mixed methods study proposal? Sketch a description of the research conditions under which you would undertake the study. Select one of the features that engage readers that fits with your study and write a brief discussion how the feature relates to your study.

4 Consider the potential influences affecting the five dimensions of complexity for a study that is of interest to you.

- What do you know about the potential influences?
- How would you assess the potential influences (see Figure 4.2)

KEY CHAPTER CONCEPTS

This chapter advances the first guiding practice for a complexity-sensitive approach to mixed methods research. It addresses the question: What does diagnosing the complexity of mixed methods research conditions involve, and how can the suitability of a complexity-sensitive approach be recognized, promoted, and conveyed? Diagnosing conditions of complexity can serve the important purpose of justifying a complexity-sensitive approach to mixed methods research that allows researchers to attend and respond to changing conditions as they occur during the study. Five dimensions of complexity provide an initial framework for which the degree of study complexity can be assessed: intentions of research problems, systems of research contexts, designs of research integrations, capacity of research interactions, and evidence of research outcomes. Researchers are encouraged to consider understandings of conditions as incomplete and with complexity under development. Guiding procedures are demonstrated for assessing and interpreting conditions of complexity, based on attending to the five dimensions of complexity.

The complexity for each of the characteristics within the dimensions is diagnosed to create a complexity study profile, as demonstrated for each of the featured studies. Creating unique complexity study profiles and then examining varying conditions across studies can create learning opportunities about how the authors of the featured studies go about describing the five dimensions of complexity in their studies. Features that will engage readers include seeking significant and unique research conditions that are highly complex and introducing the complexity diagnosis uniquely. Structures useful for conveying research conditions involve creating complexity study profiles and analysing the influences on the conditions. The next chapter introduces the complexity-sensitive practices related to framing complex mixed methods research problems.

FURTHER READINGS

The following are articles by one or more authors of the six featured mixed methods studies. These resources are offered as complementary readings for the featured studies. Readers may find it interesting to see how authors position their previous work or report their work across multiple publications. Readings denoted with an asterisk are available on the companion website for this book.

Corkalo Biruski, D., & Ajdukovic, D. (2016). Young adults' perspective of social reconstruction in three post-war communities in Croatia and Bosnia-Herzegovina. In M. Fisher & O. Simic (Eds.), *Transitional justice and reconciliation: Lessons from the Balkans* (pp. 169–192). New York: Routledge.

Written by two of the authors of the featured study on postconflict risk, this chapter reports young adults' perspectives on social reconstruction in three post-war urban communities in Vukovar and Knin (Croatia), and Banja Luka (Bosnia-Herzegovina).

*Cheng, K. K.-Y., Chui, W. H., & Ong, R. (2015). Providing justice for low-income youths: Publicly-funded lawyers and youth clients in Hong Kong. *Social & Legal Studies, 24*, 577–593.

Written by the two authors of the featured study on law clients, this study draws on in-depth interviews with 40 youth defendants and defence lawyers. It examines the ways in which the welfare and justice imperatives are negotiated within the Hong Kong juvenile justice system.

Dickson, V., Tkacs, N., & Riegel, B. (2007). Cognitive influences on self-care decision making in persons with heart failure. *American Heart Journal, 154*, 424–431. https://doi.org/10.1016/j.ahj.2007.04.058.

Written by two of the authors of the featured study on heart care, this publication contributes to the understanding of heart failure self-care by exploring the cognitive deficits for decision-making.

Primack, B. A., Soneji, S., Stoolmiller, M., Fine, M. J., & Sargent, J. D. (2015). Progression to traditional cigarette smoking after electronic cigarette use among US adolescents and young adults. *JAMA Pediatrics, 169*, 1018. doi: 10.1001/jamapediatrics.2015.1742.

Written by one of the authors of the featured study on vaping culture, this longitudinal cohort study involving 694 participants from a national US sample found an association between use of electronic cigarettes and progression to traditional cigarette smoking.

Vollman, A. R., Thurston, W. E., Meadows, L., & Strudsholm, T. (2014). *Leadership competencies for public health practice in Canada: Environmental scan.* St. John's, NS: Community Health Nurses of Canada. Retrieved from https://www.chnc.ca/documents/LCPHPC_Project-EnvironmentalScan_Sep2014Final.pdf.

Written by four of the authors of the featured study on leadership competencies, this publication reports the findings from the environmental scan that informed the first phase of the mixed methods study.

Zea, M. C., Reisen, C. A., Bianchi, F. T., Gonzales, F. G., Betancourt, F., Aguilar, M., & Poppen, P. J. (2013). Armed conflict, homonegativity, and forced internal displacement: Implications for HIV among Colombian gay, bisexual, and transgender individuals. *Culture, Health, & Sexuality, 15*, 788–803. doi: 10.1080/13691058.2013.779028.

Written by all the authors of the featured study on safe spaces, along with others, this article reports findings from 19 key informants. It provides information about internal displacement of sexual minorities and life history interviews with 42 participants.

Apply your mixed methods knowledge with videos, activities, SAGE journal articles and project templates at **https://study.sagepub.com/poth**

5

FRAMING INTENTIONS OF COMPLEX MIXED METHODS RESEARCH PROBLEMS

By the end of this chapter, you will be able to answer the following questions:

- Why frame intentions of mixed methods research problems?
- What opportunities exist to frame complex mixed methods problems?
- Why can literature-based framing become hazardous for mixed methods researchers?
- What guides the framing of complex mixed methods research problems?
- What features engage readers with complex mixed methods research problems?
- What writing and diagram innovations are useful for framing complex mixed methods research problems?

By the end of this chapter, you will be familiar with the following terms:

- Framing perspectives
- Literature search parameters

- Grey literature
- Published literature

This chapter advances the adaptive practice for guiding a complexity-sensitive approach to mixed methods research. It addresses the question: *What does the framing of complex mixed methods research problems involve and how can the need for innovation-focused mixing intentions and evolving background influences be recognized, promoted, and conveyed?'* Think about the last time you read an introduction to a research proposal or report. Were you persuaded of the significance of the problem and the need for the study? Why or why not? Consider which of the following questions were clearly addressed and what remained ambiguous after reading the introduction: Why was the problem worth pursuing? What purpose guided the focus of the study? Who are the intended study audiences? A well-written introduction to a mixed methods study familiarizes the reader with the background to the study problems, the conceptual foundations guiding the study, and the purpose for integration (Creswell & Plano Clark, 2018; DeCuir-Gunby & Schultz, 2017). Ideally the study introduction conveys cohesive reasoning for the significance of the problem, the need for the study, and the purpose(s) of mixing that then set the stage for the entire mixed methods research proposal or report. The researcher then provides further details in subsequent parts of a research proposal or report such as the literature review and methods description. Let us now consider how framing a complex mixed methods research problem is distinctive.

Among the initial challenges for mixed methods researchers addressing complex problems is focusing the background descriptions in a way that conveys the problem's research significance and the study's need for innovation. These difficulties are attributable to the highly complex nature of problems that involve nonlinear background influences and uncertain study methods and outcomes (see Chapter 2 for initial discussion). As a result, researchers are challenged to describe the interdependent societal issues and generate understandings of topical and methodological literature directly relevant to the complex research problem in order to underpin the significance of the problem and the need for the study. This situation contrasts starkly with research problems that are considered less complex because they are easily described by relatable literature with well-established study methods with which to identify a mixing purpose from existing typologies. To that end, framing the significance of complex mixed methods research problems is the focus of this chapter because the background descriptions and focus of innovation as the mixing purpose have important impacts on how the study is implemented, what the study generates as outcomes, and who the study audiences are with a vested interest.

Work on this chapter was informed by my experiences as an instructor, mentor, and reviewer as I have grappled to guide others in developing a complexity-sensitive mentality. Specifically, in seeking to frame the mixing intentions involved in complex mixed methods research problems, I draw upon my previous experiences of conducting mixed literature reviews and my thinking about Onwuegbuzie and Frels's (2016) resource guiding a seven-step comprehensive literature review process and Heyvaert, Hannes, and Onghena's (2017) eight-step mixed methods research syntheses approach. There is no agreed-upon approach for framing mixed methods research problems, yet there seem to be commonalities that underpin current practices. A comprehensive process is naturally iterative and draws upon relevant literature topics and research approaches.

Embedding the featured mixed methods studies in this chapter reflects a continued effort to address the practice gap in many textbooks and to provide authentic examples of published articles that represent varying conditions of complexity related to research problems. Specifically, assuming our understandings of complex mixed methods research problems as dynamic and evolving over time – and that problems where our understandings are considered to be incomplete yet are *worthy of pursuit* and are indeed *possible to pursue* using a complexity-sensitive approach to mixed methods research. In so doing, there is a need to make explicit the actions involved in developing initial understandings of complex problems in order to propose mixed methods studies and then assimilate and report new understandings of the complexities from the standpoint of completed mixed methods research. This leads to a new approach to framing the intentions of complex problems. From there we can consider the opportunities afforded to researchers and the hazards related to **framing perspectives** that influence our understandings of complex mixed methods research problems and the iterative guiding procedures. As a starting point, let us consider the iterative procedures to guide researchers in framing complex mixed methods research problems.

Why Frame Intentions of Mixed Methods Research Problems?

Researchers are tasked with the responsibility of conveying the significance of the problem – for a complexity-sensitive approach, this involves framing the need of the complex mixed methods research problems. The important roles for problems to shape study designs and implementation have been described. The descriptions of research problems can include information about background influences and literature gaps. The purpose of framing is to introduce the reader to the demand for innovation-focused integration purposes underlying the pursuit of the complex problem. The new framing approach for complex problems responds to the dilemmas experienced with a lack of understanding of background influences on the problems and availability of guiding practices. Thus, the traditional mixed methods research practice focused on rationalizing the integration purpose based on content and methodological gaps identified in existing literature is not suitable under conditions of higher complexity. Instead an adaptive practice for framing the intention of problems is more appropriate, given the uncertainty of the purposes for integration. The framing of research problems is realized through ongoing integrative thinking with complexity about the background influences. In so doing, the researcher is better able to assimilate and respond to emerging understandings of research problems in a way that both influences and is influenced by the changing conditions surrounding the mixed methods research.

Framing the complex mixed methods research problems plays a crucial role in demonstrating congruence among the interrelated research topic, problem, purpose, and questions underpinning the mixed methods research (see initial discussion in Chapter 2). The approach by which to establish and maintain methodological congruence within our designs for tackling complex mixed methods research is understandably considered iterative in response to dynamic influences. Demonstrating methodological congruence begins with exploring the topics that are of interest to study, identifying a clear problem in need of investigation, advancing the primary purpose of the study, and specifying the questions guiding the study design. This is essential because these decisions related to topics, problem, purpose, and questions provide the foundation on which to base subsequent design decisions. Examine the guiding framework in Figure 5.1 to highlight the interrelatedness of this narrowing process.

An effective framing of complex research problems requires pinpointing integration purposes for innovation and I have sought, over the last decade, to develop a practice for guiding the necessary integrative thinking with complexity. This work came about from my experience of students and colleagues describing having abandoned studies because they had assumed (and been guided in the false notion) that they needed to have what they called a complete understanding of their research problem before they undertook such studies. Further queries to explore what a complete understanding would look like revealed common

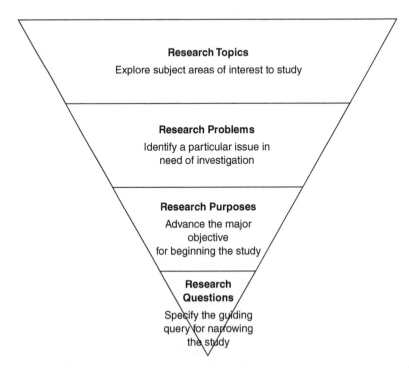

Figure 5.1 Interrelating study research topics, problems, purposes, and questions
Adapted from Creswell and Poth (2017, p. 129). Used with permission from Sage Publications.

aspects of their responses, such as referring to relevant topical and methodological literature that could point to specific deficiencies that were in need of investigation.

What I came to realize is that many students and researchers seemed to be constrained to pursue less complex research problems because they felt it was too risky to pursue problems that did not have relevant related literature. Thinking back to my own methodological training experiences, this made sense. We had been taught to follow the linear sequence of identifying a problem, describing what we know about the problem, searching what others have done related to the problem, defining a topical and/or methodological gap that needed to be pursued, and designing a study. I came to realize the need to shift this mentality and the related assumptions I held about research problems and create guiding practices for complexity-sensitive research that would no longer limit researchers because of what they (and their advisors and colleagues) assumed were possible problems to pursue. The highly complex nature of complex problems involving nonlinear background influences and uncertain study methods and outcomes creates challenges for researchers. A frame can be created by describing the relevant societal issues and existing literature that is directly relevant to the complex research problem which underpins the need for the study. To that end I set about reassuring those who are pursuing (such as researchers), assessing (such as journal reviewers, editors and funders), and guiding (such as book authors and supervisors) that mixed methods studies can be (and indeed should be) pursued based on the need for innovation in addressing complex research problems in complex conditions. Examine Researcher Spotlight 5.1, from the perspective of an emerging scholar from South Africa, featuring the need for researchers to explore new ways of approaching complex mixed methods research problems.

 **Researcher Spotlight 5.1**

Christo Ackermann on the need for exploring new practices for addressing complex mixed methods research problems

The complex research world we operate in will call more and more on mixed methods approaches to contribute to or solve problems. Thus failure to know about and understand mixed methods as a research approach will be detrimental to researchers in being able to face research problems head-on.

It is therefore key that we step out of our comfort zones and explore the best possible means to address complex research problems. This, in my opinion, is what mixed methods is all about: taking us out of our comfort zones and assisting us in making a real contribution to complex research problems.

Framing Opportunities and Hazards for Mixed Methods Researchers

Innovation-Focused Intention Opportunities

To focus on a particular form of innovation provides an important reference point for subsequent study decisions when addressing complex mixed methods research problems. Complex mixed methods research problems often tackle unchartered territory in terms of yet-to-be-discovered relationships among topical and disciplinary areas of study, yet-to-be-described research approaches and designs, and yet-to-be-revealed innovative insights and solutions. The role of framing to focus the study need on a particular form of innovation means identifying the specific mixing purpose. So far, my work has revealed four types of mixing purposes focused on innovation. A study need for novel insights is not unique to complex mixed methods research problems, yet what is new is making the case through relevant literature in the absence of guiding literature related directly to the topic. A study need for integrative interactions may already exist in the literature on the rationale for the use of research teams, yet it may not yet be explicitly expressed that these interactions are not based on predetermination of how the diverse disciplines and expertise will be integrated. A study need for dynamic responses may already be happening in practice, yet perhaps not well reported. A study need for new designs is well established in the literature (Creswell & Plano Clark, 2018) and ongoing efforts are reflected. The innovation-focused mixing purposes should naturally be considered to be in progress and will evolve over time. To distinguish among four mixing purposes focused on innovation, I describe the nature of innovation and research contributions in Table 5.1. The differing foci of the research contributions on insights, interactions, responses, and designs can be helpful for pinpointing the type of mixing purposes and creating the mixing purpose statement.

The pioneering opportunities afforded by tackling complex mixed methods research problems can be attractive to researchers, yet the reality of limited guidance and access to successful research and funded proposals can hinder these pursuits. For these reasons, I consider framing the significance of the complex problem and conveying the study's need for innovation as representing the most important yet most challenging part of a complexity-sensitive mixed methods research project because of the risks involved.

Table 5.1 Distinguishing among four mixing purposes focused on innovation

Types of mixing purposes	Nature of innovation	Research contributions
1 Generating *novel insights* to address complex mixed methods research problems	Innovation through accessing previously unknown understandings and making the case through relevant literature	Illuminating novel insights for enhancing background connections and implications
2 Developing *integrative interactions* to capitalize on mixed methods research capacities	Innovation through developing relationships, perspectives, and transcending disciplinary and methodological boundaries	Clarifying how integrative interactions create capacity for emergence
3 Supporting *dynamic responses* to assimilate evolving mixed methods research conditions	Innovation through adapting an existing design to changeable research influences	Developing, documenting, and providing feedback about impacts of emergent influences
4 Advancing *new designs* to focus on points of interface	Innovation through describing the procedures involved in an original mixed methods research design	Elaborating the ways in researchers realize agility in procedures and design legitimacy of studies with more than one purpose for mixing

Literature–Based Framing Hazards

The way a mixed methods research problem is framed can dramatically influence the study design, implementation, and outcomes. This can be attributable to the interrelatedness of the problems with the purposes, topics, and designs, and complicated by the complexity of the conditions under which the study is undertaken. I propose an artwork frame as a metaphor for introducing complex mixed methods research problems to readers. The frame on a piece of artwork enhances the viewer's experience by presenting and protecting the exhibit. We enhance the reader's experience of a study by describing the perspective from which the complex research problem is posed and providing the reasons for which the study need for innovation is based. The task requires being explicit about our understandings of the complex mixed methods research problem because without proper framing, the study is at risk of being misunderstood and underappreciated.

Thus, framing plays an important role in guiding the readers' perceptions and understandings of the research problem and need for the study. This is particularly important, given the degree of choices researchers make about relevant issues and literature surrounding the problems because of the low degree of stability and uncertainty inherent in complex research problems. To that end, there exist infinite ways researchers may frame the same complex research problem; each one affects our understanding of the background of the problem and the need for the study. We only need to look to experimental research demonstrated in the classic study undertaken by behavioural scientists Amos Tversky and Daniel Kahneman (1981) for evidence of the phenomenon known as the *framing effect*.

The framing effect may have major implications for how we communicate complex mixed methods research problems in our study proposals and reports. Tversky and Kahneman (1981) asked two groups to imagine that the USA is preparing for the outbreak of an unusual disease, which is expected to kill many people, and to make a choice between two programmes, A and B. Each of the groups was presented with similar information, but from different perspectives – either those who were saved or those who were killed. The researchers attributed the differences to the framing effect, where markedly dissimilar responses resulted from information about the same problem were simply presented from different perspectives. Consider this effect now within the research context: if you were to present the same problem using identical information yet different words representing different framing perspectives, you can see how a reader could be lead to interpret the significance of the problem differently. Researchers have to carefully consider the information they use in framing their problems.

You might now be asking: how likely are the hazards of framing perspectives for mixed methods researchers and how can mixed methods researchers avoid framing effects? It may not be surprising that mixed methods research problems that are considered to have higher complexity are also at a greater risk from framing effects. This is because there is less agreement and stability in the literature related to the nature of and background influences on complex mixed methods research problems than there is on those that are considered less complex. Researchers are cautioned to pay close attention to what sources and perspectives are relied upon and how they convey the information when framing, that is, the words they choose to use, as the researchers may be at risk of framing effects when describing their complex mixed methods research problems and studies. There is no simple solution for avoiding framing effects, although increased awareness of the perspectives that a researcher brings to the description of the complex mixed methods research problem and need for the study represents an important first step. In Practice Alert 5.1, I consider some of the missed framing opportunities I have observed during oral consultations and when reviewing written proposals, and I invite you to do the same. In so doing, I am enhancing my understandings of the influences of framing perspectives when situating my mixed methods research problem.

 Practice Alert 5.1

What influences your framing perspectives as a mixed methods researcher?

Readers and many reviewers of mixed methods research proposals are more interested in assessing *why you are doing the study* than *what design you are using.* When mixed methods researchers define themselves by the design, they are forever defined by that rather than by what problem they are pursuing. They may miss the opportunity to convey their framing perspective representing how they are 'thinking differently' than anyone else about a complex research problem. Some examples of framing perspectives involve clear personal connections to the research topic or to relevant literature. Establishing the uniqueness and significance of the study problem and purpose creates the foundation for successful funding proposals and published manuscripts.

Try this now – sketch your ideas about what influences your framing perspective on a research problem. Then consider the effects on how the significance of the study is conveyed.

An Iterative Process for Framing Complex Mixed Methods Research Problems

There is no simple solution for avoiding framing effects, yet embedding certain safeguards can be helpful, such as integrating a variety of sources, accessing feedback from multiple perspectives, and employing systematic search procedures. To guide researchers in describing complex mixed methods research problems and studies, I outline an iterative framing process. This process involves six tasks that are interdependent and iterative – not to be considered as a set of procedures or linear steps (see Figure 5.2). I purposefully depict the role of integrative thinking and interactions as the central source of the continual emergence of new ideas and understandings. Because of this, it is essential that the framing of complex mixed methods research problems be considered *in progress,* meaning that our understandings of the significance of the problem are constantly evolving and we assimilate new information that informs the study. Indeed, the wonderful opportunities afforded by a complexity lens (see also the initial discussion in Chapter 3) include the need for assuming nonlinearity, self-organization, unpredictability, and responsiveness in the research process. Specific to framing, these assumptions explain why understandings of the background to the problem are subject to continual development with uncertain outcomes yet greater than what a sole researcher could have produced alone and responsive to changing conditions. In Guiding Tip 5.1, a Commonwealth scholar from the UK and doctoral candidate at Auckland University of Technology (New Zealand) offers new ways of thinking about the research problem as evolving.

━ ◁ ━ Guiding Tip 5.1 ━━━━━━━━━━━━━━━━━━━

Amrit Dencer-Brown advising how to navigate the framing of complex mixed methods research problems

Be dynamic. Be open to the evolution of your research problem. Do not simplify. Embrace and harness complexity. It is OK to change your framework as you understand more about your research. Maintain flexibility and adaptability.

Special attention to each of the tasks involved in framing a complex mixed methods research problem is warranted because the initial description of the problem and focus of innovation have important impacts on why we pursue the complex problem, what guides our mixed methods researcher approach, and how we focus the mixing purpose. There is no

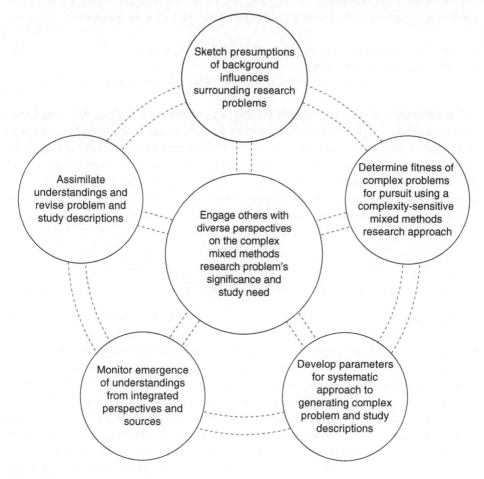

Figure 5.2   An iterative process for framing complex mixed methods research problems

fixed way to frame complex mixed methods research problems, and you should feel free to adapt to your particular study conditions, but the following tasks can help you get started.

Engage Others in Framing Processes

At the heart of the framing process is the engagement of others whose diverse perspectives will inform understandings of the complex mixed methods research problems and study. Throughout the framing process, researchers consult others, including team members representing a range of research roles, expertise, and experiences, such as librarians, disciplinary experts, and methodological experts. The researchers seek diverse perspectives to create collective understandings influencing the framing of the problem and the study. Embedding the practice of engaging others provides a feedback mechanism for informing ongoing development of understandings throughout the study.

In making explicit the need for consultations within and beyond mixed methods research teams, I build confidence in my background descriptions drawn from others representing relevant fields, roles, and expertise. The resulting revisions enhance confidence in the validity of the outcomes of the overall iterative framing process. Before engaging others, consider who could best contribute to the framing process by asking the following questions:

- Who may collaborate effectively with others offering diverse perspectives?
- Who may be open to mixed methods research?
- Who may bring new perspectives to areas of study relevant to the complex problem?

From the further readings in Chapter 4, you can begin to see evidence of long-term programmes of research focused on particular research topics by the connections between the featured studies in this book and the authors' previous work and publications. Noteworthy are some changes to the authors in the publications, and these changes are attributable to numerous factors. While I do not have knowledge specific to these authors, from my own experience, some changes to membership of research teams seek the inclusion of new perspectives and expertise for taking the programme in new directions. The authors might have made the connections, as appropriate, between past and present work and team members more explicit in the featured studies.

Sketch Presumptions of Background Influences

The framing process involves identifying and then sketching initial understandings of a problem so that you can discover the presumptions researchers are bringing. A variety of sources exist for complex research problems; among the most common origins for research problems are those that involve real-life experience, reading about historical and current events, identifying literature gaps and future research directions, and deriving ideas as part of an advisor's research agenda (Creswell, 2014). Along with other leaders in this field, I have long recognized the capacity for mixed methods research to address pressing issues that our colleagues and students discuss across their respective fields yet do not yet fully understand how to study. What is not always apparent is what the researcher brings to the study in terms of theoretical perspectives, personal connections, and research orientations. These are areas that have important implications for why and how the research is ultimately pursued.

The key to testing presumptions for me is to write down my initial understandings of the background influences to the complex research problem. I find capturing my ideas both in writing and in diagrams can be helpful for identifying areas of strengths and weaknesses in my understandings of problems. See the template in Figure B.1 in Appendix B, an editable version of which is also available on the companion website for the book. The template was useful for making explicit my understandings between my presumptions about the complex problem and societal, personal, literature, and study connections. Only once I recognized my personal motivations, potential target audience, and gaps in understanding the problem am I able to focus the **literature search parameters** and engage others. Before testing presumptions, consider what contributes to current understandings of the complex research problem by asking the following questions:

- How might the problem be considered relevant to society in terms of current and historical events?
- How might the problem connect to existing literature?
- How might the problem be personally relatable to the researchers?
- How might the problem generate outcomes that are of interest?

The featured studies provide some evidence of such efforts; for example, the authors of the postconflict risk study provide a robust description of the social context of the research as taking place in Vukovar, 'a mid-sized city affected by the ethnic violence following Croatia's declaration of independence in 1991' (Taylor et al., 2017, p. 3). Although the authors only provide a cursory description of the well-established collaborations the University of Zagreb team has with local schools and non-governmental organizations, it can be assumed that members of these groups can relate personally to the research problem. The authors might have made these descriptions more explicit by further references; for example, about how the problem was personally relatable to the researchers by describing who had lived through the war, and the relationships among researchers by describing the nature of the past collaborations.

Determine Fitness of a Complexity-Sensitive Approach

There are key framing determinants that establish the suitability of a complexity-sensitive approach. Among these is whether a selected problem requires mixed methods research and meets the defining characteristics to be considered complex (see Chapter 1 for initial discussion). When a study warrants innovation and meets certain conditions, a complexity-sensitive mixed methods approach is suitable for addressing the complex mixed methods research problems. Despite establishing the need for mixed methods research as an essential step and important quality criterion (O'Cathain, 2010), the use of mixed methods research often remains insufficiently justified in the descriptions of research problems (Bryman, 2007; Onwuegbuzie & Poth, 2016).

Justifying the significance of the research problem requires first assessing and then describing the levels of complexity related to the dimension characteristics of clarity of problem dynamics, integration purpose, and study insights (see Chapter 2 for initial discussion). Only when I can justify the problem or its study as pioneering in some way can others consider a complexity-sensitive approach as needed. Before determining a problem's fitness, consider the demand for a complexity-sensitive mixed methods research approach by asking the following questions:

- Why has this problem not yet been addressed? What are the sources of complexity?
- What is it about the problem that demands mixed methods research?
- What innovation does the problem require the study to focus on?

All the featured studies describe their problems as necessitating mixed methods research, and several allude to sources of complexity and mixing purposes. Yet none of the featured studies identifies specific mixing purpose innovations beyond developing new insights for the problems pursued. For example, in the featured study on leadership competencies, the authors establish the use of mixed methods for investigating complex problems and the necessity of the multiphase mixed methods design 'to address the complex character of leadership in a multifaceted public health context' (Strudsholm et al., 2016, p. 8). The authors might have made their descriptions of how their problem is complex more explicit, beyond simply referring to the project and problem as complex, by adding further details.

Develop Parameters for Literature Search

The development of search parameters is essential because it bounds a systematic approach to generating understandings of background influences surrounding the complex mixed methods research problem and study. The need for bounding the work by identifying search parameters has become even more essential as the quantity of **published literature** and **grey literature** increases. The need to consider a range of formats of information as well as the extent to which the materials are considered trustworthy and valid is common across perspectives of a mixed methods literature review (Leech, Dellinger, Brannagan, & Tanaka, 2010; Onwuegbuzie & Frels, 2016). There is wide recognition that the root causes of complex problems cannot be distilled because many are yet unknown (Mertens et al., 2016b). This is one of the key challenges for researchers pursuing complex mixed methods research problems. The result is that identifying problems requires calculated guesswork using search terms related to the problem.

Many resources are available for guiding literature reviews, yet few adopt a mixed methods perspective for guiding how both qualitative and quantitative evidence can be sought, evaluated, and integrated. A current resource describing an eight-step mixed methods research syntheses involves initial steps for documenting methodological and substantive choices by writing a protocol and then selecting a sampling strategy for your literature search (Heyvaert et al., 2017). This can provide important guidance specific to mixed methods research for developing a documentation system tracking evolutions in search decisions and results to create a means for others to audit your search processes and provide feedback, thus supporting the iterative actions involved in collecting, assessing, and synthesizing information – as new information is discovered, it is documented, evaluated, and integrated. As part of the evaluation process, literature is reviewed for keywords and citations that can lead to new areas of literature, and so on.

My consideration of literature reviews as an integrative and dynamic research activity and the need for guiding practices is not new. Indeed, researchers have long admonished doctoral programmes for not adequately preparing students for the tasks involved in analysing and synthesizing research and attributed improvements that are key to advancing research implications (Boote & Beile, 2005; Fink, 2013). A thorough and sophisticated review of literature that is considered a dynamic process is necessary for messy, complex problems (Boote & Beile,

2005) – and, in my opinion, this is especially important when seeking literature reflective of qualitative, quantitative, and mixed methods research. Software can be helpful in organizing and managing documents as well as diagrams for capturing and describing parameters. Reference management computer software has been available for over two decades, and has become more refined and helpful in organizing documents and easing the information retrieval and reference citation processes (Fenner, Scheliga, & Bartling, 2013). Of interest for research teams are the recent open source and web-based versions which enhance availability of collaborative aspects for collecting references, annotating documents, and writing manuscripts. See the template in Figure B.2, an editable version of which is available on the companion website for the book. This template is useful for documenting decisions points and results involved in a literature search. This documentation of a systematic approach provides evidence for enhancing confidence in the comprehensiveness of the understandings of the background influences on the complex problem. In developing search parameters, consider what topical areas of research contribute to understanding the complex research problem by asking the following questions:

- What disciplinary and topical areas of study relate to the problem?
- What do the initial searches reveal about keywords, time periods, availability, and deficiencies of relevant material?
- What citations within relevant materials might inform revisions to my parameters?

All the featured studies describe their problems by referring to disciplinary and related topical areas of study as well as pointing to areas of deficiencies. The featured study on leadership competencies (Strudsholm et al., 2016) was unique in identifying the search parameters as part of a first phase focused on a literature review. Among the parameters identified were the electronic databases of published literature, keywords, language, and date of publication. Interestingly, the purpose of the search was to identify personal characteristics of leadership in addition to enablers and barriers to public health leadership. The authors might have made their descriptions more fulsome beyond simply referring to the search parameters and included details of how they evaluated the quality of these studies more explicit beyond their description of qualitative analysis.

Monitor Emergence of Background Influences

A key aspect of the iterative process is integration across different formats of information to generate descriptions of the background influences to position the significance of the complex mixed methods research problem and need for study. Despite many resources emphasizing the need for synthesis of a wide array of literature forms in literature reviews throughout the study, there remains a need for moving beyond simply summarizing literature that is published and discovered prior to beginning of the study (Onwuegbuzie & Frels, 2016). Indeed, creating conditions for emergence describes the capacity for researchers to accommodate the products of their integrations of a variety of perspectives and sources – throughout the study.

The process of generating descriptions that integrate a variety of data sources is best described as assembling a jigsaw puzzle where the pieces can fit together in different ways to create several pictures. This metaphor represents the many ways researchers can integrate different information sources: the foundations are ever evolving, and the result is not yet known. There is no right way of doing it. Rather, a merging of individual ideas creates unique descriptions of the problem's significance that will continue to evolve throughout the study. Few resources are available for guiding the integration of and detailing specific procedures for qualitative, quantitative, and mixed methods research literature across a variety of formats. A current resource describing a seven-step comprehensive literature review involves a sixth integration step for analysing and synthesizing information involving creating analysis questions and responding to emergent issues (Onwuegbuzie & Frels, 2016). This can provide important guidance on how teams can integrate and interpret background influences for describing mixed methods research problems and making the case for the study need.

My evidence of emergence can take different forms; the rigorous analysis and integration of a wide variety of sources, including theoretical writings, empirical studies, online blogs, and topical reviews, may reveal new possible relationships and audiences as well as topical and methodological deficiencies. My review of documentation and seeking feedback can inform revisions to the parameters and may, in turn, assist in developing new perspectives of relationships among topical areas and disciplinary fields of study. In this way, I am no longer limited by current understandings, and begin to see emergent possibilities that were previously unknown. Before drafting my problem description and study need, I consider what and who could best contribute to creating conditions for emergence by asking the following questions:

- What sources of information are missing in the search protocol that may be important to the problem and study?
- What connections and relationships related to the problem have not yet been considered?
- What areas in the preliminary background descriptions and study need could benefit from greater or less detail?

All the featured studies make the case for their study need within relevant existing literature and highlight the gap that their study will address. The featured study on vaping culture (Colditz et al., 2017) relies greatly on the recent literature synthesis by Snelson (2016) related to use of social media within mixed methods studies to situate itself. Colditz et al. might have made their case more strongly by identifying what the literature synthesis contributed and what was missing and by providing more information about the search parameters beyond the number of studies and range of publication dates. Consider Researcher Spotlight 5.2 describing the challenges students may face when proposing mixed methods dissertations, from the perspective of a veteran supervisor and professor emerita from the Educational Research and Evaluation Program in the School of Education at Virginia Polytechnic Institute and State University (USA) and visiting senior scholar at the University of Michigan.

 Researcher Spotlight 5.2

Elizabeth Creamer on advocating the value of mixed methods research dissertations for tackling societal issues

It is a rite of passage for doctoral students to be required to demonstrate their capacity to conceive and execute independent research before they move on to join the academic community and the world of research that is increasingly multiphase, interdisciplinary, and team-based. Despite the irrefutable compatibility of mixed methods with the complex social problems that face educators, health practitioners, and evaluators addressing policy issues, faculty members often discourage graduate students from utilizing mixed methods because they consider it too ambitious for the scope of a dissertation.

There is ample evidence of excellent mixed methods dissertations to refute the admonition that it is overly taxing of resources and expertise to undertake a dissertation that utilizes both qualitative and quantitative approaches with the intent to integrate them at one or more points. My recommendation is not to shy away from envisioning a research purpose that tackles an important social issue, including those that contribute to the quest for equity, that have long-term and sometimes world-wide implications, and that have theoretical significance. At the outset, I suggest that students consult the literature to sketch a type of concept map that includes a long list of possible research questions and multiple ways to pursue them. This kind of vision makes it possible to subsequently carve out an initial project with a narrower focus, but one that can serve as a springboard for future research. A concept map like this can form the basis of a long-term research agenda that is so integral to launching a career that involves research.

Assimilate Understandings of Problem Significance

Assimilating understandings to inform revisions to the problem and study descriptions is a challenging task because it requires researchers to develop new connections between existing ideas and then to pay attention to emerging understandings that further forge connections and ideas. Framing processes involving descriptions of my problem's significance and the need for the study are continual and reinforcing – as new information is discovered, the connections are investigated and integrated into revising the background descriptions and study need. For example, articulating a societal purpose involves considering how the study fits within larger, more complex, pressing societal issues in order to identify the historical and current trends and priorities associated with the study problem.

In offering my 'higher' purpose for pursuing the study, my description of the complex mixed methods research problem conveys my personal motivations and literature deficiencies in addition to the background details related to societal purpose and the study's need for innovation. When integrating new information, consider the impact of the information on the description of the problem and study by asking the following questions:

- How does the new information converge or diverge with existing understandings of the research problem and study approach?
- What understandings of the problem's significance and study need are well supported by evidence, and what understandings require further development?
- How have the descriptions of problem and study evolved over time?

Not surprising, none of the featured studies explicitly describe their understandings of the complex problems by describing how they have evolved over time in the introduction. Instead these studies follow the conventions of discussing how their understandings of the problem have been influenced by the study in the discussion and conclusions. For example, in the featured study on law clients (Chui & Cheng, 2017) the discussion was focused on addressing the stated research problem: How do young offenders perceive fairness and satisfaction towards their lawyers in Hong Kong's criminal justice system? To that end, the authors suggest that the inadequacy of the interactions between young defendants and their duty lawyers influenced perceived fairness and satisfaction. They also stated: 'The results confirmed that young offenders' perception of fairness and satisfaction with lawyers have a positive association with views about the legitimacy of the justice system' (2017, p. 281). The authors might have provided greater authenticity in their conclusions had they further described the complexity inherent in the individuals, their interactions, and the justice system beyond the brief list of possible limitations.

Features that Engage Readers with Complex Research Problems

It is advantageous for researchers to distinguish their studies. Research problems are a great place to start differentiating your study under conditions of complexity. The following list provides some ideas from my own experiences as researcher, as a reviewer of mixed methods research proposals for funding and of manuscripts for publication, and from working with graduate students as an instructor, supervisor, and examiner. See also the featured studies for illustrative examples of some of these engaging features.

- *Seek timely societal issues that underpin your complex mixed methods research problem.* Go to conferences, look at websites, and talk to researchers to confirm that your ideas are in line with current topics and issues. This will help you pose timely research topics and complex problems that align with research and funding priorities.
- *Focus on pressing complex mixed methods research problems.* There are various places where ideas for complex mixed methods research problems can originate. Review recently published research and attend conference presentations to ensure that your problem has not yet been pursued. This will help position the unique contributions of your study and avoid simply replicating the work of others.
- *Introduce your mixed methods study uniquely.* Catch readers' attention with a statistic, quote, or personal narrative relevant to your complex mixed methods research problem. Review literature that others have not sought before. This will help you create reader interest in your study right from the start.
- *Assume unconventional perspectives in your mixed methods study.* Consider new roles for theory or theoretical perspectives, involve research team members from disciplines not yet reflected in studies, or assume research paradigms that have not yet been adopted in the literature. This will help you to see beyond what might be expected of your complex research problem.

Consider Researcher Spotlight 5.3 reimagining the mixed methods research space to activate actionable agendas and thus lessen the focus on designs, from the perspective of a renowned research professor in the Department of Adult Education and Youth Development at the University of South Africa.

 **Researcher Spotlight 5.3**

Norma Romm on orienting mixed methods research to incorporate an action agenda

Many mixed methods researchers have yet to sufficiently recognize how the research space itself might be used to activate novel (less restrictive or deficit-based) discourses and actions, while capitalizing on the complexity of the research situation (including research participants' and stakeholders' various expectations and hopes). Thus far it seems to me that many mixed methods researchers follow the notion that the role of research (and researchers) in society is to try to 'find out' or 'better understand' the patterning and dynamics of social realities; but how the research is oriented to incorporate an action agenda (and how co-responsibility is taken for this) is not sufficiently deliberated upon. The focus seems to be on designing research – including emergent designs – with a view to explaining or exploring realities, rather than contributing, via the research, to the development of the worlds being 'investigated'. The way in which research influences (impacts upon) the unfolding of realities in the making – by reproducing/stultifying or potentially altering/transforming discourses and actions – thus becomes obscured. The creativity highlighted in this book should include developing ways of proceeding that are responsive to opportunities to make a difference which is felt to be constructive, especially for those most marginalized in the social fabric (and also in relation to 'nature', which is often marginalized rather than revered). This would allow researchers to increase their involvement in the unfolding situations of which they, with others, are part.

Innovations in Framing Complex Mixed Methods Research Problems

Researchers working under conditions of complexity are tasked with clearly describing the mixed methods research problem and presenting the literature connections to justify the study purpose in a written proposal or report. Also important, yet often underreported, are details about the study connections with society in terms of historical events, pressing issues, current trends, and funding priorities, as well as with the researchers' personal motivations and perspectives. Descriptions of research problems vary widely and may be attributable to the range of audiences for proposals and reports, from supervisors and committee members to reviewers for funding and publication. It is not surprising that there is little agreement about format for framing a mixed methods research proposal or report, yet several writers do suggest topics to be included in an introduction and highlight brevity as a requirement. Further framing details are often found elsewhere in proposals and reports under the headings of literature review and methods. I see common structures in introductions across the differing formats for mixed methods research proposal and reports (Creswell & Plano Clark, 2018; Dahlberg, Wittink, & Gallo, 2010). The challenge with many of these descriptions of introductions is that they are simply not sufficiently detailed to be of great assistance and do not account sufficiently for the unique conditions inherent in complex mixed methods research problems.

Framing of complex mixed methods research problems can appear quite different across studies due to the differing research conditions under which the studies are conducted. In the same way, the introduction in a completed study report can be quite different from the introduction in the research proposal because understandings naturally emerged and new information was assimilated. Specifically for research problems, this can involve adapting the connections among relevant literature to emerging background influences. There is an ongoing iterative process of framing complex mixed methods research problems; it begins with a proposal drafted before the study, continues during the study implementation, and is finalized with the writing of the report once the research is completed. To that end, variations are expected in structures across the proposals and reports that you will encounter. The inherent nature of different researcher perspectives, research contexts, and stages of research commands it. In this section I describe two innovations for communicating and tracking the framing of complex mixed methods research problems.

Diagrams Representing Understandings of Study Intentions

It is uncommon to see diagrams in a study introduction of the research problem. In addition to conveying information, diagrams have proven to be an effective format for tracking evolutions in my presumptions of the connections among the study, society, literature, and researchers to the complex problem. To focus on the various connections represents a unique approach to framing complex mixed methods research problems. I find this focus helpful because by making explicit my researcher presumptions, I then have a foundation upon which I can test and track my evolving understandings. This is important because this positions my researcher mindset as open to new possibilities of understandings for:

- Why the complex mixed methods research problems are worthy of pursuit
- How my presumptions and understandings of the complex research problems evolve over time.

Connections-oriented diagrams can provide essential evidence of the links among the problem and the study, society, literature, and researchers. Furthermore, a diagram captures my understandings at a point in time, and over time I can refine the diagram to reflect what understandings of the new and existing connections have emerged during the study. In so doing, it supports creative and integrative thinking by creating a structure for managing the input of ideas. I often use visual maps to describe my dynamic schemes of understanding connections in a diagram. I am often inspired by concept, visual, and mindmapping techniques because of their usefulness for representing 'words, themes, tasks, or other items linked to and arranged around a central key word or idea' (Wheeldon & Åhlberg, 2012, p. 24). There is no set format – visual maps are intended to reflect personal preferences and styles. Their appearance varies considerably as a result – sometimes I use pictures and other times words.

What I like most about visual mapping is that it can be undertaken by different configurations of people and using various materials. Although I often use visual mapping as an individual to capture my initial sketches of problem presumptions, I find it most valuable as a group process – so it is especially well suited for testing assumptions among mixed methods research team members or seeking feedback from others. Researchers and research teams can also use variations of visual mapping, from a low-tech approach incorporating freehand drawing, to high-tech use of computers to analyse the input, generate an aggregate group product, and create a visual representation. In Figure 5.3, I provide a diagram example conveying the connections that are made explicit by the authors of the featured study on vaping culture (Colditz et al., 2017) to frame their complex research problem: What can contextualizing vaping culture in social media add to our understanding? Note that the diagram is limited to my interpretation of the information described in the article about the connection between the problem and the study, society, literature, and researchers. Note the obvious connections from the diagram, and, the absence of information related to researcher motivations.

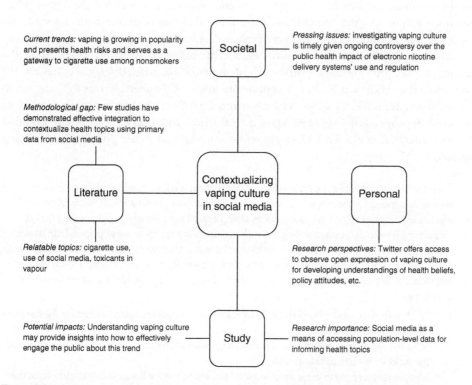

Figure 5.3   Diagram example conveying societal, study, personal and literature connections framing the complex mixed methods research problems

Writing Ideas for Framing Research Problems

It is uncommon to see a researcher explicitly convey their understandings of a mixed methods research problem as incomplete and under development. I find such accounts especially useful for mixed methods researchers who are new to tackling complex problems. This is important to position the researchers' mindset as open to new possibilities of understandings for:

- What background influences will be considered as relevant for understanding the complex problem.
- What innovative research outcomes are sought from the study needs identified.

Under conditions of complexity, understandings of the features of the complex problem are considered to be evolving and the researcher is tasked with the following question: How can the existing literature and understandings of relevant topics contribute to framing the complex mixed methods research problem necessary for pinpointing a study need for innovation?

Consider designing an introduction to the problem in need of a mixed methods research approach. I often use outlines to frame my arguments – there is no set format and researchers should adapt to their own preferences. Preparing an outline allows me to review the logic of my writing and to seek feedback from others before I engage in the writing process. Researchers and research teams can use outline diagrams to organize the headings and structures for proposals and reports. First examine the writing ideas described below and the four related illustrative excerpts from the featured study on vaping culture (Colditz et al., 2017) contextualizing vaping culture in social media using a convergent parallel mixed methods design. This reflects a focus on interrelating the research topics, problems, and purposes for demonstrating methodological cohesion. We now know that under conditions of complexity many of the contributors to understanding the research problem are not yet known and are influenced by changes in conditions and evolving understandings of background influences and links with literature. Examine the four interrelated elements of an authentic introduction to the problem that is being pursued in the study:

- *Describe the research topics and societal connections to the study.* Here, familiarize the readers with your understandings of the research topics as well as societal issues, current trends, historical events, and funding priorities surrounding the study problem. Researchers generally begin by making the case for pursuing the problem using a writing tool such as advancing a key controversy, personal narrative, or statistic. The sentences that follow should introduce the topical areas surrounding the study problem and define key terms. Summarize the key reasons for pursing the study by linking to societal needs in a single sentence, if at all possible. Researchers may find the following questions useful for guiding their topical descriptions:
  - What do readers need to know about the relevant research topics to better understand the literature connections to the problem?
  - What do readers need to know about the pressing issues and funding priorities to better understand the societal connections to the problem?
  - What do readers need to know about historical events and current trends to better understand the timeliness of study pursuit of the problem?

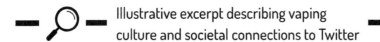 **Illustrative excerpt describing vaping culture and societal connections to Twitter**

The Twitter social media platform provides an opportunity to observe consistently sized units of salient content; Twitter messages, known as 'tweets,' are a maximum of 140 characters. Twitter is also a 'public-facing' platform, with an estimated 88% of users allowing their content to be viewed publicly (Beevolve Inc., 2014). Researchers have used public Twitter data to examine content of messages about topics such as quitting smoking

(Prochaska, Pechmann, Kim, & Leonhardt, 2012) and electronic cigarette marketing (Huang, Kornfield, Szczypka, & Emery, 2014). Twitter use is highest among adolescents and young adults (Duggan & Brenner, 2013; Kim et al., 2013), which are populations that have high and increasing incidence of electronic nicotine delivery systems (ENDS) use (Arrazola et al., 2015; Chapman & Wu, 2014). Twitter users, and those who are also ENDS users in particular, are regularly exposed to ENDS marketing messages on this platform (Emery, Vera, Huang, & Szczypka, 2014). Analysis of Twitter content may be particularly valuable in exploring cultural contexts of ENDS use (Clark et al., 2014) – a phenomenon which is more broadly referred to as 'vaping culture' (Budney, Sargent, & Lee, 2015; Gostin & Glasner, 2014).

Source: Colditz et al. (2017, p. 2). Used with permission from Sage.

- *Discuss the background to the complex problem in need of mixing methods research.* Researchers identify the goals of the study and the use of a mixed methods research approach. Sentences should briefly outline features positioning the level of complexity of the problem. Summarize the key reasons justifying the suitability of mixed methods research and the need for a focus on innovation. Researchers may find the following questions useful for guiding their methodological rationales:
  - What do readers need to know about the study's need to integrate qualitative and quantitative data to better understand the suitability of mixed methods research?
  - What do readers need to know about the features of the mixed methods research problem to better understand the sources and levels of complexity inherent in the problem?
  - What do readers need to know about the study's need for innovation to better understand the potential for and importance of a mixed methods research approach to the problem?

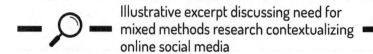

Illustrative excerpt discussing need for mixed methods research contextualizing online social media

Mixed methods research approaches have much to offer the study of online social media. Data from social media platforms are both quantitatively large in breadth (i.e., 'big data') and qualitatively complex in depth (e.g., unstructured text, linguistically and culturally nuanced). With respect to breadth, mixed methods researchers have posited that content derived from social media is, in some cases, comprehensive enough to be considered population-level data (Mertens et al., 2016b). This raises methodological questions about how to appropriately subsample the data for feasibility of analyses, how to quantitatively verify the representativeness of a sample within the population, and what qualitative methods are appropriate to incorporate into such frameworks.

Source: Colditz et al. (2017, p. 1–2). Used with permission from SAGE.

- *Situate the problem within related literature and personal perspectives.* Researchers familiarize the readers with their understandings of the background influences and motivations for pursuing complex mixed methods research problems. The sentences that follow should briefly outline a literature synthesis and point to topical and methodological deficiencies. Summarize the key intended study impacts and potential target audiences.
  - What do readers need to know about the researchers' experiences to better understand the real-life impetus for the study?
  - What do readers need to know about the literature gaps the problem seeks to address within relatable topical and methodological research?
  - What do readers need to know about the importance and necessity of the problem in light of research innovation needs?

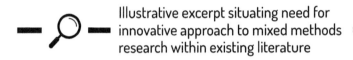

Illustrative excerpt situating need for innovative approach to mixed methods research within existing literature

Snelson (2016) reviewed the literature and identified 55 mixed methods studies relating to social media, published from 2007 through 2013. Of studies that focused on particular social media platforms, those emphasizing Facebook were more prevalent than those related to Twitter and YouTube combined. Methodological approaches generally incorporated two or more primary data sources such as interviews and surveys, as opposed to using multiple methods to approach primary data from social media platforms. Recent studies focusing on primary data from social media platforms tend to implement computational linguistic approaches such as Natural Language Processing (Ruths & Pfeffer, 2014). While effective for quickly categorizing a large breadth of data, computational linguistic approaches may not effectively synthesize the depth of lived experience from social media content. Yet such approaches can be integrated with qualitative syntheses, within mixed methods frameworks, to capture both breadth and depth of meaning from primary social media data.

Source: Colditz et al. (2017, p. 2). Used with permission from Sage.

- *Justify the study mixing purpose focused on innovation.* Here, researchers convey to readers their understandings of the study need for a mixing purpose focused on innovation. Researchers generally begin by making the case for the demand for mixed methods research innovations and justifying the use of a complexity-sensitive mixed methods study approach for innovation. Summarize the key justifications for the mixing purpose focused on innovation. Researchers may find the following questions useful for guiding their mixing purpose rationales:
  - What do readers need to know about the complexity of the research problem to better understand the need for the complexity-sensitive mixed methods study?
  - What do readers need to know about why the mixed methods research approach is warranted to better understand the focus of the mixing purpose on innovation?
  - What do readers need to know about the type of research innovation needed to better understand the significance of the complex mixed methods research problem and the need for a complexity-sensitive approach?

Illustrative excerpt justifying mixing purpose focused on generating innovative understandings of vaping culture

In mixed methods research, it is additionally useful to describe how such quantitative and qualitative methods are integrated for 'added value' over the sum of individual methods themselves (Fetters & Freshwater, 2015). To this end, Venkatesh, Brown, and Bala (2013) have presented a framework which can help guide such integrations toward 'meta-inferences' for information systems research, but this is not specifically attuned to analysis of primary social media data or health-related content. To date, few studies have demonstrated effective integration of combined quantitative and qualitative approaches to contextualize health topics using primary data from social media Twitter … Understanding vaping culture, particularly with respect to health beliefs and policy attitudes, may provide insights into how to effectively engage the public about this trend. For example, public health advocates may risk alienating ENDS users if intervention efforts are perceived as ill-informed, overly restrictive, or paternalistic. Collecting relevant data from the Twitter platform offers an opportunity to observe open expression of vaping culture and to ultimately gain better understandings of health beliefs, policy attitudes, and other potentially salient aspects of this phenomenon.

Source: Colditz et al. (2017, p. 2–3). Used with permission from Sage.

CHAPTER CHECK-IN

1   Can you discern the differences and similarities in the introductions across the authors of the six featured mixed methods studies? Compare how the authors of at least two of these articles describe the following:

- Background for the complex research problem
- Rationale for the study mixing purpose.

Consider what your analysis tells you about their descriptions.

2   Do you recognize the hazards of framing effects and the strategies for avoiding them when initiating a new study? Select a published study in an area that is of interest to you or one of the featured mixed methods studies.

- Examine the study limitations and areas for future directions. Select one idea to pursue.
- Sketch initial ideas for a related complex mixed methods research problem. What topics would be involved? What is the mixing purpose for the study to be investigated? (Use Figure 5.1 to guide your thinking.)
- Briefly describe how you would go about framing the complex mixed methods research problem (use Figure 5.2 to guide the iterative process). For example:
    o   Who would you engage to seek diverse perspectives?
    o   What presumptions of background influences do you bring to or observe for the problem?
    o   What are the conditions of complexity surrounding the problem?
    o   What parameters would underpin your initial search protocol?

     o   How would you bring together the sources of information?

     o   How would you make sense of your evolving understandings?

- Create a flow diagram for documenting your decision points related to the literature search (see Figure B.2, an editable version of which is available on companion website for the book).

3   Can you frame a complex mixed methods research problem and the need for a study that is of interest to you? Apply the guiding questions presented in this chapter to structure your outlines:

- Describe the complex research problem that is the focus of your study in a few sentences.
- Discuss the extant research literature, its contributions to your study, and the deficiencies your study intends to address.
- Present the study mixing purpose.
- Review the draft and create a visual map to organize your writing (see Figure B.1). Note which elements were easy and which are more difficult to include.

4   What features for engaging readers can you use to begin creating your complexity-sensitive mixed methods study proposal? Access a complex mixed methods research problem that you would like to pursue. Sketch a description of the problem and need for the study. Select one of the features for engaging readers that fits with your study and write a brief discussion on how your study engages the reader.

KEY CHAPTER CONCEPTS

This chapter advances the second practice for guiding a complexity-sensitive approach to mixed methods research. It addresses the question: What does communicating the significance of a complex mixed methods research problem involve and how can the study need for innovation be conveyed? The rationale for framing complex mixed methods research problems is grounded in the need for conveying the significance of the problem when the understandings are considered to be evolving and incomplete. The purpose of framing is to demonstrate congruence among interrelated research topics, problems, purposes, and questions underpinning the need for a mixed methods study. Opportunities for identifying the focus of the study on one of four mixing purposes focused on innovation are presented, as are framing effects to avoid. Six tasks are demonstrated for framing complex mixed methods research problems involved in an iterative process: engage others in framing processes, sketch presumptions of background influences, determine fitness of a complexity-sensitive approach, develop parameters of literature search, monitor emergence of background influences, and assimilate understandings of problem significance. Features that will engage readers include focusing on timely social issues and unique perspectives. Innovations in framing complex mixed methods research problems involve visual diagrams and writing ideas. The next chapter introduces the complexity-sensitive practices related to positioning interrelated mixed methods research systems.

FURTHER READINGS

The following resources are offered as introductory references for planning research and framing research problems. The list should not be considered exhaustive. Readers are encouraged to seek out additional readings in the end-of-book reference list. Readings denoted with an asterisk are available on the online resources website for this book.

Creswell, J. W. (2015). *A concise introduction to mixed methods research*. Thousand Oaks, CA: Sage.

John W. Creswell's focus on brevity makes this accessible resource ideal for those seeking an overall introduction to mixed methods. Particularly noteworthy is Chapter 5 which focuses on how to draw a diagram of procedures.

DeCuir-Gunby, J. T., & Schutz, P. A. (2017*). Developing a mixed methods proposal: A practical guide for beginning researchers*. Thousand Oaks, CA: Sage.

Jessica DeCuir-Gunby and Paul Schulz provide a practical guide aimed at supporting beginning researchers in developing mixed methods proposals. Each chapter describes a feature in the process and provides questions, exercises, and resources for guiding researchers.

Fenner, M., Scheliga, K., & Bartling, S. (2013). Reference management. In S. Bartling and S. Friesike (Eds.), *Opening Science: The evolving guide on how the internet is changing research, collaboration and scholarly publishing* (pp. 125–137). Heidelberg: Springer Open. doi: 10.1007/978-3-319-00026-8_8.

Martin Fenner, Kaja Scheliga, and Sönke Bartling provide an important historical foundation and overview of important trends in reference management computer software. The authors offer information for guiding choice by distinguishing software features such as collaborative possibilities, expanded storage of content formats, and open source options.

Heyvaert, M., Hannes, K., & Onghena, P. (2017). *Using mixed methods research synthesis for literature reviews*. Thousand Oaks, CA: Sage.

In this recent addition to the field, Mieke Heyvaert, Karin Hannes, and Patrick Onghena provide an accessible guide to mixed methods research synthesis. The authors describe eight steps for making choices when aggregating, combining, and communicating research from diverse methodological traditions.

Onwuegbuzie, A. J., & Frels, R. (2016). *7 Steps to a comprehensive literature review*. London: Sage.

Anthony Onwuegbuzie and Rebecca Frels explain the contributions and procedures for seven steps in this innovative approach to a comprehensive literature review. Particularly noteworthy is the excellent guidance provided on the exploratory, integration, and communication aspects of the mixed research literature review.

Apply your mixed methods knowledge with videos, activities, SAGE journal articles and project templates at **https://study.sagepub.com/poth**

6

DEFINING SYSTEMS OF COMPLEX MIXED METHODS RESEARCH CONTEXTS

.... **KEY CHAPTER QUESTIONS**

By the end of this chapter, you will be able to answer the following questions:

- Why define systems of complex mixed methods research contexts?
- What opportunities exist to define complex mixed methods research contexts?
- Why can a proximity focus become hazardous for mixed methods researchers?
- What guides the relational systems approach for defining complex mixed methods research contexts?
- What features engage readers with complex mixed methods research contexts?
- What writing and diagram innovations are useful for defining complex mixed methods research contexts?

.... **NEW CHAPTER TERMS**

By the end of this chapter, you will be familiar with the following terms:

- Complex mixed methods research contexts
- Environmental influences
- Interpersonal contexts
- Personal contexts

- Proximity focus
- Relational systems approach
- Social contexts
- Systems perspective

This chapter advances the adaptive practice for guiding a complexity-sensitive approach to mixed methods research. It addresses the question: *What does defining complex mixed methods research contexts involve, and how can the interrelated systems and evolving environmental influences be recognized, promoted, and conveyed?* Think about a recent study account you read. What contexts were described by the author? Did the description clearly convey the places and people involved in the research? Did the descriptions situate the research within the relevant organizational, historical, political, and societal contexts? Were there any indicators of dynamic influences within or across the contexts, or were they presented as stable? A comprehensive description of contexts alerts the reader to the key environmental features shaping a study such as the participants, sites, and researchers, as well as their surrounding environments. Ideally, the description of the study contexts conveys the interdependencies of many contexts and suggests that contexts are subjected to dynamic and nonlinear environmental influences. Let us now consider how defining **complex mixed methods research contexts** is distinctive.

One of the typical dilemmas experienced by mixed methods researchers addressing complex problems is not being able to predetermine the specific contexts in which the study occurs. This represents a departure from what are traditionally early considerations in planning mixed methods research based on what is known about the problem: specifically, identifying *who* provides insights into the problem and *where* these participants are situated. The absence of such contextual information under some conditions of complexity triggers dilemmas for researchers with the traditional mixed methods research practices associated with designs and implementations. Recall from the discussions in Chapter 5 that these dilemmas can be attributable to the uncertainty in purposes and background influences for highly complex research problems. The uncertainty for planning is intensified by a lack of guiding literature. If researchers are not able to specify the study sites, describe the participants or researchers, then they are not able to predetermine site access or the nature of the interactions among participants and researchers. Researchers are thus challenged to describe the interrelated contexts relevant for a particular research problem and must adjust their descriptions of the contexts throughout the study to assimilate emerging understandings of those involved and the dynamic environmental influences. This situation contrasts markedly with research contexts that are considered less complex which can be described by drawing upon relevant literature to identify appropriate participants, sites, and researchers, as well as the surrounding environments for the research problem. To that end, defining the complex mixed methods research contexts is the focus of this chapter because the system descriptions and influence recognitions have important implications for study plans, implementations, and outcomes.

Work on this chapter was informed by my experiences as a researcher, instructor, mentor, and reviewer as I have grappled to guide my own work as well as others in developing a complexity-sensitive mentality. Specifically, in seeking to define the interrelated systems involved in complex mixed methods research contexts, I draw upon my previous work using ecological systems theory (Bronfenbrenner, 1979) for generating understandings of the **environmental influences** that shape students – understandings which must be considered when developing educational interventions that centre on holistic and systemic change for complex needs populations (Poth et al., 2014). I am not alone in seeing the application of this theory in identifying and planning research; Onwuegbuzie, Collins, and Frels (2013) used the systems theory to frame quantitative, qualitative, and mixed methods research and highlight the implications for generalizations. More recently, Onwuegbuzie and Hitchcock (2017) use systems theory to determine the level at which the context takes place in a mixed methods theory-based impact evaluation. Importantly, as you will see, this work is also shaped by the socio-ecological conceptual framework for the field of mixed methods advanced by Plano Clark and Ivankova (2016). Whereas some commonalities exist across the ideas related to the interrelated contexts that shape mixed methods research practice, the socio-ecological conceptual framework is more comprehensive in that it 'identifies the major topics addressed in the field of mixed methods research and describes how these topics relate to the mixed methods research process' (2016, p. xxi). There is no agreed-upon systems approach for defining mixed methods research contexts, yet there seem to be commonalities that underpin current practices. Research is a social process and so it involves interactions among people, and people are shaped by the contexts in which they live.

Embedding the featured mixed methods studies in this chapter reflects a continued effort to address the practice gap in many textbooks and to provide authentic examples of published articles that represent varying conditions of complexity related to research contexts. Specifically, by looking at completed research we can trace backwards and assume their (and our!) understandings of complex mixed methods research contexts are dynamic and evolving over time in response to changing conditions. To enhance an approach to defining mixed methods research contexts in light of the uncertainties researchers face under conditions of increased complexity, three pressing needs exist. First, to position the need for a systems approach that embeds integrative thinking with complexity about research contexts and the hazards associated with a **proximity focus**. Next, to advance procedures for defining complex mixed methods research contexts based on relationships among interrelated systems and assimilating current and emerging understandings of the environmental influences and research problems. Finally, to identify features for engaging readers with writing and to diagram innovations useful for explaining complex mixed methods research systems in proposals and reports. To get us started, let us consider the need for defining systems within complex mixed methods research contexts.

Why Define Systems of Complex Mixed Methods Research Contexts?

Researchers are tasked with the responsibility of situating the study within the surrounding research contexts – for a complexity-sensitive approach, this involves assimilating current understandings of the interrelated systems with emerging understandings of the effects of dynamic environmental influences on the evolving study contexts. The important roles for contexts to shape study designs, implementations, and interpretations have been described. The descriptions of research contexts can include a range of information about the physical study locations; historical, political, and economic landscapes; social influences on the people and communities; and relationships among those involved in the research. The purpose of defining these contexts is to situate the reader to the interrelated personal, interpersonal, and social systems and the related global-, community-, and individual-level research details that are important for understanding the study's plans, implementations, and outcomes (Plano Clark & Ivankova, 2016). Examine Figure 6.1 for a visual representation of three nested mixed methods research contexts reflective of an ecological **systems perspective** that is further described below. (See Figure B.3, an editable version of which is also available on the companion website for the book.)

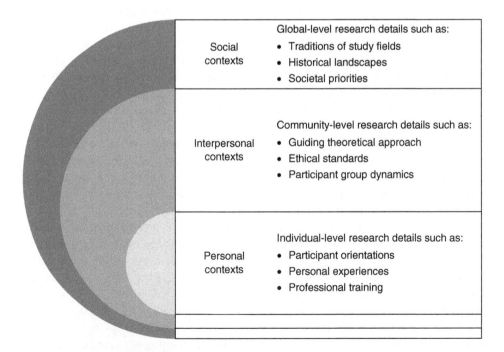

Figure 6.1   Interrelated social, interpersonal, and personal contexts involved in mixed methods research

Social Contexts

The outermost layer involves global-level details of the influences on both interpersonal and **personal contexts** involved in the study such as traditions of the fields or disciplines of study, the historical, political, and economic landscape of countries or institutions involved, as well as societal priorities such as funding or pressing foci. This description aligns well with the definition provided by Plano Clark and Ivankova (2016, p. 249): 'The institutional structures, disciplinary conventions, and societal priorities that shape mixed methods research practice'. Information about the **social contexts** is often described in research proposals and reports under the heading 'study context', either as part of the study introduction or research method sections. Examine Table 6.1 for examples of the many global-level details related to the social contexts across the featured studies. Notice the many details describing the relationships among the three contextual features of the six studies; for example, the physical locations are clearly represented by the institutional structures for which the societal foci can be examined and the influence of the disciplinary conventions on the societal foci. Information about social contexts is essential for generating understandings of the phenomena studied; for instance, studying postconflict risk in 2010 in Croatia following its declaration of independence in 1991 would be quite different from studying it in the Democratic Republic of the Congo following its declaration of independence in 1959.

Table 6.1 Situating the social contexts of the featured studies through global-level research details

Featured study	Disciplinary conventions	Societal foci	Institutional structures
Law clients (Chui & Cheng, 2017)	Justice systems require legitimacy to be respected	Understand perceptions of procedural fairness and satisfaction of young offenders towards their lawyers	Hong Kong's criminal justice system
Postconflict risk (Taylor et al., 2017)	Psychological risk factors manifest themselves in a variety of ways	Understand insecurity effect of political violence on youth development	Postconflict setting specific to Vukovar, Croatia
Heart care (Dickson et al., 2011)	Health favours blinding investigators to data	Assess clinical effect of cognitive function and knowledge of heart failure self-care because heart failure is prevalent and self-care is patient-directed	Heart failure clinics in US urban settings
Safe places (Zea et al., 2014)	Social change through egalitarian dialogue in health and gender disciplines	Inform social policies guiding development of safe places for internally displaced Colombian gay and bisexual men and transwomen	Marginalized populations at risk in Colombia
Leadership competencies (Strudsholm et al., 2016)	Public health disciplines vary widely	Identify leadership competencies for public health practice	Public health systems across Canada
Vaping culture (Colditz et al., 2017)	Twitter use points to potential for health technology	Inform health promotion policies for vaping culture in social media	Global 'World Vaping Day' on Twitter

Interpersonal Contexts

The middle layer involves community-level details of the interrelations among those actively involved, such as the theoretical approach and ethical standards guiding researchers in their interactions with one another and with their participants. This description aligns well with the definition provided by Plano Clark and Ivankova (2016, p. 218), except that their definition also highlights the influence of publication review processes: 'Research ethics and researchers' relationships with study participants, research teams, and editorial and review boards that shape mixed methods research practice'. Information about the **interpersonal contexts** is often scattered in various places in research proposals and reports under headings such as 'guiding theoretical approach', 'ethical considerations', and 'research team backgrounds'. This information is highly pertinent for researchers to make explicit and for readers to learn from, yet the level of detail provided in proposals and reports varies considerably. In my experience as a reviewer of manuscripts and proposals, it is not common to see the influence of editorial and review boards explicitly described. Examine Table 6.2 for examples of the few relational-level details related to the interpersonal contexts offered across the featured studies. The following descriptors are used to represent the nature of relationships with participants: *New* refers to a lack of previous relationship whereas *existing* refers to a relationship that pre-existed the study. *Distanced* refers to a less intense relationship whereas *close* refers to a relationship that is considered intense characterized by frequent interactions. Notice the limited details describing the relationships among the three contextual features; for example, the guiding theoretical framework for the featured study on safe places was the only one to explicitly describe the ethical considerations for the interactions among researchers and participants. Also, while all the studies provided some detail of the guiding theoretical approach, the authors of the featured study on vaping culture did not provide details of ethical considerations (see Chapter 7 for further discussions on research procedures). While no study explicitly stated the nature of the relationship with participants, this could be extrapolated and categorized as new or existing and distanced or close. The limited details make the relationships among the contextual features less obvious to the reader, yet no less important (see Chapter 8 for further discussions on research interactions). Information about interpersonal contexts is essential for generating understandings of the phenomena studied; for instance, studying youth social patterns across ethnic groups from an insider perspective in postconflict Croatia in 2010 would be quite different from studying familial social patterns across ethnic groups without any existing relationships to the community.

Personal Contexts

The innermost layer involves individual-level details of the orientations of those actively involved and the influences shaping their backgrounds. From their immediate personal environments such as families, colleagues, and communities, people develop personal and professional experiences, expertise, beliefs, worldviews, and assumptions that create the orientations people bring to bear on the research. This description aligns well with the definition provided by Plano Clark and Ivankova (2016, p. 193): 'The philosophical assumptions, theoretical models, and background knowledge that shape mixed methods research practice'. Providing information about backgrounds of those involved in the research, their

Table 6.2 Situating the interpersonal contexts of the featured studies through relational-level research details

Featured study	Nature of relationships with participants	Guiding theoretical framework	Ethical considerations
Law clients (Chui & Cheng, 2017)	New and distanced	Procedural justice theory for understanding the client–lawyer interactions	Well-being of vulnerable youth guides informed consent and confidentiality measures
Postconflict risk (Taylor et al., 2017)	Existing and close	Emotional security theory for understanding the community interactions	Well-being of vulnerable families guides informed consent and confidentiality measures
Heart care (Dickson et al., 2011)	Existing and distanced	Self-care model for understanding patient and doctor interactions	Well-being of vulnerable patients guides informed consent and confidentiality measures
Safe places (Zea et al., 2014)	New and close	Theory of communicative action for guiding researcher interactions using non-coercive dialogue to create a safe environment	Well-being of vulnerable participants guides informed consent and confidentiality measures
Leadership competencies (Strudsholm et al., 2016)	New and distanced	Understanding value of mixed methods research	Informed consent and confidentiality measures
Vaping culture (Colditz et al., 2017)	New and distanced	Understanding value added of mixed methods research	—

relationship to the study topic and with each other remains varied and somewhat atypical. What is becoming increasingly common is for researchers to convey their philosophical assumptions. This information is valuable for researchers and readers to consider, yet in my experience it is more common to find this information in dissertations than in published articles under the heading 'researcher positionality'. Examine Table 6.3 for examples of the few individual-level details related to the personal contexts offered across the featured studies. Notice the few details describing the nature of the two contextual features; for example, the little background information about the researcher orientations in the featured study on law clients limits the readers' ability to understand what assumptions, beliefs or experiences influenced their research. In contrast, comprehensive background information about the researchers involved in the featured study on safe places provided the reader with a fulsome understanding of the assumptions, training, and expertise of the researchers as well as the participants. The lack of details means the relationships among the contextual features remain unknown to the reader. Information about personal contexts is essential for generating understandings of the phenomena studied and making overt the researchers' influences on data collection and analysis; for instance, having access to information about researchers' background in postconflict resolution and orientations would be quite different from having no access.

Table 6.3 Situating the personal contexts of the featured studies through individual-level research details

Featured study	Researcher orientations	Participant characteristics
Law clients (Chui & Cheng, 2017)	Two researchers affiliated with different Hong Kong universities; no other information provided	Young offenders within Hong Kong who are recruited through interactions with youth outreach teams and transitional housing facilities and have either public or private lawyers
Postconflict risk (Taylor et al., 2017)	Five researchers affiliated with UK, Croatian, and US universities, in addition to undergraduate and graduate researchers; no other information provided	Youth, mothers, and fathers who are recruited from the area
Heart care (Dickson et al., 2011)	Three researchers affiliated with different US universities; no other information provided	Heart failure patients who attend two US outpatient heart failure specialty clinics associated with a large urban medical centre
Safe places (Zea et al., 2014)	Five researchers affiliated with three US universities and two with Colombian community organizations; detailed description of philosophical assumptions, methodological training, and disciplinary backgrounds of each member	Internally displaced Colombian gay and bisexual men and transwomen from Bogotá recruited through snowball sampling
Leadership competencies (Strudsholm et al., 2016)	Five researchers affiliated with two Canadian universities, and detailed description of team member's backgrounds in terms of training, research, and practice expertise	Canadian Public health workforce and leaders who reply to a Listserv request
Vaping culture (Colditz et al., 2017)	Five researchers affiliated with three US universities; no other information provided	Randomly selected ENDS users who are also users of Twitter

Defining Opportunities and Hazards for Mixed Methods Researchers

Interrelated Systems Approach Opportunities

I remain surprised at how little attention defining research contexts has received in our guiding resources, given the important role these understandings play in the mixed methods research process.

Perhaps it can be attributed to aspects in need of reconsideration under conditions of increased complexity. Our methodological training provides guidance for identifying study contexts based on some assumptions of stability with the problem. Thus, the idea that we can pursue research with incomplete understandings of who and where the study occurs presents a stark departure from our training. Yet we regularly make decisions in our everyday lives based on incomplete information, and in so doing we are constantly assimilating information and being influenced by our changing environmental conditions as we go. As such, we can be considered complex adaptive systems. In the same way, defining research contexts based on incomplete information and assimilating new information into our evolving understandings responds to the dilemmas experienced under conditions of higher complexity.

An opportunity is presented in realizing an interrelated systems approach for defining research contexts through ongoing integrative thinking with complexity about the environmental influences. By positioning the research contexts as nested and interrelated with one another, we are better able to see the research contexts as parts of a dynamic system that is affected by environmental influences. Adopting a complex adaptive systems perspective allows us to monitor and describe the environmental influences and subsequent effects on the systems over time. Only once we recognize environmental influences can we begin to discern what influences in a system matter, how they interact, and to what effect. Thus, what integrative thinking with complexity about the systems involved in research allows us to do is to focus on the interdependent and emergent properties of contexts. Interdependencies focus on interactions and how the choices in one affect the other, whereas emergence describes how small effects can, in turn, influence the system. In other words, if we consider our interrelated research systems as complex adaptive systems (see also Chapter 3) then we shift our mindset to assume that the research contexts are constantly evolving in light of the dynamic environmental influences. This makes sense given our understandings from Plano Clark and Ivankova's (2016) socio-ecological framework that positions individual's personal contexts as constantly influenced by their interpersonal and social contexts. What this does is point to the need for researchers to pay attention to the emerging effects of these influences on systems. In so doing, the researcher is better able to assimilate and respond to emerging understandings of research systems in a way that both influences and is affected by the changing conditions surrounding the mixed methods research. It also highlights the challenges researchers encounter under conditions of complexity when they remain focused on only the contextual features that are proximal to and known about the problem being studied. Consider the challenges experienced by a senior educational scientist at the Royal College of Physicians and Surgeons of Canada when working within dynamic contexts and described in Researcher Spotlight 6.1.

 Researcher Spotlight 6.1

Elaine Van Melle on challenges when working under conditions of increasingly complex conditions

The randomized controlled trial (RCT) is well entrenched as *the* gold standard in the field of medicine. The majority of my role involves working with clinicians. It is therefore assumed that the RCT is also the gold standard when evaluating programmes. However, educational programme change takes place under conditions of complexity. There are numerous variables, outcomes can be unpredictable, and local context heavily influences how the educational innovation, in this case competency-based education, is implemented. The challenge then is to convince stakeholders that outcomes can only be well understood to the extent that the relationship between programme implementation and outcomes has been made explicit.

Proximity Focus Defining Hazards

When interrelated systems are evolving in response to dynamic environmental influences, a proximity focus for defining mixed methods research contexts is not suitable. Consider an illustrative example of the guidance provided to researchers related to the study context in a resource for developing a mixed methods proposal:

> It is important to understand the environments in which you want to understand your participants. As such, providing a description of the research context is an important aspect of the participant description component. For example, if you are conducting a case study on the incorporation of an organic lunch program within a particular school context, the school environment itself is central to your investigation. You cannot understand how the lunch program has been implemented without understanding the school environment. As such, the more details you can provide about your preferred research context(s), the better your readers will be able to understand the possible outcomes for your study. (DeCuir-Gunby & Schutz, 2017, p. 112)

In no way should highlighting this excerpt be interpreted as a critique, because indeed the authors provide *some* guidance related to defining the study contexts – which is not the case for all introductory resources. The authors also illustrate the importance of interpreting the study findings to define contexts based on the problem. This is essential for any eventual comparing and evaluating among studies; for example, did the studies use similar populations? Were there particular political or historical influences at work that need to be taken into consideration?

It would be remiss of me not to highlight the pressing hazards I consider to be based in the proximity focus often reflected in our traditional mixed methods research practice that focuses on predetermining the contextual boundaries based on proximity to the study problem and the relevant literature under conditions of higher complexity. While the proximal study environment remains an important consideration, we now recognize that selecting who is involved in the research and where the research is situated is not as straightforward under conditions of increased complexity. Complexity science can guide us in attending to the patterns that emerge from the intersections of interrelated research systems. This thinking aligns with what others have done, for example, in applying the principles of complexity science – and specifically, system effects – to understanding global events such as the 2008 US housing bubble and the 2011 Arab Spring (Jones-Rooy & Page, 2012). In describing their research context, the authors state: 'the political, economic, social, and environmental worlds are systems. If we want to make sense of and improve these worlds, we need to understand how the systems affect each other. We need to explore both the boundaries of, and the connections between, systems' (p. 314). The authors acknowledge this is no easy task, yet for mixed methods research under conditions of complexity the benefits of understanding systems would be more strategic responses to environmental influences and being able to predict the effect of the influences within the systems on the whole system.

We have to begin to think about research contexts not as separate entities from the research but as systems involved and influenced by relationships. The emphasis with a systems perspective shifts from parts (individual contexts) to the organization of parts, recognizing that interactions of the parts are not static and constant but are dynamic processes. It makes sense that, because research is highly social, our considerations of research systems must focus on relations among those involved in the research and the influences we cannot predict. We now recognize the benefits of understanding the systems both in part and as a whole. By looking at the common patterns we can develop greater insight into the behaviours of the research system as a whole. A relational systems approach is a new way of defining mixed methods research contexts. In so doing, we co-create the reality in which we situate research.

Relational Systems Approach to Defining Complex Mixed Methods Research Contexts

Among the many challenges mixed methods researchers face under conditions of complexity is the lack of guidance on how to define research contexts when predefined contexts based on existing literature are not an option. A **relational systems approach** involves a focus on the way two or more research systems are connected. Given the infinite possibilities, I consider my relational systems approach more in line with creating options for mixed methods researchers under conditions of complexity than a descriptive approach would be. To that end, it is my hope that readers realize my intention to present the approach as iterative, and that readers will make informed choices for themselves based on the research conditions in which they are working. Based on my ideas about integrative thinking about complexity related to research contexts as interrelated systems, I advance procedures for defining complex mixed methods research contexts based on identifying features of four relationships among interrelated systems and assimilating current and emerging understandings of the environmental influences and research problems. Examine Figure 6.2 for a visual representation of the four relationships that are further described below: (A) relationships among social and interpersonal systems; (B) relationships among social and personal systems; (C) relationships among interpersonal and personal systems; and (D) relationships among social, interpersonal, and personal systems. To illustrate how one might go about these procedures in a study that they are conceptualizing, in addition to drawing upon completed research such as the featured studies, I will also include a discussion about the housing programme example that I have referred to throughout this book. See Table 6.4 for a summary of the key tasks, desirable outcomes, and potential implications for the housing study example across the four relationships. Through this example, I advance the role for mixed methods researchers in attending to the systems effects generated by evolving environmental influences and in informing appropriate responses to changing conditions.

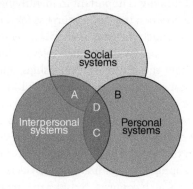

Figure 6.2 Four relationships among interrelated systems for defining complex mixed methods research contexts

Relationships among Social and Interpersonal Systems

Many relationships exist and are possible among the social and interpersonal systems. Any of these may be useful in generating initial understandings of contextual study features and influences. Specific threats to keeping up the pace of our understandings of social and inter-personal system relationships with the study realities would involve relying on our initial understandings and not attending sufficiently to the emerging environmental influences such as shifts to societal priorities with political elections or groups that are served by particu-lar programs. To mitigate this threat, researchers need to pay attention to sources and effects of emerging influences that can initiate anywhere and have nonlinear effects. For example, in the featured study on law clients, shifts in judicial policies guiding the roles of lawyers with young offender clients would influence the interactions these lawyers have with their clients.

Deciphering relationships among social and interpersonal systems when information is lacking to guide who is involved in the research and where the research takes place is natu-rally challenging. Pursuing opportunities for dialogue with those involved in relevant social and interpersonal systems for the problem may, over time, generate understandings of the societal features and group participant characteristics involved in addressing the research problem. These understandings have important potential implications because it is the possible global features and community relations among researchers and participants that contribute to building rapport and establishing access to participants and sites, developing appropriate data procedures for the groups, and informing group interpretive and dissemina-tion considerations.

Key among the initial considerations is what is known (or emerging understandings) about the social contexts. How do these help to identify potential relationships relevant for the research problem being pursued? Any information about the disciplines, societal foci, and institutional structures involved in the problem can be useful in identifying potential par-ticipant groups situated within target social contexts. For example, in the featured study on law clients (Chui & Cheng, 2017), information about the Hong Kong justice system – such as the conventions within the judicial processes and options for young offenders to select either a private or public lawyer to represent them – are important to be able to select appropriate participant samples and recruitment strategies. In the housing example, previously discussed, familiarity with the institutional structures offering housing initiatives and the government priorities guiding policy and funding is important in identifying participant groups who are considered 'hard to house', even when the mixing purpose for the study has yet to be defined.

Another initial consideration might be what is known (or emerging understandings) about the relationships to identify potential societal features relevant for the research problem being pursued. Any information about the nature of relationships, appropriate guiding theoretical frameworks, or essential ethical considerations can be useful in identifying potential societal contexts. For example, in the featured study on heart care (Dickson et al., 2011), information about the self-care model and ethical considerations related to studying patients within the health system are important to be able to select appropriate sites for the research. In the hous-ing example, familiarity with the relationships that service providers build with their clients is important in identifying the appropriate organizational providers for the problem. When defin-ing complex mixed methods research contexts, consider the information available on existing and possible relationships among the social and interpersonal systems. Many of our approaches to mixed methods research can be reconsidered in light of the relationships among contextual systems. Consider Researcher Spotlight 6.2 about reconfiguring our positions as mixed methods researchers towards greater understandings of the interconnections between our social and ethical responsibilities, from the perspective of a research professor in the Department of Adult Education and Youth Development at the University of South Africa.

 **Researcher Spotlight 6.2**

Norma Romm on reconfiguring our mixed methods research positions about our social and ethical responsibilities

I believe that the research community employing mixed methods research (and justifying its use) needs to face the challenge of considering in more depth and in more forums our ethical responsibilities in relation to participants involved in the research – so as to develop ideas on creative use of the research space (in conjunction with those concerned) to actively contribute to 'better' futures for human and ecological life. The mixed methods community needs to be careful of formulating a myriad of designs designed to try to find out about the world (as if the finding-out exercise itself can be regarded as more or less neutral). Energy should be directed in the research community towards encouraging researchers, with others, to intervene constructively in the development of options for better living in the face of experienced and expressed problems, as defined and (re)constructed in the contexts in question. With some 'stretching' of all the underpinnings which currently are used to justify mixed methods research projects, our responsibilities as professional researchers (with participants and stakeholders) for the potentially constructive influence of research in/on the social fabric can be better accounted for. The intricacy of having on hand to draw on – and learn from – positions such as postpositivist, constructivist, transformative, pragmatic, and Indigenous-oriented bases as underpinnings of research work can become an opportunity to consider how the positions can be reconfigured by focusing on our responsibilities with others involved/concerned with making a future which is yet to be, through the way in which research becomes (innovatively) handled.

Relationships among Social and Personal Systems

Many relationships exist and are possible among the social and personal systems. Any of these may be useful for generating initial understandings of contextual study features and influences. Specific threats to keeping up the pace of our understandings of social and personal system relationships with the study's realities would involve relying on our initial understandings and not attending sufficiently to the emerging environmental influences, such as shifts to societal priorities with political elections or individuals that are served by particular programmes. To mitigate this threat, researchers need to pay attention to sources and effects of emerging influences that can initiate anywhere and have uncertain outcomes. For example, in the featured study on postconflict risk (Taylor et al., 2017), shifts in government policies for different ethnic groups would influence individual experiences and orientations in the wider community.

Deciphering relationships among social and personal systems when information is lacking to guide who is involved in the research and where the research takes place is naturally challenging. Pursuing opportunities for dialogue with those involved in relevant social and personal systems for the problem may, over time, generate understandings of the societal features and individual participant characteristics suitable to address the research problem. These understandings have important potential implications because it is the possible global features and individual characteristics among researchers and participants that contribute to building rapport with individuals, developing appropriate data procedures for individuals, and informing individual interpretive and dissemination considerations.

Key among the initial considerations is what is known (or emerging understandings) about the social contexts to identify potential individual orientations relevant for the research problem being pursued. Any information about the disciplines, societal foci, and institutional structures involved in the problem can be useful in identifying potential participant characteristics related to target social contexts. For example, in the featured study on safe places (Zea et al., 2014), information about how an egalitarian dialogue can transform social change in gender and health disciplines is important when selecting researchers with complementary experiences, backgrounds, and expertise for working with marginalized populations such as internally displaced Colombian gay and bisexual men and transwomen. In the housing example, previously discussed, familiarity with the institutional structures offering housing initiatives and the government priorities guiding policy and funding is important when identifying the individual characteristics of those who can contribute to the problem even when understandings of the background influences to the problem are under development.

Another initial consideration might be what is known (or emerging understandings) about the personal contexts. How does this help identify potential societal features relevant for the problem? Any information about the individual orientations held by participants or researchers involved in the problem can be useful in identifying potential disciplines, institutions, or societal foci related to target personal contexts. For example, in the featured study on leadership competencies (Strudsholm et al., 2016), information about the large project group of researchers affiliated with two Canadian universities and detailed description of team members' backgrounds in terms of training, research, and practice expertise would help identify which disciplines to involve. When defining complex mixed methods research contexts, consider the information available on relationships that exist and that are possible among the social and personal systems. Examine Researcher Spotlight 6.3 considering the personal contexts and relationships with social impacts, from the perspective of a pre-eminent mixed methods researcher and professor emeritus from Gallaudet University in Washington, DC (USA).

 Researcher Spotlight 6.3

Donna Mertens on realizing societal intentions of complex mixed methods research problems

The key challenge that occurred for me under conditions of complexity is related to addressing power differentials, inclusion of stakeholders, resistance to change, and use of findings for social change. I evaluated a nine-year project designed to improve the preparation of teachers of the deaf through the use of technology. The first planning meeting for the project revealed that the team consisted of about 20 hearing people. I asked: What needed to change to be inclusive of deaf people on the team? How would the quality of the project be impacted by the absence of deaf members? As the evaluator, I raised these questions as a way to challenge the existing power structure and to provide an opportunity for inclusion of deaf participants. I assured the project director that these would be questions that I would need to address in the evaluation design. From that point onward, I used a transformative mixed methods design to collect data about inclusion of diverse stakeholders and the impact of having deaf people and people of colour on the team. I was able to document a significant shift in terms of who was included and the nature of the activities that were undertaken. In the final years of the project, the team had an objective to increase the number of teachers who are deaf and of colour through the use of technology.

Relationships among Interpersonal and Personal Systems

Many relationships exist and are possible among the interpersonal and personal systems. Any of these may be useful in generating initial understandings of contextual study features and influences. Specific threats to keeping up the pace of our understandings of interpersonal and personal system relationships with the study realities would involve relying on our initial understandings and not attending sufficiently to the emerging environmental influences such as shifts in researcher or participant orientations. To mitigate this threat, researchers need to pay attention to the sources and effects of emerging influences that can initiate anywhere and have nonlinear effects. For example, in the featured study on heart care (Dickson et al., 2011), shifts in a doctors' orientation towards self-care of heart failure patients would influence their interactions with patients.

Deciphering relationships among interpersonal and personal systems when information is lacking to guide who is involved in the research and where the research takes place is naturally challenging. Pursuing opportunities for dialogue with those involved in relevant personal and interpersonal systems for the problem may, over time, generate understandings of the individual and group participant characteristics that will be addressing the research problem. These understandings have important implications because it is the possible personal features and community relations among researchers and participants that contribute to building rapport, developing appropriate data procedures, and informing interpretive and dissemination considerations.

Key among the initial considerations is what is known (or emerging understandings) about the interpersonal contexts. This helps identify potential individual orientations relevant to the research problem being pursued. Any information about the nature of relationships, appropriate guiding theoretical frameworks, or essential ethical considerations can be useful in identifying potential participant group characteristics related to target personal contexts. For example, in the featured study on postconflict risk (Taylor et al., 2017), shifts in communal relations among ethnic groups would influence individual experiences and orientations in the wider community. In the housing example, I have discussed familiarity with the relationships among the organizations delivering housing services is important when identifying individual characteristics of those who can contribute to the problem even when understandings of the background influences to the problem are under development.

Another initial consideration might be what is known (or emerging understandings) about the personal contexts to identify potential relationships relevant to the problem. Any information about the nature of researcher or participant characteristics can be useful in identifying potential participant group characteristics related to target interpersonal contexts. For example, in the featured study on postconflict risk (Taylor et al., 2017), shifts in personal experiences of individuals would influence interactions within the wider community. In the housing example, familiarity with the individual receiving the housing programme services is important when identifying group characteristics of those who can contribute to the problem's study, even when understandings of the background influences to the problem are under development. When defining complex mixed methods research contexts, consider the information available about existing and possible relationships among the personal and interpersonal systems. In Guiding Tip 6.1, a professor emeritus from Gallaudet University in Washington, DC (USA) offers new ways of thinking about the importance of understanding our own researcher orientations because of the implications of our interactions during the mixed methods research process.

 Guiding Tip 6.1

Donna Mertens advising how to navigate the complexity of mixed methods research

Researchers need to understand the diverse philosophical frameworks that are available in the mixed methods research community and the implications of situating themselves in each framework. Methodological implications are derived from assumptions about the nature of ethics, reality, knowledge, and systematic inquiry. It is important to engage in critical self-reflection to become aware of the assumptions that reflect each of our worldviews. Technical expertise in quantitative and qualitative methods is a necessary foundation for the conduct of mixed methods research, but it is not sufficient to inform choices of appropriate approaches to research. If an individual is not skilled in both quantitative and qualitative methods, then skills need to be developed to work with teams of researchers who represent different areas of expertise. This might entail the need to recognize that within some disciplines, monomethod approaches have traditionally dominated. Clarity about assumptions that undergird methodological decisions can provide the ground for meaningful discussion about methodological choices. Mixed methods researchers need to articulate the benefits of the use of mixed methods and be able to do so in a respectful manner. Referring to complexity theory is one of the strategies that can be useful to clarify the need for collecting more than one type of data and for integrating the results of both quantitative and qualitative data collection.

Relationships among Social, Interpersonal, and Personal Systems

Many relationships exist among the social, interpersonal, and personal systems. Any of these may be useful in generating initial understandings of contextual study features and influences. Specific threats to our understandings of personal, interpersonal and social system relationships keeping pace with the study realities involve relying on our initial understandings and not attending sufficiently to the emerging environmental influences, such as shifts in researcher or participant orientations, changes in access to participants, or fluctuations in political agendas. Such nonlinear and unpredictable influences create ripple effects that can only be recognized after they have occurred. To mitigate this threat, researchers need to pay attention to sources and effects of emerging influences that can initiate anywhere and be unpredictable. Important initial considerations involve what is known (and emerging) about any environmental considerations that are likely to influence the contexts and how the systems might be affected. Only then can we begin to discern what influences in a system matter, how they interact, and to what effect. In Practice Alert 6.1, I consider some of the assumptions and influences on my thinking about relationships relative to the housing research, and I invite you to do the same for a research project under formulation. In so doing, I have enhanced my understandings of the influences on defining systems in mixed methods research contexts.

Table 6.4   Key considerations, desirable outcomes, and potential threats across the four system relationships

System relationships	Key considerations	Desirable outcomes	Potential threats
(A) Social/ interpersonal	What is known (and emerging) about the social contexts to identify potential relationships relevant to the problem?	Identify potential social contexts in which participant groups are situated	Relying upon what is initially known and not paying sufficient attention to the effects of emerging environmental influences
	What is known (and emerging) about the interpersonal contexts to identify potential societal features relevant to the problem?	Identify potential participant groups situated within target social contexts	
(B) Social/ personal	What is known (and emerging) about the social contexts to identify potential individual orientations relevant to the problem?	Identify potential social contexts related to target participant characteristics	
	What is known (and emerging) about the personal contexts that help identify potential societal features relevant to the problem?	Identify potential participant characteristics related to target social contexts	
(C) Interpersonal/ personal	What is known (and emerging) about the interpersonal contexts to identify potential individual characteristics relevant to the problem?	Identify potential participant characteristics related to the target interpersonal contexts	
	What is known (and emerging) about the personal contexts to identify potential relationships relevant to the problem?	Identify potential participant groups situated within the target personal contexts	
(D) Social/ interpersonal/ personal	What is known (and emerging) about any environmental considerations that are likely to influence the contexts and how the systems might be affected?	Generate initial understandings of environmental influences and discern what influences in a system matter, how they interact, and to what effect across the personal, interpersonal, and social contexts	

—⟳— Practice Alert 6.1 ▬▬▬▬▬▬▬▬▬▬▬▬▬▬▬▬▬▬▬▬▬

What might you bring to bear on integrative thinking with complexity about the relationships and influences among systems in mixed methods research contexts?

Careful consideration of the assumptions and influences on my thinking helps me to create authentic descriptions of my initial understandings of the systems surrounding research. As an illustrative example, let us consider what I (am aware that I) bring to bear on the housing project that we are currently formulating. I have always been drawn to mixed methods research where the mixing purpose allows the possibility of generating insights reflective of a divergence in findings and perspectives. In general, I am interested in how we, as researchers, resolve (or not) these tensions. This interest may stem from my extensive work in case studies where I have tended to be drawn to what are called 'negative cases' (sometimes also referred to as deviant or discrepant cases) in which respondents' experiences or viewpoints differ from the main body of evidence. My reading a decade ago of Flyvbjerg's (2006) work identifying a bias towards verification as one of the five misunderstandings about case study research highlighted the usefulness of explaining such negative cases for strengthening the explanation of the more typical case. In so doing, this thinking resonates with Greene's (2007) dialectic approach to mixed methods research, in which divergent perspectives are used to deepen, rather than simply broaden or confirm, one's conclusions. What this means for me, when formulating mixed methods research, is that I have a preference, when choosing among multiple suitable mixing purposes, for completion-focused designs that allow me to compare and contrast the qualitative and quantitative findings. So, this means that in the housing project, I must carefully consider all the possible mixing purposes by first generating an initial understanding of the complex systems in which the research problem can be pursued. In this case, we have already discussed some of the global-level details of housing, especially for those considered 'difficult to house' or vulnerable populations. The fields of study that solutions for housing draw upon are mainly from health and social services disciplines. The possible interpersonal contexts involve the service delivery personnel and the clients receiving housing services. The personal contexts involve the researchers as well as participants across all organizational levels in service provision and receipt. If, after carefully considering the options, the mixing purposes end up being focused on completion, I want to be confident it is because it is the optimal mixing purpose, not just my preference. It is thus important for our teaching and guiding resources of mixed methods to encourage researchers to build awareness of the assumptions and influences you bring to your research so that you can recognize the effects of your research orientation (Mertens et al., 2016a). To do so, articulate your orientation and situate yourself as being influenced by and as influential to the interrelated mixed methods research systems.

Try this now – sketch your ideas about what assumptions and influences you bring to bear on your research and consider the potential effects on relationships within and across the research systems. Then as a reader, assess evidence of any philosophical assumptions in your contextual descriptions and what distinguishes your research system.

Features that Engage Readers with Complex Research Contexts

It is advantageous for researchers to distinguish their studies. Research contexts are a great place to start differentiating a study under conditions of complexity. The following list provides some ideas from my own experiences as researcher, as a reviewer of mixed methods research proposals for funding and of manuscripts for publication, and from working with graduate students as an instructor, supervisor, and examiner. See also the featured studies for illustrative examples of some of these engaging features.

- *Seek participants situated in unique complex mixed methods research contexts.* There are various personal, interpersonal, and social contexts in which to situate research. Review the literature for ideas. This will help you create reader interest right from the start.
- *Focus on atypical combinations of interrelated research systems.* Consider new ways of integrating various systems into your research contexts. Review resources for populations and sites that others have not sought to combine before. This will help you position the unique contributions of your problem and avoid replicating the work of others.
- *Introduce your mixed methods research context uniquely.* Catch readers' attention with an interesting context for your study and visual representation of the interrelated systems. This will help you clearly communicate the study's contexts to the reader.
- *Assume unconventional perspectives to guide your mixed methods research.* Consider new roles for theory or theoretical perspectives, involve research team members from disciplines not yet reflected in studies, or assume research paradigms that have not yet been adopted in the literature. This will help you see beyond what might be expected of your complex research contexts.

Innovations in Defining Complex Mixed Methods Research Contexts

Mixed methods researchers define their research systems to reflect the situatedness of their research within and across interrelated contexts. Researchers working under conditions of complexity are tasked with defining contexts based on identifying features of four relationships among interrelated systems and assimilating current and emerging understandings of the environmental influences and research problems. Descriptions of research contexts tend to be oriented at the global level, with some detail from the community level, and often few details from the individual level. Also important, yet underreported, are details about dynamic environmental influences and subsequent effects on the systems over time. The lack of contextual details can be attributed to a lack of focus on the relationships among contexts. This has only recently been noted in guiding resources and has yet to be widely adopted in published manuscripts. There may appear to be agreement about how to situate a study's context through descriptions of the social context and participant groups, yet existing descriptions should often be considered incomplete. I believe access to illustrative examples will be key to enhancing our contextual descriptions under conditions of complexity.

Descriptions of complex mixed methods research systems can appear quite different across studies, related to the differing research conditions under which the studies are conducted. This happens in the same way that definitions of the social, interpersonal, and personal contextual details can appear quite different from those in the research proposal because understandings naturally emerged and new information was assimilated. Specific to research systems, differences can arise as a result of assimilating the contextual definitions with emerging environmental influences. There is an ongoing iterative process of defining complex mixed methods research contexts: it begins with a proposal, continues during implementation, and is finalized with the writing of the report once the research is complete. To that end, variations are expected in structures across the proposals and reports that you will encounter. The inherent nature of different researcher perspectives, research problems, and stages of research commands it. In the following sections, I describe two innovations for communicating and tracking the definitions of complex mixed methods research contexts.

Diagrams Representing Understandings of Interrelated Research Systems

It is uncommon to see diagrams of the research context, yet I believe this is an untapped opportunity! In addition to conveying information, diagrams have proven to be an effective format for tracking evolutions in my understandings of the interrelated research systems and dynamic environmental influences on the personal, interpersonal, and social contexts. To focus on the relations among systems represents a unique approach to defining the complex mixed methods research contexts. I find this focus helpful because by making explicit my initial understandings, I then have a foundation upon which I can assimilate my evolving understandings of systems and environmental influences. This is important because this positions my researcher mindset as open to new possibilities of understandings for:

- Why the complex mixed methods research contexts are appropriate for studying the problem
- How my initial understandings of the complex research contexts and environmental influences evolve over time.

Interrelated systems diagrams can provide essential evidence of the relationships among the personal, interpersonal, and social contexts involved in the study. Furthermore, a diagram captures my understandings at a point in time, and over time I can refine the diagram to reflect what understandings of the new and existing connections have emerged during the study. In so doing, this process supports creative and integrative thinking by creating a structure for managing the input of ideas. I often use systems diagrams to describe my dynamic schemes for understanding system components, their interactions, and their environments. Inspired by the diagrams often used in engineering, such as system context diagrams (Kossiakoff, Sweet, Seymour, &, Biemer, 2011), many variations of systems diagrams exist. What I like most about systems diagrams is that they can be undertaken by different configurations of people and using various materials. I have found the process of creating systems diagrams to be useful on my own and even more useful to explore contextual possibilities among mixed methods research team members. In Figure 6.3, I provide a diagram example conveying the interrelated contexts that are made explicit by the authors of the featured study on law clients (Chui & Cheng, 2017) to define their complex research problem: How do young offenders perceive fairness and satisfaction towards their lawyers in Hong Kong's criminal justice system? Note that the diagram is limited to my interpretation of the information described in the article about the personal, interpersonal, and social study contexts. Note the obvious relationships from the diagram, and the absence of information related to researcher orientations.

Writing Ideas for Defining Research Contexts

It is common to see descriptions of contexts in mixed methods research, but less common for a researcher to explicitly convey their contextual descriptions as incomplete and under

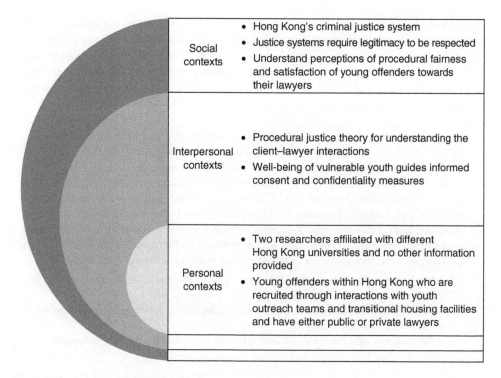

Figure 6.3 Diagram example conveying interrelated societal, interpersonal, and personal systems defining the complex mixed methods research contexts

Source: Author generated from narrative information provided by Chui and Cheng (2017).

development. It is also uncommon practice for researchers to present a comprehensive research systems description that includes interrelated personal, community, and global research contexts as well as the important intersections among researchers, participants, and problems. More comprehensive contextual descriptions are especially useful for mixed methods researchers who are new to conceptualizing studies under conditions of complexity. This is important to position the researchers' mindset as open to new possibilities of understandings for:

- What environmental influences will be considered relevant in defining the complex research contexts
- What innovative research interactions, participant samples, and site dispersions are sought from the contexts identified.

Under conditions of complexity, understandings of the considerations for the complex systems are considered to be evolving. The researcher is tasked with the following question: How can the existing design approaches and understandings of design considerations contribute to describing the complex mixed methods research integrations necessary to guide the study procedures for integrations?

Consider describing the context using an outline. First examine the writing ideas described below and the four related illustrative excepts from the featured study on postconflict risk

(Taylor et al., 2017) identifying community-level risk factors and related emotional insecurity responses using an exploratory sequential design. This reflects the idea that the contexts are both nested and interdependent. We now know that under conditions of complexity many of the contributors to understanding the research context are not yet known and are influenced by changes in conditions and evolving understandings of environmental influences. Examine the four interrelated contexts involved in a mixed methods study:

- *Articulate the social study contexts.* Here, familiarize the readers with your understandings of the global-level research system. Researchers generally begin by identifying or describing the physical study location and any pertinent political, historical, social, cultural aspects. Depending on ethical considerations, researchers may name the specific city, country, organization, or institution, such as 'the Strathroy Middlesex General Hospital in the UK', or may choose to describe it in more general terms, such as 'an urban hospital in the county of Middlesex in south-east England'. The sentences that follow should introduce the societal features surrounding the study's problem and define key information. Many researchers use these details to position the study's significance for the reader. You may find the following questions useful in guiding your social context descriptions and need for the study rationales:

  o   What do readers need to know about the relevant physical study location to better understand its contextual connections to the problem?

  o   What do readers need to know about the pressing issues and priorities to better understand the societal connections to the problem?

  o   What do readers need to know about historical events and current literature trends to better understand how the problem is appropriate to the study's context?

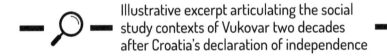

Illustrative excerpt articulating the social study contexts of Vukovar two decades after Croatia's declaration of independence

Vukovar is a 'textbook example of a disrupted multi-ethnic community that used to be well integrated and proud of its ethnic diversity before the 1991-1995 war' (Ajdukovic & Corkalo Biruski, 2008, p. 338). Located in eastern Croatia bordering Serbia, Vukovar is a mid-sized city affected by the ethnic violence following Croatia's declaration of independence in 1991. The war that followed not only caused thousands of deaths and destroyed infrastructure, but also tore the social fabric that had united this once peaceful city. ...

The continuation of ethnic tension in Vukovar is reflected in the relatively separate patterns of daily life. As a protection of minority rights specified in the 1995 Erdut Agreement, separate schooling for minority children is offered (Corkalo Biruski, 2012). ... Like other postconflict societies, despite being born after the height of the war, young people continue to be socialized in a context of intergroup division (Reidy et al., 2015).

Source: Taylor et al. (2017, p. 587). Used with permission from Sage

- *Convey the interpersonal study contexts.* Identify the participants involved in the study and information about existing relationships to familiarize readers with your understandings of the community-level research systems. If applicable, the theoretical framework for guiding the interactions of those involved in the study should be described. The sentences that follow should briefly outline ethical measures taken for ensuring the well-being of participants – these might include information about sampling, criteria for inclusion/exclusion, consent and confidentiality procedures. You may find the following questions useful for guiding your interpersonal contexts descriptions and methodological rationales:

o   What do readers need to know about the target participant groups to better understand the suitability of the recruitment, consent, and sampling procedures?

o   What do readers need to know about the researcher group to better understand their interactions with participants?

o   What do readers need to know about those involved in the study to better understand the appropriateness of the guiding theoretical framework?

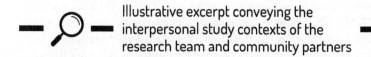

Illustrative excerpt conveying the interpersonal study contexts of the research team and community partners

The University of Zagreb team has well-established collaboration with local schools and non-governmental organizations; these partners helped to purposefully recruit a sample that balanced ethnicity (Croats/Serbs) and gender among the youth in each target age group. Focus group participants also received a modest compensation (US$20). All youth and parent participants provided signed assent and consent, respectively, for Studies 1 and 2, and all procedures were approved by the [institutional review board] at participating universities.

Source: Taylor et al. (2017, p. 590). Used with permission from Sage.

•   *Communicate the personal study contexts.* Familiarize readers with your understandings of the individual-level research systems related to background influences and the experiences of those involved in the research. Sentences in the methodology sections should rationalize the appropriateness of the data procedures. You may find the following questions useful for guiding your personal contexts descriptions and research methods rationales:

o   What do readers need to know about the individual researchers' experiences to better understand the orientations they bring to bear on the study?

o   What do readers need to know about the individual participants' experiences to better understand the orientations they bring to bear on the study?

o   What do readers need to know about those involved in the study to assess the appropriateness of the study procedures?

Illustrative excerpt communicating the personal study contexts of participants

Focus groups were designed to learn about the viewpoint of the participants, and to strike a balance between informal talk and structured interviews. Focus groups allow for a flexible and fluid conversation (Denzin & Lincoln, 2005). ...

(Continued)

(Continued)

This process led to 10 focus groups, each with five to nine participants, homogeneous by ethnicity (N = 66; 47% Croat, 53% Serb). To get a more complete picture of the risks facing young people, we conducted two mixed-gendered youth focus groups (50% male) for each of three age groups (11, 13, and 15 years). This range was selected because young people of this age are reliable report-ers of their emotional and cognitive states and experiences (Cummings et al., 2014). In addition, youth of this age are able to make social distinctions between salient ethnic identities and they increasingly spend more time outside the home which may expose them to varying degrees of risk with age (Cummings et al., 2014). However, family perspectives still play an important role in this age group (Reidy et al., 2015); as the majority of the children came from two-parent house-holds (74%), we also conducted two focus groups for mothers (age: *M* = 41.17, *SD* = 6.90) and two for fathers (age: *M* = 41.75, *SD* = 4.33). The parental perspectives inform how families shape youth perceptions of risk and their responses. Only one child from each family could participate.

All focus groups were conducted in May 2010 by University of Zagreb professors and trained graduate students. The semistructured focus group guide ... was developed for both parents and youth and included a series of catalyst questions and follow-up prompts to help partici-pants share rich, contextual details (Smith & Dunworth, 2003). To ensure the comprehensibil-ity and applicability of the guide, all questions were pretested in focus groups with youth and parents in a community with a similar ethnic composition as Vukovar. In Vukovar, focus groups were convened in a neutral site at a local hotel. Each focus group discussion was recorded and lasted between 60 and 90 minutes. Dialogues were transcribed by Croatian graduate students and translated into English by the Croatian co-investigators.

Source: Taylor et al. (2017, p.590–591). Used with permission from Sage.

- *Describe the relationships and influences across the study contexts.* Here, convey to readers your understandings of the study's significance across the study's contexts. Researchers generally begin by making the case for the demand for mixed methods research innovations and what this particular study context will contribute. You should summarize the key justifications for the context and contributions focused on innovative insights. You may find the following questions useful in guiding your mixing purpose rationales:

  o   What do readers need to know about the complexity of the research context to better understand the significance of the complexity-sensitive mixed methods study?
  o   What do readers need to know about why the mixed methods research context is warranted to tackle the problem?
  o   What do readers need to know about the type of research innovation needed to better understand the significance of the complex mixed methods research context and the need for the study?

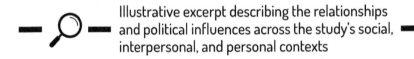

Illustrative excerpt describing the relationships and political influences across the study's social, interpersonal, and personal contexts

This study builds on previous research on the importance of security perceptions to psychological adjustment for adults in contexts of political violence (e.g., Bar-Tal & Jacobson, 1998), by examining an adolescent sample and examining two forms of community insecurity. Past research with adolescents in such settings has found that emotional insecurity processes outside of the family environment have implications for youth well-being and adjustment (Cummings et al., 2010; 2013). Moreover, previous studies have also shown that multiple forms of emotional insecurity may interact with each other over time (Cummings et al., 2016). Notably, past research has found no gender differences in the relation between experiences of intergroup risk and related insecurity (Cummings et al., 2010), a finding that was replicated in this study. The current study also found that ethnic tensions remain salient for young people, consistent with findings based on similar factors in Northern Ireland (Cummings et al., 2014). Yet, previous research has only focused on forms of emotional insecurity at the community level related to intergroup threat (Goeke-Morey et al., 2009).

Source: Taylor et al. (2017, p.603-604). Used with permission from Sage.

CHAPTER CHECK-IN

1   Can you discern the differences and similarities in the interrelated systems of the research contexts across the six featured studies? Compare how the authors of at least two studies describe the following and consider what your analysis tells you about their descriptions (use Figure 6.1 to guide your thinking):

- Personal contexts
- Interpersonal contexts
- Social contexts.

2   Can you recognize hazards of a proximal focus and the strategies for avoiding them when defining study contexts under conditions of complexity? Select a published study in an area that is of interest to you or one of the featured studies.

- Examine the study limitations and areas for future directions. Select one idea to pursue related to a complex problem.
- Sketch preliminary ideas for people and places to situate a related complex mixed methods research design.
    - What disciplines, societal foci, or institutional structures might be involved in the social contexts? (Use Table 6.1 to guide your thinking.)
    - What guiding theoretical framework or ethical considerations might influence the interpersonal contexts? (Use Table 6.2 to guide your thinking.)
    - What researcher orientations or participant characteristics might be appropriate for the personal contexts? (Use Table 6.3 to guide your thinking.)

3   Can you define a complex mixed methods research context for a study that is of interest to you? Apply the guiding questions presented in this chapter to structure an outline.

- Discuss what is known about the social study contexts to identify potential relationships relevant to the problem such as study location, disciplines, and foci.
- Discuss what is known about the interpersonal study contexts to identify potential societal features relevant for the problem, such as nature of relationships, guiding theoretical framework, and ethical considerations.

- Discuss what is known about the social study contexts to identify potential individual orientations relevant to the problem, such as researcher and participant backgrounds.
- Discuss what is known about the personal study contexts to identify potential societal features relevant to the problem, such as historical and political details.
- Discuss what is known about the interpersonal study contexts to identify potential individual characteristics relevant to the problem, such as researcher experiences with particular theoretical frameworks.
- Discuss what is known about the personal study contexts of the study to identify potential relationships relevant to the problem, such as the nature of the existing relationships.
- Discuss what is known about any environmental considerations that are likely to influence the contexts and how the systems might be affected.
- Review the draft (see Table 6.4 to guide your thinking) and create a system diagram (see also Figure B.3). Note which details are present in your description and which are not yet known.

4   What features for engaging readers can you use to begin creating your complexity-sensitive mixed methods study proposal? Access a complex mixed methods research problem that you would like to pursue. Sketch the problem and need for the study. Select one of the features for engaging readers that fits with your study and write a brief description of an engaging context in which to address this problem.

KEY CHAPTER CONCEPTS

This chapter advances the third adaptive practice for guiding a complexity-sensitive approach to mixed methods research. It addresses the question: What does defining complex mixed methods research contexts involve, and how can the interrelated systems and evolving environmental influences be recognized, promoted, and conveyed? The purpose of defining the complex mixed methods research contexts is the focus of this chapter because the system descriptions and influence recognitions have important implications for study plans, implementations, and outcomes. A systems perspective is a noteworthy opportunity to represent the interrelated context, and a proximity focus illustrates a hazard for researchers under some conditions because of the uncertainties related to complex problems. The rationale for the use of a relational systems approach for defining complex research contexts is grounded in the need to situate the people and places for the study when the understandings of the social, interpersonal, and personal contexts are considered to be evolving and incomplete. To that end, integrative thinking with complexity about the systems involved in research allows us to focus on the interdependent and emergent properties of contexts and is guided by procedures for identifying features of four relationships among interrelated systems and assimilating current and emerging understandings of the environmental influences and research problems. Features that will engage readers include seeking participants situated in unique complex mixed methods research contexts and focusing on atypical combinations of interrelated research systems. Innovations in defining complex mixed methods research contexts involve system diagrams and writing ideas. The next chapter introduces the complexity-sensitive practices related to describing designs of complex mixed methods research integrations.

FURTHER READINGS

The following resources are offered as introductory references for systems theory and defining research contexts. The list should not be considered exhaustive. Readers are encouraged to seek out additional readings in the end-of-book reference list. Readings denoted with an asterisk are available on the online resources website for this book.

Jones-Rooy, A., & Page, S. E. (2012). The complexity of system effects. *Critical Review, 24*(3), 313–342. doi: 10.1080/08913811.2012.767045.

Jones-Rooy and Scott Page provide an illustrative example of applying the principles of complexity science and, specifically, systems effects to understanding recent global political events, including the 2008 US housing bubble and the 2011 Arab Spring.

Onwuegbuzie, A., Collins, K. M. T., & Frels, R. K. (2013). Foreword: Using Bronfenbrenner's ecological systems theory to frame quantitative, qualitative, and mixed research. *International Journal of Multiple Research Approaches, 7*(1), 2–8. doi: 10.5172/mra.2013.7.1.2.

This article uses Bronfenbrenner's (1979) ecological systems theory to frame quantitative, qualitative, and mixed research. This resource provides essential understandings of the theory and the author's application to generalizations.

Plano Clark, V. L., & Ivankova, N. V. (2016). *Mixed methods research: A guide to the field.* Thousand Oaks, CA: Sage.

This book introduces a unique socio-ecological framework for understanding the field of mixed methods research. This resource is an excellent overall introduction to the field – in particular, the focus of Part III on the personal, interpersonal, and social contexts that shape mixed methods research practice.

*Levitt, H. M., Bamberg, M., Creswell, J. W., Frost, D. M., Josselson, R., & Suárez-Orozco, C. (2018). Journal article reporting standards for qualitative primary, qualitative meta-analytic, and mixed methods research in psychology: The APA Publications and Communications Board task force report. *American Psychologist, 73*(1), 26–46. http://dx.doi.org/10.1037/amp0000151.

The authors describe standards for guiding what should be included in a qualitative or mixed methods research report. The standards are intended for use by authors in the process of writing prior to submission and by reviewers and editors during the peer review process.

*Marti, T. S., & Mertens, D. M. (Eds.) (2014). Special Issue: Marginalized populations. *Journal of Mixed Methods Research, 8*(3), 207–321.

To explore the potential of mixed methods to contribute to social change, two different features are discussed in this special issue: a researcher's responsibility to inform policies when working with marginalized populations, and involving the participants to generate more accurate and useful knowledge. This issue is an essential read for anyone pursuing mixed methods research under conditions of complexity because of its particular methodological strategies aimed at including the people who are being 'researched'.

Stroh, D. P. (2015). *Systems thinking for social change: A practical guide to solving complex problems, avoiding unintended consequences, and achieving lasting results*. White River Junction, VT: Chelsea Green Publishing.

David Stroh offers an accessible guide to understanding and applying systems thinking to problem-solving, decision-making, and strategic planning. This resource provides essential information about systems thinking for planning complex mixed methods research studies.

Apply your mixed methods knowledge with videos, activities, SAGE journal articles and project templates at **https://study.sagepub.com/poth**

7

DESCRIBING DESIGNS OF COMPLEX MIXED METHODS RESEARCH INTEGRATIONS

By the end of this chapter, you will be able to answer the following questions:

- Why describe designs of complex mixed methods research integrations?
- What opportunities exist to describe complex mixed methods integrations?
- Why can the design orientation become hazardous for mixed methods researchers?
- What guides the descriptive design approach for complex mixed methods research integrations?
- What features engage readers with complex mixed methods research integrations?
- What writing and diagram innovations are useful for describing complex mixed methods research integrations?

- Complex mixed methods research integrations
- Interactive, system-based design approach
- Descriptive design approach
- Intensity of mixing
- Design orientation
- Point of interface

- Emergent mixed methods research designs
- Research ethics
- Evolving mixed methods research designs
- Research design typology
- Fixed mixed methods research designs
- Typology-based design approach

This chapter advances the adaptive practice for guiding a complexity-sensitive approach to mixed methods research. It addresses the question: *What does describing complex mixed methods research integrations involve and how can key design considerations and evolving feasibility influences be recognized, promoted, and conveyed?* Consider an occasion when a colleague explained their desired design for a mixed methods study. Did their description provide sufficient detail about how the research would be undertaken? What procedures were involved in generating each of the qualitative and quantitative data strands? Where and how did the integration take place? What ethical considerations were discussed? What design adaptations occurred during implementation? A well-written methodology section provides a rationale for the choice of mixed methods research approach, describes the design selected, and describes the data collection, analysis, and integration procedures guiding the study's implementation (Creswell & Plano Clark, 2018; DeCuir-Gunby & Schultz, 2017). Ideally, the description of the integration procedures will also convey the feasibility considerations under which the research is implemented and embed agility in the procedures for responding to unexpected situations. Let us now consider how describing **complex mixed methods research integrations** is distinctive.

Not being able to predetermine the specific directions for guiding integration procedures traditionally associated with mixed methods research designs is one of the dilemmas experienced by mixed methods researchers addressing complex problems. If researchers are not able to pinpoint the study's need for integration, the timing of the data strands or the priority for the data strands, then they are not able to identify if their procedures fit an existing typology or specify how their procedures meet the standards for conduct of ethical research. The lack of ability to predetermine procedures and to select from an existing **research design typology** have emerged as key dilemmas experienced by researchers under conditions of complexity. Dichotomies described in the literature illustrate some situations that create unintended constraints on design possibilities. For example, Creswell and Plano Clark (2018) categorize mixed methods designs as either fixed or emergent. A **fixed mixed methods research design** involves procedures that are described at the start of the research process which are then implemented as planned. **Emergent mixed methods research designs** are described as 'studies in which the use of mixed methods arises due to issues that develop during the process of conducting the research' (Creswell & Plano Clark, 2018, p. 52).

Let us examine the challenges created by the false dichotomy of fixed or emergent types of mixed methods design. First, the likelihood of any design being implemented *exactly* as planned is exceedingly small in my experience, and others also counsel that researchers 'need to be flexible and that your study may indeed have emergent elements' (DeCuir-Gunby & Schutz, 2017, p. 108). Yet this unlikely experience is how many 'fixed' designs are reported and conveyed in published studies. More authentic accounts of design implementations are especially necessary for those undertaking research in varying conditions of complexity. Procedural adaptations *are likely to occur* during implementation of designs under all research conditions and *will almost certainly occur* during implementation of designs under conditions of greater complexity. The need to embed agility within our integration procedures inherent in complex mixed methods research designs cannot be overstated, given the uncertain and evolving conditions under which some research occurs. Second, the very definition of emergent mixed methods designs conveys a lack of intention for integration. Whoa! Does that mean that all mixed methods designs are either implemented as planned (i.e., fixed) or not originally intended to be mixed methods research (i.e., emergent)? There is a pressing need for a third design type within mixed methods research. I suggest **evolving mixed methods research designs** as studies in which the integration procedures evolve as understandings emerge and adaptations occur in response to changing conditions during the process of conducting the research. A focus on evolving research designs advances the possibility of guiding integration procedures that are yet to be known and embedding agility to respond to changing conditions. This is the niche occupied by a **descriptive design approach** to complex mixed methods research integrations.

Work on this chapter was informed by my experiences as an instructor, mentor, and reviewer as I have grappled to guide others in developing a complexity-sensitive mentality. Embedding the featured mixed methods studies in this chapter reflects a continued effort to address the practice gap in many textbooks and to provide authentic examples of published articles that represent varying conditions of complexity related to research integrations. Specifically, a complexity-sensitive approach to mixed methods research assumes our designs for complex mixed methods research integrations are evolving over time in response to changing conditions. To optimize an approach to mixed methods research design in light of the uncertainties researchers face under some conditions of complexity, three pressing needs exist. First, to position the need for a descriptive design approach that embeds integrative thinking with complexity about implementation plans. Next, to advance procedures for describing complex mixed methods research designs that draw upon our current and emerging understandings of design considerations and feasibility influences. Finally, to identify features for engaging readers with writing and diagram innovations useful for explaining complex mixed methods research designs in proposals and reports. As a starting point, let us consider the need for a focus on integrative thinking with complexity to guide researchers in describing complex mixed methods research integrations.

Why Describe Designs of Complex Mixed Methods Research Integrations?

Researchers are tasked with the responsibility of conveying the design guiding the study procedures; for a complexity-sensitive approach, this involves assimilating emerging understandings of the design considerations and feasibility influences determining the data integrations. The important roles of a design to shape a study have been described. The design itself has been described as 'a centrepiece in mixed methods methodology' (Creswell & Plano-Clark, 2018, p. 295). The purpose of describing complex mixed methods designs is to make explicit the underlying considerations and embed agility within the procedures for responding to the evolving conditions underlying any implementation plans. The new descriptive design approach responds to the dilemmas experienced with a lack of guidance when understandings of the integration procedures are evolving and when fit with existing design typologies is not possible.

To further delineate the advantages of a descriptive design approach, let us consider the current design approaches within the field of mixed methods research. The topic is probably familiar from your readings and experiences because mixed methods design is adeptly described as having been 'widely debated and discussed' (Creswell & Plano Clark, 2018, p. 52). There is no agreed-upon design approach for mixed methods research, yet two approaches seem to underpin most traditional mixed methods research practice tendencies: a **typology-based design approach** and an **interactive, system-based design approach** (Creswell & Plano Clark, 2018).

The typology-based approach has received extensive attention in the literature. Researchers are often guided to choose among the many design typologies (e.g., Creswell, 2015a; Creswell, Fetters, & Ivankova, 2004; Creswell & Plano Clark, 2007, 2011, 2018; Greene, 2007; Greene & Caracelli, 1997; Morse, 1991; Morse & Niehaus, 2009; Plano Clark & Ivankova, 2016; Sandelowski, 2000; Teddlie & Tashakkori, 2009). Typologies are a system of classifying designs by study purpose and emphasize the selection of a design from among the various classifications based on differences in timing, priority, and level of interaction across the qualitative and quantitative data strands involved in a research study or programme (Creswell & Plano Clark, 2018). You are probably familiar with designs such as explanatory sequential and convergent concurrent, as described by Creswell and Plano Clark (2007; 2011; 2018), but did you know many more typologies exist such as qualitative follow-up (Morgan, 1998) and concurrent nested (Creswell, Plano Clark, Gutmann, & Hanson, 2003)? Indeed, researchers embrace diversity in mixed methods designs and have long recognized the value of the various systems of classification (Caracelli & Greene, 1997; Maxwell & Loomis, 2003; Tashakkori & Teddlie, 1998). A typology-based design approach is represented in many published reports of mixed methods research and is seen as providing necessary guidance for those new to mixed methods research. Yet the existing classifications of mixed methods research typologies remain limited in their capacity to represent complex designs (Guest, 2013). This limited capacity of existing classifications is understandable because we have yet to 'know' the possible diversity of complex mixed methods designs.

In contrast, the interactive, system-based design approach has received significantly less attention in the literature despite its potential for representing complex designs and the relationships among design components. The interactive, system-based approach guides the researcher in considering the five interconnected components influencing research designs – the study's goals, conceptual framework, research questions, methods, and validity considerations – as well as the researcher's skill, situational constraints, ethical standards, funding agendas and prior research (Maxwell, 2012; Maxwell, Chmiel, & Rogers, 2015; Maxwell & Loomis, 2003). It also means that the interactive, system-based design approaches emphasize thinking about the interrelationships and influences among study components throughout the design process. Many researchers simply are not familiar with this approach, and its potential for representing complex designs remains relatively untapped.

Common to both typology-based and interactive, system-based design approaches is a **design orientation** focused on the research study or programme details. I define a design orientation as the point of reference for the research design to be labelled. I conceptualize that these design approaches represent a design orientation from research or a programme of study because the designs reflect the research or study-level features. For example, typology-based designs reflect features such as timing, priority, and level of interaction between the data strands, whereas interactive, system-based designs reflect interconnected research components. It thus means that these research or study-level features must be predetermined, which we have come to understand is not always possible under some conditions of complexity.

The shortcomings of the typology-based approach are concisely described by Guest (2013, p. 141): 'current systems of classification although useful for simple and less fluid types of mixed methods research, are not capable of capturing the complexity and iterative nature of large, more intricate research projects'. When fit within existing typologies is not possible, the traditional mixed methods research practices focused on design orientations of the research study or programme are not suitable. Mixed methods researchers should be guided to abandon the need to simplify their research designs to fit existing typologies and begin to think about the processes involved in realizing integrations as iterative and developmental in nature. This is particularly important because of the limited capacity for a typology-based approach to accommodate multifaceted research designs involving broad purposes and more than one **point of interface** (Guest, 2013). 'Point of interface' refers to the point or points where mixing of qualitative and quantitative data strands occurs in a mixed methods research design.

Two additional design approaches that have been advanced warrant some attention here. Hall and Howard (2008) described a dynamic approach that shares some similarities with the interactive, system-based approaches yet that embeds a unique combination of structure and flexibility they called the synergistic approach. Guest (2013) advanced an alternative approach that shifts the design orientation to the points of interface. The shift from a design orientation of the research study adopted by the typology-based design approaches allowed Guest to reduce the descriptive dimensions to only two: timing and purpose of data integration. Yet common to both the typology-based and alternative design approaches is their fixedness – that is, their design dimensions are predetermined and intended to be implemented as planned. The dilemma faced by those working under conditions of high complexity is that the understandings of the design dimensions are often incomplete or unknown and adaptations are almost certain as implementation unfolds. Consider Researcher Spotlight 7.1, which describes the pressing challenge of responding to complex conditions from the perspective of a professor of educational psychology and university faculty scholar in the Department of Teacher Education and Learning Sciences at North Carolina State University in Raleigh (USA).

 ━━ Researcher Spotlight 7.1 ━━━━━━━━━━━━━━━━━

Jessica DeCuir-Gunby on the need for flexibility within complex mixed methods designs

I feel there are several challenges for the field of mixed methods. The first major challenge is the need for more complex mixed methods designs. The standard/common mixed methods designs are not always flexible enough to capture the range of complexity that can occur within the data collection and analysis phases of a study. Researchers frequently have to piece elements of different mixed methods research designs together, often creating a lot of confusion for readers. As research studies become more intricate, researchers will naturally engage in more complex mixed methods designs. Because of this, new designs need to be created.

A design orientation that draws upon emerging understandings of feasibility considerations from the research study or programme as well as the points of integration is intuitive because the study's need to integrate qualitative and quantitative data strands is a distinguishing feature of mixed methods research. Examine the guiding framework in Figure 7.1 to highlight the interconnecting considerations across design orientations for complex mixed methods research integrations. The very nature of complex designs involving nonlinear feasibility influences and uncertain integration procedures and outcomes creates challenges for researchers. Indeed, describing research designs is realized through integrative thinking with

Research study design orientation

```
                    ┌─────────────┐
                    │    Logic    │
                    │considerations│
                    └─────────────┘
                           │
                           ▼
┌──────────────┐     ┌──────────┐     ┌──────────────┐
│   Framing    │ ──▶ │  Design  │ ◀── │    Ethics    │
│considerations│     │description│     │considerations│
└──────────────┘     └──────────┘     └──────────────┘
                           ▲
                           │
                    ┌─────────────┐
                    │  Procedural │
                    │considerations│
                    └─────────────┘
```

Point of interface design orientation

Figure 7.1 Interconnecting considerations across design orientations for complex mixed methods research integrations

complexity about the feasibility considerations related to framing, logic, ethics, and procedures. In so doing, the researcher is better able to assimilate emerging understanding of research integrations and respond to the changing conditions surrounding the mixed methods research through an adaptive practice for describing the designs of integrations.

Describing Opportunities and Hazards for Mixed Methods Researchers

Descriptive Design Approach Opportunities

A focus on a descriptive design approach for complex mixed methods research integrations opens new possibilities for innovative designs addressing complex mixed methods research problems. Complex mixed research problems often tackle uncharted territory requiring yet-to-be-designed procedures for integration. A descriptive design approach is very much shaped by the particular conditions in which the research takes place by drawing upon the design orientations of the research study as well as the points of interface. It creates the opportunity for more authentic study proposals and reports under conditions of complexity.

An authentic design description of complex mixed methods research integrations involves detailing information as transparently as possible, and I have sought over the last decade to develop a practice for guiding the necessary integrative thinking with complexity. This work came about from hearing my students and colleagues alter their desired studies because they had assumed (and had been guided in the false notion) that they needed to fit their integration procedures into an existing design typology. For example, one of my students wanted to do an intervention study where the emphasis would be on quantitative data generated by standardized assessments, but because they were working with an understudied and difficult-to-access population it was important to qualitatively assess whether the quantitative assessments were capturing the impacts of the intervention on the constructs they were supposed to measure. A complementary use of the integrated findings was to inform the development of the intervention over time. Their initial understandings of the needs of the population and the constructs the intervention would likely impact were based on their experiences as a clinician working with this population and their reading of the impacts of the intervention with populations with similar needs. The design they proposed is represented in Figure 7.2 and reflects the practicality that the sample size would likely involve four to six participants. As denoted by stars and letters, the design involves eight points of interface between quantitative standardized assessments and qualitative interviews. The pre-intervention data would be collected the week before the six weekly sessions of the intervention would occur, and the post-intervention data would be collected one week following the completion of the intervention. The diagram also depicts the possibility for a longitudinal study and thus potential further data collections are represented for 6, 12 and 18 months post-intervention. In addition to comparing and contrasting the data at each point of interface, the student proposed a possible time series analysis across the quantitative data as well as a thematic analysis across the qualitative data performed post-intervention.

Further discussions revealed that many students reported being dissuaded from tackling problems that could not be addressed with an established mixed methods research design typology. What I came to realize is that many students and researchers seemed constrained to using less complex research designs because of the examples they read in published literature and described creating their own mixed methods research designs as too risky. Three key design dilemmas emerged from these discussions that sparked my interest:

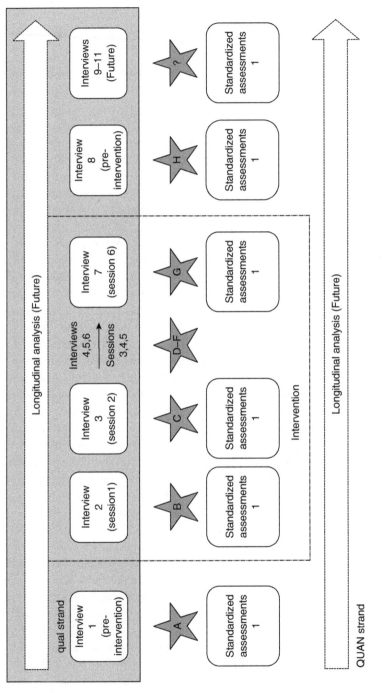

Figure 7.2 Example of a complex mixed methods research design in need of a descriptive approach

1   What to do when understandings of integration procedures are incomplete and guiding examples are not available in the literature.
2   What to do when a desired design does not fit within the existing mixed methods research design typologies.
3   What to do when the procedures cannot be implemented as planned.

What we noticed was that there was no clear fit within an existing typology. At the time in 2014, we used the embedded notion of data sequencing and priority advanced by Creswell and Plano Clark (2011) to describe a multi-case embedded mixed methods research design. This design described the qualitative data as embedded within and complementing the quantitative data. Each participant became a case, and comparing across the cases generated new understandings of this understudied population and informed both the intervention and constructs for measuring impacts. I am pleased to see that the field has continued to evolve; the most recent edition of Creswell and Plano Clark's influential introductory text (2018) reflects complex designs related to case study, intervention, and evaluation. When I think back to this design, it appears to me that this could be couched within any of these three types of complex mixed methods research designs.

Notice that it is much easier to identify the points of interface from a diagram than from a narrative description. I am well known to grab a pen and paper or marker and whiteboard as soon as someone wants to talk through a study. I find diagramming to be a great strategy for working through the design procedures without feeling constrained by a typology. Consider Researcher Spotlight 7.2, describing future data source opportunities for mixed methods researchers from the perspective of a veteran supervisor and professor emerita from the Educational Research and Evaluation Program in the School of Education at Virginia Polytechnic Institute and State University (USA) and visiting senior scholar at the University of Michigan. It is noteworthy that no current design typologies (that I know of!) explicitly involve big data sets.

 Researcher Spotlight 7.2

Elizabeth Creamer on attending to emerging data source opportunities for mixed methods researchers

Social and behavioural scientists are arriving at the doorstep of the era of big data. This trend will further cement the relationship between mixed methods and research involving complex social and health problems because it involves a shift towards, among other things, open access data and journals, interdisciplinary teams, machine learning, and artificial intelligence. At the same time, researchers are increasingly confronted with obstacles to recruiting sufficient participants to contribute in thoughtful ways to conventional strategies for collecting data through interviews and survey research.

The emerging presence of research that involves large data sets in quantitative research and machine learning in qualitative research has the potential to change the way that research is routinely conducted. Social media platforms, for example, offer the opportunity for access to almost unlimited data that can be extracted and analysed in qualitative software. Digital libraries, such as the database created by National Public Radio called Story Corps from pairs of people who step

(Continued)

(Continued)

into a booth to record a conversation about a shared experience, offer free access to interviews and images that are well suited to be qualitative and mixed methods research approaches.

While there will always be a place in the literature for qualitative studies with a small sample size, doctoral students and early-career academics seeking to leverage their research into a long-term agenda will find that the trend towards big data will challenge them to expand their skill repertoire to include fluency in sophisticated qualitative and quantitative software that may not be part of the required course work in a graduate programme.

Considering my own methodological training experiences, these dilemmas associated with 'deviating' from typologies resonate with me. I had been taught to use mixed methods design typologies because of the advantages offered according to Teddlie and Tashakkori (2009). They said that typologies

- Provide tools that help researchers design their studies
- Establish a common language for the field
- Help provide structure to the field
- Help legitimize the field
- Are useful pedagogical tools.

It is time to shift our design approaches and to reconsider the related practice assumptions and create guiding practices for complexity-sensitive research that would no longer constrain researchers because of what they (and their advisors and colleagues) assumed were possible designs and design approaches. Consider the desirability of an adaptive mixed methods practice for designs that embeds integrative thinking with complexity, is descriptive, and embeds responsiveness in the implementation plans under varying conditions of complexity. Then we can create reports of research that detail the procedural adaptations that were made and the influences on these decisions. Mixed methods researchers would benefit from an elaboration on how to realize adaptive practices under conditions of complexity which is what my descriptive design approach intends to do. Consider Researcher Spotlight 7.3, which describes the pressing challenge of time and temporality under conditions of complexity from the perspective of an associate professor at the Centre for Interdisciplinary Methodologies at the University of Warwick (UK).

 Researcher Spotlight 7.3

Emma Uprichard on researching complex social objects that are changing in situ

Approaching the social world from a complexity perspective assumes that the social world is dynamic, nonlinear, and emerges from complex multidimensional interactions. These kinds of issues raise a whole host of methodological challenges. The ones I have been most interested in come under the broad umbrella of time and temporality. For example, when might a social phenomenon change or even have the capacity to change? To what extent might the change radically alter continuity? To what extent does the *timing* of an intervention matter to the success or failure of that intervention?

In other words, when we study a complex social object, we have to account for the fact that the object itself is subject to change *as we are studying it.* Furthermore, social systems involve actors – individuals who are reflexive and can remember and reflect on the ways things were in the past, are still in the present, and could be, should be and potentially will be in the future. Even the methods and data of what we are studying may change over the course of the research period, so those aspects need to adapt and be adapted.

Design Orientation Hazards

The design orientation from which the integration procedures are described can dramatically influence the way a study is conceptualized. So far, we have discussed approaches that represent two different design orientations: the typology-based and interactive approaches represent the research study orientation, whereas the alternate approach represents the point of interface orientation. I propose a bird's-eye view as a metaphor for differentiating these viewpoints and introducing design orientation effects to mixed methods researchers. Adopting the research study orientation can be thought of as the viewpoint from a bird flying high above the ground. This bird's-eye perspective permits a far-reaching view of the general landscape but few details. In the same way, designing a research study from this perspective takes into account the general need of the study for integration and procedures based on assumptions of stability for the methods to be implemented as planned. Yet the high viewpoint does not allow close attention to be paid to the changing conditions on the ground. The assumptions of stability allow the researcher confidence in the predictability of the outcomes based on previous experiences. In contrast, a bird flying low to the ground permits a more granular view of the conditions on the ground related to the individual points of interface among the data strands and greater responsiveness to changing conditions. What may be missing from this perspective are understandings of the contributions of each point of interface to the study's overall need for integration. Both perspectives are valuable for the bird and the researcher as navigator, and thus are valuable to the reader because they provide different but complementary information for informing designs.

Thus, describing rather than selecting a design typology plays an important role in guiding the readers' perspectives and understandings of the research design to avoid design orientation effects. This is particularly important, given the many choices related to sampling, methods, and mixing strategies and the roles that feasibility plays in the decisions. It should be noted that while discussions referring to potential limitations of typology-based approaches have been present in the literature for over a decade (Guest, 2013; Maxwell & Loomis, 2003), the need for thinking beyond the existing typologies and using alternate design approaches have also led to suggestions for using alternate approaches once a researcher gains expertise with typology-focused approaches to mixed methods designs:

> We do not advocate that researchers adopt a typology-based design like a cookbook recipe but instead use it as a guiding framework to help inform design choices. As researchers gain more expertise with mixed methods, they are better able to effectively design their studies using an interactive or dynamic approach. (Creswell and Plano Clark, 2018, p. 59)

The challenge of course is that many researchers do not follow the advice. In my experience, once researchers are trained in selecting mixed methods research designs from typologies, it is difficult to convince them of the need for a different approach – thus the unintended effect of typologies. I am not alone in highlighting the effect of typologies in mixed methods research as constraining innovations in designs; others have also raised similar concerns referring to typology 'as failing to capture the actual diversity of mixed methods studies' (Mertens et al., 2016b, p. 19). Further discussion on how to capitalize on design typologies for those new to mixed methods research is warranted to 'foster discussion on ways of classifying designs, again with rigidly imposing a particularly typology' (p. 16). In situations that warrant it, a description-focused approach can provide freedom from the restrictions of having to select from existing mixed methods designs.

Among the key challenges for those pursuing more complex mixed methods research is the assumption that an aspiring researcher can learn how to conduct this form of inquiry by reading a published study. This thinking is flawed because examples exist that are easily accessible and provide access to thinking behind the design decisions and adaptations. A description-focused approach offers a mechanism for describing complex mixed methods designs and does not assume that a design reflective of the study's particular integration processes already exists. In Practice Alert 7.1, I consider some of the influences underpinning design decisions for a research proposal I observed in my own experience as a supervisor and researcher. I invite you to do the same. In so doing, I am enhancing my understandings of the influences on integration procedures when conveying my decisions underpinning a mixed methods research design.

 Practice Alert 7.1

What influences your design decisions underpinning a complex mixed methods research design?

Readers and many reviewers of mixed methods research proposals and manuscripts are more interested in assessing *what underpins your integration procedures* than *what design you are using.* When mixed methods researchers define themselves by the design, they are forever defined by that rather than by what procedures they are using. They may miss the opportunity to convey their design decisions that represent how they are 'thinking differently' than anyone else about a complex research problem. Some examples of design decisions involve clear personal connections to the research participants and to considerations about the methods that would be appropriate to the sample. Establishing the uniqueness and appropriateness of the integration procedures and designs creates the foundation for successful funding proposals and published manuscripts.

Try this now – sketch your ideas about what influences your design decisions for a research problem. Then consider the effects on how the decisions underpinning your integration procedures are conveyed.

A Descriptive Design Approach for Complex Mixed Methods Research Integrations

Rather than offering a how-to perspective, I consider my descriptive design approach as more in line with creating options for mixed methods researchers under conditions of complexity, advancing some options given my experiences and reading of the literature, and then letting readers make informed choices for themselves. There exists no simple solution for avoiding design orientation effects in research designs, yet adopting an approach that draws upon both the research study and points of interface provides a suitable perspective for describing adaptive designs. I can share how I approach describing designs under conditions of varying complexity using four tasks that are interdependent and iterative – not to be considered as a set of procedures or linear steps (see Figure 7.3): articulating framing sensitivities guiding study foundations; examining logic features guiding data integrations; attending to ethical concerns guiding research procedures; and assimilating procedural adaptations guiding research responses. By purposefully situating the practice of describing complex mixed methods research integrations encircled by the four tasks, I depict the central role of integrative thinking with complexity about designs and the dynamic feasibility influences that can be an essential source of the continual emergence of new ideas and understandings. Because of this, it is essential that the descriptions of complex mixed methods research designs be considered *in progress*, meaning that our understandings of the procedures for integration are constantly evolving and we must assimilate new information that informs the study. Indeed, amid the wonderful opportunities afforded by a complexity lens (discussed in Chapter 3) are the need to assume nonlinearity, self-organization, unpredictability and responsiveness in the research process. Specific to designs, these assumptions explain why understandings of the framing, logic, and ethics considerations along with the procedural adaptations are subject to continual development with uncertain outcomes and the necessity of procedural agility under changing conditions. An approach for describing complex mixed methods research designs departs from the traditional mixed methods research practice tendency to select an existing design that best fits the problem. Yet if the

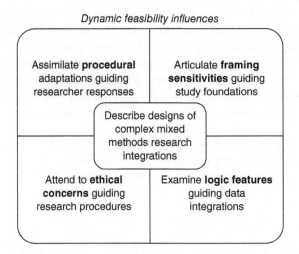

Figure 7.3 Tasks involved in a descriptive design approach for complex mixed methods research integrations

design description fits an existing typology, the researcher may be well served to employ it along with the additional descriptive information. See Table B.2, an editable version of which is also available on the companion website for the book.

Articulate Framing Sensitivities Guiding Study Foundations

Several framing sensitivities guide how the researcher approaches the design. Key among these sensitivities are detailing the guiding theoretical framework, the rationale for the study's need for integration (see Chapter 5), and the **intensity of mixing** during the study. These aspects are all important foundations for introducing the study and the significance of its design (Creswell & Plano Clark, 2018; DeCuir-Gunby & Schutz, 2017). To illustrate how this is done under conditions of complexity, I turn to the evidence of framing sensitivities provided in the design descriptions of the featured studies (see Table 7.1). Four of the six featured studies identify a substantive content theory guiding their theoretical frameworks (DeCuir-Gunby & Schutz, 2017), whereas two refer to the value of mixed methods research as their guiding interpretive framework. Interestingly, the studies adopting this interpretive framework were also those that were considered to have some of the highest conditions of complexity (see Chapter 4). Despite the plans of some researchers to identify the mixing purpose and predetermine the extent to which mixing (also known as level of interaction between data strands) occurs, the intensity of mixing often emerges as the study unfolds. This is because under conditions of higher complexity the mixing purpose may not be easily identified in the existing typologies, and whether the study reflects fully or partially integrated mixing is often dictated by the emerging understandings of the research outcomes.

All of the featured studies identified a need for integration; whereas three were easily categorized by the existing typologies (explanation and completeness), the other three were innovation-focused for the purpose of generating new insights. Not surprisingly, it was the case that these innovation-focused mixing purposes were identified in studies with high conditions of complexity. None of the featured studies illustrated fully integrated mixing. That would involve mixing across all aspects of the research process, including during the definition of the purpose and research questions, during data collection, during data analysis, and while drawing conclusions or inferences. Common across all the featured studies was the focus on partial integration referring to mixing that occurs during some aspects of the research process. The majority of studies involve mixing during inferences followed by data analysis. When describing a complex mixed methods research integration, consider the information available from the following questions related to framing considerations:

- What do I know about theoretical frameworks that could guide the study?
- What do I know about the possible needs for integration in the study?
- What do I know about the extent of intensity of mixing in the study?

Examine Logic Features Guiding Data Integrations

Several logic features guide how the researcher realizes the integration procedures of the design. Key among these features are the timing and weighting of data strands as well as strategies for sampling, generating data, and mixing. The featured studies provide some evidence

Table 7.1 Summary of framing sensitivities of the six featured mixed methods designs

Featured study	Guiding theoretical framework	Study's need for integration	Intensity of mixing (research stage)
Law clients (Chui & Cheng, 2017)	Procedural justice theory	Explain initial quantitative findings	Partial (inferences)
Postconflict risk (Taylor et al., 2017)	Emotional security theory	Deepen understanding by developing a quantitative instrument	Partial (inferences)
Heart care (Dickson et al., 2011)	Self-care model	Triangulation for congruence	Partial (inference)
Safe places (Zea et al., 2014)	Theory of communicative action	Generate new understandings of social change to inform policies and innovative interventions through use of refined quantitative instrument	Partial (inference)
Leadership competencies (Strudsholm et al., 2016)	Value of mixed methods research	Identify new public health leadership competencies	Partial (data analysis)
Vaping culture (Colditz et al., 2017)	Value added of mixed methods research	Generate new understandings of vaping culture in social media	Partial (inference)

of logic features in their design descriptions (see Table 7.2). For example, four of the featured studies describe the sequential timing of qualitative and quantitative data collection and analysis – that is, that data strands were separated temporally, one following the other. The timing of the data strands of the other two featured studies was described as parallel and concurrent, meaning that both data strands were generated at relatively the same time. Despite the best intentions to determine when data strands will interface, sometimes sequencing emerges in relation to participant access or because the intent of data mixing changes as a result of a previous point of interface.

Weighting of data strands refers to how qualitative and quantitative data are conceptually prioritized relative to each other at their point of interface. All but one of the featured studies identify the weighting assigned to the data strands; two gave the quantitative data priority, two gave the qualitative data priority, and one gave them equal emphasis. Only the featured study on postconflict risk (Taylor et al., 2017) did not explicitly identify weighting. Weighting often emerges during integration because it depends on how the intent of data mixing and logic of data strands ultimately play out in the implementation (Guest, 2013; Teddlie & Tashakkori, 2009). Thus, under conditions of complexity, weighting is often dictated by the emerging understandings of the implementation of integration procedures.

Sampling strategies describe the procedures used for decisions related to the number of participants to select and how to select them (Onwuegbuzie & Collins, 2007). Mixed sampling refers to the strategies used for both qualitative and quantitative research samples. The featured studies demonstrate some evidence of nested, identical, and multilevel mixed sampling strategies. Three of the six featured studies described nested samples featuring subsamples of the initial sample used across the data strands yet different schemes. The scheme for the featured study on law clients (Chui & Cheng, 2017) was stratified purposive in that equal numbers of young offenders who had chosen either public or private lawyers were selected to participate in interviews following their participation in a questionnaire. The featured study on safe places (Zea et al., 2014) used a snowball scheme (also called respondent driven) whereby participants in life history interviews and focus groups were asked to identify further survey participants. The featured study on leadership competencies (Strudsholm et al., 2016) used a mixed purposeful scheme to choose more than one sampling strategy, comparing the results from the public health workforce and the public health leadership. Two of the six featured studies described identical samples (also called matched) featuring the same sample across the data strands yet different schemes. The featured study on heart care (Dickson et al., 2011) offered an example of a criterion scheme because the group from the clinic of heart failure patients met particular criteria, whereas the featured study on vaping culture (Colditz et al., 2017) used a random purposeful scheme where cases were randomly chosen from Twitter postings. Finally, the featured study on postconflict risk (Taylor et al., 2017) demonstrated multilevel sampling and a convenience scheme where the individuals were chosen based on their availability and willingness to participate, such as the youth, mothers, and fathers from Vukovar, Croatia. Sampling decisions have important implications for interpretations of study outcomes.

Creating and selecting strategies for generating data offers many options. The featured studies offer some more traditional combinations of data as well as more innovative ones. Among the more traditional combinations are the focus groups or interviews with questionnaires or quantified scales in three of the featured studies. The three featured studies that are considered the most complex involved data generating strategies that had been specially tailored to the populations (e.g., social media and life history interviews). The featured studies describe their various mixing strategies as linking, converging, or developing. A linking strategy (also called connecting) has one data strand inform the sampling of the other. Converging (also called merging) brings together quantitative and qualitative data for analysis and comparison. A developing strategy (also called building) occurs when one form of data informs the data collection of the other data strand (Fetters, Curry, & Creswell, 2013). Despite the potential desire of some researchers to predetermine mixing strategies, under some more complex conditions, the mixing strategy can emerge because it depends on how the intent of data mixing and logic of data strands ultimately play out during implementation (Bazeley, 2018). When describing complex mixed methods research design, consider the information available from the following questions related to logic considerations for the study:

- What is the desired timing of data strands with respect to one another?
- What conceptual weighting of the data strands might be appropriate?
- What mixed sampling strategies might be suitable?
- What data generating strategies might be appropriate for the sample?
- What are relevant mixing strategies?

Consider Researcher Spotlight 7.4, which introduces some design challenges faced by those who are new to mixed methods research from the perspective of a professor in the Department of Curriculum and Instruction in the College of Education & Health Professions at the University of Arkansas – Fayetteville (USA).

Table 7.2 Summary of logic features of the six featured mixed methods studies

| Featured study | Data strands | | | Strategies | |
	Timing	Weighting	Mixed sampling	Generating data	Mixing strands
Law clients (Chui & Cheng, 2017)	Sequential	Quantitative	Nested (stratified purposive)	Quantitative questionnaire with young offenders and follow-up qualitative interviews	Linking
Postconflict risk (Taylor et al., 2017)	Sequential	—	Multilevel (convenience)	Qualitative focus groups with youth, mothers, and fathers and follow-up youth quantitative questionnaires	Linking
Heart care (Dickson et al., 2011)	Concurrent	Equal	Identical (criterion)	Heart failure patient qualitative interviews and quantitative standardized measures	Converging
Safe places (Zea et al., 2014)	Sequential	Qualitative	Nested (snowball)	Qualitative life history interviews and focus groups with internally displaced Colombian gay and bisexual men and transwomen and follow-up quantitative survey	Linking
Leadership competencies (Strudsholm et al., 2016)	Sequential	Qualitative	Nested (mixed purposeful)	Literature review, online survey with public health workforce and leaders, focus group webinars with public health leaders, modified Delphi	Developing, linking
Vaping culture (Colditz et al., 2017)	Parallel	Quantitative	Identical (random purposeful)	Twitter, social media platform with electronic nicotine delivery system	Converging

 Researcher Spotlight 7.4

Kathleen Collins on the pressing challenge for novice mixed methods researchers to focus the design on the research intent, not on methods

I teach graduate-level courses and present workshops on design and application of mixed methods research at selective universities and conferences. These courses and workshops draw novice researchers who represent different disciplines and who have varying levels of experience designing qualitative and quantitative research. Typically, these novice researchers share the perception that mixed methods research design is a method-centric approach. A method-centric approach is to assume incorrectly that the choice of method drives design decisions rather than assume correctly that the choice of question drives these decisions. A challenge that I experience is how to expand novice researchers' levels of awareness that mixed methods research is a cyclical process centred on addressing a research question or multiple interrelated questions. Also, I stress in these courses and in the workshops that the research process begins by articulating one's philosophical assumptions about what constitutes a viable research question and what comprises quality data. The process continues with the researcher formulating decisions in the areas of research design, sampling design, and validity design.

Attend to Ethical Concerns Guiding Research Procedures

Research procedures are guided by the three principles for the conduct of ethical research: respect for persons, concern for welfare, and concern for justice. Specifically, mixed methods researchers would benefit from increased attention to **research ethics** in their designs. This is because there is a dearth of literature about ethical issues specific to mixed methods research (Collins, Onwuegbuzie, & Johnson, 2012; Hesse-Biber & Johnson, 2013) and there is a potential for research ethics concerns to become intensified for different designs (Hesse-Biber, 2010). The potential for unique ethical issues can be attributed to the definition of mixed methods research as requiring the collection, analysis, and integration of two types of data followed by the generation of inferences which address the study purpose. Indeed, as Hesse-Biber and Johnson (2013, p. 106) noted: 'Ethical issues reside across the research process. It is crucial for [mixed methods] researchers to continually reflect on their ethical standpoints throughout their research project, as they may encounter thorny ethical issues after [a mixed methods] project is in progress.' Among the key challenges for mixed methods researchers is the need to attend to ethical issues specific to mixed methods research in addition to those inherent in qualitative and quantitative research in isolation (for further guidance, see NIH Office of Behavioral and Social Sciences, 2018; Curry & Nunez-Smith, 2015; Plano Clark & Ivankova, 2016). It is noteworthy that all but one of the featured studies described having applied for and received study approval from an institutional ethical review board before work commenced, and there was no mention of any further amendments during the studies (see Table 7.3). Despite the best intentions of some researchers to mitigate ethical issues by proactively planning for anticipated issues, researchers must also be prepared to respond to emergent issues at any time during the process, because issues depend on how the procedures ultimately play out in their implementation (Hesse-Biber & Johnson, 2013).

Respect for persons encompasses the treatment of persons and their data involved in the mixed methods research process. Respecting autonomy is a key consideration; seeking a person's free, informed, and ongoing consent is an important research mechanism. In so doing, the consent process requires that a person's choice to participate is free and without interference; informed and aware of the research purpose and procedures; and confirmed on an ongoing basis, with opportunities to withdraw once the research has started. Among the ethical issues that may be introduced by procedures inherent in mixed methods research are ongoing consent between more than one data strand, explanation of the study procedures, and seeking of informed consent. In particular, two of the featured studies described seeking consent for the different data collection methods. Interestingly, both these studies featured online questionnaires followed by in-person interviews or focus groups. While one study did not elaborate much on explaining or seeking consent, they did refer to the exclusion of youth without parental consent and thus demonstrated the researchers' mindfulness of working with vulnerable populations where their ability to exercise autonomy may be compromised due to youth, cognitive impairment, or other issues.

Limited evidence was noted for demonstrating concern for welfare among the designs of the featured studies. Concern for welfare involves researchers ensuring adequate protection of participants by minimizing harm and maximizing benefits of the mixed methods research. The featured study on safe places (Zea et al., 2014) stands out for its integration of an

Table 7.3 Summary of ethics concerns of the six featured mixed methods studies

Featured study	Respect for persons	Concern for welfare	Concern for justice
Law clients (Chui & Cheng, 2017)	• Procedures for explaining the study to those completing the questionnaire • Separate procedures for written consent for the follow-up interviews	• Assurance of confidentiality for the questionnaire • Private room for interviews • Pseudonyms used in data transcription	• Questionnaire recruitment through social workers of youth from a transitional housing facility for young offenders and various youth outreach teams • Purposive sampling of young offenders who completed the questionnaire and equal private/public lawyers
Postconflict risk (Taylor et al., 2017)	• All youth and parent participants provided signed assent and consent for interviews • Youth provided assent prior to the survey	• Modest financial incentive for interview • Reference to exclusion of youth without parental consent	• Recruitment through well-established collaboration and specified recruitment procedures • Exclusion of youth without parental consent
Heart care (Dickson et al., 2011)	• Procedures for written consent, explanation of study procedures	• Modest financial incentive was described	• Recruited by clinicians because participants were clinic patients and met specific eligibility and gave verbal consent to be referred to the research team
Safe places (Zea et al., 2014)*	• Procedures described for informed consent	• Life history interviews through egalitarian/non-coercive dialogue • Participants had complete control over what and how much to disclose • Confidentiality was assured and carefully guarded • Participant benefits included enhanced access to information and care	• Recruitment was undertaken by developing partnerships and participant trust • Eligibility criteria clearly described • Administration of survey ensured wide distribution within the target population
Leadership competencies (Strudsholm et al., 2016)	• Online consent form for survey • Procedures for informed consent for focus groups • Procedures for informed consent for modified Delphi process	—	• Survey recruitment through wide distribution of email to membership of seven public health professional associations • Recruitment for focus groups by email to a particular set of leadership • Recruit panel of public health experts for modified Delphi process
Vaping culture (Colditz et al., 2017)	• Twitter feed was publicly accessible	• User's handle removed prior to coding to protect confidentiality	• No evidence

*This study alone was not described as having gained institutional approval by ethics review boards.

egalitarian/non-coercive dialogue approach and it was the only study to highlight benefits related to health care access. The researcher is obliged to assess and take all reasonable measures to augment the potential benefits and mitigate the foreseeable risks to confidentiality and ensure security of data storage. Assurances of confidentiality were only provided to participants in two of the studies; the use of pseudonyms or blinded data was only mentioned in two studies as well. There was only evidence of explicit participant benefits in three of the studies (two referred to monetary incentives) and no mentions of foreseeable risks, discomfort, or adverse effects including any limits to confidentiality. Interestingly, there was no mention of data storage at all.

Justice refers to the need to treat people fairly and equitably and concerns all who participate in the mixed methods research; carefully considered recruitment strategies are an important research mechanism. The researcher should clearly state and justify the criteria for inclusion and exclusion and should be especially vigilant not to perpetuate systemic privileging of research involving specific populations at the exclusion of others. All but one of the featured studies described their recruitment strategies. No recruitment was necessary for the featured study on vaping culture (Colditz et al., 2017) because the researchers retrieved public Twitter content. The featured studies also included details about inclusion and eligibility criteria, with a few delineating exclusion criteria. When describing complex mixed methods research design, consider the information available from the following questions related to ethics considerations:

- What procedures promote respect for persons?
- What procedures mitigate concerns for welfare?
- What procedures uphold justice in the study?

Consider Researcher Spotlight 7.5, describing the challenges mixed methods researchers face under conditions of complexity related to developing relevant expertise for thinking mindfully about research methods and designs, from the perspective of a prominent mixed methods research scholar and adjunct professor at Western Sydney University (Australia).

 **Researcher Spotlight 7.5**

Pat Bazeley on challenges with designing mixed methods research for adapting to the research conditions

My desire, ultimately, is to get people to just think about (and be excited by) doing research, using whatever methods are appropriate and accessible at the time, rather than thinking about and deciding first whether they are going to use qualitative, quantitative, or even mixed methods, however that might be defined. The challenges in doing so are threefold: first, to break down stereotypical, rigidly divided views of how research methods should be thought about and taught; second, to have people teaching research methods who are adequately trained and experienced, so that they can move beyond dependence on a textbook with 'recipes' for doing research, and the limitations of their own doctoral project, to teach (and demonstrate to) students how to flexibly respond to the complexity of a new research problem; and third, to have people think about writing research results that address the topic of their research, rather than the methods they used to investigate it.

Assimilate Procedural Adaptations Guiding Researcher Responses

Among the key procedural adaptations guiding researcher responses are the extent of possible agility of the procedures, the ability of the design to assimilate adaptations as needed due to feasibility constraints, and the fit of any existing design typology to the description. There is a need for agility in data procedures and for researchers willing (and able) to anticipate and adapt to the unexpected. This means that a focus on planning is important, but so also is navigating the research process by adapting to changing conditions. It likely means that aspects of research design such as data sources, participants, and contexts may change in terms of what data is collected, who the data is collected from, and where the data is collected. Only three featured studies report procedural adaptations during implementation and only two were considered evolving designs (see Table 7.4). Feasibility constraints can refer to anything that limits the ability to achieve the design – from human resources to necessary time. Not surprisingly, increased resources are highlighted as being a challenge for researchers because more of everything is needed in mixed methods research than would likely be necessary in either qualitative and quantitative research alone (Creswell & Plano Clark, 2018). Increased monetary needs have been noted by those undertaking both types of data collection, ranging from increased costs of transcription to incentives. Increased researcher capacity needs have been noted, because researchers need expertise not only in qualitative and quantitative data collection and analysis but also in mixed methods research. Increased time has been noted by those undertaking sequential points of interface simply because of the need to complete one data strand before beginning the other. Despite the best intentions to mitigate resource and time issues by planning ahead, researchers may face emergent issues at any time because of how procedures ultimately play out.

Once you have described the design, then you can assess whether the mixing purposes and data procedures are categorized within an existing mixed methods design typology. If it fits an existing design typology, it can be described more succinctly. All of the featured studies described their designs using a familiar typology. You will note that the design typology *multiphase* of the featured study on leadership competencies (Strudsholm et al., 2016) does not convey any design information about the timing of the data strands or mixing purpose, and that in the recent edition of their book Creswell and Plano Clark (2018) no longer refer to it. When describing complex mixed methods research design, consider the information available from the following questions related to ethics considerations:

- What are some possible ways of embedding agility in the study procedures?
- What do I know about the feasibility constraints for the study?
- Would any design typology be suitable for the study description after all?

Table 7.4 Summary of procedural adaptations of the six featured mixed methods studies

Featured study	Design typology	Procedural adaptations	Nature of design
Law clients (Chui & Cheng, 2017)	Explanatory sequential	No evidence: intended timeframes were reported as met	Fixed
Postconflict risk (Taylor et al., 2017)	Exploratory sequential	No evidence	Fixed
Heart care (Dickson et al., 2011)	Concurrent triangulation	Adaptations during interviews were considered deviations	Fixed
Safe places (Zea et al., 2014)	Transformative	Many adaptions were made to procedures, and the transformative design was responsive to study findings and to upholding the desire to create non-coercive dialogue	Evolving
Leadership competencies (Strudsholm et al., 2016)	Multiphase	Many adaptions to procedures were made in the focus group phase in response to recruitment challenges	Evolving
Vaping culture (Colditz et al., 2017)	Convergent parallel	No evidence	Fixed

Examine Researcher Spotlight 7.6 highlighting the challenges wicked mixed methods research problems present and the need for preparing future mixed methods researchers for the pressing issues they will tackle, from the perspective of an assistant professor at the University of Michigan (USA).

 **Researcher Spotlight 7.6**

Tim Guetterman on designing mixed methods research under conditions of complexity

In my view, the two most important concepts in conducting mixed methods under conditions of complexity are to have a rationale behind our methodological decisions, and to understand what methodological options already exist. Under what conditions is a certain design appropriate? How do we make that decision with intentionality? Decisions about methods depend on your research questions. Jennifer Greene (2007, p. 97) reminds us that 'Methodology is ever the servant of purpose, never the master'. Principles that guide all of my mixed methods work are to have a rationale and to employ systematic procedures, something I learned from John Creswell and Vicki Plano Clark. That means that we do not simply collect some data or apply terms like mixed methods or grounded theory, but that we are employing systematic proce-dures in conducting research. Because mixed methods is still developing, we all have a great opportunity right now to write methodological articles that guide other researchers.

Features that Engage Readers with Complex Mixed Methods Research Integrations

It is advantageous for researchers to distinguish their studies. Research designs are a great place to start differentiating a study under conditions of complexity. The following list pro-vides some ideas from my own experiences as researcher, as a reviewer of mixed methods research proposals for funding and of manuscripts for publication, and from working with graduate students as an instructor, supervisor, and examiner. See also the featured studies for illustrative examples of some of these engaging features.

- *Seek unique recruitment and sampling strategies for populations to study in the complex mixed methods research design.* There are various places to recruit and strategies for mixed sampling. Review the literature for ideas. This will help you create reader interest right from the start.
- *Focus on atypical combinations of data collection and analysis strategies.* Consider new ways of integrating technology into your data collection and analysis strategies. Review resources for ways that others have not sought to combine before. This helps position the unique contributions of your data and avoid replicating the work of others.
- *Introduce your mixed methods design uniquely.* Catch readers' attention with an interesting name and visual representation for your design. Review the literature about diagramming conventions and then adapt as needed. This will help clearly communicate your design to the reader.
- *Assume unconventional perspectives for framing your mixed methods design.* Consider new roles for theory or theoretical perspectives, involve research team members from disciplines not yet reflected in studies, or assume research paradigms that have not yet been adopted in the literature. This will help you see beyond what might be expected of your complex research design.

In Guiding Tip 7.1, a research professor in the Department of Adult Education and Youth Development at the University of South Africa offers advice for enhancing innovations in mixed methods research designs.

 Guiding Tip 7.1

Norma Romm advising new ways of thinking about mixed methods research designs

Put the focus less on formulating research designs to guide research and to later classify it, and more on innovative ways of working with key participants and stakeholders to create opportunities for developing (what are felt to be) constructive discourses and actions via the research process.

Innovations in Describing Complex Mixed Methods Research Integrations

Researchers working under conditions of complexity are tasked with embedding agility within the procedures and explaining the frame, logic, ethics, and procedural considerations underpinning the study's design. Also important, yet often underreported, are details about any feasibility influences and possible procedural adaptations in a written proposal and report. Descriptions of research designs tend to be very typology-based. The following ideas are often used in structuring a methods section. Identify the mixed methods design typology, and then the logic of the selected design dictates the presentation of the descriptions of participants, qualitative and quantitative data collection and analysis procedures (Creswell & Plano Clark, 2018; DeCuir-Gunby & Schutz, 2017). The lack of variation in structures can be attributable to the accessible guidance for those new to the field through examples in instructional resources and published manuscripts. It is not surprising that great variability in level of detail occurs, yet several writers do suggest the need for adequate information to convey the rigour of the qualitative and quantitative data procedures as well as increasing attention to the procedures for integration (Bazeley, 2018) and hopefully (in my view at least) to ethical considerations. Sometimes the information related to procedures for enhancing the rigour and conduct of ethical research is embedded within the data procedures rather than in standalone sections. The challenges with a typology-based approach that dominate descriptions of methods are that under some conditions of complexity, predetermining the procedures, fitting them into an existing typology, or implementing a design as planned is simply not possible. The dominant typology-based approach to mixed methods designs is problematic as researchers employ mixed methods under conditions of increasing complexity because developing new ways of integration through integrative thinking with complexity will be key to expanding the designs we use. I believe access to illustrative examples will be key to building researcher confidence in learning how to plan, implement, and convey innovative designs under conditions of complexity.

Descriptions of complex mixed methods research designs can appear quite different across studies due to the differing research conditions under which the studies are conducted. In the same way, the methods section in a study's report can appear quite different from that in the research proposal because understandings naturally emerged and new information was assimilated. Specific for research designs, differences can arise from adapting the data procedures to emerging feasibility influences. There is an ongoing iterative process of describing complex mixed methods research integrations: it begins with a proposal, continues during implementation, and is finalized with the writing of the report once the research is completed. To that end, variations are expected in structures across the proposals and reports that you will encounter. The inherent nature of different researcher perspectives, research designs, and stages of research commands it. In this section I describe two innovations for communicating and tracking the descriptions of complex mixed methods research integrations.

Diagrams Representing Understandings of Study Designs

Over the last decade, it has become increasingly common to see design diagrams in the methods section of a mixed methods research proposal and report. The logistical challenge of describing in words the multiple procedures involved in a mixed methods design can be (somewhat) alleviated through the complementary use of a visual representation. A visual representation can be used in one of two ways: as an advance organizer (before the written description) or as a summary (following the written description). Extensive guidance on the design of diagrams is accessible yet varied: from a simple notation system first described by Morse (1991) to the more detailed system of Ivankova, Creswell, and Stick (2006) and more recently of Creswell and Plano Clark (2018). The notation system has been widely adopted, and many illustrative examples exist to guide researchers who adopt a typology-based approach. As we move beyond the existing typologies, there are few examples, yet the role of diagrams becomes intensified under conditions of complexity. Guest argues for using a visual representation of the research process as part of a detailed description for any complex study, saying 'Diagramming is critical for accurate and cogent description of complex study designs' (2013, p. 142). A diagram can reduce the number of words necessary for the design description, which is important for disseminating mixed methods studies with complex designs where word limitations associated with many peer-reviewed journals are challenging. The current notation system can be applied and expanded to diagrams for monitoring the evolutions in complex mixed methods designs as understandings of the integration procedures emerge.

Diagrams representing descriptions of complex mixed methods research can appear quite different across studies due to the differing information that might be available. In the same way, the design diagram in a report can be quite different from that in a proposal because understandings naturally emerged and new information was assimilated between the two products. A design generated by a descriptive approach to complex mixed methods research integrations represents the emerging understandings of design considerations from the design orientation of the research study alongside those of the points of interface. To focus on both units of reference represents a unique approach to describing the complex mixed methods research integrations. Yet I find this focus helpful because by making explicit my design considerations, I have a foundation upon which I can test and track my evolving understandings. This is important because this positions my researcher mindset as open to new possibilities of understandings for:

• Why the complex mixed methods research integrations address the study's need for integration
• How my understandings of the framing, logic, ethics, and procedure considerations for the study design evolve over time.

Descriptive designs can look different each time they are described because the diagram captures available information. Because of this, the diagram can also be used as a tool for monitoring evolving understandings of the design. In Figure 7.4, I provide a sample diagram conveying the procedures as described by the authors of the multiphase featured study on leadership competencies (Strudsholm et al., 2016). Note that the diagram is limited to my interpretation of the information described in the article about the framing, logic, ethical, and procedural information. Also note the places where information was provided and where it is missing – for example, the three points of interface are made more explicit, adaptations were made to the Phase III procedures, and analysis of Phase II lacked information.

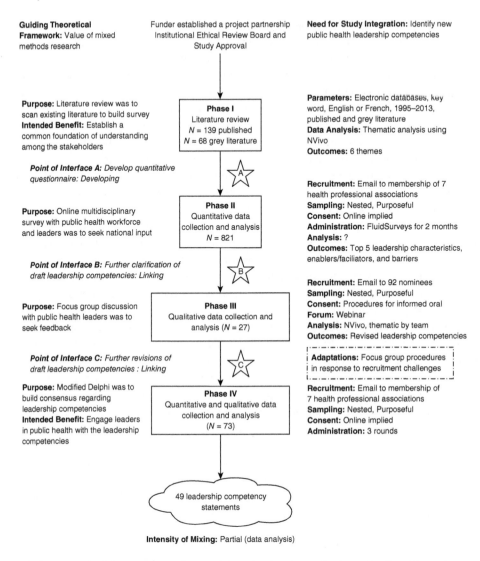

Guiding Theoretical Framework: Value of mixed methods research

Funder established a project partnership
Institutional Ethical Review Board and Study Approval

Need for Study Integration: Identify new public health leadership competencies

Purpose: Literature review was to scan existing literature to build survey
Intended Benefit: Establish a common foundation of understanding among the stakeholders

Phase I
Literature review
N = 139 published
N = 68 grey literature

Parameters: Electronic databases, key word, English or French, 1995–2013, published and grey literature
Data Analysis: Thematic analysis using NVivo
Outcomes: 6 themes

Point of Interface A: Develop quantitative questionnaire: Developing

Ⓐ

Purpose: Online multidisciplinary survey with public health workforce and leaders was to seek national input

Phase II
Quantitative data collection and analysis
N = 821

Recruitment: Email to membership of 7 health professional associations
Sampling: Nested, Purposeful
Consent: Online implied
Administration: FluidSurveys for 2 months
Analysis: ?
Outcomes: Top 5 leadership characteristics, enablers/facilitators, and barriers

Point of Interface B: Further clarification of draft leadership competencies: Linking

Ⓑ

Purpose: Focus group discussion with public health leaders was to seek feedback

Phase III
Qualitative data collection and analysis (*N* = 27)

Recruitment: Email to 92 nominees
Sampling: Nested, Purposeful
Consent: Procedures for informed oral
Forum: Webinar
Analysis: NVivo, thematic by team
Outcomes: Revised leadership competencies

Point of Interface C: Further revisions of draft leadership competencies : Linking

Ⓒ

Adaptations: Focus group procedures in response to recruitment challenges

Purpose: Modified Delphi was to build consensus regarding leadership competencies
Intended Benefit: Engage leaders in public health with the leadership competencies

Phase IV
Quantitative and qualitative data collection and analysis
(*N* = 73)

Recruitment: Email to membership of 7 health professional associations
Sampling: Nested, Purposeful
Consent: Online implied
Administration: 3 rounds

49 leadership competency statements

Intensity of Mixing: Partial (data analysis)

Figure 7.4   Sample diagram conveying framing, logic, ethical, and procedural considerations of complex mixed methods research integrations

Source: Author generated from narrative information provided by Strudsholm et al. (2016).

Writing Ideas for Describing Research Integrations

It is uncommon to see a researcher explicitly convey their design for a mixed methods research study as incomplete and under development. It is also infrequent practice for researchers to describe the adaptations to their design plans. This is unfortunate, as I find such accounts especially useful for mixed methods researchers who are new to implementing designs under conditions of complexity. This is important to position the researchers' mindset as open to new possibilities of understandings for:

- What feasibility influences are considered relevant for planning the complex design
- What innovative research designs are sought from the procedures identified.

Under conditions of complexity, understandings of the considerations for the complex design are considered to be evolving. The researcher is tasked with the following question: How can the existing design approaches and understandings of design considerations contribute to describing the complex mixed methods research integrations necessary to guide the study procedures for integrations?

Consider common structures for organizing the methods section of a mixed methods research report. I often use headings to organize my sections. There is no set format; researchers should follow their own preferences. Preparing heading structures allows me to review the organizational flow of my writing and to seek feedback before I engage in the writing process. Examine the writing ideas described below and the four related illustrative excerpts from the featured study on leadership competencies (Strudsholm et al., 2016). These illustrate the benefits of using a multiphase mixed methods design to identify public health leadership competencies that could be applied to public health practice across Canada. This structure reflects a focus on both units of reference: those of the research study and of the two points of interface. We now know that under conditions of complexity, many considerations in describing the research design are not yet known and are influenced by changing conditions and evolving understandings of feasibility influences. Examine the four tasks involved in an authentic design for guiding the problem that is being pursued:

- *Articulate the study's needs for integration by creating interest in the frameworks guiding the study.* Here, familiarize readers with understandings of the potential for the study to generate new understandings. Researchers generally begin by linking the study's need for integration to the complexity of research design. The sentences that follow should introduce the mixed methods literature related to its usefulness for addressing complex problems. Key reasons for pursuing the research problem using a mixed methods design are summarized in a single sentence, if at all possible. You may find the following questions useful for guiding descriptions of the integration need of the study.
  - ○ What do readers need to better understand about the reasons underpinning the use of a mixed methods research approach rather than either qualitative or quantitative approaches alone?
  - ○ What do readers need to know about the need for integrations to generate new understandings necessary for addressing the complex mixed methods research problem?
  - ○ What do readers need to know about the guiding frameworks in order to better understand their potential for guiding mixed methods research?

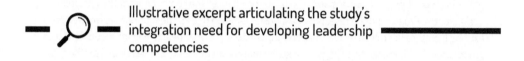

Illustrative excerpt articulating the study's integration need for developing leadership competencies

The debate over what constitutes a mixed methods research continues (Johnson, Onwuegbuzie, & Turner, 2007). The work plan [was] developed for the Public Health Leadership Competencies Project, hereafter called the Project ... A growing body of literature strongly

(Continued)

(Continued)

supports the use of mixed methods as appropriate and necessary for research quality (Ivankova & Kawamura, 2010). Much has been written (e.g., Johnson & Onwuegbuzie, 2004; Weir & Fouche, 2015) about research designs that involve the use of mixed methods research approaches in order to investigate complex problems, such as those in health care and public health. One challenge of mixed methods, however, is methodological congruence (Richards & Morse, 2013; Thurston et al., 2008) … The study design and methods presented in this article were used in the Project, with the aim of articulating leadership competencies for public health practice in Canada.

Source: Strudsholm et al. (2016, pp. 1–2). Used with permission from Sage.

- *Convey the mixing details related to the study by referring to the desired intensity of mixing, weighting of data strands, and timing of data strands.* Here, researchers illuminate how the data strands contribute to the study's overall need for integration. Researchers identify the desired intensity of mixing (partial or full), weighting of data strands (qualitative, quantitative, or equal emphasis), and timing of data strands (sequential, concurrent, or embedded). Key details of logic for the study are summarized in a single sentence, if at all possible. The following questions are useful for guiding descriptions of the mixing details of the study:
    - What do readers need to better understand the reasons underpinning the mixing details?
    - What do readers need to know about the integrative potential for each data strand to contribute to the study's overall need for integration?
    - What do readers need to know about the design logic, in order to assess fit with an existing mixed methods design typology?

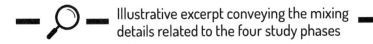 Illustrative excerpt conveying the mixing details related to the four study phases

A focus on process and points of intersection within a mixed methods design provides means of accurately describing the study and identifying critical checkpoints along a study's progression. These checkpoints may correspond with markers along a decision trail and also signal opportunities for iterative reflection and verification … Table 1 represents the elements of the Project designed to support congruence and to elucidate points at which reflection and decisions regarding Project progress were made. The table summarizes the components of the research design for the Project and the research questions(s) for each phase. The four phases focused on existing literature (literature review), national input (survey), public health leaders' feedback (focus groups), and building consensus regarding leadership competencies (modified Delphi method).

Source: Strudsholm et al. (2016, p. 2). Used with permission from Sage.

- *Rationalize procedures for each point of interface for addressing the complex research problems and mixing purposes focused on innovation.* Here, researchers illuminate the purpose of and procedures guiding each point of interface and potential contributions to the overall intensity of mixing for the study. Key ethics, recruitment, sampling, data collection, and analysis procedures for the data strands are summarized. The following questions may be useful in guiding descriptions of the point of interface:

o What do readers need to know about the data procedure activities related to ethics, recruitment, sampling, data collection, and analysis to have confidence in the rigour of each data strand?

o What do readers need to know about the contribution of each point of interface to the study's overall need for integration?

o What do readers need to know about the mixing purpose of each point of interface to assess the fit of the data procedures to the study's overall design?

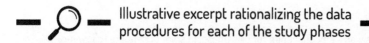 **Illustrative excerpt rationalizing the data procedures for each of the study phases**

The survey was developed using FluidSurveys™ software and based on the results of Phase 1, including lists of knowledge areas, skills, behaviors, enablers, and barriers identified in the literature. Participants were asked to rank the top 5 items in each list. The opportunity for comments was available in all components of the survey. An online consent form that included a link to the survey was distributed widely via e-mail to the membership of seven public health professional associations, remaining live for 2 months, from November 20, 2013, to January 20, 2014. Responses were collected from all seven disciplines from across Canada ... The Phase III objective was to assemble responses from recognized leaders in public health about the results of the online survey ... and to capture details about the context of public health leadership. Data collection was undertaken using a focus group technique (Meadows, Strudsholm, Vollman, Thurston, & Henderson, 2014). Participants for the focus groups were nominated by members of the [Expert Advisory Committee] as being experts in public health. The 92 nominees were from across Canada and worked at all levels of the public health hierarchy. Recruitment for each focus group was undertaken through an e-mail invitation to nominees that briefly described the overall Project and provided a summary of the online survey results. A copy of the University-approved consent form also was sent with the invitation ... The Delphi process is a flexible group facilitation technique that uses an iterative multistage process. It is designed to transform opinion into group consensus through several rounds of structured questionnaires or surveys (Hasson & Keeney, 2011). In this Project, the Delphi panelists were asked to participate in three Delphi rounds in which they completed an online survey designed to collect both qualitative and quantitative data. In each round, an e-mail invitation was sent to each panelist and included a consent form and link to the online survey. Informed consent was implied by willing participation in the survey.

Source: Strudsholm et al. (2016, pp. 3–6). Used with permission from Sage.

• *Describe feasibility evidence for procedural adaptations. Here, researchers explain the procedural adaptations in response to changing conditions.* Key feasibility influences and their impact on the planned procedures are summarized. Researchers may find the following questions useful for guiding their descriptions of procedural adaptations:

○ What do readers need to know about feasibility considerations in order to better understand their potential influence on procedural adaptations?

○ What do readers need to know about the integration procedures in order to better understand anticipated and potentially emerging feasibility considerations?

○ What do readers need to know about the design considerations in order to better understand feasibility constraints on the planned procedures?

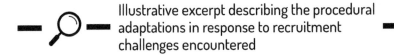

Illustrative excerpt describing the procedural adaptations in response to recruitment challenges encountered

Recruiting participants was a key challenge for this phase. In spite of sending follow-up reminders and receiving signed consent forms from those who stated that they would participate, each focus group had members who did not show up. As it became apparent that the number of participants was going to be low, the research team decided to invite all nominees again and added a fifth focus group.

Source: Strudsholm et al. (2016, p. 2). Used with permission from Sage.

CHAPTER CHECK-IN

1   Can you discern the differences and similarities in the designs of the integration procedures across the six featured studies? Compare how the authors of at least two studies describe the following and consider what your analysis tells you about their descriptions:

- Preliminary framing considerations
- Design logic considerations
- Ongoing ethical considerations.

2   Can you recognize hazards of design orientation effects and the strategies for avoiding them when designing study integrations under conditions of complexity? Select a published study in an area that is of interest to you or one of the featured studies.

- Examine the study limitations and areas for future directions. Select one idea to pursue relating to a complex problem.
- Sketch preliminary design ideas for a related complex mixed methods research study. What theoretical frameworks could guide the study? What study needs for integration might be involved? What is the intended intensity of mixing for the study? (Use Table 7.1 to guide your thinking.)
- Briefly describe how you would go about building the logic underpinning the complex mixed methods research design. (Use Figure 7.2 to guide your thinking.) For example:

   ○ What might be the desired timing of data strands with respect to one another?
   ○ What might be the relevant mixing strategies?
   ○ What conceptual weighting of the data strands might be appropriate?

- Briefly describe how you would go about anticipating the ethical issues for the complex mixed methods research design. (Use Figure 7.4 to guide your thinking.) For example:
  - What issues related to respect for persons might arise in the procedures?
  - What issues related to concerns for welfare might appear?
  - What issues related to justice might need attention?
- Create a summary table (see Table B.2).

3 Can you design a complex mixed methods research integration for a study that is of interest to you? Apply the guiding questions presented in this chapter to structure an outline:

- Describe the study's need for integration and frameworks guiding the design, in a few sentences.
- Discuss the desired mixing details by referring to the extent of mixing, weighting of data strands, and timing of data strands.
- Present the purpose and procedures for each point of interface and provide a rationale for its contribution to the study.
- Describe any feasibility considerations that are likely to influence the procedures and how the procedures might be adapted.
- Review the draft (see Figure 7.4) and use that description to create a diagram of your design. Note which details are present in your description and which are not yet known.

4 What features for engaging readers can you use to begin creating your complexity-sensitive mixed methods study proposal? Access a complex mixed methods research problem that you would like to pursue. Sketch the problem and need for the study. Select one of the features for engaging readers that fits with your study and write a brief description of an engaging design for addressing this problem.

KEY CHAPTER CONCEPTS

This chapter advances the fourth adaptive practice for guiding a complexity-sensitive approach to mixed methods research. It addresses the question: What does describing complex mixed methods research integrations involve and how can key design considerations and evolving feasibility influences be recognized, promoted, and conveyed? The rationale for describing complex mixed methods research integrations is grounded in the need to guide design implementations when the understandings are considered to be evolving and incomplete. The purpose of describing integration procedures is to create designs that reflect the study needs rather than being constrained to fitting into existing design typologies. Opportunities for creating more authentic accounts of integration procedures are presented, as are design orientations to avoid. Four interdependent and iterative tasks guide the descriptive design approach: articulate the framing considerations guiding the study; examine the logic considerations underpinning the design; attend to the ethical considerations during the research; and assimilate procedural adaptations throughout the implementation. Features that will engage readers include seeking unique populations to recruit and focusing on atypical combinations of data collection and analysis strategies. Innovations in describing complex mixed methods research problems involve visual diagrams and writing ideas. The next chapter introduces the complexity-sensitive practices related to developing the capacity of mixed methods research interactions.

.... FURTHER READINGS

The following resources are offered as introductory references for research designs and describing research integrations. The list should not be considered exhaustive. Readers are encouraged to seek out additional readings in the end-of-book reference list. Readings denoted with an asterisk are available on the companion website for this book.

Creswell, J. W. (2014). *Research design: Qualitative, quantitative, and mixed methods approaches* (4th ed.). Thousand Oaks, CA: Sage.

John Creswell presents an excellent resource across three approaches to research. Using the research process as the organizing structure allows the reader to see how each approach is operationalized in a study.

*Guest, G. (2013). Describing mixed methods research: An alternative to typologies. *Journal of Mixed Methods Research, 7,* 141–151. doi: 10.1177/1558689812461179.

Greg Guest offers a thoughtful critique of the use of typologies for designing mixed methods research. He also offers an alternative approach to design, shifting the focus from the research study to the individual points of interface among data strands.

*Hall, B., and Howard, K. (2008). A synergistic approach: Conducting mixed methods research with typological and systemic design considerations. *Journal of Mixed Methods Research, 2*(3), 248–269. doi: 10.1177/1558689808314622.

Bronwyn Hall and Kirsten Howard described the core set of principles of a synergistic approach to bring the principles of typological and systemic design approaches together. They describe the synergistic approach within the context of mixing methods in a randomized controlled trial.

Teddlie, C., & Tashakkori, A. (2009). *Foundations of mixed methods research.* Thousand Oaks, CA: Sage.

Charles Teddlie and Abbas Tashakkori provide an introduction to and overview of the field of mixed methods research that follows the process from design to conclusions. Of particular interest is the typology of designs presented by the authors.

Apply your mixed methods knowledge with videos, activities, SAGE journal articles and project templates at **https://study.sagepub.com/poth**

8

DEVELOPING CAPACITY OF COMPLEX MIXED METHODS RESEARCH INTERACTIONS

.... KEY CHAPTER QUESTIONS

By the end of this chapter, you will be able to answer the following questions:

- Why develop capacity of mixed methods research interactions?
- What opportunities exist to promote conditions for complex mixed methods research interactions?
- Why can leader-centric interactions become hazardous for mixed methods researchers?
- What guides the capacity development of mixed methods interactions?
- What features engage readers with complex mixed methods research interactions?
- What writing and diagram innovations are useful for explaining the integrative outcomes of mixed methods research interactions?

.... NEW CHAPTER TERMS

By the end of this chapter, you will be familiar with the following terms:

- Complex mixed methods research interactions
- Leader-centric effects
- Integrative interactions
- Team-centric leadership style

This chapter advances the adaptive practice for guiding a complexity-sensitive approach to mixed methods research. It addresses the question: *What does developing capacity for mixed methods research interactions involve, and how can the conditions for emergence among those involved in the research and evolving social influences be recognized, promoted, and conveyed?* Consider a time when you worked with other researchers on a project with a shared goal. Would you describe your experience as more like individuals working independently but in parallel and creating an outcome reflective of combined efforts, or as individuals working collaboratively and creating an outcome that was greater than the sum of the individual efforts? While both scenarios involve two or more individuals connected by social relationships based on some similarities such as a shared research goal, the latter describes the outcomes from interactions among researchers working as a team, and the former describes collective efforts among researchers working as a group. Research teams and working groups represent worthy configurations for drawing upon individual contributions, yet most complex mixed methods research problems require the integration of diverse member expertise, experiences, and intuitions beyond what is accessible from individual members. Thus, distinguishing the desirable interactions becomes essential when working under conditions of complexity because *not all research groups are teams and not all research teams can be considered integrative* – even though most literature has yet to define a conceptual and practical distinction among the terms. Let us now consider how developing **complex mixed methods research interactions** is unique.

Initial research on mixed methods research interactions among members has established the usefulness of teams and points to benefits and challenges as well as the need for careful formation and development (Bowers et al., 2013; NIH Office of Behavioral and Social Sciences, 2018; O'Cathain, Murphy, & Nicholl, 2008). Research teams have increasingly been recognized as an optimal configuration for addressing mixed methods research problems (Curry et al., 2012, 2013), and especially for those considered to be wicked and complex problems (Mertens et al., 2016a). A well-written introduction to a mixed methods study has involved highlighting the compositions of those involved in the research by briefly describing the relationship among research members (if applicable), background expertise, and expected (or realized) contributions. In so doing, researchers promote the study's feasibility by explaining the researchers' collective capacity for addressing the research problem which then sets the stage for the entire mixed methods research proposal or report. Ideally the study conveys cohesive reasoning about the contributors and their individual and collective contributions to the research, including details about the study need for various disciplinary and methodological expertise and the people who will fulfil the necessary study roles for realizing the anticipated study outcomes. Further details are then interspersed across the research proposal or report using various section headings such as descriptions of researcher members and research team composition. Let us now consider the desirability of an adaptive practice focused on forming and developing capacity for complex mixed methods research interactions.

Among the initial challenges for mixed methods researchers addressing complex problems are identifying researchers with suitably diverse expertise and experiences and then developing the integrative capacity among researchers for addressing a problem that has uncertain background influences and study methods. As researchers begin to work together, team members must capitalize on their differences in perspectives, experiences, and assumptions to contribute yet-to-be-known roles for addressing the complex mixed methods research problem. As the team develops collaborative routines, it is hoped that members create conditions of emergence harnessing the integrative potential of individuals, and then sustain these interactions for generating yet-to-be-known insights addressing the complex problem that are greater than the sum of individuals' contributions. This situation contrasts starkly with mixed methods research problems and interactions that are considered less complex because the necessary expertise, researcher roles, study contexts, and study methods for addressing the problem are well established, and fewer background, environmental, social, and mixing influences enable greater predictability of outcomes. To that end, developing **integrative interactions** in mixed methods research is the focus of this chapter because the need for ongoing adaptations to research conditions has important impacts on how we form research teams with relevant diversity, what interactions generate integrative outcomes, and why development of integrative capacities is desirable. Optimizing mixed methods research interactions under conditions of complexity does not typically happen accidentally or speedily, rather the conditions for emergence result from the intentional development of integrative capacity over time.

Work on this chapter was informed by my experiences as a mixed methods researcher, research team leader, and member of diverse research teams as I have grappled with how to best advise those planning and tackling complex mixed methods research questions. Specifically, in seeking to develop the capacity involved in complex mixed methods research interactions, I draw upon my previous work exploring the role of mixed methods practitioners within educational research teams (Poth, 2012) and my understandings of others' work recognizing research teams as an optimal configuration for addressing mixed methods research problems (Curry et al., 2012, 2013). Importantly, this work is also shaped by my roles as graduate supervisor, supervisory committee member, and consultant to numerous students as they grapple with formulating, conducting, and reporting their own graduate work. It is important for me to clarify here, at the beginning of this chapter, that my use of research teams literally means those involved in the research. It should be obvious that while graduate programs assess students' ability to undertake research independently, students are *never really alone*. I am told students naturally form research teams, yet the contributions of those members understandably differ in scope. For some their supervisor will contribute greatly, whereas for others perhaps supervisory committee members, mentors or peers may fill those roles. Experience tells me that the extent to which others contribute to students' work varies greatly. Research is a social process and so it involves interactions among people and people are shaped by the context in which they live and were trained.

Embedding the featured mixed methods studies in this chapter reflects a continued effort to address the practice gap in many textbooks and to provide authentic examples of published articles that represent varying conditions of complexity related to research interactions. Distinguishing the important role for and describing how to intentionally focus on developing integrative mixed methods research interactions was essential because creating conditions for emergence remains elusive to many of us. From there we can strategize the development and innovations from integrative mixed methods research interactions. As a starting point to developing capacity, I distinguish the desirability and niche for integrative thinking with complexity for guiding mixed methods research interactions within a complexity-sensitive approach to mixed methods research. Then, I advance a developmental strategy for developing integrative capacity among those involved in mixed methods research under conditions of complexity. Finally, I identify features for engaging readers' and writing and diagram innovations useful for explaining the integrative capacity for mixed methods research interactions in proposals and reports.

Why Develop Capacity in Complex Mixed Methods Research Interactions?

Researchers are tasked with the responsibility of explaining their capacity for undertaking the research. For a complexity-sensitive mixed methods study, this involves developing the conditions for emergence among those involved in the research. The purpose of developing capacity for emergence is to generate novel insights for addressing complex mixed methods research problems that are greater than the sum of individual researcher contributions. The new approach for developing capacity in researchers and research teams responds to the dilemmas experienced with a lack of understanding of social influences on the integrations and availability of guiding practices. Thus, the traditional mixed methods research practice focused on predetermining the roles for researchers based on expertise for the study is not suitable under conditions of higher complexity. Instead an adaptive practice for developing the interactions is more appropriate, given the uncertainty of the need for researcher expertise. Developing research capacity is realized through integrative thinking with complexity about the researcher interactions and social influences. In so doing, the researcher is better able to assimilate and respond to emerging understandings of research capacities in a way that both influences and is influenced by the changing conditions surrounding the mixed methods research.

By drawing upon team members' collective experiences, expertise, and intuition to generate outcomes that are otherwise inaccessible, mixed methods research teams benefit from creating conditions of emergence when working under conditions of complexity. Given the importance of emergence for addressing complex problems, I have sought, over the last decade, to articulate complexity-sensitive practices which develop and maximize researcher capacity for emergence in mixed methods research interactions. My work, which focused on forming and developing mixed methods research team capacity for integrative interactions, stemmed from my own experiences and from those of students and colleagues. Common to these experiences were feasibility issues associated with such difficulties as working with diverse research teams whose roles were yet ill-defined, resolving differences in philosophical orientations, disciplinary and methodological expertise among individual researchers, and lack of collaboration experiences among team members. A review of the literature revealed numerous reports of mixed methods research team experiences and lessons learned, yet (so far!) there are few examples specific to conditions of complexity. Perhaps the most alarming to me is the continuing lack of opportunities for training specific to developing mixed methods research teams, especially given the increased calls for team configurations for addressing pressing societal issues. Consider Researcher Spotlight 8.1 describing future challenges for preparing mixed methods researchers for their work as team members under conditions of complexity, from the perspective of a well-known mixed methods researcher and professor of health services research at the School of Health and Related Research at the University of Sheffield (UK).

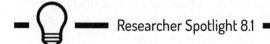 **Researcher Spotlight 8.1**

Alicia O'Cathain on developing capacity of mixed methods research team interactions

A key challenge for the future is teaching and training in mixed methods research. Courses need to offer a range of detailed guidance on designs, integration, quality and reporting, but also real-world issues such as team working. Teaching this early in a career trajectory can help researchers to value team working and spend time on empowering team members to work together when they lead research projects.

Among my initial steps to begin addressing the dearth of team-focused training opportunities in mixed methods research was delving into the literature distinguishing teams from a working group that is now more than two decades old. In so doing, I recognized the relevance of some key criteria to what I had also experienced as an effective team member related to a collective effort, manageable size, specified roles, and limited duration of membership (Salas, Dickinson, Converse, & Tannenbaum, 1992). Yet under conditions of complexity, I realized some of these assumptions were limited in their application and instead I found their more recent expansion of teams to be more relevant. In this work, Salas and colleagues highlight the importance of a team's ability to adapt their collaborative strategies involving (among others) coordination, communication, and collective understanding of the ever-changing task (Salas, Fiore, & Letsky, 2012). This literature helps make the case for adaptive practices guiding team formations and development of capacity for mixed methods research interactions.

A complexity-sensitive approach to developing team capacity for integrative mixed methods research members calls into question three traditional mainstays for forming mixed methods research teams: roles, interactions, and outcomes (see Table 8.1). Mixed methods research members working under conditions of lower overall complexity are well suited for predetermined roles aligned with the expertise needs of the study, interactions that are variously interrelated, and outcomes that are anticipated to reflect a summation of individual contributions. This is because greater predictability in roles and required expertise characterizes the efforts of mixed methods research teams who pursue less complex problems featuring a high degree of stability, a clearly defined mixing purpose, and a certainty regarding outcomes. In contrast, mixed methods research teams working under conditions of high overall complexity are well suited for roles that are responsive to the emergent expertise needs of the study, interactions that are intensively collaborative, and outcomes that are integrative beyond the sum of individual contributions.

The need for capacity in interactions was apparent in the featured study on safe places where the authors provide a detailed description of the development of the team (Zea et al., 2014). The researcher roles were not predetermined and concerted efforts were made by the transdisciplinary and transculturally diverse members to develop egalitarian relationships to enable intensive collaborations that are detailed throughout the study. Collaboratively, team members generated validation evidence for the mixed insights that would not have been accessible by individual contributions. Such study characteristics demonstrate the integrative interactions necessary for pursuing highly complex problems featuring a low degree of stability, an innovation-focused mixing purpose, and uncertain outcomes. Creating the team capacity for integrative mixed methods research interactions requires specific skills for drawing upon individual and collective learnings from experience, inferences from expertise, beliefs from intuition, and generating new insights.

The recent Mixed Methods International Research Association (MMIRA) task force report highlights the need for skills beyond the methodological and disciplinary expertise of members to include collaboration, negotiation, and resolution, stating 'given the complex nature of wicked problems, future challenges for mixed methods researchers include how to bring multidisciplinary teams together to share their expertise in respectful ways' (Mertens et al., 2016a, p. 225). Mertens et al. (2016b) specifically point to the potential for researchers to provide opportunities for in-team mentoring while generating innovative outcomes for complex and challenging mixed methods research problems. Creating conditions for emergence well positions mixed methods research teams to respond to complex problems by drawing upon

Table 8.1 Contrasts between traditional and complexity-sensitive practices for mixed methods research members

	Traditional practices for mixed methods research members	Complexity-sensitive practices for mixed methods research members
Roles	• Predetermined by study needs	• Responsive to emergent study needs
Interactions	• Variously interrelated	• Intensively collaborative
Outcomes	• Summation of individual contributions	• Integrative beyond the summation of individual contributions

the capacity of the diverse membership. It should be noted that there is no reason to think that developing capacity is limited to what has been discussed – there are lots of examples in business, politics, and education where this has also been beneficial. This book is not the place to tackle those examples, but in describing how integrative teams can be realized within mixed methods research, perhaps the lessons from this book can be extrapolated elsewhere. What remains to be further explained is what conditions promote emergence among mixed methods researchers. In Guiding Tip 8.1 an emerging scholar from Canada living in Australia offers advice for working with others and seeking mentoring.

 ══ Guiding Tip 8.1 ══════════════

Mandy Archibald advising engaging in deep learning from others to navigate the complexity of mixed methods research

'Going deep' into a research area is often advised. Yet, because diversity enhances creativity, and creativity is needed to respond to complexity, I also advise 'going broad'. Going broad involves reading well beyond your discipline, working beyond your comfortable skill set, and seeking vertical and lateral mentorship when and wherever possible.

Developing Opportunities and Hazards for Mixed Methods Researchers

Promoting Conditions for Emergence Opportunities

Emergence is not something that can be executed by members of a mixed methods research team based on a plan – rather, teams have to be attentive to whatever emerges from the conditions they create. Researchers working under conditions of complexity should assume the unexpected and be responsive to whatever happens. These are not easy positions for many of us to adopt, given that much of our methodological training has assumed stability in the context and focused on careful planning and implementation of research plans. Furthermore, developing the capacity for integrative mixed methods research interactions requires fostering the conditions for emergence – which we do not yet fully understand. The lack of control and predictive power remains a challenging reality for researchers tackling complex mixed methods research problems.

Emergence results from the ability of complex adaptive systems to self-organize and be affected by one another. As humans, we continue to evolve – we did not always look the way we do now, and the same is true of how we think and interact with one another within teams. Integration of past and present has become necessary, especially in this information technology age where we must draw on data from diverse perspectives and experiences to make sense of complex situations. An illustrative example of the contributions of a diverse research team is provided in one of the studies I describe as part of a cross-case comparison of the contributions of a mixed methods practitioner within educational research teams (Poth, 2012). In conceptualizing the use of a parallel convergent mixed methods research design the research team drew upon the individual expertise of the team members to generate a comprehensive understanding of the impact of a team instructional approach on student access to constructive feedback and an effective learning environment. Although specific tasks were assigned to individual members of the research team, a core element of the implementation was the weekly team members who facilitated communication and adaptations to the procedures to respond to changing conditions and emerging findings. In so doing, the research as well as the team members benefited from the individual contributions and the learning that occurred among members. In so doing, the research team maximized (in my view!) the potential contributions of different team members and generated insights that were beyond what could have been achieved individually or even collectively. There was something that happened during the team development that supported the capacity for the team to integrate their individual contributions – in this paper, I attribute this to the roles of the mixed methods practitioner that I describe as a boundary spanner and issue mediator. In so doing, I make the case that 'opening up new ways of researching established fields is one avenue for novel contributions to be made. Classroom teaching and learning environments are complex and multifaceted and are, thus, well suited to a mixed methods research approach' (Poth, 2012, p. 329). I will freely admit that my thinking has become more sophisticated in relation to team dynamics and social influences, but this provided impetus for my thinking about the potential for the conditions of emergence within mixed methods research teams.

Experiences, where I saw a new, unpredictable outcome arise from intensive collaboration of team members across different roles, were unique in generating an outcome that could not be easily understood by reductionism. I consider the outcomes unlikely (even impossible) to have been achieved individually. I came to recognize that understanding the conditions that promoted these remarkable outcomes could provide insight into developing capacity in mixed methods research interactions. Creating the conditions for emergence and promoting integrative interactions among diverse mixed methods research team members may be simply necessary because we cannot predict our desirable outcomes under conditions of research complexity. The idea that each mixed methods research team member is a valued contributor to something that has not yet been determined can be motivating and open new possibilities and discoveries about what members can generate through their integrative interactions.

To provide previously inaccessible ways to move research forward towards addressing complex problems, team members interact in a way that integrates their individual and collective learnings from experience, inferences from expertise, and beliefs from intuition. In so doing, integrative interactions serve to draw on past experiences, current expertise, and intuition in order to invent the future. Thus, mixed methods research teams with capacity for integrative interactions are well positioned to respond to the emergent and dynamic realities inherent in the environments in which complex mixed methods research problems occur. Three conditions promoting emergence have been revealed in my work as a mixed methods research team member. I describe them below so that they can be used to guide the integrative interactions among members of mixed methods research teams tackling complex problems (see also Figure 8.1). Integrative mixed methods research members must be willing to:

- *Commit to diverse roles that are yet to be defined and are not limited to methodological and disciplinary contributions.* A pressing need remains for mixed methods research teams to proactively avoid many of the misunderstandings alluded to by other researchers related to role definitions by methodological and disciplinary expertise (Curry et al., 2013; O'Cathain et al., 2008). This is especially relevant for diverse research teams tackling complex mixed methods research problems who rely on the team's collective expertise yet whose roles are not yet clear but require mutual respect and collaboration.

- *Contribute individual experiences, expertise, and intuition in a way that others can draw upon and integrate with their own.* This helps to avoid some of the tensions that may arise when there is a lack of communication and interaction between researchers completing independent tasks documented by others (e.g., Bowers et al., 2013; Morgan, 2014). This is especially relevant for the integrative interactions required for research teams tackling complex mixed methods research problems who rely on the team's ability to clearly communicate and navigate differences.
- *Develop a team-focused identity in which individual members consider themselves part of an entity, adopting a distributed leadership style.* **Leader-centric effects** can be avoided on mixed methods research teams when each member shares in the responsibility that comes with collective engagement for a common purpose; that is, no single researcher directs the team interactions (e.g., Hemmings, Beckett, Kennerly, & Yap, 2013; Sharp et al., 2012). This is especially relevant for integrative mixed methods research teams tackling complex mixed methods research problems who rely on the team's individual and mutual accountability as an approach to leadership.

The featured study on leadership competencies (Strudsholm et al., 2016) provides an illustrative example of meeting the conditions promoting emergence. First, the authors do not identify particular roles for researchers, rather they point out that an important feature of the project was a team structure providing access to multidisciplinary expertise and diverse methodological strengths among members. Second, Strudsholm et al. describe how they go about drawing upon individual expertise and experiences at different points in the study – in particular, how the team undertook focus group analysis through engaging in intensive collaborations over time. Third, the authors describe their distributed leadership approach as team-centred by assigning a lead investigator for each of the four project phases. They also

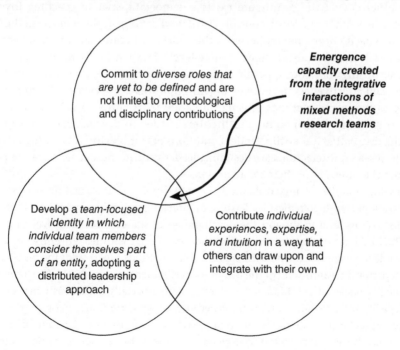

Figure 8.1 Conditions promoting emergence of integrative mixed methods research teams

note that the lead investigator was not assigned sole responsibility because they were supported by other members as appropriate and provided with administrative support.

Leader-Centric Hazards for Capacity Development

Leader-centric effects are hazardous to developing integrative mixed methods research interactions because of the influential roles of leaders on teams. Under conditions of high complexity, the adoption of a team leadership style is particularly influential because of the uncertainty surrounding the research problem, interrelatedness of research contexts, diversity among team members, and agility of research designs. As a result, members must attend to dynamic influences and assimilate new conditions for emergence on an ongoing basis in a way that is appropriate for the mixed methods research. I propose an athletic coaching metaphor to delineate the leader-centric effects on developing the integrative capacity of mixed methods research teams because both leadership and coaching styles exist under complex conditions and have been described along similar continuums. Given the influential roles of athletic coaches and research leaders on the lives of their team's members, their team's colleagues and families, and their team's wider communities, their actions and consequences must be taken carefully into account during team formations and capacity developments.

At one end of the continuum exists an autocratic style of coaching involving a commander-like function for the athletic team. With control residing with the coach, the unit of focus for capacity development becomes the individual because such a leader-centric style involves one person directing the individual actions of many team members. At the other end of the continuum exists a democratic style of coaching involving a facilitator-like function. With control distributed among team members, the unit of focus for capacity development becomes the collective because such a team-centric style involves each team member assuming some level of responsibility for leadership. It may not be surprising that both types of leadership styles have been described in the literature on team effectiveness in complex organizations (Zaccaro, Heinen, & Shuffler, 2009). Specific to the mixed methods research literature (NIH Office of Behavioral and Social Sciences, 2018), have also pointed to the time needed to develop the team capacity for assuming distributed leadership. Under conditions of complexity where integrative mixed methods research interactions are desirable, leader-centric approaches have the potential to hinder the intensity of their collaborations.

A growing number of mixed methods examples point to the need for diverse research teams to adopt non-hierarchical leadership, to interact frequently using means that enhance open discussions, and to support the development of shared leadership over time (Bowers et al., 2013). Many of the problems researchers encounter with leader-centric styles can be attributable to an approach where the single 'mixed methods expert' adds the mixed methods research perspective at the end of the research development process (NIH Office of Behavioral and Social Sciences, 2018). Leader-centric effects are especially hazardous when developing team capacity for integrative interactions because, under conditions of complexity, it is not possible to predict how the mixed methods researcher will need to adapt and an authoritarian style has the strong potential to undercut team trust by removing the decision-making power of the team and micromanaging tasks that could otherwise be distributed.

While studies indicate the vital role of effective leadership, descriptions of the roles and responsibilities for mixed methods research team leaders have often been vague and a need for practical strategies remains (Bowers et al., 2013). A point of consensus seems to be the need for someone to bring together the team and to establish the shared leadership early on (e.g., Bowers et al., 2013; Curry et al., 2012). Also common to the leadership roles described by NIH Office of Behavioral and Social Sciences (2018) and Curry et al. (2012) are broad, sweeping roles for the team leader. These descriptions suggest a more distributed leadership model, perhaps involving different researchers taking on responsibility for leading within their area of expertise. Reconceptualizing leadership 'as a role rather than an individual characteristic' (Curry et al., 2013, p. 16) permits the mixed methods practitioner to support the contributions of individual members and to provide leadership as needed in the areas of technical, situational, interpersonal, and management skills. The idea that leadership roles emerge and change over time in response to shifts within the research process and within the team itself is aligned with the conceptualization of research processes as nonlinear entities influenced by contextual and human factors. Therefore, a leader-centric approach to forming and developing a mixed methods research team under conditions of complexity can hinder these conditions for emergence and indeed hinder the integrative capacity development of the team. There is no simple solution for avoiding leader-centric effects, although increased awareness of the leadership assumptions and influences that a researcher's leadership style preferences bring to their work as a team member represents an important first step. In Practice Alert 8.1, I consider some of the assumptions and influences on my leadership style preferences, and I invite you to do the same. In so doing, I have enhanced my understandings of the influences on developing conditions of emergence in mixed methods research interactions.

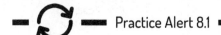 **Practice Alert 8.1**

What assumptions and influences might your leadership style preferences bring to mixed methods research interactions?

Careful consideration of the expertise needed for the study by lead researchers often means the team description is focused on roles rather than on past and anticipated interactions.

When mixed methods researchers bring a record of effective past collaborations, they are more likely to be seen as credible in a proposed research effort (NIH Office of Behavioral and Social Sciences, 2018). It is thus important to highlight the novel products that demonstrate the team capacity, or in the case of newly formed teams, what efforts will be undertaken to support the development of team capacity for generating innovative products. To do so, establish the uniqueness of the team capacity and situate the team development as having the potential for significant contributions.

Try this now – sketch your ideas about what influences your leadership style towards developing teams and consider the effects on how the significance of the team is conveyed in a research proposal. Then as a reader, assess evidence of any leader-centric effects in your rationales for a research team and what distinguishes your team capacity.

A Strategy for Developing Complex Mixed Methods Research Interactions

Lack of guidance about creating functioning mixed methods teams with the capacity to overcome challenges is among the key challenges faced by researchers (Curry et al., 2012; Sharp et al., 2012). In my experience, this need is even more acute under conditions of complexity. In Figure 8.2, I advance four interrelated elements that comprise a strategy for developing complex mixed methods research interactions: forming for diversity, capitalizing on differences, norming of relations, and performing as a team. These elements are based on my readings of the literature and professional experience. Together the four interrelated elements support development of complex mixed methods research interactions by committing interest, promoting candour, nurturing accountability, and transcending boundaries. As will be described, these abilities are necessary under all conditions of complexity, but especially under those that have greater complexity.

The importance of development for enhancing the outputs of mixed methods research teams is well established, as are the challenges team members face in their work together (e.g., Curry et al., 2012; O'Cathain et al., 2008). Conceptualizing capacity development for integrative mixed methods research interactions as ongoing is essential in preparing research members not only for the realities they currently face but also for an unknown future. Each of the elements is described in this section and summarized in Table 8.2. Integrative mixed methods research interactions are best developed by considering diversity beyond methodologies and disciplines – often we fill mixed methods research teams with those who simply

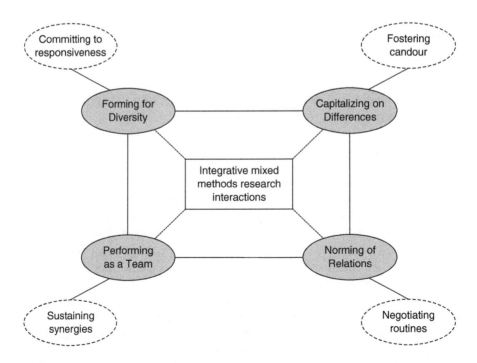

Figure 8.2 A developmental strategy for integrative mixed methods research interactions

bring the expertise without considering whether they work well together as a whole (Bowers et al., 2013). Differences are best discussed openly – often, as research team members, we are tempted to withdraw when tensions arise without mechanisms for conflict resolution (Curry et al., 2012). Relations are best nurtured with intention – often we do not ensure conditions and time for meaningful interactions. Teams are best sustained with continued development – often we are focused on forming and implementing mixed methods research teams without reflecting on the experiences and lessons learned.

Forming for Diversity of Expertise

When expertise can be predetermined, the study needs drive membership in mixed methods research teams in order to develop 'members with expertise in the range of methods employed within a study' (O'Cathain et al., 2008, p. 1579). Under conditions of complexity, we seek to create integrative mixed methods research interactions that draw upon members' broad diversity in expertise, experiences, and intuition in ways that cannot be predetermined. Not everyone should or can commit to working collaboratively when mixing purposes require creating conditions for emergence and generating integrative outcomes that are not accessible through individuals working in parallel. Drawing upon broad diversity is essential when adapting to unexpected and unknown study needs inherent in complex mixed methods research problems. Thus, developing integrative mixed methods research interactions requires determining the team members' commitment to working together and establishing team members' responsiveness to emergent study needs. Whereas some abilities may be easy for researchers to articulate, others may not be obvious, and so teams must discover the broad diversity of expertise, experiences, and intuition each member brings.

Deciphering what individuals bring to integrative mixed methods research interactions requires establishing a rapport among those involved. Among the challenges when determining the extent of researchers' commitment to working together are a lack of rapport and shared language, as well as limited interest in the problems and issues being pursued. Through opportunities for dialoguing, team members may, over time, convey their record of successful research collaborations, background description of interest in study issues and, for some, develop a shared language. In particular, curiosity and dedication to the study topics and a shared language have been identified as teamwork facilitators (Bowers et al., 2013; Curry et al., 2012; Hesse-Biber, 2016; Szostak, 2015). Bowers et al. describe how a shared language may help teams to establish rapport and avoid some of the consequences of language miscommunications, saying that 'differences were numerous, and not always obvious, posing a risk for team division, marginalization, and misunderstanding' (2013, p. 2170). Practical suggestions for mitigating challenges involved in committing to work together include seeking members who are willing to share, and are interested in, each other's background stories, and creating opportunities for sustained dialogue over time, such as collaborative online forums and meetings designed to foster sociability.

A team's capacity for pursuing complex mixed methods research problems is dependent upon the members' willingness to adapt to emerging conditions and study needs. The current lack of authentic mixed methods research literature for guiding the pursuit of mixed methods research under conditions of complexity is key among the many challenges teams may encounter. Specific mixed methods research expertise and experiences have been identified

Table 8.2 Four interrelated elements for developing integrative mixed methods research teams

Strategy elements	Desirable outcomes	Key activities	Potential challenges	Suggestions for mitigating Challenges
Forming for Diversity	• Determine commitment to work together	• Establish rapport and decipher individual expertise, experiences, and intuition	• Lack of shared language • Limited issue and topical interests	• Seek members willing to share • Create opportunities for sustained dialogues
	• Promote responsiveness to emergent needs	• Assess ability for team to pursue complex mixed methods research	• Lack of access to guiding literature and familiarity with complex research problems • Lack of access to mixed methods research expertise	• Seek members with (or willing to develop) mixed methods research expertise and complexity-sensitive mindsets • Dedicate time in meetings for learning over time
Capitalizing on Differences	• Encourage candour for differing perspectives	• Cultivate safe space	• Absence of open communication and mutual respect • Absence of conflict resolution mechanisms	• Seek members willing to actively listen and offer considerate responses • Create opportunities for understanding each other's perspectives
	• Foster team trust for collaborative work	• Encourage risk taking	• Lack of access to guiding literature for establishing trust • Lack of guidance and collaborative experiences among diverse teams	• Seek members with collaborative experiences and those willing to develop trust among one another • Establish a balance for fostering relationships with tasks
Norming of Relations	• Negotiate roles in response to emerging need	• Foster shared identity	• Lack of focus on team development • Lack of mutual accountability	• Seek members committed to developing team-centric leadership capacity • Establish meeting agendas with time dedicated to discussing team roles
	• Co-create routines for integrative interactions	• Maintain engagement	• Lack of time for development • Lack of opportunities for meaningful interactions	• Seek adequate resources to support team development • Establish routines with dedicated time for creativity
Performing as a Team	• Sustain assimilations of new understandings	• Support learning about and from each other	• Lack of attention to team dynamics • Lack of member introspection	• Seek members who recognize the potential for ongoing development • Establish opportunities for reflection
	• Prioritize synergy	• Create conditions for emergence	• Lack of team-focused training opportunities • Lack of transcending boundaries	• Embed opportunities for learning together • Seek team members with interdisciplinary experiences

by several authors as desirable for a mixed methods research team (Arnault & Fetters, 2012; NIH Office of Behavioral and Social Sciences, 2018); yet few studies point to a broader view of diversity beyond the methodological expertise for dealing with the messiness associated with complex problems. Indeed, while the lack of access to team members with mixed methods research expertise remains an impediment to successful teamwork (O'Cathain et al., 2008), scant guidance exists for the types of expertise needed to adapt under conditions of complexity. Specifically, familiarity with complex mixed methods research, including the need for teams to be adaptable to new and uncertain conditions, may help avoid some of the challenges that researchers working under conditions of complexity experience because they no longer assume stability. Practical suggestions for assessing the ability of newly formed teams to pursue complex mixed methods research include seeking members with, and those who are willing to develop, mixed methods research expertise and complexity-sensitive mindsets. Developing teams with the potential for integrative mixed methods research interactions emphasizes practices for drawing upon members' broad diversity in expertise, experiences, and intuition in ways that cannot be predetermined and that are responsive to the uncertainty inherent in complex research problems.

The featured studies provide some evidence of forming for diversity among teams and commitment to responsiveness. In particular, the authors of the safe places (Zea et al., 2014) and leadership competencies (Strudsholm et al., 2016) studies provided evidence of establishing a strong commitment to work together. Zea et al. described in great detail their efforts realizing an egalitarian dialogue among researchers and participants, while Strudsholm et al. described their development of a collaborative approach among team members. Common to these studies were references to frequent interactions among diverse team members drawing upon a variety of disciplinary and methodological experiences and expertise. Indeed, Zea et al. referred to the research team composition as transdisciplinary and transcultural. Strudsholm et al., (2016, p. 2) state: 'An important feature of the Project was the team structure that made available multidisciplinary expertise and diverse methodological strengths among members. The training, research, and practice expertise of members included public health, population health, psychology, community health, sociology, primary care, education, anthropology.' It is noteworthy that none of the featured studies referred specifically to any members' mixed methods research expertise or previous experiences with complex research problems.

Capitalizing on Differences in Perspectives

That diverse mixed methods research members can give rise to challenges within teams is well established and often attributable to factors including differing disciplinary perspectives (Bowers et al., 2013; Bryman, 2006; Szostak, 2015), methodological backgrounds (Curry et al., 2012; O'Cathain et al., 2008), and social dynamics (Curry et al., 2013; Sharp et al., 2012). Under conditions of complexity we seek to capitalize on the diversity within and among mixed methods research members by negotiating differences in members' perspectives to enable integrative mixed methods research interactions. It never ceases to amaze me how much precious time we spend as mixed methods researchers trying to convince people of our thinking – instead of coming together with a recognition that we each have something to contribute to the team as well as to learn from others. The ability for diverse mixed methods researchers to discuss areas of differences in perspectives provides an example of the essential type of dialogue for developing integrative interactions. Thus, team candour for diverse perspectives and fostering trust for collaborative work is how teams can capitalize on their differences in addressing a complex mixed methods research problem. Where some attributes may be easy to establish, others may not be, and so collaboration among team members is necessary to navigate assumptions and conflicts that individuals bring to their interactions. Consider Researcher Spotlight 8.2 describing the key pressing challenge for developing capacity for interdisciplinary interactions, from the perspective of a well-known mixed methods researcher and professor of health services research at the School of Health and Related Research at the University of Sheffield (UK).

 Researcher Spotlight 8.2

Alicia O'Cathain on developing the capacity for interdisciplinary team interactions to yield integrative outcomes

Team working is a real-world issue when undertaking mixed methods research. Mixed methods research can be undertaken by a single researcher, for example a PhD candidate. However, it is more usual to have a diverse team delivering a study – researchers with different methodological expertise and understandings as well as different levels of topic expertise. In some teams, the quantitative components of a study are delivered by one sub-team and the qualitative components delivered by a different sub-team. This team configuration can lead to the separation of the qualitative and quantitative components, a lack of integration and thus no potential for insights from such integration. It is important for team members to sit with each other at the start of the study and discuss their understandings of the topic under study, get to know the 'other' methods, and think about how their part of the study can be influenced by and interact with the other parts. This communication can help to identify differences in language and values, develop interdisciplinary working and create the environment for integration of qualitative and quantitative data and findings to ensure that the whole is greater than the sum of the parts of the study.

Cultivating safe space for integrative interactions requires a willingness to engage productively with differing perspectives. Among the challenges for diverse teams are the absence of open communication and mechanisms for resolving conflicts, as well as a failure to develop mutual respect. Through opportunities for open acknowledgement of differences, team members may, over time, convey their implicit and explicit assumptions; some may convey their willingness to assimilate new understandings. The importance of these understandings cannot be overemphasized. Team members must be attentive to their histories obstructing expressions of new ideas from integrative mixed methods research interactions. Engagement with differences is more likely to occur when team members feel safe, heard, and have room to appreciate other perspectives. Several researchers suggest that open acknowledgement early on as well as sustained dialogue will help mixed methods research teams to effectively respond to disciplinary and methodological differences (Bowers et al., 2013; Robins et al., 2008). Developing such mechanisms for resolving conflicts is key, because of the necessary ability for research teams to face the tension of differing ideas constructively and to generate innovative ideas. Curry et al. (2012) describe the outcomes from members who are willing to engage productively with differing perspectives, saying: 'When researchers expect and embrace differences, diversity can bring both excitement and new ways of thinking to our work. Yet we typically tend to avoid differences, address them only superficially, or silently wish they did not exist' (p. 11). Active listening and considerate responses, as well as creating opportunities for understanding each other's perspectives over time are two practical suggestions for developing team candour.

Encouraging risk-taking among team members contributes to developing integrative mixed methods research interactions. Risk-taking happens when team members consider different perspectives than their own. As a mixed methods research community, we would benefit from greater guidance in the literature for taking risks and fostering trust. This is because nurturing and sustaining respect is deemed helpful in addressing challenges inherent in groups (Curry et al., 2012). Differences in the collaborative team experiences may not be as obvious (O'Cathain et al., 2008), nor are the types of collaborative relationships necessary for successful mixed methods research obvious (Aboela et al., 2007). Indeed, we seek to better understand what Creswell et al. (2011, p. 12) describe as 'sufficient capacity for researchers to support and challenge one another in each aspect of the research so as to produce the highest quality research'. What remains to be further investigated in the literature is how trust is successfully fostered within a diverse mixed methods research team and what features of collaborative work should be valued under conditions of complexity. Practical suggestions for encouraging risk-taking among members of newly formed teams involve seeking members with collaborative experiences and those willing to develop trust with one another. Also, establishing a balance for fostering relationships with tasks such as dedicated time during a meeting for building relationships as well as for discussing tasks. Capitalizing on integrative mixed methods research interactions emphasizes practices for discussing areas of differences in members' perspectives through candour and considerate procedures in ways that draw upon the diversity needed to address complex research problems. Consider Researcher Spotlight 8.3 describing challenges with cross-disciplinary work under complex mixed methods research conditions, from the perspective of an assistant professor at the University of Michigan (USA).

 Researcher Spotlight 8.3

Tim Guetterman on developing a mixed methods way of thinking among diverse team members

Working in interrelated contexts, disciplines, and diverse teams has been a rewarding challenge for me. The work often requires some gentle leading and education about mixed methods to lift collaborators into a mixed methods way of thinking. Reading books, such as this one,

(Continued)

(Continued)

and other literature is so important to help us think through complex issues as a team. Another challenging experience is the disciplinary silos. Dealing with complex conditions takes a team effort and requires truly engaging with collaborators across those silos. Every time I talk with someone using or thinking about using mixed methods in a different field, I learn and leave with new insights. Seeing what others value and understanding their perspectives produces better collaboration and better research. I realize it is easier said than done, especially when egos are involved and not everyone may be as compromising as you! I hear way too often researchers dismissing literature from other disciplines, such as saying 'but that's education research' or 'but that's in health'. Really? None of it applies? Granted, I see research through the lens of methodology, so I often filter out content to focus on the research procedures. Disciplines see things differently, or at least they think they do. Personally, I see more similarity than differences among disciplines, especially as most of our work is increasingly blurring those lines. My advice, though, is to remain open and try to understand diverse views and values about research.

The featured studies provide some illustrative examples of capitalizing on differences among team members and fostering candour. Specifically, the authors of the safe places study encouraged an openness for differing perspectives: 'Many hours of planning, developing mutual trust, establishing different means of communication across countries (e.g., face-to-face meetings, e-mails, Skype meetings), as well as honoring diverse styles of communication (e.g., more or less philosophical, analytic, political, direct) were needed to develop an egalitarian relationship among team members' (Zea et al., 2014, p. 215). In addition, these authors described their concerted efforts to build trust among the researchers: 'the different world-views of the U.S.-based researchers and the Colombian participants were bridged by the Colombian team members who shared some of the perspectives and experiences of both groups' (p. 215). It is noteworthy that only two of the featured studies – those on safe places and heart care (Dickson et al., 2011) – referred specifically to any previous collaborations or experiences among the diverse teams.

Norming of Relations among Researchers

As member interactions become routine, a shared vision is ever important to maintain as a guide to collaborative efforts. Under conditions of complexity, we seek to normalize relations among mixed methods research team members by creating routines for integrative interactions to occur. Such interactions represent the sources of emergence and opportunities for team members to self-organize and accommodate the products of their integrative actions. Thus, norming team relations for addressing a mixed methods research problem requires negotiating roles in response to emerging study needs and co-creating routines involving integrative interactions. Whereas some roles may be easy to negotiate in response to emerging needs, the challenges inherent in others may not be so obvious and so co-creating routines for team integrative interactions is necessary for promoting conditions for the emergence of innovative outcomes.

Fostering a shared identity when norming relations among team members requires an appreciation of what the members contribute as an entity, which is difficult to do if team members view themselves solely as individuals working together. Among the challenges for negotiating roles in response to emerging study needs are a lack of focus on team development and a lack of mutual accountability. By focusing on team development, team members may, over time, begin to shift their unit of focus from individual contributions to that of a collective entity with integrative capacity. Establishing mutual accountability can be valuable, yet few examples exist in mixed methods research literature of real-world efforts. Key among the few examples are a 'sign-off' process in which each team member acknowledges their comfort with the interpretations and conclusions being reached and disseminated by other team members through a formal acknowledgement of the report (Bowers et al., 2013). Practical suggestions for cultivating a team identity include nurturing team function and procedures by seeking members who are committed to adopting a **team-centric leadership style** and establishing time to discuss team roles during meetings.

A committed membership is required in order to maintain team engagement when norming relations among team members. Among the challenges for teams are a lack of time allocation to team development and opportunities for meaningful interactions (Creswell et al., 2011). Integrative interactions are more likely to occur with intensive team collaborations because that increases opportunities for communication – and with more intensive interactions comes an increased likelihood of emergence and serendipity. These unexpected outcomes were observed by Bowers et al. and described as 'unexpected and sometimes unforeseen opportunities for processes and aims to inform one another' (2013, p. 2173). When interacting, members learn from one another, assimilate their new understandings, and apply their new ideas to creatively resolve salient features of complex problems. Practical suggestions for maintaining team engagement include nurturing team function and procedures by seeking adequate resources that support team development and by establishing routines that include time dedicated to creativity. Norming integrative mixed methods research interactions emphasizes practices for cultivating shared identities and maintaining team engagement in ways that optimize the possibilities inherent in complex research problems.

The featured studies provide some indications of norming of relations among team members and how they went about negotiating their routines. Among the key examples from the featured study on safe places are the authors' descriptions of their efforts to create egalitarian relationships: 'We worked to avoid the assumption that the expertise came from U.S. universities or from existing, standardized surveys' (Zea et al., 2014, p. 215). Team engagement was evident in the featured study on leadership competencies (Strudsholm et al., 2016) where the authors created routines involving every researcher in all the research activities, thus following a fully integrated mixed methods research model. What is not as apparent in any of the featured studies is how the members' routines and interactions as well as roles and contributions evolved during the study.

Performing as a Team with Capacity

The ultimate performance of integrative mixed methods research interactions cannot be reliably predicted. Specific team circumstances, including extended time and opportunities for engagement (Bowers et al., 2013), ability to resolve conflicts (O'Cathain et al., 2008) and commitment to the process, have been noted as effective supports. Under conditions of complexity, we seek to perform integrative interactions and adapt to changing study conditions as they arise. The ability to assimilate dynamic influences while also maintaining methodological cohesion in the study represent important aspects for a complexity-sensitive approach to mixed methods research. Thus, performing integrative mixed methods research interactions addressing a mixed methods research problem requires assimilating each other's experiences, expertise, and intuition as well as the creation of conditions for emergence that will generate innovative ideas.

To support team synergies, the members must focus on continuing their intensive interactions rather than ending that support after forming and implementing the team, as is often the case. Among the challenges to sustaining integrative interactions are a lack of attention to social dynamics and a lack of team introspection. Through greater focus on organizational structures, integrative mixed methods research interactions have the strong potential to provide the mechanism that will support ongoing collaborations. This is because reflection on the experiences and lessons learned helps to ensure the longevity of the team. Practical suggestions for supporting team synergies are to seek others who also recognize the potential of ongoing team development and to establish opportunities for reflection.

Creating conditions for emergence when performing integrative mixed methods research interactions requires a focus on effective negotiation of traditional methodological and disciplinary boundaries. Among the challenges for prioritizing integrative interactions are the lack of collaborative-focused training opportunities and a lack of experience with boundary transcendence. 'Transcend' means there is a shared sense of involvement and achievement that goes beyond simple mixing of interdisciplinary boundaries. A key characteristic for integrative interactions among team members is successful negotiation of traditional boundaries and, so far, this desired transcendence has been limited in the literature to methodological and discipline-specific boundaries. More and more literature is documenting that the ability of research members to transcend disciplinary boundaries encourages the generation of innovative solutions to complex problems (Hesse-Biber & Johnson, 2013). The training challenge as noted by Hesse-Biber (2016, p. 650; emphasis in original) is that:

> researchers *do not practice interdisciplinarity well.* This is because, in part, they do not actively seek out ways to tap into the potential synergy of a team–based mixed methods project. They ethnocentrically do not see past their own comfort zone or horizon for theories, questions, and methods. I further argue that there is a *lack of conscious reflexivity on the part of the research team;* instead, the team often buys into the idea of 'inherent' synergy contained in these types of research configurations and designs. *Working in a group does not necessarily mean that you are working as a team.*

Through transcendence of traditional boundaries, team members promote conditions for emergence that are generative of fresh ideas. Practical suggestions for encouraging conditions for emergence involve seeking team members with interdisciplinary experiences and embedding opportunities for the team to learn together, as well as performing integrative mixed methods research interactions emphasizing practices that support team synergies and creating conditions for emergence in necessary ways to address complex research problems. Consider Researcher Spotlight 8.4 on the future challenges for mixed methods researchers' team performance, from the perspective of a Canadian nurse holding a research-only post-doctoral position as a Canadian Institute for Health research fellow and National Health and Medical Research Council post-doctoral research officer in the College of Nursing and Health Sciences, Flinders University (South Australia).

Researcher Spotlight 8.4

Mandy Archibald on exploring the intersections of interdisciplinary teams through integrative thinking

The challenge reflects my diverse roles as an artist, nurse, and mixed-methods researcher in the applied health sciences, a combination that invariably places in tension (and potential harmony) the standpoints of the reflexive practitioner, the experiences of individuals, and population-level outcomes. In health care, uniformity within groups is often assumed or inferred based on specific clinical indicators (e.g., frail, non-frail). Individual preferences are easily overlooked in place of casual efficacy. Buried further is how individuals construct and attribute meaning to their experiences within complex adaptive systems. Research methods that reflect these differences are necessary to achieve desired outcomes, and can be aided by an understanding of complexity science – for a particularly useful resource, see Braithwaite et al.'s (2017) white paper on complexity science in health care. In response to these challenges, I have been incorporating various arts-informed and arts-based methods, such as visual elicitation and reflexive art making, with more conventional narrative and statistical approaches. Guidance is generally lacking on integrating arts and mixed methods research, despite arts-based and mixed methods research approaches having similar ontological and epistemological positioning, such as recognition of intersubjectivity and a dialectical approach to knowledge production. In my current work I am exploring these intersections, creating a framework for arts–mixed methods research applications. Further, because the preference of some research methods and realities reflects the influence of power and privilege, a key (and underdeveloped) role exists for researcher reflectivity in mixed methods research, specifically one that questions and challenges the positioning of self and method in broader sociopolitical contexts.

The featured studies provide some indications of performing as a team and sustaining synergies. In particular, the authors of the safe places (Zea et al., 2014) and leadership competencies (Strudsholm et al., 2016) studies provide evidence of reflection upon their experiences and outcomes as well as learning about and from one another. Zea et al. (2014, p. 215) reflected upon the validity of the research outcomes: 'participation of the entire interdisciplinary team enabled the incorporation of the native perspective and the generation of ecologically valid, socially relevant knowledge'. Similarly, but with a different focus, Strudsholm et al. (2016, p. 9) reflected upon the usefulness of the processes involved in mixed methods research: 'The challenges of this national, complex, multidisciplinary Project were well served by the use of a mixed methods research design. The study provided a responsive research strategy that could reach a national, diverse, and busy population of public health professionals.

Furthermore, the design supported integrated [knowledge translation] among Project partners' (Strudsholm et al., 2016, p. 9). It is noteworthy that none of the featured studies report engaging in any formal team training opportunities to develop and sustain their interactions. In Practice Alert 8.2, I consider some of my experiences as a member and leader of mixed methods research teams, and I invite you to do the same. In so doing, I have enhanced my understandings of the social influences on developing capacity in mixed methods research interactions.

 Practice Alert 8.2

What might my reflections upon past experiences illuminate about potential interactions as a mixed methods research team member?

Reflective practices can yield insights that would otherwise be inaccessible. In the case of revisiting my experiences in leading the development of mixed methods research teams, I have come to realize that I focused my attention largely on the logistical aspects of writing the proposal, identifying and inviting team members to participate, managing budgets, and developing an initial work plan (Poth, 2012). What I did not do as much as I do now is focus upon diagnosing the complexity of research contexts and building synergies across researchers and projects.

Try this now – consider an experience you have had as a member of a team. How did you develop the team capacity, and what was effective? In what ways might your approach change under differing conditions of complexity?

Features that Engage Readers with Integrative Mixed Methods Research Interactions

It is often advantageous for research to be distinctive. The description of the research interactions – those who are involved, how conditions are developed, and what are the intended outcomes – is a great place to distinguish a study. The following list provides some ideas from my own experiences as a researcher, as a reviewer of mixed methods research proposals for funding and of manuscripts for publication, and from working with graduate students as an instructor, supervisor, and examiner. See also the featured studies for illustrative examples of some of these engaging features.

- *Highlight the diversity of the individuals involved in the research.* By bringing together new combinations of diverse expertise and experiences, researchers may gain new insights into well-established research areas. This helps to predict the probability of your study generating innovative contributions.
- *Describe creative opportunities for members to interact collaboratively.* By providing unique opportunities for frequent and meaningful interactions, the members are more likely to develop their integrative capacity. This will help make the case for resources to support development of integrative team capacity.

- *Seek to develop the integrative capacity of members in an atypical way.* Consider new ways to bring team members together beyond the typical telephone conference call or in-person meeting. This will help highlight the potential for your team to develop unique synergy.
- *Present descriptions of member diversity and integrative capacity in an unusual way.* There are various ways to describe research member skills and experiences. This will help justify your use of a team configuration as well as highlight the unique contributions of individual team members to the collective team.

Innovations in Developing Integrative Mixed Methods Research Interactions

Researchers working under conditions of complexity are tasked with clearly justifying the research team membership and describing the backgrounds of individual mixed methods research members as well as their study roles and contributions. Also important, but often underreported in written proposals and reports, are details about the nature of the researcher interactions, intended team outcomes, and capacity development efforts. Differences in accounts may be attributable to various influences involving personal, disciplinary, and methodological conventions evidenced in proposal and publication requirements. Furthermore, differing expectations among target audiences may play an important role; for example, a funding reviewer may expect greater detail about those involved in the research than a journal editor. It is not uncommon to find only a scant mention of the use of a team configuration within mixed methods research without further detailing of researcher backgrounds, research processes, and team development. The lack of illustrative examples is problematic for the field of mixed methods research in general and is intensified for research under conditions of complexity because developing the capacity for integrative thinking with complexity about interactions is key to generating new, mixed insights. It has become apparent to me that only when researchers have access to the thinking and processes behind successful capacity development for complex mixed methods research interactions can they learn how to plan, implement, and convey their own such efforts under conditions of complexity.

In the same way, the description of the research interactions in a completed study report may be quite different from the initial description in the research proposal. This is because, as the study unfolds and new information is assimilated, understandings related to researcher backgrounds and study contributions as well as researcher relations and study outcomes naturally evolve. There is little agreement about the format for describing researcher backgrounds and their interactions in a mixed methods research proposal or report, yet several writers do suggest topics to be included and highlight brevity as a requirement. What remains missing (but may soon be expected) is a description of how the integrative capacity of the researchers will be realized during the study (as part of a proposal) or was accomplished (as part of a report). To that end, there exists a need for guiding how researchers convey developing the integrative capacity of those involved in the mixed methods research over time; it begins with a proposal drafted before the study, continues during the study implementation, and is finalized with the writing of the report once the research is completed. In this section, I describe two innovations for communicating and tracking the development of integrative mixed methods research interactions.

Diagrams Illuminating Understandings of Researcher Capacities

It is not common to see diagrams in a study introduction of those involved in the research. In addition to conveying information, diagrams have proven to be an effective format for documenting evolutions in my understandings of differences among researchers. To focus on researcher differences represents an uncommon approach when introducing those involved in a study. Yet I find this focus helpful because identifying researcher differences (and similarities!) is only possible once I develop an adequate understanding of what individual researchers bring to the study. This is important because these understandings help make the feasibility case given the team capacity for:

- Why the specific team configuration is well positioned to pursue the complex research problem
- How my understandings of the relevant collective expertise and experiences for the study evolve over time.

Background-oriented diagrams can provide essential evidence of the methodological and disciplinary capacity of those involved in the research. Furthermore, a diagram captures my understandings at a point in time and, over time, I can refine the diagram to reflect what understandings have emerged during the study. I am often inspired by Venn diagrams (Wheeldon & Åhlberg, 2012) and stakeholder diagrams (from my evaluation world) to convey this information. I see the theoretical foundations to this approach to diagramming grounded in representational group theory. To that end, an approach to diagramming able to represent the unique background aspects of individuals as well as some areas of commonality among the backgrounds of research team members can be helpful for depicting these contributions. That individual team member characteristics influence both individual behaviour as well as our interactions with others is aligned with the description advanced by Curry et al. (2012, p. 8; emphasis in original):

> When we work on teams, we participate *both* as individuals and as members of a variety of groups. As individuals, our personality characteristics (e.g., assertive, reserved, critical) affect both the way we behave in groups and the way others respond to us through interpersonal interactions. However, what is less often appreciated is the fact that we also bring our multiple organizational, professional, and identify group membership (e.g., professional or functional training and experience, religious affiliation, gender, race) with us to the team.

This type of diagram assumes that our backgrounds potentially influence our personality characteristics as well as choices for group memberships. Obviously, there is no set format – these visuals are intended to reflect the study context. Their appearance and development vary considerably as a result – sometimes I use few words and create it independently; other times words are central to the diagram, as is the group process in generating or revising the diagram. In Figure 8.3, I provide an example diagram conveying certain individual and group characteristics representing the backgrounds and methodological capacity of those involved in the featured study on safe places research (Zea et al., 2014) to address their complex mixed methods research problem: What does developing safe places involve for internally displaced Colombian gay and bisexual men and transwomen? Note that the diagram is limited to my interpretation of the information described in the article about the five-member research team related to their backgrounds and relationships with the Lesbian, gay, bisexual, and transgender (LGBT) community. Notice the obvious features from the diagram and the absence of any reference to mixed methods research expertise. See also Figure B.4, an editable version of which is also available on the companion website for the book.

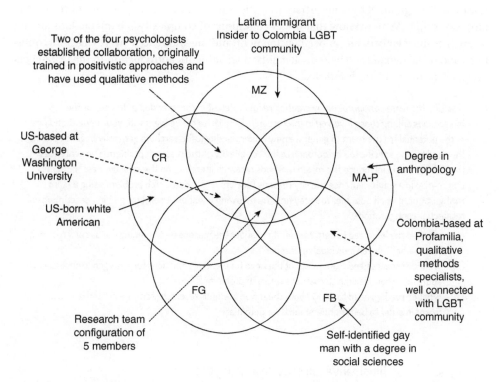

Figure 8.3 Diagram example conveying backgrounds and some methodological expertise

Source: Author generated from narrative information provided in Zea et al. (2014).

Writing Ideas for Developing Research Interactions

It is unusual to convey the development of capacity among mixed methods researchers. I find these accounts are especially helpful for researchers new to developing and writing mixed methods research proposals. It is important to convey these understandings to help make the feasibility case given the team formation and development plans for:

• How the integrative capacity will be sufficiently developed
• What research outcomes can be realistically expected from the anticipated integrative interactions.

Under conditions of complexity, understandings of the features of the complex problem are considered incomplete and the researcher is tasked with the following question: How can the diverse researcher experiences contribute to developing the integrative team capacity necessary for the innovation-focused purpose addressing the complex mixed methods research problem?

Consider designing an introduction to the researchers involved in a mixed methods study proposal. First examine the writing ideas described below and the four related illustrative excerpts from the featured study on safe places (Zea et al., 2014) exploring the subjective, objective, and social worlds of internally displaced Colombian gay and bisexual men and transwomen represented. This structuring reflects a focus on illuminating the differences in researcher backgrounds to demonstrate that those involved have the capacity to realize the proposed study. We now know that under conditions of complexity the interactions among research team members are under development and are influenced by changes in conditions and social dynamics. The four elements of an authentic introduction to the researchers involved in the study are as follows:

- *Describe the team configuration by creating reader interest in the intended outcomes of the interactions among those involved in the research.* Familiarize the readers with your understandings of the potential for the team to generate new understandings. Researchers generally begin by linking the need for the specific team approach to the complexity of the research problem. The sentences that follow should introduce the mixed methods research literature on the effectiveness of teams. Summarize in a single sentence the key reasons for pursuing the research problem using a team configuration, if at all possible. You may find the following questions useful for guiding descriptions of researcher configurations:
  - What do readers need to better understand about the reasons underpinning the use of a research team rather than an individual researcher?
  - What do readers need to know about the need for creating conditions for emergence necessary to address the complex mixed methods research problem?
  - What do readers need to know about the mixed methods research literature related to research teams in order to better understand their potential?

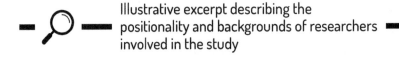

Illustrative excerpt describing the positionality and backgrounds of researchers involved in the study

In addition to the broad social context for GBT individuals in Colombia, we recognize that a research project creates its own social and cultural context that participants in a study encounter. We believe that researchers' positionality exerts an important influence over every aspect of the research process (Curry et al., 2012; Lunde et al., 2013; Mertens, 2007). The group that wrote the grant application funding this study was based in the United States and was composed of four psychologists who have been working together for more than 15 years on HIV among gay and bisexual Latino men. Two are Latina immigrants, and two are U.S.-born White Americans. Although all four had been originally trained in positivistic approaches, the team has incorporated broader perspectives and has used qualitative methods to capture experiences of groups who have little voice in much of psychological research. The first author is an insider to the Colombian LGBT community but at the same time has the privilege of an academic position in the United States.

Source: Zea et al. (2014, pp. 214–215). Used with permission from Sage.

- *Discuss the collective expertise and experiences by referring to individuals' disciplinary and methodological backgrounds.* Researchers illuminate differences in individual contributions to convey the collective team capacity for addressing the complex research problem. Researchers identify the disciplinary, methodological, and collaborative expertise and experiences of members in relation to the study needs. Summarize the key justifications for the selection of individual members and their anticipated (or realized) roles and responsibilities as team members adopting a team-centric leadership approach. You may find the following questions useful for guiding their background descriptions:

  - What do readers need to better understand about the reasons for choosing each of the individual members?
  - What do readers need to know about the integrative potential of team members in addressing the complex mixed methods research problem?
  - What do readers need to know about the mixed methods research literature on the role of distributed leadership, in order to better understand the team-centric approach adopted by the team?

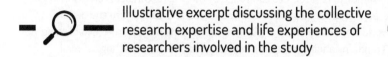

Illustrative excerpt discussing the collective research expertise and life experiences of researchers involved in the study

Important partners were two Colombian qualitative methods specialists (second and third authors of this article) who helped develop interview guides, conducted key informant and life history interviews, handled recruitment, administered quantitative surveys and HIV testing, and delivered HIV pre– and posttest counseling. Among their many contributions was their ability to provide the 'native' perspective. One of these individuals is a self-identified gay man with a degree in social sciences, and the other is a woman with a degree in anthropology. Both were very connected with the LGBT community in Colombia; they knew the sociocultural context, as well as the geographic areas where [men who have sex with men] socialize in Bogotá. Their familiarity and local perspective facilitated the process of recruiting and gaining the trust of participants. The active participation of these two team members was essential for ensuring that the research reflected the concerns of the community. Additionally, the different world-views of the U.S.-based researchers and the Colombian participants were bridged by the Colombian team members who shared some of the perspectives and experiences of both groups.

Source: Zea et al. (2014, p. 215). Used with permission from Sage.

- *Explain the processes involved in developing integrative interactions for addressing the complex research problems and mixing purposes focused on innovation.* Researchers describe how they go about capitalizing the team diversity, normalizing the team relations, and sustaining the team performance. Summarize the key interactions and outcomes for addressing the mixing purpose focused on innovation. Researchers may find the following questions useful for guiding their processes descriptions:

  - What do readers need to know about how the activities related to differences among team members function in order to better understand challenges and outcomes they experienced and the integrative team capacity they developed?
  - What do readers need to know about the activities related to norming relations among team members in order to better understand the challenges and outcomes they experienced and the integrative team capacity they developed?

      o   What do readers need to know about the activities related to team performance to better understand the challenges and outcomes that were experienced and the integrative team capacity developed?

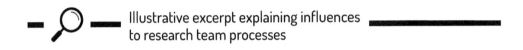

Illustrative excerpt explaining influences to research team processes

Because team members came from diverse national, ethnic, theoretical, and disciplinary backgrounds, there were many opportunities to identify differences in assumptions, approaches, assets, and knowledge (Hemmings et al., 2013). Similar processes to those that take place in the global context can occur among team members of first- and third world societies. For example, the resources controlled by the U.S. researchers can result in a power differential, an attitude analogous to an imperialist stance, and a 'use and discard' approach to third-world staff. Many hours of planning, developing mutual trust, establishing different means of communication across countries (e.g., face-to-face meetings, e-mails, Skype meetings), as well as honoring diverse styles of communication (e.g., more or less philosophical, analytic, political, direct) were needed to develop an egalitarian relationship among team members. We worked to avoid the assumption that the expertise came from U.S. universities or from existing, standardized surveys.

Source: Zea et al. (2014, p. 215). Used with permission from Sage.

- *Provide evidence of integrative outcomes for demonstrating development of integrative mixed methods research interactions.* Researchers describe the outcomes generated by the study and characterize the innovative insights as previously inaccessible. Summarize the key qualities and innovations of the outcomes addressing the complex mixed methods research problem. Researchers may find the following questions useful for guiding their outcomes descriptions:
  - o   What do readers need to know about the study outcomes in order to distinguish the outcomes as having been generated by mixed methods research interactions?
  - o   What do readers need to know about the conditions of emergence in order to have confidence that these outcomes required integrative interactions?
  - o   What do readers need to know about how the integrative outcomes were generated to address the complex mixed methods research problem?

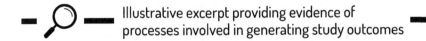

Illustrative excerpt providing evidence of processes involved in generating study outcomes

The participation of the entire interdisciplinary team enabled the incorporation of the native perspective and the generation of ecologically valid, socially relevant knowledge.

Source: Zea et al. (2014, p. 215). Used with permission from Sage.

---

1   Do you discern the differences and similarities in the descriptions of research interactions across the authors of the six featured mixed methods studies? Compare how the authors of at least two of these articles describe the following. Consider what your analysis tells you about their descriptions:

- Rationale for the research team configurations
- Background descriptions for individual researchers
- Evidence of team-focused development efforts
- Nature of the study outcomes from researcher interactions (integrative or collective?).

2   Do you understand the hazards of leader-centric effects and the strategies for avoiding them when initiating a study? Select a published study in an area that is of interest to you or one of the featured mixed methods studies.

- Examine the study limitations and areas for future directions. Select one idea to pursue.
- Sketch initial ideas for a related complex mixed methods research problem and the conditions promoting emergence. What individual experiences, expertise, and intuition would the study require to draw upon? (Use Figure 8.1 to guide your thinking.)
- Briefly describe how you would go about developing the integrative mixed methods research interactions. (Use Figure 8.2 to guide your thinking.) For example:
  - How would you commit to forming a diverse team to meet study needs?
  - How would you foster candour to capitalize on differences among researchers?
  - How would you go about the norming of relations among those involved in the research?
  - How would you optimize leadership for performing as a team?
- Create a diagram of desirable background and expertise characteristics for research members (see Figure B.4).

3   Can you describe the formation and development of integrative mixed methods research interactions and rationalize the need for a team configuration for a study that is of interest to you? Apply the guiding questions presented in this chapter to structure your outlines:

- Describe, in a few sentences, the study need for integrative interactions by justifying the specific team configuration for tackling the complex research problem that is the focus of your study.
- Discuss the collective study contributions by identifying individual methodological, disciplinary and collaborative experiences and expertise.
- Explain how the diversity of the team will be sought, how the differences among team members will be negotiated, how the integrative interactions among team members will be encouraged, and how the performance as a team will be sustained (see Figure 8.2 and Table 8.2 to guide description of activities and avoidance of challenges).
- Consider what evidence you would seek to demonstrate the development of integrative mixed methods research interactions. What developmental processes would be necessary?

4   What features for engaging readers can you use to begin creating your complexity-sensitive mixed methods study proposal? Access a complex mixed methods research problem that you would like to pursue. Sketch a description of the research team members and justify the need for the team configuration. Select one of the features for engaging readers that fits with your study and write a brief discussion of how your study engages the reader.

.... KEY CHAPTER CONCEPTS

This chapter advances the fifth adaptive practice for a complexity-sensitive approach to mixed methods research. It addresses the question: What do integrative mixed methods research interactions involve and how can integrative capacity among research team members be developed? The essential functions for complex mixed methods research interactions are linked with the need for emergence of as yet unknown understandings and member roles for addressing complex research questions. The purpose of explaining the integrative capacity is to demonstrate feasibility of the study. By considering leader-centric effects, researchers are cautioned to avoid allocating leadership responsibilities to a single person or small group of people by instead adopting a more distributed and shared approach to team leadership. A four-part iterative process is presented for developing integrative mixed methods research teams involving forming for diversity, capitalizing on differences, norming of relations, and performing as a team. Features that will engage readers include highlighting the diversity of those involved in the research and describing creative opportunities for members to interact collaboratively. Innovations in explaining the capacity for developing integrative mixed methods research interactions involve visual diagrams and writing ideas. The next chapter introduces the complexity-sensitive practices related to generating evidence of complex mixed methods research outcomes.

.... FURTHER READINGS

The following resources are offered as introductory references for research teams and developing research interactions. The list should not be considered exhaustive. Readers are encouraged to seek out additional readings in the end-of-book reference list. Readings denoted with an asterisk are available on the online resources website for this book.

Bowers, B., Cohen, L. W., Elliot, A. E., Grabowski, D. C., Fishman, N. W., Sharkey, S. S., ..., & Kemper, P. (2013). Creating and supporting a mixed methods health services research team. *Health Services Research, 48*, 2157–2180. doi: 10.1111/1475-6773.12118.

These authors draw upon their experiences from a health services research evaluation to offer practical guidance for developing mixed methods research teams. Findings call for 'creative optimization' of resources for team development along with frequent communication, creation of collaborative policies, commitment to the work, and flexibility for responding to opportunities.

NIH Office of Behavioral and Social Sciences (2018). Best practices for mixed methods research in the health sciences (2nd ed). Bethesda: National Institutes of Health. Retrieved from https://www.obssr.od.nih.gov/wp-content/uploads/2018/01/Best-Practices-for-Mixed-Methods-Research-in-the-Health-Sciences-2018-01-25.pdf.

This second edition offers authors a guiding resource for US-based National Institute of Health investigators focused on how to rigorously evelop and evaluate mixed methods research applications. Among the key best practices identified is the advice related to team formations, mixed methods research training, and reviewing mixed methods research applications.

Curry, L. A., Krumholz, H. M., O'Cathain, A., Plano Clark, V. L., Cherlin, E., & Bradley, E. H. (2013). Mixed methods in biomedical and health services research. *Circulation: Cardiovascular Quality and Outcomes, 10*(1), 119–123. doi: 10.1161/ CIRCOUTCOMES.112.967885.

These authors provide a concise overview of key principles to facilitate mixed methods research best practices for the readers of biomedical and health services journals. In so doing, the authors offer practical advice about focal topics that are well suited for mixed methods research.

*Curry, L. A., O'Cathain, A., Plano Clark, V. L., Aroni, R., Fetters, M., & Berg, D. (2012). The role of group dynamics in mixed methods health sciences research teams. *Journal of Mixed Methods Research, 6*(1), 5–20. doi: 10.1177/1558689811416941.

These authors explore the group dynamics of mixed methods health sciences research teams, identify challenges, and propose guiding principles. Noteworthy are the discussions about developing meaningful interactions and handling conflict and tension.

*Hesse-Biber, S. (2016). Doing interdisciplinary mixed methods health care research: Working the boundaries, tensions, and synergistic potential of team-based research. *Qualitative Health Research, 26*(5), 649–658. doi: 10.1177/1049732316634304.

Sharlene Hesse-Biber examines the range of factors and issues that need to be considered to facilitate efficient interdisciplinary team-based mixed methods research. Of particular note are the discussions related to definitions of interdisciplinary research and practical considerations.

*O'Cathain, A., Murphy, E., & Nicholl, J. (2008). Multidisciplinary, interdisciplinary, or dysfunctional? Team working in mixed-methods research. *Qualitative Health Research, 18*(11), 1574–1585. doi:10.1177/1049732308325535.

These authors identify three distinct models of teamwork – multidisciplinary, interdisciplinary, and dysfunctional – from an empirical study involving interviews with 20 researchers who had worked on mixed methods studies in health research services.

Poth, C. (2012). Exploring the role of mixed methods practitioner within educational research teams: A cross case comparison of the research planning process. *International Journal of Multiple Research Approaches, 6*(3), 315–332. doi: 10.5172/mra.2012.6.3.314.

I illustrate the role of a mixed methods practitioner by comparing the processes involved in two multi-year, educational-focused mixed methods research studies. Of particular note are the roles for the mixed methods practitioner related to boundary spanner and issue mediator.

Apply your mixed methods knowledge with videos, activities, SAGE journal articles and project templates at **https://study.sagepub.com/poth**

9

GENERATING EVIDENCE OF COMPLEX MIXED METHODS RESEARCH OUTCOMES

By the end of this chapter, you will be able to answer the following questions:

- Why generate evidence of complex mixed methods research outcomes?
- What opportunities exist to generate evidence for complex mixed methods outcomes?
- Why can 'black box' interpretations become hazardous for mixed methods researchers?
- What guides the generative evidence approach for complex mixed methods research outcomes?
- What features engage readers with complex mixed methods research outcomes?
- What writing and diagram innovations are useful for generating evidence of complex mixed methods research outcomes?

NEW CHAPTER TERMS

By the end of this chapter, you will be familiar with the following terms:

- 'Black box' interpretations
- Practical influences

- Complex mixed methods research outcomes
- Quality criteria

This chapter advances the adaptive practice for guiding a complexity-sensitive approach to mixed methods research. It addresses the question: *What does generating complex mixed methods research outcomes involve, and how can the evidence of methodological rigour and evolving practical influences be recognized, promoted, and conveyed?* Consider a research study you recently read. Did the authors present sufficient evidence about the methodological rigour of the study for you to have confidence in the outcomes? Were you persuaded that the study outcomes are worthy of attention? What evidence is presented and what strategies contribute to building your confidence in the study's outcomes? A well-written methodology section outlines the rationales and strategies for generating evidence of methodological rigour, whereby the findings section reports the evidence underpinning the outcomes that are then considered within the discussion section. Ideally, the subsequent study conclusions describe the potential implications and their audiences and present key limitations and future directions for research. Let us now consider how generating **complex mixed methods research outcomes** is distinctive.

Not being able to specify the research outcomes and predetermine the processes for generating the mixed insights are key dilemmas experienced by mixed methods researchers addressing complex problems. These dilemmas can be attributed to the interdependency of the practice for generating evidence for research outcomes within the organic mixed methods research process discussed in Chapter 2. Specifically, as understandings of the intentions of research problems, systems of research contexts, designs of research integrations, and capacity of research interactions evolve throughout the study, so do the understandings of the necessary evidence of methodological rigour for building confidence in the research outcomes. This is because under conditions of high complexity, the research outcomes are yet to be known and thus researchers must adjust their processes and products for generating the evidence to assimilate evolving understandings of the conditions and the dynamic **practical influences** throughout the study. If researchers are not able to predetermine the intentions, systems, designs, and capacities for tackling complex problems, then they are not able to plan to generate the evidence that meets the standards associated with rigorous research. Researchers are thus challenged to describe how the evidence underpinning methodological rigour will be generated at the beginning of a study.

Before we go too far in this chapter, it is imperative that I wade through the diverse terminology associated with evaluating quality of mixed methods research and clearly plant our feet in my operational definition of methodological rigour: the strength of the underlying logic of the research and the confidence with which conclusions can be drawn. The seminal work developed by the Task Force on Reporting of Research Methods in American Educational Research Association Publications (AERA, 2006) and adopted by the AERA Council in 2006 provides useful guidance for defining the evidence necessary for research to be considered rigorous. According to AERA (2006), warrantedness and transparency are key criteria that need to be met. Whereas *warranted* implies sufficient evidence is presented to justify the findings and subsequent inferences, *transparent* implies sufficient evidence is presented regarding the research process. Similar to the assertion made by Onwuegbuzie and Corrigan (2014), I believe these criteria are highly suitable for describing rigorous mixed methods research. In practice, this means mixed methods research proposals and reports must be defensible and transparent. In this chapter, I suggest a way for evidence of methodological rigour to be generated as understandings emerge and adaptations occur in response to changing conditions during the process of conducting mixed methods research under conditions of complexity. A focus on generative evidence advances the possibility of meeting the criteria of warrantedness and transparency associated with methodological rigour when mixed methods research outcomes and processes are yet to be known through embedding responsiveness to evolving conditions. This is represented by a **generative evidence approach** to complex mixed methods research outcomes.

Work on this chapter was informed by my experiences developing a complexity-sensitive mentality and specifically, my reading of the recent recommendations and reporting standards by the American Psychological Association (Appelbaum et al., 2018; Levitt et al., 2017, 2018) and those advancing discussions and practices for enhancing quality of mixed methods research (Creamer, 2018; Creswell, 2015b; Fàbregues & Molina-Azorín, 2017) and legitimation and validity of mixed methods research outcomes (Collins, 2015; Collins et al., 2012; Collins, Onwuegbuzie, & Jiao, 2007; Creswell & Plano Clark, 2018; Onwuegbuzie, Johnson, & Collins, 2009). A pivotal moment for my thinking about research rigour occurred during the writing of our evidence-based guidelines for reviewing mixed methods research manuscripts as guest editors of a special journal issue (Onwuegbuzie & Poth, 2016). I realized that while reviewers of mixed methods manuscripts could generally articulate the type of evidence they sought, many of our resources lacked guidance for generating such evidence. This was especially true for designs that did not easily fit an existing typology. Connections were forged with the Task Force on Reporting of Research Methods in American Educational Research Association (AERA) Publications (2006), resulting in two of our meta-themes relating to the lack of warrantedness and lack of transparency regarding inappropriate, inadequate or missing evidence. Embedding the featured mixed methods studies in this chapter reflects a continued effort to address the practice gap in many textbooks and to provide authentic examples of published articles that represent varying conditions of complexity related to research outcomes. Specifically, a complexity-sensitive approach to mixed methods research assumes our approaches to generating evidence for complex mixed methods research outcomes are evolving over time in response to changing conditions.

To optimize an approach to generating evidence of rigour in mixed methods research outcomes in light of the uncertainties researchers face under some conditions of complexity, three pressing needs exist. The first is to position the need for a generative approach that embeds integrative thinking with complexity about research outcomes and the hazards associated with **'black box' interpretations**. The second pressing need is to advance strategies for generating evidence of complex mixed methods research outcomes that draw upon our current and emerging understandings of the warrantedness and transparency criteria associated with methodological rigour across qualitative, quantitative, and mixed methods research as well as the practical influences on the dynamic research conditions. The third pressing need is to identify features for engaging readers and those writing and diagram innovations that are useful for explaining evidence of complex mixed methods research outcomes in proposals and reports. As a starting point, let us consider the need for a focus on integrative thinking with complexity to guide researchers in generating evidence of complex mixed methods research outcomes.

Why Generate Evidence of Complex Mixed Methods Research Outcomes?

Researchers are tasked with the responsibility of generating evidence of methodological rigour for building confidence in their research outcomes – for a complexity-sensitive approach, this involves assimilating understandings of the effects of dynamic practical influences on the evolving study outcomes while meeting the criteria of warrantedness and transparency associated with rigorous research. The importance of generating persuasive evidence of the rationales, processes, and outcomes of mixed methods research cannot be understated. As recently noted, 'quality is one of the most debated topics in the recent history of mixed methods research. A growing number of authors are currently discussing how the quality of mixed methods research should be conceptualized and operationalized, with the ultimate aim of promoting well designed and properly implemented mixed methods studies' (Fàbregues & Molina-Azorín, 2017, p. 2847). Indeed, considerations about quality remain key to, if not *the most important* aspect of, mixed methods research, although suffering from lack of agreement related to terminology and practical guidance. Among the many challenges, especially for those new to mixed methods research, is the number of differing terms that are used for this topic and the lack of specific criteria to evaluate studies with.

Let me provide some foundational ideas that draw on differing perspectives including my own (note that I do not claim the following to be representative of all diverse perspectives or that my viewpoint should be adopted). What is perceived as research quality is highly context dependent (Collins et al., 2012), and I consider **quality criteria** to be a useful overarching term and as referring, in part, to strategies for defending the warrantedness of the study's outcomes and for building credibility of the researcher's inferences through transparency in mixed methods research. It is noteworthy that others have included warrantedness and transparency within larger frameworks of quality criteria (Bryman, 2014; Creamer, 2018 Fàbregues & Molina-Azorín, 2017; Onwuegbuzie & Poth, 2016). You will note my previous references to the need for innovations in quality indicators when generating evidence of mixed methods research outcomes under conditions of complexity in Chapter 3. I am using just two aspects of methodological rigour, warrantedness and transparency, in this discussion of complex mixed methods research outcomes to begin addressing the concerns that quality frameworks are too large and complex and therefore of little use to those new to mixed methods research (Bryman, 2014).

Generating evidence of efforts to enhance methodological rigour on the part of the researcher is a key quality indicator (Creamer, 2018). It requires being explicit about rationales underpinning decisions and being transparent in describing the processes. Sources of potential evidence for methodological rigour are embedded throughout the mixed methods research process. Examine Figure 9.1 highlighting six sources of evidence for methodological rigour in mixed methods research as follows:

- *Participant samples.* Details about who is involved in mixed methods research are important for assessing the relevance of the participant samples, and the mixed sampling strategies and outcomes for generating evidence.
- *Data collections.* Details about how the data is collected in mixed methods research are important for assessing the relevance of the data sources, and the data strand procedures and outcomes for generating evidence.
- *Data analyses.* Details about how the data is analysed in mixed methods research are important for assessing the relevance of the strategies, and the intensity of mixing and outcomes for generating evidence.
- *Findings representations.* Details about how the findings are represented in mixed methods research are important for assessing the relevance of the displays, and the extent of mixing and outcomes for generating evidence.
- *Interpretation approaches.* Details about how the inferences are interpreted in mixed methods research are important for assessing the relevance of the insights and outcomes for generating evidence.
- *Insight discussions.* Details about how the insights are discussed in mixed methods research are important for assessing the relevance of the implications and outcomes and for generating evidence.

The purpose of generating evidence is to build confidence in the mixed methods research outcomes. The new approach to generating evidence under conditions of complexity responds to the dilemmas experienced with a lack of understanding of practical influences on the integrations and availability of guiding practices. Thus, the traditional mixed methods research practice focused on evaluating research outcomes based on predetermined expectations of methodological rigour is not suitable under conditions of higher complexity. Instead an adaptive practice for assessing evidence of outcomes is more appropriate, given the uncertainty of the processes and products necessary for methodological rigour. Generating research evidence is realized through integrative thinking with complexity about the research outcomes and practical influences. In so doing, the researcher is better able to assimilate and respond to emerging understandings of research evidence in ways that both influences and are influenced by the changing conditions surrounding the mixed methods research. Examine Figure 9.1 depicting the potential sources of evidence as embedded throughout mixed methods research. See Table B.3 in Appendix B, an editable version of which is also available on the companion website for the book.

Determining the quality of a study should reflect responsiveness to changing conditions and researchers' professional judgements of their interpretation of the most consistent evidence, with special considerations given to the evidence most relevant to the research. In this way, researchers play a key role in the generation and assessment of outcomes evidence. They need to be adequately prepared for this. In Guiding Tip 9.1, a professor of international communication at Aoyama Gakuin University in Tokyo (Japan) offers advice for expanding discussions about the specific capacity needed for evaluating mixed methods research.

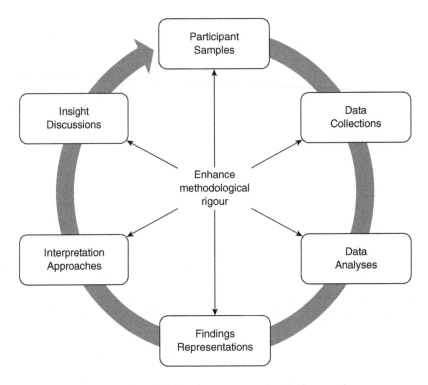

Figure 9.1 Sources of evidence of methodological rigour in mixed methods research

Guiding Tip 9.1

Hisako Kakai advising how to navigate the evaluative criteria specific to mixed methods research

The mixed methods literature also needs to expand discussion on the kinds of evaluation criteria that are unique to and reasonable for epistemologically diverse types of mixed methods research.

Generating Opportunities and Hazards for Mixed Methods Researchers

Generative Evidence Approach Opportunities

Among the opportunities for mixed methods researchers is the ability to capitalize upon the recommendations for designing and reviewing research advanced by others as they consider specific guidelines for mixed methods research. Further to the AERA (2006) guidelines discussed earlier by AERA (2006), noteworthy are the recent publications by the American Psychological Association (APA) Publications and Communications Board Task Forces on the journal article reporting standards for quantitative research (Appelbaum et al.,

2018) and for qualitative and mixed methods research (Levitt et al., 2018) are noteworthy. The significance can be attributed to the catalysis of the APA's work in establishing journal article reporting standards which was described as 'a mounting concern with transparency in science' (Appelbaum et al., 2018, p. 3). The expansion beyond quantitative research to also include qualitative and mixed methods research represents a significant milestone acknowledging their unique contributions and indicating acceptance by the field. Like the authors of the article on reporting standards for qualitative and mixed methods, I can also see a similar opportunity for what they call 'an ethic of transparency' (Levitt et al., 2018, p. 29) to inform research practices in other areas. That the recursive nature of data collection and analysis inherent in qualitative approaches may bring shifts in the procedures as the study unfolds can also be helpful for those struggling under conditions of complexity with the inability to predetermine research processes and outcomes. Consider Researcher Spotlight 9.1 describing the challenges future mixed methods researchers may face under conditions of complexity related to keeping pace with the changing research world, from the perspective of a prominent mixed methods research scholar and adjunct professor at Western Sydney University (Australia).

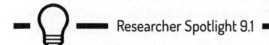 Researcher Spotlight 9.1

Pat Bazeley on future challenges with researcher methodological capacity

Methods are constantly evolving; increasingly so in an increasingly digitized world. On the one hand, researchers are faced with the difficulty of keeping up with new developments, especially those that involve coming to grips with constantly evolving and new computer programs and algorithms. On the other hand, the basic foundations of methods are in danger of becoming lost, as researchers are beguiled by new methods and what computers can do. Researchers still need to be trained in those basic foundational skills of obtaining data – which involve building relationships regardless of the data type, recording and managing data, and especially, immersing oneself in and interpreting data. The computer can assist, but it cannot replace the capacity of the human mind to flexibly and contextually respond to data; to creatively imagine data; and to understand, evaluate, and make sense of data.

The need to remain open to new possibilities, shifts in thinking, and conditions of research should inform how we approach generating evidence of methodological rigour. Alan Bryman was ahead of his time in his recognition of the unpredictability of some mixed methods research outcomes: 'while a decision about design issues may be made in advance and for good reasons, when the data are generated, surprising findings or unrealized potential in the data may suggest anticipated consequences of combining them' (Bryman, 2006, p. 99). This points to the need for researchers to be agile in their thinking about evidence and adaptive in their strategies for generating it. Further and more recently, Bryman (2014, p. 125) suggested the need for researchers to adhere to the quality expectations of the data strands and the 'need for the quantitative and qualitative components of a mixed methods project to be implemented in a technically competent manner'. I would agree, and further expand the need for competencies specifically related to mixed methods research. In Practice Alert 9.1, I consider how my previous research experiences using data analysis software can contribute to my capacity for integrating qualitative and quantitative data in mixed methods research, and I invite you to do the same. In doing this analysis, I am enhancing my understandings of the influences of my qualitative and quantitative research experiences on my thinking about mixed methods research outcomes.

 Practice Alert 9.1

What might my previous research experiences contribute to my capacity for generating evidence of mixed methods research outcomes?

Careful consideration of some existing strategies for enhancing methodological rigour in qualitative and quantitative research has illuminated potential applications of mixed methods research under conditions of complexity. As an illustrative example, let us consider my use of computer software applications for data analysis. For years, I have used different software applications for the analysis of quantitative and qualitative data. Over the last few years, I have become more aware of (and perhaps open to) the use of computers in mixed methods data integration, but I must provide a caveat to the uses I will discuss below. The processes used for integration are the same for what can be done by hand – either through computation of statistics or hand-coding of themes. Computers in mixed methods research for data integration might be worthwhile to consider. How the researcher intends to use the software for organizing and memoing as well as retrieval and representations are key considerations. My experiences point to three tasks where software can be especially useful during data analysis and integration. These tasks align with those also described by Kuchartz (2014) and Bazeley (2018):

- Importing and exporting data is easy because the software helps with organization; for example, I can effortlessly link between qualitative and quantitative data files.
- Searching and retrieving data is quick because the software facilitates searches; for example, I can easily locate a variety of materials – whether this material is an idea, a statement, a statistic or code definition.
- Exploring and generating insights is facilitated because the software creates visual representations; for example, I can examine connections among qualitative themes and quantitative findings.

What this means for me, as I begin to use computer software for integration, is that I can build upon my existing practices rather than starting anew. I am excited by the increasing capacities of computer software where the only limitations may be my creativity in use! I also heed the sage advice offered by Pat Bazeley (2003b, pp. 418–419): 'the role of the researcher remains paramount in deciding issues relating to the meaning of codes, the appropriateness of samples, the choice of techniques for manipulating data and methods of analysis and the interpretations of the data tables and displays produced using the computer'.

Try this now – sketch your ideas about how you might use computer software in your mixed methods research. Download a trial version of one of the programs considered most useful for combining quantitative with qualitative data for analysis: Dedoose (www.dedoose.com), MAXQDA (www.maxqda.com), NVivo (www.qsrinternational.com) and QDA Miner (provalisresearch.com). Then upload and process some files to assess the particular strengths of each of the different software programs.

'Black Box' Interpretation Hazards

The extent to which evidence of the processes and products of integration is presented can dramatically influence the quality assessment of the study. This can be attributed to integration offering researchers the opportunity to advance an area that is considered 'undertheorized and understudied' (Greene, 2007, p. 125) but an essential characteristic of mixed methods research. Uprichard and Dawney (2016, p. 2; emphasis in original) posit: 'the possibility of data integration lies in the extent to which data from different methods can be interpreted *together* in a meaningful way.' That researchers continue to struggle with data integration is not new (Bazeley, 2018; Bryman, 2006; 2007; O'Cathain, et al., 2008). The various aspects of these struggles range from whether integration actually takes place (or can) to the procedures guiding integration. For example, an examination of reports and publications from 48 mixed methods projects funded by the UK Department of Health highlighted a lack of evidence in 51 % of the studies of attempts to integrate data (O'Cathain, Murphy, & Nicholl, 2007). Another example highlights the limited variety in how integration was performed or reported in a review of 232 social sciences articles in which qualitative and quantitative research were combined (Bryman, 2006). In her book focused on integration, Bazeley (2018, p. 10) highlights the ongoing challenge for the field of mixed methods research and its readers:

> The challenge of integration becomes most evident when results from studies purporting to use mixed methods are reported separately; or when separately developed components are reported sequentially within a dissertation, a report or article. When specific findings derived from different components of a study are reported in parallel, it can appear as if the tasks of integrating them is the responsibility of the reader.

I propose a 'black box' as a metaphor for the 'darkness' or lack of knowledge ascribed to the actual interpretation procedures undertaken related to the integrated findings to generate the mixed insights. I use a black box to represent how the integration and interpretation processes are often presented to readers. Often authors spend a great deal of effort describing the data procedures for the qualitative and quantitative data strands and discussing the outcomes from the integration but provide few details about the actual integration and interpretation procedures leading to the mixed insights. I make the case for moving beyond the darkness because it is not enough to simply report the inputs and outputs; researchers have to explain how it was done and why.

The problem, of course, is the lack of transparency in these tasks, and generating evidence of complex mixed methods research outcomes requires being explicit about our understandings of the processes and products involved in the research. This is particularly important for the topic of integration where the field could benefit from greater transparency and guidance for a future we cannot yet imagine. Consider Researcher Spotlight 9.2 which describes the key future challenges related to data sources and possible integrations, from the perspective of an associate professor at the Centre for Interdisciplinary Methodologies at the University of Warwick (UK).

 Researcher Spotlight 9.2

Emma Uprichard on two future challenges related to data sources and possible integrations, and questions that will need addressing

The first challenge relates to being able to deal with a huge variety of data: data that is both qualitative and quantitative, and also data that is a bit of both – hybrid data, if you like. For example, YouTube, Facebook, and data from a variety of new and old social media sites and networks. How can these kinds of data challenge the mixed methods paradigms? How might these data sources dismantle or challenge some of the a priori assumptions upon which mixed methods research takes place in the first place? For example, how might these new forms of data challenge the very notion that data can be either quantitative or qualitative? The second challenge is about new forms of digital data with many more time and space points than ever before. How might mixed methods researchers critically engage with these new kinds of data? How do these new kinds of data allow for alternative ways to 'mix' and 'integrate' data? How might these kinds of large sources of data, which in some cases may be available in almost 'real time' and 'real space', provide opportunities for mixed methods researchers to consider the complex dynamics of change and continuity?

A Generative Evidence Approach for Complex Mixed Methods Research Outcomes

With the focus on researchers' responsiveness and professional judgements of their interpretation of most consistent evidence, with special considerations given to evidence most relevant to the research, the generative evidence approach represents a departure from traditional practices associated with evaluating research outcomes based on predetermined expectations of methodological rigour. There is no simple way to avoid black box effects in research outcomes, but adopting an approach that emphasizes transparency of processes and products provides a suitable place for generating adaptive evidence. I can share how I approach generating evidence under conditions of varying complexity using six contributors to methodological rigour in mixed methods research as the organizing framework depicted in Figure 9.2, summarized in Table 9.1, and discussed below: accounts of participant samples, procedures for data collections, strategies guiding data analyses, displays of findings representations, conveying interpretation approaches, and relating insight discussions.

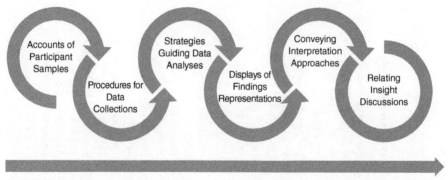

As understandings of the research conditions evolve, so does the contributing evidence of each component for methodological rigour

Figure 9.2 A generative evidence approach for complex mixed methods research outcomes

Accounts of Participant Samples

Participant samples can be differentiated by their composition and relationships. Making the mixed sampling characteristics explicit as they become known is a key aspect of enhancing methodological rigour in mixed methods studies under conditions of high complexity. The field of mixed methods research is fortunate to be able to draw upon the extensive work of others in relation to sampling. For example, Collins (2015) describes an inclusive sampling model for mixed methods research which extends her previous work identifying sample schemes (see also Onwuegbuzie & Collins, 2007). Other seminal works in this area include the comprehensive description by Teddlie and Yu (2007) of a taxonomy involving five types of mixed methods sampling techniques. Each of these typologies can be drawn upon under conditions of varying complexity if the sampling strategy fits the description of the sampling processes undertaken. Generating evidence to describe exactly who is involved in a study sample (and who is not) when the target population is not defined at the beginning of the study is naturally challenging.

Through documenting sampling decisions throughout the study, the researcher can create an account of participant samplings. These understandings have important potential implications for interpreting the integrated findings and for how the outcomes can be used beyond the specific study contexts. Key among the considerations is what is known (and emerging) about the sample and the sampling strategy. Any information about the relationships among the samples, among participants and researchers, and their larger populations and contexts can be useful for describing participant samples. The featured studies provide some evidence of accounts of participant samples (see Table 9.2). For example, all of the featured studies provided information about the qualitative and quantitative samples as well as indicators of the relationship among the samples. In the featured study on safe places (Zea et al., 2014), although a nested mixed sampling strategy is not explicitly identified we can assume that this might be the case for at least some of the 42 qualitative research participants and 113 quantitative research participants because of the small size of the vulnerable and

Table 9.1 Summary of desirable evidence for methodological rigour of qualitative, quantitative and mixed methods research

Sources of evidence	Contribution to methodological rigour	Generative mixed methods research evidence	Quantitative research evidence	Qualitative research evidence
Accounts of participant samples	Who is involved is important for assessing relevance of the participant samples to the complex mixed methods research problems and outcomes for generating evidence	Descriptions of rationales, processes and outcomes for the participant samples and representations about how understandings of the mixed samples evolved throughout the study	Descriptions of quantitative samples related to: • Sampling strategy • Response rates • Incentives/compensation • Inclusion/exclusion criteria • Demographic information • Margin of error • Confidence interval • Confidence level	Descriptions of qualitative samples related to: • Sampling strategy • Participation rates • Incentives/compensation • Inclusion/exclusion criteria • Common and unique characteristics • Personal, interpersonal and social contextual information
Procedures for data collections	How data is collected is important for assessing the relevance of data sources and data strand procedures to the complex mixed methods research integrations and outcomes for generating evidence	Descriptions of rationales, processes and outcomes for data collections and representations about how understandings of the data strands evolved throughout the study	Descriptions of quantitative data collections related to: • Theoretical frameworks identifying variables and constructs • Rationale for choice of scales and instruments • Composition of scales and instruments and established reliability • Procedures for piloting/pretesting scales and instruments • Procedures for administering scales and instruments	Descriptions of qualitative data collections related to: • Rationale for choice of research strategy/method • Development of protocols/instruments • Composition of protocols and instruments • Pretesting/piloting protocols/instruments • Administration procedures for protocols and instruments

Sources of evidence	Contribution to methodological rigour	Generative mixed methods research evidence	Quantitative research evidence	Qualitative research evidence
Strategies for data analyses	How the data is analysed in mixed methods research is important for assessing the relevance of strategies and intensity of mixing to the complex mixed methods research integrations and outcomes and for generating evidence	Descriptions of rationales, processes and outcomes for data analyses and representations about how understandings of the mixed analysis strategies evolved throughout the study	Descriptions of quantitative data analysis related to: • Analysis software • Data preparations and missing data strategies • Exploratory analysis procedures – descriptive analysis and assessment of instrument reliability • In-depth analysis procedures such as inferential statistics and structural equation modelling	Descriptions of qualitative data analysis related to: • Analysis software • Data preparations and checking transcripts for accuracy • Exploratory examinations of transcripts or files and create memos • In-depth analysis procedures such as development of coding schemes, audit trails, and member checking
Displays of findings representations	How the findings are represented in mixed methods research is important for assessing the relevance of the displays and the extent of mixing for the complex research problems and outcomes and for generating evidence	Descriptions of rationales, processes and outcomes for integrated findings and representations about how understandings of the points of interface evolved throughout the study	Descriptions of quantitative findings related to: • Exploratory analysis findings such as reliability of scales and effect sizes • In-depth analysis findings such as models and correlations	Descriptions of qualitative findings related to: • Coding, theme and category structures and quotes and inter-rater reliabilities
Conveying interpretation approaches	How the inferences are interpreted in mixed methods research is important for assessing relevance of the insights to the complex research problems and outcomes and for generating evidence	Descriptions of rationales, processes and outcomes for interpretations and representations about how understandings of the inferences evolved throughout the study	Descriptions of quantitative interpretations related to: • Level of statistical significance • Comparisons to hypothesis • Specific scale interpretations guidelines	Descriptions of qualitative interpretations related to: • Key themes and quotes • Development of visual models or tables
Relating insight discussions	How the insights are discussed in mixed methods research is important for assessing the relevance of implications to the complex research problems and outcomes for generating evidence	Descriptions of rationales, processes and outcomes for mixed insights and representations about how understandings of the implications evolved throughout the study	Descriptions of quantitative insights related to: • Existing literature • New understandings and study implications—Limitations • Future directions for research	Descriptions of qualitative insights related to: • Existing literature • New understandings and study implications—Limitations • Future directions for research

marginalized Colombian population of gay and bisexual men and transwomen who had experienced internal displacement due to violent conflict, social cleansing, and homonegativity. A further feature of this particular participant sample was understanding the existing relationships of the researchers with members of this hard-to-reach sample. As well, any information about common characteristics and practical limitations to participation can be useful in identifying potential sampling bias. For example, all of the featured studies reported their sample sizes, yet none of them reported population statistics or even how many participants might have been recruited. The exception might be the information provided by the featured study on heart care (Dickson et al., 2011) which reported 41 participants out of a possible 42 who were referred to the research team and explained why the one participant no longer met eligibility criteria.

When generating evidence for complex mixed methods research outcomes, consider the information available from the following questions related to the participant sample and sampling considerations:

• What do we know about the relationships among the participant samples? (Identify any sampling typologies, if applicable.)
• What do we know about the mixed participant sample characteristics?
• What do we know about the possible practical influences on the sampling rationales, processes, and outcomes?

Procedures for Data Collections

The procedures guiding data collection play an essential role in generating information to address research questions. Making explicit the sequencing of data strands as well as the rationales and procedures underpinning these decisions is a key aspect of enhancing methodological rigour. When it is not possible to predetermine a design and outline exactly why, when, and how the data is collected, our understandings of what evidence is necessary related to the data collection procedures evolve throughout the study. These understandings have important potential implications for building confidence in the findings and eventual study outcomes. Key among the considerations is what is known (and emerging) about the data strand sequencing and rationales underpinning the selection of research methods. Any information about the designs and established research methods can be useful for describing data collections.

The featured studies provide extensive evidence of the procedures for data collections (see Table 9.3). For example, all the featured studies include information about the timing of the data strands, mixing purposes, and how the data is collected in terms of instruments and protocols, yet only two – those on heart care (Dickson et al., 2011) and vaping culture (Colditz et al., 2017) – provide a visual design diagram. The featured study on leadership competencies (Strudsholm et al., 2016) provides a summary table of the design features. It is interesting to note that all the featured studies provide a rationale for their use of the quantitative research method selected, whereas less information about rationales underpinning qualitative methods and protocol development is provided. In the featured study on law clients (Chui & Cheng, 2017), the authors describe their use of a quantitatively led sequential design using follow-up interviews to explain the results of established scales. They ground their rationale for the use of three scales in their theoretical framework.

Table 9.2 Summary of evidence generated by the accounts of participant samples in the featured studies

Featured study	Mixed methods research evidence	Quantitative research evidence	Qualitative research evidence
Law clients (Chui & Cheng, 2017)	Nested mixed sampling of youth who had experience with lawyers described, but typology not identified	Convenience sample of 168 and inclusion criteria described and demographic information included: age, gender, education, ethnicity, previous experiences within judicial system	Purposeful sampling of 30 described from initial quantitative sample Demographic information: age, gender, education, employment status, income, conviction rates, crimes committed, previous lawyer experiences
Postconflict risk (Taylor et al., 2017)	Multilevel sampling of mothers, fathers, and adolescents living in the same larger context setting of intergroup conflict described but typology not identified. Well-established collaboration of researcher with local communities described	Convenience sample of 227 youth with inclusion criteria described and demographic information included: age, gender, ethnicity, family composition	Convenience sample of 66 mothers, fathers, and adolescents with inclusion criteria described and demographic information included: adolescent and mother age range, compositions relative to ethnicity and gender
Heart care (Dickson et al., 2011)	Identical samples of heart failure patients including criteria for inclusion/exclusion related to clinical features, age, English ability; 41 of 42 possible participants. Referral process of potential participants described as occurring from the clinical team to the research team		
Safe places (Zea et al., 2014)	Nested sampling assumed, but typology is not identified. Existing relationships of the researchers within the vulnerable and marginalized Colombian GBT community, who had experienced internal displacement due to violent conflict, social cleansing, and homonegativity, are described	Convenience sample of 113 out of possible 1000 respondents and inclusion criteria related to age, gender, sexual orientation (but not displacement)	Snowball sample of 42 participants that met eligibility criteria described related to age, gender, sexual orientation, and displacement status
Leadership competencies (Strudsholm et al., 2016)	Nested sampling but typology is not identified. Relationship of several members of the research team as part of the targeted sample is described	Population sample sought, 821 responses and inclusion criteria related to association members on email list of seven public health professions	Purposeful sample of 27 recognized leaders in public health out of 92 nominated by the project's expert advisory committee
Vaping culture (Colditz et al., 2017)	Identical random purposeful samples of 768 out of 5149 possible tweets created by electronic nicotine delivery system users who post on Twitter during the 3rd Annual World Vaping Day		

Another important consideration might be what is known about the instruments and protocols used to collect data. Any information about their development, previous use, administration, and practical limitations can be useful in identifying potential researcher or respondent bias. For example, two featured studies (those on law clients and heart care) provide fulsome descriptions of the quantitative scales, and that on postconflict risk (Taylor et al., 2017) provides the scales in the appendices. The other three provide no details of the quantitative scales – common to all of these was that the scales are researcher developed from initial quantitative data, yet no information about their development is provided. All the featured studies provide information about the procedures guiding the qualitative data collection, yet only two (those on heart care and postconflict risk) describe the development and include the protocols in the appendices. The law clients study provides examples of the interview question within the text.

When generating evidence for complex mixed methods research outcomes, consider the information available from the following questions related to data collection and procedures considerations:

- What do we know about the rationales underpinning decisions about the selection of methods for data collection and procedures?
- What do we know about the data collection sequencing, protocols, and instruments? (Identify any design typologies, if applicable.)
- What do we know about the possible practical influences on the data collection rationales, processes, and outcomes?

Table 9.3 Summary of evidence generated by the descriptions of data collection procedures in the featured studies

Featured study	Mixed methods research evidence	Quantitative research evidence	Qualitative research evidence
Law clients (Chui & Cheng, 2017)	Quantitatively led sequential design identified whereby the interviews were intended to explain the results of the initial statistical analysis	Description of three scales comprising survey instrument (perception of fairness in lawyer–client interactions, satisfaction with lawyers, and understanding about lawyers): authors, measurement scale, number of items, and constructs measured. Scales included in appendices	No information about interview protocol development, but example questions provided in text. Description of semi-structured interview procedures: length of time and language
Postconflict risk (Taylor et al., 2017)	Explanatory sequential, but typology not identified, whereby quantitative scales were developed from initial focus groups	Rationale provided and description of researcher-developed items briefly mentions pretesting and scale type and number of items, but no information provided about how items were developed. Scale included in appendix	Rationale of semi-structured focus group provided and procedures included: length, language and location. Training of facilitators and pre-testing referred to and protocol provided in appendix
Heart care (Dickson et al., 2011)	Concurrent triangulation mixed methods design identified and represented in a diagram.	Description of survey instruments included four scales	Rationale for use of semi-structured interviews provided and protocol

Featured study	Mixed methods research evidence	Quantitative research evidence	Qualitative research evidence
	whereby qualitative interviews and quantitative standardized assessments collected at the same time. Summary table of qualitative and quantitative data collection procedures provided	(Dutch heart failure knowledge, digit symbol substitution test, probed memory recall, self-care heart failure index) and information about established reliability, authors, purpose, procedures including measurement scale, number of items, and constructs measured	included in appendix. Administration procedures detail audio recording, length, training of researchers, and capturing of adaptations in field notes
Safe Places (Zea et al., 2014)	Design theoretically informed by transformative and social justice but no typology identified. Quantitative instrument was developed from qualitative findings	Brief description of survey instrument, but references to details provided in other publications. Administered through computers at a relevant organization providing safe places. Revised following piloting	Description of rationale for use of semi-structured life history interviews, focus groups, and key informant interviews using a non-coercive dialogue approach to guide narratives of internal displacement, risks, and survival. Audio recordings were produced. References to other publications with further details
Leadership competencies (Strudsholm et al., 2016)	Multiphase. Summary table of project components describes data collection methods in relation to research questions	Survey instrument was developed based on five categories resulting from a literature review. No information about	Rationale for use of focus group and references to established practices were provided, including sizes and audio recording. No information about the protocol
		item development or pilot testing was provided	other than that presentation slides were used to communicate survey results. Protocol was piloted among the researchers. Detailed description of procedures included adaptations in response to recruitment challenges
Vaping culture (Colditz et al., 2017)	Convergent parallel design identified and represented in a diagram, whereby tweets were collected and analysed qualitatively and quantitatively.	Protocols for decoding and creating a textured text file involved time-stamp, textual content of the tweet, and user's Twitter handle. Parameters of data collection were described in relation to: dates and times of postings, English language, and key search words	

Strategies Guiding Data Analyses

Among both the pressing challenges and opportunities for mixed methods researchers is how to go about integration. As noted by Bazeley (2018, p. xi), 'some of these [integration] methods are long established, but many are fresh and developing, as researchers capitalize on and share their creative skills'. It may not surprise you to learn that many typologies for integrated analysis exist and have generally been associated with particular designs and mixing purposes (Creswell & Plano Clark, 2018; Fetters et al., 2013; Teddlie & Tashakkori, 2009). Another approach to integration typologies involves identifying 13 dimensions to create analysis typologies. This offers the advantage of listing an extensive range of qualitative and quantitative analyses that could be used 'in an almost unlimited number of combinations' (Onwuegbuzie & Combs, 2010, p. 420). These attempts to create typologies for integrated analysis are well intended and may be beneficial to some, but under conditions of complexity they may be problematic and necessitate more advance mixed analysis processes such as those advanced by Onwuegbuzie and Hitchcock (2015). As Pat Bazeley (2018, pp. 63–64) highlights, 'typological models of analysis, like their design counterparts, become a problem when they constrain researchers' choices or when they focus the researcher's attention on concerns in analysis that are not especially relevant to their current situation'. She goes on to advise the need to focus on 'what data are available (or accessible) with which to answer [the question of interest], and what analysis processes can best be used to maximize the benefit of combining the different sources and types of data' (p. 65).

Similar to what we often see in published reports, some of the featured studies provide extensive evidence of the procedures for data analysis of quantitative and qualitative research, yet almost all lack information about integration processes (see Table 9.4). For example, four of the featured studies describe preparation, exploration, and in-depth analysis of the quantitative data and all provide at least comparable information about the qualitative data analysis, yet only two provide sufficient descriptions of the mixed analysis. The featured study on vaping culture (Colditz et al., 2017) provides a comprehensive description of the separate analyses and then how the coders move between the qualitative and quantitative data to assess convergence.

When generating evidence for complex mixed methods research outcomes, consider the information available from the following questions related to data analysis and procedures:

• What do we know about the rationales underpinning decisions about the data analysis strategies?
• What do we know about the qualitative, quantitative and mixed analysis strategies? (Identify any analysis typologies, if applicable.)
• What do we know about the possible practical influences on the data analysis rationales, processes, and outcomes?

Displays of Findings Representations

The initial work involves bringing together the differing records of evidence from the analyses and integration. Then there is a need to assess what makes sense to represent the findings: a table or a joint display. While I have used qualitative and quantitative software separately for this function, newer approaches for producing joint displays are emerging (see also Guetterman, Creswell, & Kuchartz, 2015). Making explicit the findings from the exploratory and in-depth analyses as well as rationales and procedures underpinning these decisions is a key aspect of enhancing methodological rigour. These understandings have important potential implications for building confidence in the findings and eventually study outcomes. Key among the considerations is what is known (and emerging) about the extent to which the data is integrated and the rationales that underpin the procedures.

Table 9.4 Summary of evidence generated by the descriptions of data analysis strategies in the featured studies

Featured study	Mixed methods research evidence	Quantitative research evidence	Qualitative research evidence
Law clients (Chui & Cheng, 2017)	Data integration occurs at inference, but little information about processes for linking quantitative data to qualitative data to explain initial (and prioritized) quantitative findings	Description of procedures for performing exploratory analysis (reliability coefficients) and ordinary least squares regressions	Description of transcription and translation to English. Thematic coding procedures identified, but procedures limited in description as guided by quantitative constructs
Postconflict risk (Taylor et al., 2017)	Data integration occurs at inference, but little information about linking of qualitative themes to develop quantitative scales	Description of procedures for performing exploratory factor analysis and generating evidence of internal consistency, factor loadings, and bivariate correlations	Description of transcription procedures involves translation into English. Procedures for constant comparative analysis method are detailed and include multiple coders
Heart care (Dickson et al., 2011)	Data integration occurs during interpretation to assess concordance between the qualitative and quantitative results	Description of computer software and procedures for data preparation and protection against skewed data with small sample size and linear regressions testing relative influence	Description of line-by-line checking of transcript, use of analysis software, and content analysis based on a priori codes from theoretical framework. Procedures for inter-rater reliability reported. Within- and across-case analysis described as iterative
Safe places (Zea et al., 2014)	Data integration is described as occurring during interpretations, so development of quantitative instrument is assumed from qualitative findings	No information provided about analysis	Use of computer software and egalitarian dialogue maintained during analysis. Multiple coders contributed to the coding process
Leadership competencies (Strudsholm et al., 2016)	Multiphase includes linking across three phases	No information provided about analysis	Use of computer software and multiple coders involved in thematic line coding
Vaping culture (Colditz et al., 2017)	Data integration occurs during interpretations through well-described convergence between qualitative and quantitative data about how the coders moved between the data sources	Quantitative content analysis was used to guide transformation procedures involving multiple coders. Use of computer software and performance of exploratory descriptive and inter-rater reliability statistics	Three broad a priori coding categories was the starting point. The codebook was refined through an iterative process involving multiple coders

I use the metaphors advanced by Bazeley and Kemp (2012), in one of my favourite articles, for describing how the findings in the featured studies are presented – related to linking, jigsaws, sprinkling, and fusion. The featured studies provide varying evidence of the findings representations (see Table 9.5). For example, all the featured studies (with the exception of that on safe places) present some evidence of quantitative and qualitative findings. Three provide extensive evidence of the quantitative scales alongside descriptions of the qualitative findings organized thematically. Information about the scale reliabilities and confidence intervals is more consistently represented in table form, whereas only one featured study – that on vaping culture (Colditz et al., 2017) – represented the coding structures in a table and reported inter-rater agreement. The extent to which integrated findings were represented also varied greatly: whereas only one featured study – that on heart care (Dickson et al., 2011) provided a visual joint display to represent what I consider to be a jigsaw approach to integration, another – the vaping culture study – provided evidence of fused integration findings in a results section. Two other featured studies provided evidence of integrated findings, but they were in the discussions.

When generating evidence for complex mixed methods research outcomes, consider the information available from the following questions related to data analysis and procedures considerations:

- What do we know about the rationales underpinning decisions about the findings representation strategies? (Identify any display typologies, if applicable)
- What do we know about the nature of the qualitative, quantitative and integrated findings?
- What do we know about the possible practical influences on the findings representation rationales, processes, and outcomes?

Table 9.5 Summary of evidence generated by the displays of findings representations in the featured studies

Featured study	Mixed methods research evidence	Quantitative research evidence	Qualitative research evidence
Law clients (Chui & Cheng, 2017)	Discussion 'sprinkled' qualitative information on significant quantitative findings. No evidence of integrated findings	Findings presented separately with four summary tables: correlations between scales and ordinary least square regressions for each scale. Reliabilities for each of three scales were reported in text	Findings presented separately and organized by four a priori themes with embedded quotes
Postconflict risk (Taylor et al., 2017)	Discussion 'linked' qualitative information to quantitative findings. No evidence of integrated findings	Findings presented separately with demonstration of discriminant validity. Path analyses established predictive validity between each type of risk and insecurity. Results of factor analysis are reported for internal consistency of revised scale. Bivariate correlations represented in summary table and results from path analysis described and represented visually	Findings presented separately and organized by four themes with embedded quotes
Heart care (Dickson et al., 2011)	Integrated findings are visually represented as a jigsaw in a joint display and then described narratively with fused findings followed by a discussion of mixed insights	Findings briefly presented separately with scores for each scale described and summarized in tables. Results were assessed by evaluating the significance of the increase in model R^2 and the direction and strength of slope coefficients and associated 95% confidence intervals. Post hoc effect sizes were calculated using Cohen's f^2. Post hoc power was also calculated imputing observed alpha, the number of predictors, sample size, and effect size	Narrative accounts summarizing consistencies and variances

Featured study	Mixed methods research evidence	Quantitative research evidence	Qualitative research evidence
Safe places (Zea et al., 2014)	No information provided	No information provided here, but reference to other publications	No information provided here, but reference to other publications
Leadership competencies (Strudsholm et al., 2016)	Little information provided about how the phases were linked	Findings presented separately with lists of characteristics of leaders as well as barriers and enablers to public leadership, but no statistical information presented	General findings are conveyed such as 'general agreement of participants with top five characteristics', but no quotes.
Vaping culture (Colditz et al., 2017)	Phenomenological synthesis processes and products described. Integrated findings presented as fused in the results	Table of descriptive statistics and statistics related to hashtags reported	Table summarized definitions of categorical codes and example tweets. Inter-rater agreement described

Conveying Interpretation Approaches

There is little guidance available for describing the approaches used by mixed methods researchers to generate mixed insights from integrated findings. One key exception is the book chapter 'From integrative analyses to warranted assertions and a coherent, negotiated account' (Bazeley, 2018). Among the key aspects described by Bazeley are to engage and document the negotiation processes as they take place. Engagement is identified as a key component to build awareness of the procedures undertaken; for example, compare or contrast? Consideration of negative cases? Attend to divergent findings? Rely on theory for guidance? Documentation is helpful to create what is known as an audit trail. Bazeley (2018, p. 291) describes generating ideas for the mixed insights through 'negotiating coherence through writing and visualizing'. Another helpful framework was recently advanced by Elizabeth Creamer (2018) in her description of criteria for interpretive comprehensiveness in her mixed methods evaluation rubric (MMER). Here she offers guidance for finding evidence of whether 'inconsistencies between the qualitative and quantitative data are identified and explained' (p. 152) or not and whether 'alternative explanations are weighed to explain inferences drawn from the analysis' (p. 152). Structures are lacking for researchers, and procedures thus far for interpreting seem to be guided by the intention of the problem, such as to confirm, expand, or explain (Creswell & Plano Clark, 2018; Fetters et al., 2013).

The featured studies provide some evidence of the approaches to interpretation (see Table 9.6). There seems to be a lack of attention to the procedures involved in interpreting the integrated findings, thus highlighting the need for these processes to be more explicit. The featured study on safe places (Zea et al., 2014) stands out for its description of how the non-coercive communication environment informed the interpretations of the qualitative findings and how participant feedback was used as evidence that this environment was achieved. The featured study on vaping culture (Colditz et al., 2017) is unique in its description and use of a validation approach to guide the phenomenological interpretations.

When generating evidence for complex mixed methods research outcomes, consider the information available from the following questions related to the interpretation approach considerations:

- What do we know about the rationales underpinning decisions about the interpretation approaches?
- What do we know about the qualitative, quantitative and mixed interpretation strategies? (Identify any interpretation typologies, if applicable.)
- What do we know about the possible practical influences on the interpretation rationales, processes, and outcomes?

Table 9.6 Summary of evidence generated by descriptions of interpretation approaches in the featured studies

Featured study	Mixed methods research evidence	Quantitative research evidence	Qualitative research evidence
Law clients (Chui & Cheng, 2017)	The key insights are described relating the contributions of the quantitative and qualitative data, but no description of the procedures provided	Descriptions of guidelines for interpreting the reliability scores of the three scales and statistical significance levels reported	Some alternative interpretations of the qualitative findings are provided
Postconflict risk (Taylor et al., 2017)	The key insight was the development of the instrument. No information provided about how the qualitative data informed the development of the instrument	Descriptions of guidelines for interpreting the path analysis	Very brief overall statements of interpretations, but no description of procedures for interpretations
Heart care (Dickson et al., 2011)	The key insights were derived from comparisons. 75% concordance was reported from triangulation efforts	Guidelines for interpreting each of the four scales are described	Interpretations drew upon diverse team member perspectives to create understandings of lived experiences
Safe places (Zea et al., 2014)	Described the participant feedback that was provided as evidence for creating a non-coercive communication environment	Described how the survey was piloted and revised, but no information about what changes were made. Described comparison of two groups (displaced and non-displaced)	Descriptions of how the team worked together, memoed, and contributed different interpretations, and provided an illustrative example
Leadership competencies (Strudsholm et al., 2016)	No information provided	No information provided	Descriptions are comprehensive as to how the team worked together to generate understandings of the qualitative data findings
Vaping culture (Colditz et al., 2017)	Created a validation approach to guide the phenomenological interpretations	Provided evidence of what was included in the coded subset and the full data set	Described the outcomes of the validation process and made explicit what tweets had not been coded

Relating Insight Discussions

The goal of integration in mixed methods research is to generate something beyond what would be accessible by either qualitative or quantitative research alone (Bazeley, 2018; Creamer, 2018; Creswell & Plano Clark, 2018; Onwuegbuzie & Poth, 2016). Others suggest that the insights produced should reflect something beyond the addition of qualitative and quantitative research. Illustrative examples remain somewhat elusive, so I was interested in the discussion of findings by Day, Sammons, and Gu (2016) to elucidate how they 'moved from conceptual and methodological integration – in which the qualitative and quantitative were, by the dictionary definition of the term, "mixed and combined to form a whole" – to synergy' (p. 331). It is this synergy that mixed methods researchers under conditions of complexity should seek by considering the question posed by Fetters and Freshwater (2015, p. 116): 'What synergy was gained by the additional work of using both qualitative and quantitative data methods?' It is thus natural that our discussions should centre on the new mixed insights and relate those insights to what we now consider to be relevant literature and point to implications. Another helpful criterion is offered by the MMER of Elizabeth Creamer (2018, p. 152): 'inconsistencies between the results and previous literature are identified and explained'. Following a discussion of literature, researchers present the limitations often focused on aspects of quality, source or types of data collected, and the qualitative, quantitative, and mixed analysis processes that might weaken the study's methodological rigour. Levitt et al. (2018) also advise describing the limits of the scope of transferability such as what readers should bear in mind when using findings across contexts. Many researchers use these details to advance future directions for further study for the reader and to highlight the value of a mixed methods approach.

The featured studies offered extensive evidence of discussions of insights grounded in relevant literature (see Table 9.7). The fact that many studies focused the discussion almost exclusively on the mixed insights reflects the desired focus on the mixed methods research outcomes. However, the descriptions of implications tended to be brief, with the exception that several studies described the value of mixed methods research. The limitations were almost exclusively focused on the quantitative findings, which does not indicate a balanced reporting of processes that might weaken the methodological rigour. Consider Researcher Spotlight 9.3, which describes future challenges for mixed methods

Researcher Spotlight 9.3

Dawn Freshwater on responsible generation of meaningful research outcomes

In my view one of the most interesting and provocative challenges for researchers currently relates to the increasing use of data-intensive discovery and the overwhelming array of data, data sets, and analytic tools available through which to view the subject matter under scrutiny. How to integrate and manage big data is of course a challenge for mixed methods researchers, specifically how to address the multiple points of data alignment and translate into meaningful and translatable outcomes that have an impact on the end user – more keenly a concern in the fields of health and medicine perhaps. The concomitant challenge is that of presenting credible and accessible outcomes built on the fact-based analysis. These challenges are not limited to mixed methods research, as I think it is interesting that we assume that the challenges faced by mixed methods researchers might be significantly different from those faced by researchers who adopt alternative methodologies and paradigms.

Table 9.7 Summary of evidence generated by descriptions of insight discussions in the featured studies

Featured study	Mixed methods research evidence	Quantitative research evidence	Qualitative research evidence
Law clients (Chui & Cheng, 2017)	Study impacts for procedural fairness discussed related to participation and trustworthiness, but few references to existing literature	Descriptions of significant findings highlighted and limitations of quantitative measures discussed	No information provided
Postconflict risk (Taylor et al., 2017)	Study impacts for future studies using the quantitative measure of emotional insecurity grounded in previous literature where measures were lacking and variables unknown	Highlighted the contribution of the development of the instrument and findings in light of relevant literature. Descriptions of limitations of quantitative measures discussed	Discussed the contributions of the qualitative strand to generate understanding of emotion insecurity and discussed relevant literature
Heart care (Dickson et al., 2011)	Discussion of mixed insights in relation to impacts for heart failure self-care interventions discussed in light of relevant literature	One quantitative finding was discussed and the rest was integrated	Discussion was integrated
Safe places (Zea et al., 2014)	Study impacts revealed differences in driving force of sex work and HIV testing and pointed to the value of mixed methods	No information provided here, but reference to other publications	No information provided here, but reference to other publications
Leadership competencies (Strudsholm et al., 2016)	Study impacts highlight importance of developing leadership competencies and the benefits and challenges related to use of mixed methods research	Limited description of the quantitative component discussion	Limited description of the qualitative component discussion
Vaping culture (Colditz et al., 2017)	Study impacts highlight importance of developing understandings of vaping culture and grounded in relevant literature	Discussion was integrated	Discussion was integrated

researchers (and researchers in general) related to generating meaningful outcomes, from the perspective of a prominent mixed methods health researcher who is vice chancellor of the University of Western Australia (Perth) and professor of mental health at the University of Leeds (UK).

When generating evidence for complex mixed methods research outcomes, consider the information available from the following questions related to insights and discussion considerations:

- What do we know about the rationales underpinning the discussions of the mixed insights?
- What do we know about the implications of the mixed insights?
- What do we know about the possible practical influences on the mixed insight discussion rationales, processes, and outcomes?

Features that Engage Readers with Complex Mixed Methods Research Outcomes

It is advantageous for researchers to distinguish their studies. Research designs are a great place to start differentiating a study under conditions of complexity. The following list provides some ideas from my own experiences as researcher, as a reviewer of mixed methods research proposals for funding and of manuscripts for publication, and from working with graduate students as an instructor, supervisor, and examiner. See also the featured studies for illustrative examples of some of these engaging features.

- *Seek unique participant samples to involve in mixed methods research under complex conditions.* There are various strategies to guide the relationship among data strands. Review the literature for ideas. This will help you create reader interest in participants right from the start.
- *Focus on innovative mixed methods research designs to guide data collection and analysis of data strands.* Consider new ways of collecting and analysing data within the qualitative and quantitative data strands. Review resources for ideas that others have not sought to combine before. This helps position the unique contributions of your design and avoid replicating the work of others.
- *Create unique ways of representing integrated findings.* Catch readers' attention with an interesting name and visual representation for your integrated findings. Review literature about diagramming conventions and then adapt as needed. This will help clearly communicate your integration to the reader.
- *Assume unconventional perspectives in your interpretations and generation of mixed insights.* Consider new roles for theory or theoretical perspectives, involve research team members from disciplines not yet reflected in studies, or assume research paradigms that have not yet been adopted in the literature. This will help you to see beyond what might be possible when generating complex research outcomes.

Consider Researcher Spotlight 9.4 and Guiding Tip 9.2 that focus on integration challenges. The researcher spotlight describes the future challenges mixed methods researchers may face under conditions of complexity related to integration of qualitative and quantitative methods, from the perspective of a professor of international communication at Aoyama Gakuin University in Tokyo (Japan). In the guiding tip a professor of education and health professions at the University of Arkansas – Fayetteville (USA) offers advice for maintaining familiarity with emerging understandings in the analysis of mixed methods research.

 Researcher Spotlight 9.4

Hisako Kakai on future challenges with high-quality integrations

Advancing creative and meaningful ways to integrate qualitative and quantitative methods and to evaluate the quality of integration may be the key future challenge for mixed methods researchers. Integration is at the core of mixed methods research and is what distinguishes this approach from other approaches. Thus, furthering our discussion, both theoretically and empirically, on creative and meaningful approaches to achieving integration that results in high inference quality is critical. One empirical example of such an approach to integration

(Continued)

(Continued)

can be found in Ungar and Liebenberg (2011). To develop a culturally sensitive resilience scale, the researchers collected both interview and questionnaire data across multiple countries, analysed the data using a grounded theory approach and exploratory factor analysis respectively, and compared and contrasted the results of these different analyses in order to integrate them. The final version of the researchers' scale consisted of a set of items validated by both the interview and the questionnaire data. In this study the researchers even retained statistically insignificant items if related concepts were recognized as meaningful through qualitative analysis. This is a good example of how mixed methods research addresses the complexity and diversity of our real world. Had the researchers depended solely on their statistical results, the cross-cultural sensitivity of the resilience scale would have been much more limited. Thus evaluation criteria for assessing the quality of integration must also be innovative, and researchers should sometimes courageously move beyond merely conforming to the procedural standard of each method. What we need is innovative fusion!

 Guiding Tip 9.2

Kathleen Collins advising keeping pace with emerging mixed methods research literature guiding data analysis

I would stress the importance of interpreting mixed methods research as a cyclical process centred on addressing a question. Also, I would advise novice researchers to attain and to maintain a familiarity with the evolving mixed methods research literature and to continue to hone their technical skills in the area of data analysis.

Innovations in Generating Evidence of Complex Mixed Methods Research Outcomes

Mixed methods researchers generate evidence to build confidence in the methodological rigour of their research processes and indicate the quality of their research outcomes. Researchers working under conditions of complexity are tasked with generating outcomes alongside evolving understandings of the research intentions, contexts, integrations, interactions and effects of the practical influences on the research processes and outcomes. Descriptions of the processes for generating evidence of research outcomes tend to occur as part of the study methods, whereas the products are often embedded across findings, discussions, and implications. Also important, yet underreported, are details about dynamic practical influences and subsequent effects on processes and outcomes over time. The lack of guidance for generating evidence specific to the integration processes and products can be attributable to the underdevelopment of these topics within the available literature. There seems to be agreement about the importance of integration to mixed methods research, yet existing descriptions of desirable evidence of research outcomes should be considered incomplete. Representations of integrated findings in the form of joint displays have only recently been addressed in guiding resources and have yet to be widely adopted in published work. Recent guidance about how to present study findings to reflect core mixed methods designs and mixed purposes exists (Creswell & Plano Clark, 2018), yet existing descriptions should be noted as somewhat constraining and not reflective of all possible complex integrations. I believe access to illustrative examples will be key to enhancing our outcomes descriptions under conditions of complexity.

Descriptions of complex mixed methods research outcomes can appear quite different across studies, related to the differing research conditions under which the studies are conducted. This happens in the same way that procedures guiding integrations can appear quite different from those in the research proposal because understandings naturally emerged and new information was assimilated. Specific to building confidence in research processes and outcomes, differences can arise as a result of assimilating the generative evidence with emerging practical influences. There is an ongoing iterative process of generating evidence of complex mixed methods research outcomes: it begins with identifying a range of possible study impacts and significance, continues during implementation, and is finalized with the writing of the report once the research is complete. To that end, variations are expected in structures across the proposals and reports that you will encounter. The inherent nature of researcher perspectives, research processes, and products of research commands it. In the rest of this chapter, I describe several innovations for communicating and displaying evidence of complex mixed methods research outcomes: diagrams and writing devices.

Diagrams Representing Evidence of Research Integrations

It is uncommon to see visual representations of the processes underpinning integration, yet I believe this is a yet-to-be-discovered opportunity. In addition to conveying information about products of integration, diagrams have proven to be an effective way of representing processes. To focus on the integrations occurring between the data strands represents a unique approach to generating evidence of the research outcomes. I find this focus helpful because by making explicit my rationales and mixed analysis procedures, I have generated evidence upon which I can build confidence and assimilate my evolving understandings of outcomes and practical influences. This is important because this positions my researcher mindset as open to new possibilities of understandings for:

- Why the complex research outcomes can be considered valid for addressing the problem
- How my initial understandings of the evidence for complex research outcomes and practical influences evolve over time.

Summary tables can provide essential evidence of the connections between evidence and procedural diagrams convey how evidence has been generated. In particular, summary tables are efficient for conveying large amounts of information concisely. In Table 9.8, I offer an illustrative example from the featured study on leadership competencies (Strudsholm et al., 2016) to represent the connections between the data strands (the authors refer to these as components of research design) and the research question. Note that the descriptors of the phases also include information about the participant samples of that phase and the research methods used for data collection.

Table 9.8 Summary table example of data strands, participants, and research questions (partially represented here) for the featured study on leadership competencies

Component of research design	Research question
Phase I A literature review of the published and grey literature on leadership competencies for public health	• What is the extent of the literature on leadership competencies for public health? • What literature exists regarding characteristics, enablers, and barriers for public health leadership?
Phase II An online survey targeted at all seven disciplines to identify their priorities for leadership competencies	• What are the top five knowledge, skills, and attributes of leaders? • What are the top five enablers and barriers to public health leadership?
Phase III Focus group webinars with nominated leaders in public health in Canada from the seven disciplines and from all geographic regions in Canada	• To what degree do public health professional leaders agree or disagree with the results of the online survey? • Should anything be added to leader characteristics, enablers or facilitators, and barriers for public health leadership?
Phase IV A modified Delphi method using experts in public health and leadership to converge toward consensus regarding the draft competencies for leadership in public health	• What is the degree of agreement among nominated public health leaders across Canada regarding leadership competencies for public health practice in Canada?

Source: Strudsholm et al. (2016, p. 3). Used with permission from Sage.

It is becoming more common to provide evidence of integrated findings in table form: 'A promising innovation to facilitate integration is the use of visual joint displays that bring data together visually to draw out new insights' (Guetterman, Fetters, & Creswell, 2015, p. 554). While these authors found that prevalent types of joint displays were statistics by themes and side-by-side comparisons, Guetterman, Creswell & Kuchartz (2015) point to innovative joint displays for connecting findings to theoretical frameworks or recommendations as having great future possibilities. These authors propose that the increased use of joint displays will assist researchers in discussing the synergy generated by the integration of quantitative and qualitative findings and thus 'may provide a structure to discuss the integrated analysis. Integration is needed to reach the full potential of a mixed methods approach and gain new insights' (Guetterman, Fetters, & Creswell, 2015, p. 560). In Table 9.9, I offer an illustrative example from the featured study on heart care (Dickson et al., 2011) representing the cross-case comparison of three participants (from sample of 41) and quantitative scores and qualitative assessments. Note that integrated findings for each of the domains are given in italics.

What is not yet common to report in mixed table form are the interpretation approaches for both quantitative instruments and qualitative protocols. In Table 9.10, I offer an illustrative example from the featured study on heart care (Dickson et al., 2011) representing the interpretation guidelines for one of the quantitative scales and the semistructured interview guide. Note the inclusion of the purpose alongside the procedures and interpretation guidelines.

Table 9.9 Summary table example of cross-case comparison using three participants and quantitative scores and qualitative assessments (partially represented here) for the featured study on heart care

Domain	Variables	Participant 1	Participant 2	Participant 3
Knowledge cognition		DHFKS total = 14 DSST = 25, PMR = 2	DHFKS total = 14 DSST = 23, PMR = 0	DHFKS total = 15 DSST = 46, PMR = 4
Self-care maintenance	SCHFI score	100	90	60
	Diet, monitoring exercise, and medication	Follows low-fat and low-salt diet, fluid 2 L restriction, weighs self daily, exercises 2–3 times per week, pillboxes for medication *Cheats (on diet) and manages (symptoms)*	Follows 2 grams low-salt diet; takes lunch to work. Checks and records blood pressure and writes weights on calendar. Exercises on treadmill each day. Medication log *Self-care maintenance as routine*	Low-salt diet 'used to be better', now has dietary indiscretions. Tries to exercise regularly but not consistent. Medication routine: medicines make the participant tired, so sometimes 'is lazy to take' *Inconsistent self-care*
Self-care management	SCHFI score	87.57	74.21	67
	Symptom monitoring, symptom recognition, symptom importance, action, symptom improvement	Checks ankles and daily weights, records data, and in presence of symptoms eats less salt; diuretic titration; energy conservation. Recognizes that increased urination and weight loss indicate improvement *Consistent self-care* *Symptom vigilance*	Daily weights, checks blood pressure symptoms such as hyperventilating. With symptoms, rests or stops activity, calls health care provider immediately. Improvement noted as breathing eases. Also has external defibrillator *Consistent self-care* *Symptom vigilance*	Daily weights (or 3 times/week). 'Knows body' and relies on intuition to identify symptoms. Often will just work through symptoms and wait to see if feels better. Does not pay attention to some symptoms (e.g., what is fatigue from heart failure, from work, and from motherhood) *Lacks vigilance* *Watches and waits on symptoms*

Source: Dickson et al. (2017, p. 177). Used with permission from Sage.

At first glance Figure 9.3 might seem hard to follow. Look again and notice that at each end are different data strands and the mixed insights are represented in the middle. This diagram is from my own work. It draws upon three data sources and seeks to represent the mixed analysis processes and products of interpretations. In so doing, it attempts to represent the synergy and provide another opportunity for making explicit the interpretation procedures. Note the identification of the mixed analysis strategy as a qualitative dominant cross-over and the relationships among the categories and codes. In Table 9.11, I offer an illustrative example from the featured study on leadership competencies (Strudsholm et al., 2016) representing the study insights and implication discussions organized by phases. Note the inclusion of the intended and observed benefits.

Table 9.10 Summary table example of data instruments and collection and interpretation procedures (partially represented here) for the featured study on heart care

Instrument	Purpose	Procedures	Interpretation
Self-Care Heart Failure Index (SCHFI)	A valid and reliable instrument measuring self-care maintenance, management, and confidence	Self-administered questionnaire with 17 items measured on a 4-point Likert-type scale (*never or rarely, sometimes, frequently, always or daily*). The items form three scales: maintenance, management, and confidence. Scores on each of the SCHFI scales are standardized to 100	Score range: 0–100. Maintenance and management scales were used in this analysis. Adequate self-care is defined as a score of ≥70 on each of the two SCHFI scales used (maintenance and management)
Semistructured interview guide	To elicit in-depth accounts of heart failure (HF) self-care and knowledge and understanding about maintenance and management behaviours	After completing the quantitative surveys, participants were asked a series of open-ended questions about daily self-care maintenance and management practices and were asked to explain what they knew about HF and the most commonly prescribed HF self-care behaviours. Interviews were audio-taped and lasted approximately 60 minutes. ATLAS.ti 5.0 software was used	Preliminary coding was based on a priori codes derived from the theoretical framework. Within-case analysis was used to identify the key elements of each individual's account of HF self-care; then across-case analysis was used to identify commonalities and variations of the themes

Source: Dickson et al. (2017, p. 173). Used with permission from Sage.

Writing Ideas for Conveying Evidence of Research Outcomes

It is uncommon to see a researcher explicitly describe the research outcomes as uncertain and unknowable. It is also infrequent practice for researchers to describe their interpretation approaches alongside their integrated findings and mixed insights. This is unfortunate, as I find such accounts especially useful for researchers who are new to the mixed methods research field and for those new to generating outcomes under conditions of complexity. This is important to position the researchers' mindset as open to new possibilities of understandings for:

- What practical influences are considered relevant for generating evidence of research outcomes
- What innovative evidence of research outcomes are sought from the procedures identified

Under conditions of complexity, understandings of the evidence for the complex outcomes are considered to be evolving. The researcher is tasked with the following question: How can the established standards of methodological rigour and understandings of specific quality considerations of mixed methods research contribute to generating the evidence necessary to build confidence in complex mixed methods research outcomes?

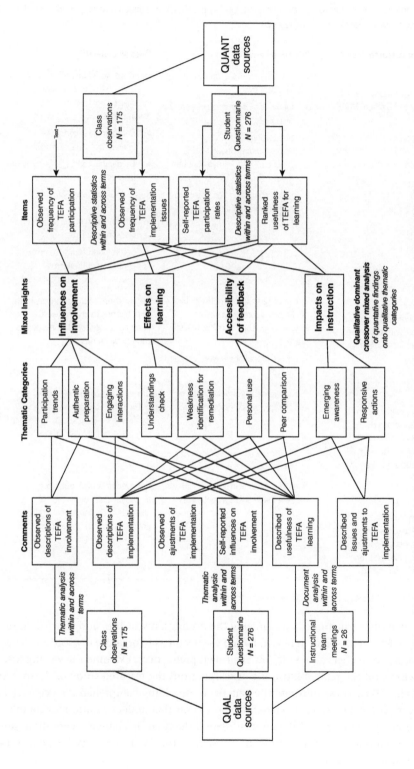

Figure 9.3 Diagram example conveying mixed analysis processes and interpretation products for a study that generated four mixed insights

Source: Poth (2018b, p. 8). Used with permission from Springer Open.

Table 9.11   Summary table example of study insights and implications discussion (partially represented here) for the featured study on leadership competencies

Component of research design	Intended benefit	Observed benefit
Phase I Mapping of disciplinary and Public Health Agency of Canada (PHAC) competencies A literature review of the published and grey literature on leadership competencies for public health	To establish common ground among stakeholders by: • Identifying commonalties across disciplines • Supporting a shared understanding about what is and is not currently known about the topic • Establishing a shared vocabulary and definition of terms	Identified lack of identification of and/or clarity on leadership competencies in public health Identified the Project's assumptions: • Competencies comprise knowledge, skills, and abilities • Leadership competencies can be learned Supported development of a shared vocabulary • Identification of the need for a glossary of terms • Seized opportunity to correct conflation of the terms 'leadership' and 'management'
Phase II An online survey targeted at all seven disciplines to identify their priorities for leadership competencies	To capture a snapshot of the public health workforce's opinion that included the scope of public health practice To ensure practitioners were engaged in the Project	Received input across Canada, from all public health disciplines, at all levels of organizations, at all points across career trajectories
Phase III Focus group webinars with nominated leaders in public health in Canada from the seven disciplines and from all geographic regions in Canada	To capture details about context of leadership competencies for public health	Gained insight into the breadth of public health practice by capturing local issues with regard to leadership competencies across Canada
Phase IV A modified Delphi method using experts in public health and leadership to converge toward consensus regarding the draft competencies for leadership in public health	To engage leaders in public health with the leadership competencies	Received national input, from all public health disciplines, at all levels of organizations, at all points across career trajectories

Source: Strudsholm et al. (2016, p. 8). Used with permission from Sage.

Consider common structures for organizing the findings, discussion, and conclusion sections of a mixed methods research report. I often use headings to organize my sections. There is no set format; researchers should follow their own preferences. Examine the writing ideas described below and the related illustrative excerpts from the featured study on heart care (Dickson et al., 2011). These illustrate the benefits of providing comprehensive evidence of how the research outcomes were generated. We now know that under conditions of complexity, some are not yet known and the outcomes are influenced by changing conditions and evolving understandings of practical influences. Examine the six tasks involved in generating evidence of research outcomes:

- *Describe the participants and mixed sampling strategies.* Familiarize the readers with your understandings of those involved as the study participant samples. Researchers generally begin by describing the relationships among the samples across the data strands: if an existing typology is appropriate, identify the mixed sampling strategy. Then familiarize the readers with your understandings of the participants by relating relevant demographic information to highlight commonalities and differences among the samples. This gives the reader a sense of who is (and is not) involved in the study. Then stipulate specific inclusion/exclusion criteria and evidence of efforts to minimize sampling bias such as those that can occur from incentives/compensation or existing relationships with researchers. Researchers often include this information under headings such as 'participants' and 'sampling and recruitment'. You may find the following questions useful in guiding your participant descriptions and sampling rationales:

  o What do readers need to know about the rationale, processes, and potential outcomes for the participant samples to better understand the contributions of the mixed samples to the research problem?
  o What do readers need to know about the efforts to enhance the methodological rigour of the participant samples?
  o What do readers need to know about the mixed sampling strategy to better understand the sampling limitations and practical influences? (Identify a mixed sampling typology if applicable.)

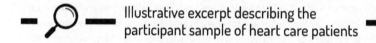

Illustrative excerpt describing the participant sample of heart care patients

Demographics and clinical characteristics of the sample of 41 are shown in Table 4. Overall, the sample was predominately Caucasian and male. Participants were primarily middle-aged adults (mean age ± SD = 49.17 ± 10.51 years, range 25–65 years). Most were NYHA functional Class III with a median length of illness of 6 years. Most had systolic [heart failure] and an implanted device to control heart rhythm.

Source: Dickson et al. (2011, p. 178). Used with permission from Sage.

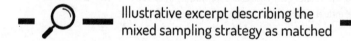

Illustrative excerpt describing the mixed sampling strategy as matched

Using a purposive homogenous sampling technique, individuals were enrolled who could provide indepth accounts of self-care (Kemper, Stringfield, & Teddlie, 2003). Patients were eligible for participation if they had documented evidence of symptomatic [heart failure] (NYHA II or III) as classified by the New York Heart Association (NYHA) criteria relating functional activity and cardiac symptoms (Zipes, Libby, Bonow, & Braunwald, 2005) for at least 3 months, were between the ages of 18 and 65 years, and could speak and read English. Those with a history of a prior neurological event that could cause dementia or inability to perform tests (e.g., inadequate vision) were excluded ... Forty-two individuals were referred

(Continued)

(Continued)

to the research team ... All 42 participants provided written informed consent and were enrolled in the study. However, one individual (Caucasian male) who initially agreed to participate withdrew from the study prior to data collection after he was added to the heart transplantation list ... Participant recruitment continued until qualitative data saturation was achieved and resulted in a sample of 41.

Source: Dickson et al. (2011, pp. 173–174). Used with permission from Sage.

- *Convey the data collection for the data strands.* Present the procedures involved in data collections. How researchers organize the descriptions of the data collection processes depends upon the choice of research methods involved in the data strands and the mixed methods research design. Common across the descriptions of data collection procedures should be a rationale for the choice of research method, the procedures involved, and efforts to enhance the methodological rigour associated with each of the research approaches. In the case of the featured study on heart care (Dickson et al., 2011), the use of four scales to measure three constructs quantitatively and the development of the interview protocol were guided by the theoretical framework for the study. The descriptions of each of the quantitative scales refer to authors, a description of the instrument, the number of items, the procedures involved in the instrument items, reported reliabilities of the scales, and guidelines for interpretations of scores. The descriptions of the qualitative semi-structured interviews include the purpose, the development of the protocol, examples of the questions, procedures in terms of length of time and question probes. Efforts to enhance methodological rigour involve the inclusion of open-ended questions and the use of field notes. As was the case for the interview protocol used in the featured study on heart care, many researchers include protocols and instruments in an appendix. A table was used to summarize both the quantitative and qualitative data collection in terms of instruments, purpose, procedures, and interpretations. You may find the following questions useful in guiding your descriptions of data collection for the data strands:

  o What do readers need to know about the rationales, processes, and potential outcomes of the data collection to better understand the contributions of the quantitative and qualitative data to the research problem? (Identify a design typology if applicable.)
  o What do readers need to know about the efforts to enhance methodological rigour of the collection procedures?
  o What do readers need to know about the data collection strategies to better understand the data limitations and practical influences?

Illustrative excerpt conveying quantitative data strands

HF [heart failure] self-care was measured by the Self-Care of Heart Failure Index (SCHFI; Riegel et al., 2004), a valid and reliable instrument with 17 items measured on a 4-point Likert-type scale. These items form three scales. The maintenance (monitoring and adherence behaviors done to prevent HF exacerbation) and management (ability to recognize and respond appropriately to symptoms) reflect self-care. In addition, self-care confidence reflects the perceived ability to engage in self-care maintenance and management behaviors. Scores on each of the SCHFI scales are standardized to 100; higher scores indicate better self-care.

In this sample, the maintenance scale had a Cronbach's alpha of .55, management .65, and confidence .86, which is consistent with prior research. Only the self-care maintenance and management scales were used in the analysis of this study. Adequate self-care was defined as a score of ≥ 70 on each of the two SCHFI scales.

Source: Dickson et al. (2011, p. 174). Used with permission from Sage.

Illustrative excerpt conveying qualitative data strands

One researcher (VVD) trained in qualitative techniques with prior experience as research assistant in two mixed methods studies conducted the interviews using a semistructured interview guide to elicit in-depth accounts of HF [heart failure] self-care and knowledge and understanding about maintenance and management behaviors. The interview guide used in this study was based on the theoretical framework guiding the study, naturalistic decision making (Lipshitz et al., 2001). The guide was adapted from a tool used by the research team in a preliminary study that examined contributors to self-care success among HF patients (Dickson et al., 2006). Through a series of open-ended questions, patients described daily self-care practices (e.g., 'Tell me what you do on a daily basis to take care of your heart failure'; see the appendix). General questions were followed by more specific questions about daily self-care maintenance and management practices that were meant to elicit narratives about the behaviors assessed on the SCHFI. Participants were also asked to explain what they knew about HF and the most commonly prescribed HF self-care behaviors ('Why is it important to follow your diet?') and to explain their understanding about the link between maintenance and management behaviors ('What does your weight today mean to you?'). Interviews were conducted after completion of the surveys and lasted approximately 60 minutes. The sequencing of data collection was purposeful to avoid biased answers on the quantitative tools as might occur after an in-depth discussion of self-care during the interview. For example, a probing question on management of weight gain may have prompted a later response on the quantitative instrument. Sequencing quantitative data collection first, as we did, also has the potential to bias the qualitative answers by prompting responses to the open-ended questions later posed by the interviewer. However, in our study, field notes documented the responses during data collection, and transcriptions of interviews recorded any reference to the surveys. For example, if individuals did not know how to answer a question on one of their surveys, they were instructed to select the answer they felt was the most appropriate for their situation. Field notes of participant observations, including any questions posed about the surveys and the researcher's response, supplemented the tape-recorded interviews.

Source: Dickson et al. (2011, p. 175). Used with permission from Sage.

- *Outline the qualitative, quantitative, and mixed analysis processes.* Describe the processes involved in data analyses. Many researchers include details about data preparation and initial explorations as well as in-depth analyses. How researchers organize the descriptions of the analysis processes depends upon the design related to sequencing of the data strands. In the case of the featured study on heart care (Dickson et al., 2011), the design guides the concurrent qualitative and quantitative data collection and analysis, with integration occurring at the inferences stage. This means that qualitative and quantitative findings are generated independently, and so the authors chose to organize their description of the data analysis processes separately beginning with presenting the quantitative and qualitative details, followed by the integration. For other combinations of complex integrations, the descriptions of processes may look very different; for example, there may be multiple points of interface or integration that occur among the data strands, without any separate qualitative and quantitative analysis presented. Common across the descriptions of analysis processes should be the preparation of data, identification of the strategies used, the procedures undertaken, and efforts to enhance the methodological rigour associated with each of the research approaches. In the case of the featured study on heart care, the quantitative data analysis refers to the software used, the performance of exploratory descriptive statistics as well as subsequent linear regressions, whereas the qualitative data analysis refers to the software used, the preparation and preliminary examinations of the transcripts, the initial coding schemes, confirmation of codes by multiple coders, and finally the within- and across-case analysis processes. Additional information about the generation of an audit trail, team meetings, and member checking was also provided. You may find the following questions useful in guiding your representations of data findings:

o   What do readers need to know about the qualitative, quantitative, and mixed methods data analysis rationale, processes, and potential outcomes to better understand the contributions of the findings to the research problem?

o   What do readers need to know about the efforts to enhance methodological rigour of the data analyses?

o   What do readers need to know about the mixed analysis strategy to better understand the integration limitations and practical influences? (Identify a mixed analysis typology if applicable.)

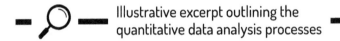

Illustrative excerpt outlining the quantitative data analysis processes

Quantitative data were analysed using SPSS (Version 14.0). Standard descriptive statistics of central tendency and dispersion were used to describe the sample. To protect against skewed data with this small sample size, Spearman's rho tests were used to assess for significant correlation between variables. Then linear regression analysis was used to determine the amount of variance in self-care explained by cognitive function and knowledge (DHFKS). The measure of cognitive function that had the highest correlation with measures of self-care was chosen for inclusion in each model. For the evaluation of self-care maintenance, we tested the influence of DHFKS total score, and then the additive influence of DSST [cognitive function] scores on variance in self-care maintenance controlling for patient age, gender, and ejection fraction, which is a measure of cardiac output (Lilly, 2003). For the evaluation of self-care management, we tested the influence of DHFKS total score and then the additive influence of PMR [Probed Memory Recall] scores on variance in self-care management. The influence of each variable on self-care was assessed by evaluating the significance of the increase in model R^2 and the direction and strength of slope coefficients and associated 95% confidence intervals (CIs). Post hoc effect sizes were calculated using Cohen's f^2. Post hoc power was also calculated imputing observed alpha, the number of predictors, sample size, and effect size.

Source: Dickson et al. (2011, p. 175). Used with permission from Sage.

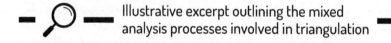

Illustrative excerpt outlining the qualitative data analysis processes

Qualitative data collected by audio-taped interviews were transcribed verbatim and analyzed by one qualitative methodologist (VVD) using content analysis to identify core knowledge and understanding about HF [heart failure] self-care and self-care practices for each individual. Transcriptions of the first three tapes were reviewed line by line for accuracy against the audiotape and then five other randomly selected tapes were audited. There was 100% accuracy in transcription ... More than 1,000 pages of double-spaced transcribed data were analyzed using ATLAS.ti 5.0. Preliminary coding was based on a priori codes derived from the theoretical framework guiding the study. The initial coding scheme resulted in data clusters related to evidence of knowledge and self-care practices. Reliability of preliminary coding was confirmed by a second independent qualitative researcher and the iterative analysis process extended to review with the research team. To achieve coding reliability, an independent qualitative methodologist coded a subset of files (n = 8). Then coding was reviewed for similarities and variations by comparing level of agreement between the two coders. Initial discrepancies were discussed, and 98% agreement was achieved suggesting that the coding scheme used was appropriate. After preliminary coding, within-case analysis was used to identify the key elements of each individual's account of HF self-care (Ayres, Kavanaugh, & Knafl, 2003). Themes that emerged from this analysis were then examined across cases to identify commonalities and variations of the themes. The within- and across-case analysis was an iterative process; the researcher moved back and forth between individual cases and across cases to track variability of themes (Ayres et al., 2003) ... Methodological rigour was also ensured in this study by maintenance of an audit trail of coding decisions, regular research team meetings and periodic peer debriefing where coding scheme and findings were discussed with colleagues knowledgeable about the phenomenon, and member checking, the process by which findings are validated as representative of the experience of the participants (Connelly & Yoder, 2000). In this study, member checking was conducted by reviewing emergent themes with three participants who had agreed to be contacted for follow-up by phone conversations.

Source: Dickson et al. (2011, p. 176). Used with permission from Sage.

Illustrative excerpt outlining the mixed analysis processes involved in triangulation

The data were then integrated during the interpretation phase using triangulation methods to assess concordance between the qualitative and quantitative results. That is, qualitative evidence of self-care and knowledge were compared with quantitative data results of the SCHFI and DHFKS for each case during data interpretation. Specifically, patient accounts of HF [heart failure] daily self-care (e.g., 'tell me how you start off your day,' 'tell me about your diet,' and 'what was your weight this morning' ... 'what did that weight mean to you')

(Continued)

(Continued)

were analyzed for evidence of self-care maintenance and management and compared with SCHFI results. These accounts of HF self-care created the anchor or base for the next steps in the analysis when the effects of cognitive function and knowledge on self-care were explored. An informational matrix ... was created to compare and contrast the emergent qualitative data with the quantitative evidence of self-care, cognitive function, and knowledge (Creswell & Plano Clark, 2006). In this way, we validated evidence of self-care and knowledge and identified cases where there was inconsistency. Themes that had emerged from the qualitative analysis including qualitative accounts of decreased cognitive function, knowledge deficits, and lack of understanding were then re-examined across cases to explicate the results. The strengths of both quantitative and qualitative methods were used to more fully understand the phenomenon.

Source: Dickson et al. (2011, p. 176). Used with permission from Sage.

- *Represent the integrated findings and, if applicable, separate qualitative and quantitative findings as well.* Present the integrated findings that are foundational to generating mixed insights which represent an essential characteristic of mixed methods research. How researchers organize the representations of findings depends upon the design related to the intensity of mixing and may or may not include separate qualitative and quantitative findings along with the integrated findings. In the case of the featured study on heart care (Dickson et al., 2011), the design guides the integration occurring at the inferences stage. This means that qualitative and quantitative findings are generated independently, and so the authors organized their representations of quantitative and qualitative findings separately followed by the integrated findings. For other combinations of complex integrations, the representations of findings may look very different; for example, there may be multiple forms of integrated findings without any separate qualitative and quantitative findings presented. The descriptions of the findings should highlight the key findings along with the appropriate validity evidence. In the case of the featured study on heart care, quantitative results for the four scales are presented in table form to represent the results of the correlational analysis and regression estimates and effect size of explained variance, with some complementary narratives reporting trends and percentage of variances explained as well as power results. Qualitative findings were organized by the themes related to the narrative accounts of self-care practices. These included participant quotes. Although 98% agreement among multiple coders for the themes was reported, the number of themes was not apparent (although the overarching theme was identified). Also, while the emergent themes were described to have been member checked with three participants, no information was provided about the processes or results. Integrated findings were presented in a cross-case comparison table (see Table 9.9) using three participants and the quantitative scores and qualitative assessments are described in the text, merging the qualitative and quantitative findings. You may find the following questions useful in guiding your representations of data findings:
  - What do readers need to know about the rationale, processes, and potential outcomes for the findings representations to better understand the contributions of the inferences to the research problem?
  - What do readers need to know about the efforts to enhance methodological rigour of the findings representations?
  - What do readers need to know about the findings representations to better understand the integrated data limitations and practical influences? (Identify a diagram or display typology if applicable.)

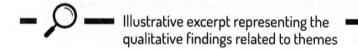

Illustrative excerpt representing the quantitative findings related to statistical evidence

When [heart failure] self-care was measured using the SCHFI [self-care of heart failure index], the majority of participants (78%) reported symptoms of ankle swelling or shortness of breath in the 3 months prior to the study, which allowed their abilities to manage symptoms to be evaluated. The mean (± SD) score of self-care management for those with symptoms was adequate (≥ 70 on the standardized scale) overall as was self-care maintenance (SCHFI management 71.28 ± 18.20; maintenance 71.54 ± 14.25). However, individually, scores were less than adequate in a considerable proportion (56%) of the sample ... There was a significant negative correlation between cognitive function (DSST) and self-care maintenance (r = -.44, p = .008). When multiple regression analysis was used to assess the relationship of cognitive function and knowledge on self-care, controlling for age, gender, and ejection fraction, knowledge did not help explain variance in self-care maintenance ... In contrast, cognitive function (DSST) scores explained 20.7% of the variance in self-care maintenance, controlling for age, gender, and ejection fraction. Higher DSST scores were associated with lower levels of self-care maintenance. Observed statistical power was 0.842.

Source: Dickson et al. (2011, pp. 178–180). Used with permission from Sage.

Illustrative excerpt representing the qualitative findings related to themes

The narrative accounts of self-care practices revealed a number of themes related to how individuals practice self-care. Some individuals were very consistent in their application of self-care, whereas others varied in their adherence to self-care maintenance, vigilance in symptom monitoring, and treatment implementation. For example, consistent with standard [heart failure] patient education, those who routinely monitored daily weights appropriately articulated the signal to take action: 'If you gain 5 or more pounds you have to report it to your doctor because it means you're retaining a lot of fluid.' However, others struggled with their ability to know what symptoms to look for and when a symptom was meaningful ('is it ... just me being winded or out of shape or my heart, I don't know that's the gray area for me') ... The overarching theme that emerged from the narrative accounts of self-care was that lack of understanding (i.e., inability to interpret or explain meaning of knowledge), not lack of knowledge, drives inconsistent self-care behavior. For example, individuals reported knowing they should weigh themselves every day but did not understand the meaning of a weight increase ('I get on the scale and see more fat each day ... so I don't get on the scale').

Source: Dickson et al. (2011, pp. 180–181). Used with permission from Sage.

Illustrative excerpt representing the integrated findings related to degree of concordance

Triangulation of the quantitative and qualitative data revealed 75% concordance between the answers on the knowledge survey and the narratives about HF [heart failure] knowledge obtained from the interviews. For example, consistent with the knowledge survey results, some individuals described having 'cold' and flu-like symptoms ... but did not link the symptoms to an exacerbation of HF symptoms ('when I get a cold ... my symptoms seem to linger longer ... I just get fatigued, I get really tired'). The modest concordance (75%) between the knowledge quantitative and qualitative data may be attributed to the format of the survey (multiple choice) compared with the open-ended interview questions where individuals had to recall knowledge unprompted. The 90% concordance between the quantitative and qualitative assessments of self-care was consistent with our previous research (Riegel et al., 2007). The integrated data revealed important insight into lapses in self-care practices by explaining the gap between knowledge and self-care practices. The two reasons that emerged were lack of understanding and cognitive impairment. The most compelling example of a gap between knowledge and self-care practice was related to adherence to daily weight monitoring, an important self-care maintenance behavior. According to the knowledge survey, all the participants knew they were supposed to weigh themselves daily. However, 37% were inconsistent in this practice.

Reasons for poor adherence that emerged from the qualitative data were a lack of understanding about the reason for daily weights and forgetting to weigh. Those who did not routinely weigh themselves explained their understanding of weighing as a weight management practice rather than a symptom-monitoring behavior. As one women woman explained, 'I learned [in weight loss programprogramme] to not look at the scale every day .. .... I don't want to see that weight go up.' An example of forgetfulness was: 'I go to weigh myself .. .... then I forget .. .... it slips my mind just like that.' Similarly, although all the participants knew that medications were to be taken as prescribed ('It is important to take my heart failure medications regularly'), many 'forgot' at times to take medication.

Source: Dickson et al. (2011, p. 181-182). Used with permission from Sage.

- *Describe the interpretation approaches for generating mixed insights.* Present information about how the findings are interpreted. How researchers organize the descriptions of the interpretation approaches depends on the intended outcomes relating to the mixing purposes and need for integration. For other studies of complex research outcomes, the processes of data interpretations may look very different. As we have already discussed, there are hazards associated with our current 'black box' approach resulting from a lack of guidance to make our interpretation approaches more explicit to the reader. In the case of the featured study on heart care (Dickson et al., 2011), the information about approaches to data interpretations emphasize the quantitative scales in the instrument descriptions presented both narratively and summarized in the data collection procedures. Only brief evidence of the interpretation processes of the within- and across-case analysis is provided in the data collection procedures. Overall a 75% concordance was reported from the triangulation efforts, yet the processes for generating this calculation are not immediately obvious (at least to me!). Some evidence is provided of the interpretation processes for integrated findings whereby one data strand elucidated understandings of the other. You may find the following questions useful in guiding your own discussion of mixed insights:

o   What do readers need to know about the rationales, processes and potential outcomes for the interpretation approaches to better understand the contributions of the insights to the research problem?

o   What do readers need to know about the efforts to enhance methodological rigour of the interpretation approaches?

o   What do readers need to know about the interpretation approaches to better understand the outcome limitations and practical influences?

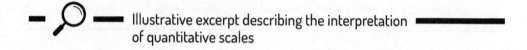

Illustrative excerpt describing the interpretation of quantitative scales

Score range: 0–100. Maintenance and management scales were used in this analysis. Adequate self-care is defined as a score of ≥70 on each of the two SCHFI scales used (maintenance and management).

Source: Dickson et al. (2011, p. 174, Table 2). Used with permission from Sage.

Illustrative excerpt describing the interpretations of qualitative codes and themes

Preliminary coding was based on a priori codes derived from the theoretical framework. Within-case analysis was used to identify the key elements of each individual's account of HF self-care; then across-case analysis was used to identify commonalities and variations of the themes.

Source: Dickson et al. (2011, p. 173, Table 2). Used with permission from Sage.

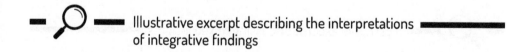

Illustrative excerpt describing the interpretations of integrative findings

The modest concordance (75%) between the knowledge quantitative and qualitative data may be attributed to the format of the survey (multiple choice) compared with the open-ended interview questions where individuals had to recall knowledge unprompted ...

(Continued)

(Continued)

In addition, the qualitative data helped elucidate the quantitative result that cognitive function was negatively correlated to self-care. Using the informational matrix, we reexamined those cases with adequate quantitative scores on the SCHFI and impaired cognitive function. Two interesting patterns were found: lack of vigilance and social support that facilitates self-care.

Several individuals (n = 7) who reported inconsistent self-care qualitatively and had inadequate SCHFI results (<70 on self-care maintenance and/or management scales) described prioritizing other daily activities over self-care. One woman who scored below the adequate level of self-care on the SCHFI explained her inconsistent practices as being less attentive[:] 'I was more careful in the beginning ... now when I am in a rush, I just grab [fast food] with the kids.'

Source: Dickson et al. (2011, pp. 181–182). Used with permission from Sage.

- *Discuss mixed insights and point to implications, limitations, and future directions for research.* Familiarize the readers with the 'so what' of the research as well as any aspects of the study processes or products that should be considered. Generally, researchers will discuss the mixed insights in relation to relevant literature and highlight theoretical, practical, and methodological contributions of the research. Then, a discussion of the limitations is given to advance directions for further study for the reader. In the case of the featured study on heart care (Dickson et al., 2011), the discussions naturally reflect the primary aim of the study to strengthen the validity of findings through congruence and complementarity of quantitative and qualitative results. As a result, the authors have emphasized the discussion of the mixed insights generated in the study, and clinical and patient self-care implications, yet have also pointed to a surprising quantitative insight as well as the advantages of a mixed methods research approach. Although making explicit the value of mixed methods research may not yet be common practice, it could be an important avenue for educating others, as advocated by Creswell and Plano Clark (2018). The authors of the featured study on heart care focused their discussion of limitations on the sample that was accessible for the study. You may find the following questions useful in guiding your own discussion of mixed insights, possible implications, limitations, and future directions:

  o What do readers need to know about rationales, processes, and potential outcomes for the mixed insights to better understand the contributions of the implications to the research problem?
  o What do readers need to know about the efforts to enhance methodological rigour of the mixed insights?
  o What do readers need to know about the mixed insights to better understand the study limitations and practical influences and value of the use of a mixed methods research approach?

 Illustrative excerpt discussing mixed insights

The results of this mixed methods study provide insight into the reasons why self-care is poor among many individuals with HF [heart failure] despite evidence of knowledge about routine maintenance and management practices. In this sample, knowledge about HF self-care was adequate overall as were reports of self-care practices. But, the qualitative data revealed that lack of understanding, not lack of knowledge, was a key driver in self-care in this sample. Furthermore, some who were inconsistent in self-care had evidence of mild cognitive impairment. Combined, these results suggest that cognitive function may have a greater influence than knowledge on self-care behaviors. That is, the gap between knowledge and understanding of self-care may be the result of poor cognitive function as well as inadequate patient education ... Our results are supported by several other studies that found that understanding of treatments was an important influence on self-care practices. Field et al (2006) defined three levels of understanding and awareness related to medication adherence by individuals with HF based on their qualitative study. In that sample of 37 patients with HF, all participants knew they should adhere to their medication regimens, but only those with high awareness were proficient in medication adherence and able to articulate understanding of their medication and HF .... The advantages of mixed methods as a research technique to study clinical phenomenon are clearly evident in this study. To date, quantitative methods alone have failed to explain the gap between knowledge and self-care that we explored in this study. By integrating qualitative data about the day-to-day self-care practices of individuals with HF and quantitative evidence of self-care and knowledge, a fuller description has emerged. Our results that misconceptions and lack of understanding lead to lapses in self-care and drive inappropriate self-care are unlikely to have been identified using other methods. Furthermore, complementarity that emerged from using mixed methods can inform future interventions to correct misconceptions and enhance understanding necessary to engage in adequate self-care .... The advantages of mixed methods as a research technique to study clinical phenomenon are clearly evident in this study. To date, quantitative methods alone have failed to explain the gap between knowledge and self-care that we explored in this study. By integrating qualitative data about the day-to-day self-care practices of individuals with HF and quantitative evidence of self-care and knowledge, a fuller description has emerged. Our results that misconceptions and lack of understanding lead to lapses in self-care and drive inappropriate self-care are unlikely to have been identified using other methods. Furthermore, complementarity that emerged from using mixed methods can inform future interventions to correct misconceptions and enhance understanding necessary to engage in adequate self-care.

Source: Dickson et al. (2011, pp. 182–184). Used with permission from Sage.

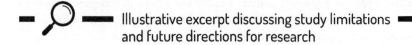 Illustrative excerpt discussing study limitations and future directions for research

The results of this study must be judged within the context of its limitations. The final sample was predominately Caucasian, male, and relatively young for a HF [heart failure] population. There were only two Hispanic patients, and both were male. Also, most of the sample had at least some college education (mean ± SD = 14.17 ± 3.28 years of education). Therefore, these findings need to be explored in a larger, more varied, and older sample of HF patients, since educational level and age have been identified as related to cognitive function in other studies (Pressler et al., 2010). Further exploration in HF patients managed outside of a specialty HF

(Continued)

(Continued)

program is also needed to determine if results differ in patients who may not be optimally managed. These individuals may have more episodes of cardiac decompensation and, therefore, experience poorer cognitive function as a result of the cerebral effects of chronic HF (Woo, Kumar, Macey, Fonarow, & Harper, 2009). Another limitation in our approach is that the purposive sampling strategy in this study was driven by the qualitative approach, which yielded a small sample for the linear regression and limited ability to test for an interaction effect of knowledge and cognition. We found minimal variance in the knowledge scores of our sample that may have resulted in failure to identify knowledge as an important determinant. The sample was well educated and high in knowledge. An effect of knowledge on both management and maintenance might well appear in a larger sample with more knowledge deficits, particularly if knowledge is a necessary but not sufficient condition. Further research is needed to determine when devoting resources to improving knowledge of HF patients is most beneficial.

Source: Dickson et al. (2011, p. 184). Used with permission from Sage.

CHAPTER CHECK-IN

1   Can you discern differences and similarities in the desirable evidence of methodological rigour across quantitative, qualitative, and mixed methods research? Compare how the authors of at least two of the featured studies describe the following sources of evidence, and consider what your analysis tells you about their descriptions (use Figure 9.1 and Table 9.1 to guide your thinking):

   • Participant samples
   • Data collections
   • Data analyses
   • Findings representations
   • Interpretation approaches
   • Insight discussions.

2   Can you recognize hazards related to 'black box' interpretations and strategies for avoiding when generating evidence of research outcomes under conditions of complexity? Select a published study in an area that is of interest to you or one of the featured studies.

   • Examine the methods section for descriptions of their interpretation approaches.
   • Examine the findings section for evidence of their interpretation processes.
   • Examine the discussion section for evidence of their interpretation products.

3   Can you describe the type of evidence you would seek for enhancing methodological rigour of complex mixed methods research outcomes. Apply the guiding questions presented in this chapter to structure an outline:

   • Describe the study's participants and mixed sampling strategies in a few sentences.
   • Describe the design guiding the data collection for the data strands by referring to the rationale, processes, and potential outcomes.
   • Outline the qualitative, quantitative, and mixed analysis processes for each point of interface and provide a rationale for the contributions of the findings to the study.

- Present plans for representing the integrated findings and, if applicable, separate qualitative and quantitative findings as well.
- Describe any anticipated interpretation guidelines for generating mixed insights.
- Discuss potential mixed insights and consider implications, limitations, and future directions for research
- Review the draft and compare the extent to which your draft includes the evidence advanced in Table 9.1. Note which details are presented persuasively in your description and which are not yet known.

4   What features for engaging readers can you use to begin creating your complexity-sensitive mixed methods study proposal? Access a complex mixed methods research problem that you would like to pursue. Sketch the problem and need for the study. Select one of the features for engaging readers that fits with your study and write a brief description of an engaging outcome for addressing this problem.

KEY CHAPTER CONCEPTS

This chapter advances the sixth and final adaptive practice for guiding a complexity-sensitive approach to mixed methods research. It addresses the question: What does generating complex mixed methods research outcomes involve and how can the evidence of methodological rigour and evolving practical influences be recognized, promoted, and conveyed? The rationale for generating evidence of complex research outcomes is grounded in the need for rigorous research when the understandings of the rationales, processes and outcomes are considered to be evolving and incomplete. The purpose of generating evidence of methodological rigour is to create research proposals and reports that are defensible and transparent not only for the specific mixed methods research aspects but also for the qualitative and quantitative data strands. Opportunities for creating more authentic accounts of rigorous mixed methods research processes and outcomes are presented, as are 'black box' interpretations to avoid. Six sources of evidence that are interdependent and iterative guide the generative evidence approach: accounts of participant samples, procedures for data collections, strategies guiding data analyses, displays of findings representations, conveying interpretation approaches, and relating insight discussions. Features that will engage readers include seeking unique participant samples and focusing on innovative mixed methods designs, findings representations, and unconventional perspectives for guiding interpretations. Innovations in describing complex mixed methods research problems involve visual diagrams and writing ideas. The next, concluding, chapter describes onward considerations for those adopting a more complexity-sensitive approach in their mixed methods research.

FURTHER READINGS

The following resources are offered as introductory references for research designs and describing research integrations. The list should not be considered exhaustive. Readers are encouraged to seek out additional readings in the end-of-book reference list. Readings denoted with an asterisk are available on the online resources website for this book.

Bazeley, P. (2018). *Integrating analyses in mixed methods research*. London: Sage.

In this book, Pat Bazeley presents various ways of integrating during the analysis of mixed methods research. The comprehensive description of eight strategies with illustrative examples offers a practical guide for any researcher.

Fàbregues, S., & Molina-Azorín, J. F. (2017). Addressing quality in mixed methods research: A review and recommendations for future agenda. *Quality & Quantity, 51*(6), 2847–2863. doi: 10.1007/s11135-016-0449-4.

Sergi Fàbregues and José Molina-Azorín examine features and trends of the literature on the quality of mixed methods research and call for an agreement on core quality criteria.

Guetterman, T. C., Fetters, M., & Creswell, J. (2015). Integrating quantitative and qualitative results in health science mixed methods research. *Annals of Family Medicine, 13*, 554–561. doi: 10.1370/afm.1865.

In this seminal work illustrating examples of effective joint displays, the authors provide essential guidance for researchers on integration and how to represent mixed methods analysis in their reports.

Onwuegbuzie, A. J., & Hitchcock, J. H. (2010). Advanced mixed analysis approaches. In S. Hesse-Biber and R. B. Johnson (Eds.), *The Oxford handbook of multimethod and mixed methods research inquiry* (pp. 275–295). Oxford: Oxford University Press.

The authors describe and illustrate advanced mixed analysis approaches with a focus on different types of cross-over mixed analysis. They make the case for the limitless combination possibilities.

*Onwuegbuzie, A., & Poth, C. (2016). Editors' afterword: Toward evidence-based guidelines for reviewing mixed methods research manuscripts submitted to journals. *International Journal of Qualitative Methods, 15*, 1–13. doi: 10.1177/1609406916628986.

In this editorial, Anthony Onwuegbuzie and I advance a framework for comprehensively reviewing a mixed methods research manuscript based on the peer reviews from two special issues. The second Appendix in this article lists the 32 items for assessing the quality of a mixed methods manuscript.

Apply your mixed methods knowledge with videos, activities, SAGE journal articles and project templates at **https://study.sagepub.com/poth**

PART III

In the final chapter I describe onward considerations for those adopting a more complexity-sensitive approach in their mixed methods research. The book concludes with three appendices which are useful to revisit as you begin to implement the adaptive practices. As an innovator it can be lonely and take time for the usefulness of practices to be recognized. I strongly believe that the time has come to continue expanding our repertoire of practices within the field of mixed methods research. It is my hope that this book has stimulated your thinking about the yet untapped potential of integrative thinking with complexity about mixed methods research practices. I am excited about the possibilities that are yet to be realized.

My intention with the concluding chapter and appendices is to help researchers implement the adaptive practices to become more complexity-sensitive in their mixed methods research endeavours. The aim of Chapter 10 is to answer two basic questions. First, why complexity-sensitive mixed methods research? Second, what are the potential challenges for complexity-sensitive mixed methods researchers? Finally, I advance some final guiding words for those seeking to implement the adaptive mixed methods research practices. The three appendices provide definitions for the new terms listed at the beginning of each chapter in the book, the complexity study profiles for each of the featured studies, and biographies of the research spotlight contributors that are interspersed throughout the book.

ONWARD CONSIDERATIONS FOR ADAPTIVE PRACTICES

The final chapter in Part III is as follows:

10

REALIZING
COMPLEXITY-SENSITIVE
MIXED METHODS
RESEARCH

By the end of this chapter, you will be able to answer the following questions:

* Why use a complexity-sensitive approach to mixed methods research?
* What challenges are associated with complexity-sensitive mixed methods research?
* How might mixed methods researchers be guided under conditions of complexity?

This chapter explores a concluding question for this book: *What distinguishes the niche for complexity-sensitive mixed methods research, and how can the six adaptive practices advanced in this book influence our integrative thinking with complexity about mixed methods research?* Writing this book has been a journey inspired by my desire to help others embrace complexity and guide integrative thinking about mixed methods research. It should not be a surprise, given our discussions about the nature of conditions of complexity, that I could not predict how this book would conclude. Now that the end is in sight, advocating for how a complexity-sensitive mixed methods research approach could be realized seems like a natural way to close the book. I begin by making the case that, while researchers no longer have the option of ignoring complexity, researchers can choose to harness complexity by adapting their practices. Two dialectic attitudes towards complexity are illustrated by Edward de Bono (1999) and David Whyte. On the one hand, de Bono (1999, p. 25) chose a more cantankerous approach in his book *Simplicity*, saying: 'Dealing with complexity is an inefficient and unnecessary waste of time, attention and mental energy. There is never any justification for things being complex when they could be simple.' On the other hand, Whyte chose a more pragmatic approach, advising against unrealistic efforts focused on reducing complexity. It may well be that the community of mixed methods researchers is simply beginning to recognize that embracing complexity is a worthwhile yet difficult endeavour. Over time, the community of mixed methods researchers may well agree with the premise advanced by Victor Hugo that timely ideas can have a greater impact than mighty armies. To that end, recognizing varying conditions of complexity and transforming traditional mixed methods practices to be more complexity-sensitive is at the heart of the six practices described in this book. In concluding this book, I want to be forthright about the challenges facing those realizing a complexity-sensitive mixed methods approach and offer some final guidance.

The Case for Complexity-Sensitive Mixed Methods Research

At the beginning of this book, I advanced several dilemmas underpinning the demand for innovations in mixed methods research practice and proposed integrative thinking with complexity science as a means for mitigating some of the constraints with traditional mixed methods research practices. To that end, I consider the six adaptive practices involved in complexity-sensitive mixed methods research as occupying a distinct niche as a response to the dilemmas I and those around me encountered when planning and conducting mixed methods research under varying conditions of complexity. Under such conditions, there is a need for adaptive responses, a benefit from integrative thinking, a demand for creative designing, and an aspiration for authentic reporting. The adaptive practices introduced in this book provide guidance and comprise these four key characteristics of a complexity-sensitive mixed methods research approach (see Figure 10.1). I will be the first to admit the tolerance for complexity-sensitive approaches to mixed methods research is not yet great, but it is getting better as researchers are increasingly seeking new ways of doing things. Integrative thinkers and the researchers that support complexity-sensitive practices can accelerate the acceptance and adoption of complexity-sensitive approaches to mixed methods research. This support is more readily realized when the need for and distinct niche of a complexity-sensitive approach is recognized by mixed methods researchers.

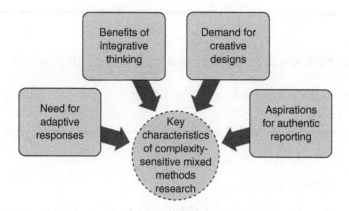

Figure 10.1   Four key characteristics of complexity-sensitive mixed methods research

Need for Adaptive Responses

Under conditions of complexity, mixed methods researchers need to continually adapt their responses since conditions are constantly changing and unpredictable. For example, as our understandings of complex mixed methods research problems evolve, adaptive responses are needed to access the expertise and data procedures to generate integrative solutions. This has certainly been the case with my work on housing programmes: as our understandings of those with a vested interest (e.g., government, organizational, and individual service providers together with their target populations and the systems in which they were situated) increase so do our understandings of the research problems to pursue so we can adjust our interactions and integrations to realize desirable outcomes. Similarly, adaptive responses are needed for responding appropriately to evolving conditions in study contexts, interactions, integrations, and outcomes. The stakes of employing adaptive responses are high – if we do not adapt as we go, then the methodological cohesion we seek cannot be maintained. Rather than being resistant, adopting a mindset that allows mixed methods researchers to respond appropriately to changing conditions is necessary to reflect the realities in which we undertake research.

Throughout the past decade, I have become increasingly aware of sources of complexity and been humbled by the effects of the varying conditions of complexity I have witnessed. Across my experiences as an instructor of research methods, graduate student supervisor, and research team member, I have discerned a common theme running through the practices of researchers who successfully navigate the complexity inherent in much of mixed methods research: researchers who attend to changing conditions and respond appropriately in their framing, planning, and conduct of research practices experience fewer dilemmas than those who do not. A responsive approach is central to the advice offered in Guiding Tip 10.1 by a senior educational scientist at the Royal College of Physicians and Surgeons of Canada for navigating the complexity of mixed methods research.

 Guiding Tip 10.1 ═══════════════════════════

Elaine Van Melle advising how to navigate mixed methods research

When using mixed methods, it is important to plan carefully, implement thoughtfully, and stay open to change.

Benefits of Integrative Thinking

Under conditions of complexity, mixed methods researchers benefit from being integrative in their thinking with complexity about their practices. This is because bringing a complexity lens to bear on what works in traditional mixed methods research practices is essential in developing adaptive practices for use under varying conditions of complexity. The tensions created by complexity can be harnessed to develop innovations in mixed insights and practices that emerge from a unique synthesis of researchers' diverse methodological and disciplinary expertise, experiences, and intuitions beyond what would be accessible individually. This new way of thinking may present challenges and perhaps even obstacles for many of us. What strikes me is that the capacity for integrative thinking with complexity is not yet often valued, and that many of our contemporary approaches to methodological training perpetuate learning about research approaches in silos with few opportunities for development across disciplines. Without exploring the contributions across research approaches, we could not have realized what we are missing – indeed, many of our innovative insights are coming from transdisciplinary collaborations. Rest assured, it is natural – as we increasingly recognize complexity in our work and the value of a complexity lens – that things will get messy and challenging along the way! Jen Sincero (2013), in her book *You are a badass: How to stop doubting your greatness and start living an awesome life*, reminds us of the power of viewing obstacles and challenges as the agents of growth. This was certainly the case with my work on housing programmes: when we brought different groups of service providers together to pursue our work, new understandings emerged that had previously not been possible. Previously they had been 'siloed' in their work and they were frustrated by the lack of progress. The timing and approach proved to be a tipping point as they realized that their synergy was greater than the sum of their contributions. Just as we can develop and refine skills to perform tasks we once considered impossible, I am convinced we can also develop the habits underpinning integrative thinking and research practices. In our daily lives, we already do much of this: we face problems that appear to have no apparent solutions and yet we draw on our existing knowledge, data, and experiences to make a decision – even if a tentative one. In the long run, the benefits of present discomforts will open possibilities that we cannot yet imagine. I believe that as the capacity for integrative thinking with complexity develops, mixed methods researchers will become better positioned to tackle many of the complex social problems.

Demand for Creative Designs

Under conditions of complexity, mixed methods researchers demand creativity in designs. This is because predetermined designs and data procedures limit creativity and promote a linear approach to mixed methods research processes even when the reality in which the research takes place is more complex. We have to get beyond the 'I can't because …' thoughts and instead see the possibilities framed with 'but I could if …'. As researchers, we are generally trained to reduce complexity to make our studies feasible. Much of our training has been biased towards simplification and specialization. As comforting as simplification can be, it simply does not translate to the realities we often face as mixed methods researchers. Mixed methods research under conditions of complexity requires embedding creativity in our everyday practices. For example, framing the mixing purpose focused on the need for innovation and employing description-focused approaches encourage innovative designs because together they free us from the unintentional constraints of existing typologies. This has certainly been the case with my work on housing programmes: as we began to conceptualize our research, we focused on mixing purposes for innovation and generated not only novel mixed insights but also creative designs in our integration of qualitative and quantitative data. As mixed methods researchers abandon the need to simplify their research plans to fit existing typologies and begin to think about the processes involved in realizing integrations as iterative and developmental in nature, researchers become better positioned to tackle many of the complex societal problems. We must enhance comfort with uncertainty and reliance in order to carry out creative work in changeable conditions.

Aspirations for Authentic Reporting

Under conditions of complexity, mixed methods researchers aspire for authenticity in their reporting. Mixed methods research under conditions of complexity can be messy and unpredictable as it unfolds and responds to dynamic influences. We need illustrative examples detailing the thinking behind how mixed methods researchers worked through their most perplexing research processes. As accounts of adaptations to our research practices become the norm, mixed methods researchers become better positioned to describe authentic research realities in their proposals and reports. Researchers can make explicit the dilemmas encountered and their adaptive responses to changing conditions, which then allows other researchers to learn from their work. The use of visuals to represent designs and procedures increasingly disseminates and provides the opportunity for illustrating adaptations to plans. This has certainly been the case with my work on housing programmes: as we begin to disseminate our work, we find ourselves relying more and more on visuals to convey discrepancies between planned and enacted procedures. We have also advocated for less emphasis on written reports and created more frequent opportunities for conveying emerging findings to different audiences with vested interests in the research outcomes. Greater acceptance of different ways of disseminating research – such as first-person accounts as described in an editorial in the *Journal of Mixed Methods Research* (Fetters & Molina-Azorin, 2017) and writing voices in dialogue (Zhou & Hall, 2016) – would contribute to expanding the ways in which we present comprehensive mixed methods research accounts. However, all researchers are cautioned to attend to the social contexts associated with specific disciplines, fields, and publications as work is generally subject to peer review.

Potential Challenges for Complexity-Sensitive Mixed Methods Researchers

A complexity-sensitive approach means transforming our research practices because we now recognize that shifting and unpredictable conditions mean that each design, procedure, and outcome will be different each time. My observations as a researcher over the past two decades allow me to infer, with some confidence, that researchers vary greatly in their discomfort with uncertainty and that some are more comfortable with the unknown. For some mixed methods researchers, the adaptive practices presented in this book will be seen as 'making it up as you go', while for others the practices offer practical guidance for responding to changing conditions. Regardless of where you currently 'sit' – with comfort or discomfort with the six adaptive mixed methods research practices described in this book – uncertainty in our research conditions is not going away. To provide some measure of comfort, I refer to the words of Trisha Greenhalgh, Penny Hawe, and Luci Lykum who, in the preface for the timely publication, *Complexity Science in Health*, state:

> [The] academic literature is steadily accumulating an evidence base on the 'the science of muddling through in real-world situations' that (mostly) complements and (occasionally) challenges the findings of more conventional basic science research, observational epidemiology and randomised controlled trials. This work points us in potential directions to explore and apply complexity science, principles and ideas. (Greenhalgh, Hawe, and Lykum, 2017, p. vi)

This quote draws attention to the limitations of our current understandings and indeed provides encouragement to think beyond our traditional research practices – similar to what this book advocates through a complexity-science approach to mixed methods research. In order to prepare for the uncertainty we most certainly will face under conditions of complexity, I identify three potential challenges to mixed methods research and offer suggestions related to training development, mindset advocacy, and resource feasibility.

Development of Situational Training

The conditions under which much research occurs are beyond what we were trained for in terms of complexity, so we must learn new skills. In Chapter 2, I described five roles of a mixed methods researcher for realizing an organic mixed methods research process:

- A *practitioner* develops a distinct ethos for and promotes the field of mixed methods research.
- An *architect* formulates the research problems and aligns the plans guiding a mixed methods study.
- An *engineer* conducts the procedures and guides the technical aspects of a mixed methods study.
- A *collaborator* facilitates the social interactions and develops capacity for a mixed methods study.
- A *manager* coordinates data management and oversees logistics in a mixed methods study.

Embedded within these mixed methods researcher roles is the notion that the competencies are naturally evolving in light of emerging understandings in the field. What has become increasingly evident is that, as mixed methods researchers develop competency, a key proficiency marker involves having hands-on experiences of working on a mixed methods project (Guetterman, 2017).

Experience as a mixed methods researcher, instructor, and team member tells me that researchers have varying capacities for dealing with complexity. It may be because our research training is generally focused on technical skills and we are just beginning to recognize the need for attending to changing conditions and develop the ability to be responsive in our practices. In so doing, some mixed methods researchers are also developing their situational proficiency. The need to develop training to enhance the capacity for adaptive practices is supported by David Byrne's assertion in his 1998 book, *Complexity and the social sciences*. He says: 'Every PhD student in everything should get to grips with the "chaos/complexity" programme, not for reasons of fashion or even legitimate career building, but because this is the way the world works and we need to understand that' (p. 161). I believe that developing competency as a mixed methods researcher takes time, and situational training requires research experiences working under varying conditions of complexity because only then do we realize the necessity of adaptive practices. Among the challenges related to developing training aimed at increasing mixed methods research competency under conditions of complexity is that advanced and individualized learning opportunities are few and far between.

Advocacy of Complexity-Sensitive Mindsets

The assumptions and mindsets we bring to research have been cultivated by many influences ranging from our training experiences and mentor interactions to our reading of literature and disciplinary norms. In Chapter 3, I advanced four opportunities afforded by complexity science for mixed methods researchers:

- Small inputs can lead to dramatically large consequences.
- Global properties flow from the aggregate behaviour of individuals.
- Slight differences in initial conditions can produce very different outcomes.
- Complex adaptive systems assimilate to their environmental interactions.

Among the challenges when working under conditions of complexity is how researchers respond to changing circumstances in real time. What has become increasingly evident is that researchers vary in their attentiveness to these dynamic influences and attitudes towards responding to the changing conditions surrounding their research.

I adapt the change curve put forward by William Bridges and Susan Bridges (2016) in their book, *Managing Transition*, to illustrate why researchers may be more or less accepting of the adaptive practices forwarded in this book. Keep in mind that researchers experience dilemmas and learnings at different rates, and so it is logical that acceptance or resistance may also occur at different rates. The key is that – as mixed methods researchers realize the limitations of current practices, referred to as 'endings' – they may express denial, confusion, and frustration before they become stuck in what is referred to as the 'neutral zone'. They then slowly work through creativity, hope, and finally enthusiasm for new practices – a stage referred to as 'new beginnings'. Thus, it is natural that, as an integrative thinker familiar with the opportunities afforded by a complexity-sensitive approach to mixed methods research, you will be called upon as an advocate to help colleagues to mitigate the dilemmas and the ripple effects of complexity that are often experienced but difficult to explain. Mindsets are difficult to change. Yet this book is a call to action and a way forward for those dealing with dilemmas experienced under conditions of complexity with our traditional mixed methods research practices. Adaptation may necessitate working with someone familiar with a complexity-sensitive approach to mixed methods research who can guide the adaptive practices. Consider Researcher Spotlight 10.1, featuring the challenges associated with transforming practices to respond to changing conditions of mixed methods research, from the perspective of a professor of empirical pedagogy at the University of Vienna (Austria).

 **Researcher Spotlight 10.1**

Judith Schoonenboom on adopting a complexity-sensitive mentality as a mixed methods researcher

Given its complexity, mixed methods research is a challenge for every researcher, and a mixed research project's path is usually complex, sometimes stressful, and never without problems. In addition, learning how to do mixed methods research is a challenging experience for beginning researchers. In the past few decades, we have gained much psychological insight into how people behave in such complex, changing environments, and what we can do to make progress easier. We know, for example, that under stress, we tend to inappropriately simplify complex situations, while positive emotions give us more options to choose from. We have learned a lot about how we can tweak environments, so that desired, but difficult behaviours become easier. We have insights into the causes of procrastination, and we know that projects are easier to start when we have the feeling that we are somehow already under way. We know that for change projects, simple goals often work, while vague goals often do not. We know that focusing on the next task works better that trying to keep an overview of the whole project. We know that unresolved tasks keep nagging – small ones to the same extent as large ones. We know a task can be better approached with a growth mindset than with a fixed mindset, and we know that a growth mindset can be developed. It is not so much my expectation or predication, but rather my wish, that we bring this knowledge together and use it to advance mixed methods research.

Feasibility of Predetermining Resources

Researchers vary in their attention to complexity and access to various human and financial resources for undertaking a mixed methods study. In Chapter 4, I advanced five dimensions for recognizing conditions of complexity within mixed methods research:

- Intentions of research problems
- Systems of research contexts
- Designs of research integrations
- Capacities of research interactions
- Evidence of research outcomes.

Embedded within these dimensions is the notion that the research conditions are naturally evolving to accommodate these dynamic influences and that researchers must attend to the changes. Predetermining time and resources when working under conditions of complexity is challenging, given the unpredictability of how the study will unfold. The question of feasibility – given time and resource constraints – is important in any mixed methods study because of the need for integrated findings generated by the collection and analysis of qualitative and quantitative data (Creswell & Plano Clark, 2018). Yet under conditions of varying complexity, time and resource requirements are intensified because of the uncertainty involved in defining problems, describing designs, and realizing outcomes. Researchers need to think carefully about how they might accommodate increases in resource needs for complexity-sensitive mixed methods research to be feasible. If mixed methods researchers are better able to meet the resource fluctuations inherent in adaptive practices, the field is better positioned to contribute to pressing complex problems. This is because, as described by Heinz Pagels in his book *Perfect Symmetry: The Search for the Beginning of Time*:

> The capacity to tolerate complexity and welcome contradiction, not the need for simplicity and certainty, is the attribute of an explorer. Centuries ago, when some people suspended their search for absolute truth and began instead to ask how things worked, modern science was born. Curiously, it is by abandoning the search for absolute truth that science has begun to make progress, opening the material universe to human exploration. (1985, p. 370)

Proposing research and writing grants for complex mixed methods research projects in a way that embeds some adaptation to resource allocations is possible, yet it may require working collaboratively as a team. An important consideration would be building a shared understanding of what a complexity-sensitive approach to mixed methods research involves to make decisions about resource allocations collaboratively.

Some Final Guiding Words

It is not often that I am at a loss for words. But here we are: I have said what needs to be said. How the ideas advanced in this book influence your mixed methods research practice remains to be seen. For me, this book has been a labour of both love and tears. Interestingly, the proposal for this book was my last piece of work before giving birth to my daughter Avery.

My recollection of those final weeks of pregnancy is fraught with concern that I would not be finished in time. While the book content and organization have evolved considerably since then, I am hopeful about its usefulness for promoting innovations in mixed methods research. Similar to Douglas Adams' experience as noted in his book, *The Hitchhiker's guide to the galaxy* (1985) that he ended up where he needed to be even though the final destination had not been planned. Let me conclude this book with the following guiding words: Be the future you seek in the field of mixed methods research. Contribute to the mixed methods research literature and practice. Find your mixed methods research community, and get involved. These guiding words have served me well.

Be the Future You Seek in the Field of Mixed Methods Research

By challenging the status quo (i.e., established practices) and advancing new mixed methods research practices, you can be an innovator. If you think complex problems are important to study, then we need researchers to delve into the 'messiness' and advance new practices because we want to demonstrate to the mixed methods research community that innovations are not only possible but desirable. This also allows us to think and act with intention: do not default to the traditional mixed methods research practices, but rather use them deliberately when appropriate for the research conditions. If we want to pursue big challenges, then it is necessary to mobilize people to experiment. Many of the highly complex problems cannot be solved with existing technical expertise. Instead, we must advance new ways of thinking and doing. Putting ourselves out there for critique can be difficult. We can even get stuck with a great idea and find ourselves unable to move it forward. The key is to figure out how to get unstuck because, as Jen Sincero highlights in her previously mentioned book, 'most of the time it's not lack of experience that's holding us back, but rather the lack of determination to do what we need to do to be successful' (2013, p. 151). Remember that done and published is better than perfect and unpublished. Figure out what part of the dissemination process is challenging to you by watching where you stop. Get yourself unstuck to get your mixed methods research ideas out there for consideration. Consider Researcher Spotlight 10.2 which describes emerging threats and opportunities for mixed methods researchers, from the perspective of a prominent mixed methods health researcher who is vice chancellor of the University of Western Australia (Perth) and Professor of Mental Health at the University of Leeds (UK).

 **Researcher Spotlight 10.2**

Dawn Freshwater on responsible production of knowledge under conditions of high mixed methods research complexity

The emerging threat to the concept of expertise and the erosion of trust in higher education, public policy, and research positions is faced by all research and researchers as we enhance our understandings of conditions of complexity. The threat is one of significant scepticism, and indeed cynicism, regarding any 'fact'-based analysis. Mixed methods researchers may be able to make an interesting contribution in relation to this challenge. Not only could they take a mixed methods research view on the problem itself (erosion of trust in Western democracy and the production of knowledge within that socio/economic/political context), but they could also ensure that knowledge produced through the mixed methods research approach takes account of and incorporates opportunities to address this specific challenge in the way they conduct and study future global challenges. Communities of scholars take on a whole new meaning when we begin to think about what constitutes scholarship in the contemporary zeitgeist!

Contribute to the Mixed Methods Research Literature and Practices

I urge you to publish and share work that contributes to societal understandings of important and pressing problems. We know that solutions are incremental, and I recognize that it will take time and resources to make significant progress in understanding many of the complex problems facing society, such as poverty, immigration, and unemployment. I continue to be inspired by the mixed methods proposals and manuscripts I read as a supervisor, reviewer, and community member. I often facilitate interactions between people who I think could benefit from networking, but all researchers need to keep an eye out for and pursue important opportunities for learning from one another. While I am pleased with the progress we have made across disciplines related to the field of mixed methods research, there are many innovations to be realized and widely shared through publications, workshops, and conference presentations. In Guiding Tip 10.2, an assistant professor at the University of Michigan (USA) offers advice for publishing your outcomes from mixed methods research conducted under conditions of complexity.

 Guiding Tip 10.2

Tim Guetterman advising the need for publishing and sharing ideas

Mixed methods research is a growing field, and it is hard to keep up with all the advances. I strongly encourage anyone who has a methodological innovation to write an article featuring the innovation to share with the mixed methods community. We can learn from each other as a community by developing literature around issues, such as how to integrate qualitative and quantitative research in increasingly complex studies. We have barely touched the surface of these topics.

Find Your Mixed Methods Research Community and Get Involved!

It is by drawing from and integrating across individuals' expertise and experiences that we can create new possibilities. As I have previously mentioned, I have both personally and professionally benefited from my interactions with the wonderfully diverse and generous global community of mixed methods researchers. I have learned more than I could have imagined and continue to be inspired by the work I read within my own disciplines related to education, psychology, health, and beyond. I often recommend that researchers seek out mixed methods researchers within their research areas and join groups if they exist. For me, this has meant joining the Mixed Methods Evaluation Topical Interest Group within the American Evaluation Association and the Mixed Methods Research Special Interest Group within the American Educational Research Association. While these have been impactful, it would be remiss of me not to highlight the obvious impact my involvement in the Mixed Methods Research Association has had on my thinking and development of complexity-sensitive mixed methods research practices. Recall Chapter 1, in which I trace the beginning of my journey as a mixed methods researcher to an initial workshop where I learned about the field. In Guiding Tip 10.3, a professor of educational psychology and a university faculty scholar in the Department of Teacher Education and Learning Sciences at North Carolina State University in Raleigh (USA) offers advice for novices preparing for a mixed methods study.

 Guiding Tip 10.3

Jessica DeCuir-Gunby advising those new to learning about mixed methods research

My advice to novices is to take time to understand the intricacies of mixed methods research before attempting to engage in a mixed methods study. Mixed methods research is much more complicated than simply putting quantitative and qualitative data together in one study.

In conclusion, I draw upon the wise words of one of my idols who has demonstrated integrative thinking in ways I can only hope to aspire to. Stephen Hawking suggested complexity would be a key consideration of many of the scientific efforts of the 21st century. A complexity-sensitive approach seems destined to play a major role in enabling mixed methods research contributions to solve societal issues because it affords creative opportunities in work on complex research problems.

CHAPTER CHECK-IN

1 Can you identify challenges you foresee as a mixed methods researcher? Compare the similarities and differences with the challenges introduced in this chapter.
2 What other roles and competencies would you identify as essential for mixed methods researchers working under conditions of complexity?
3 What guiding advice would you offer a mixed methods researcher working under conditions of complexity?

KEY CHAPTER CONCEPTS

This chapter explores a concluding question for this book: What distinguishes the niche for complexity-sensitive mixed methods research, and how can the six adaptive practices advanced in this book influence our thinking about mixed methods research? I begin by making the case that researchers no longer have the option of ignoring complexity because, under such conditions, mixed methods researchers need guidance in adaptive responses, would benefit from integrative thinking, have a desire for creative design, and aspire to generate authentic reporting. Then I introduce three potential challenges for mixed methods researchers under conditions of complexity and offer suggestions related to training development, mindset advocacy, and resource feasibility. I conclude by offering guiding advice about being the future you seek in the field of mixed methods research, contributing to the mixed methods research literature and practice, and finding your mixed methods research community and getting involved.

FURTHER READINGS

In this chapter, I depart from my usual mode and instead offer ideas for reading that have been impactful on my own thinking about mixed methods research.

Adams, D. (2017). *The hitchhiker's guide to the galaxy omnibus: A trilogy in five parts*. London: Pan Books.

Bringing together the five titles of the classic series, this edition includes an introductory, bonus short story and a previously deleted scene. In particular, the unpredictable adventures of Arthur Dent and his alien sidekick, Ford Prefect, strike me as having occurred under complex conditions.

Hawking, S. (1998). *A brief history of time*. New York: Bantam Books.

If you have not already read this bestselling classic, which is the updated and expanded tenth anniversary edition, you have been missing out! This book is noteworthy for how Stephen Hawking explains the complexities of cosmological principles and for his foreshadowing of many discoveries.

Pagels, H. (1985). *Perfect symmetry: The search for the beginning of time*. New York: Simon & Schuster.

Heinz Pagels's work is significant for his ability to explain complex scientific topics in a way that embraces rather than reduces complexity, but that is understandable all the same. This is a great example of how discoveries across quantum physics and cosmology have helped move forward our understandings of the universe, space, and time.

Sincero, J. (2013). *You are a badass: How to stop doubting your greatness and start living an awesome life*. Philadelphia: Running Press.

Jen Sincero promotes learning about oneself, how to embrace who you are, and how to move your thinking forward so that you do take risks. Written from the perspective of a success coach, one of the 'learnings' I found helpful to my own thinking is viewing obstacles and challenges as the agents of growth.

Apply your mixed methods knowledge with videos, activities, SAGE journal articles and project templates at **https://study.sagepub.com/poth**

APPENDICES

APPENDIX A

AN ANNOTATED
GLOSSARY OF TERMS

The definitions in this glossary represent new chapter terms as they are used and defined in this book. Many definitions exist for these terms, but the most workable definitions for me (and I hope for the reader) are those that reflect the content and references presented in this book.

Adaptive mixed methods research practices refer to complexity-sensitive research practices that are adapted to enhance researchers' capacity to respond to the unique and unfolding conditions under which mixed methods research studies are undertaken.

'Black box' interpretations refer to a metaphor for the 'darkness' or lack of knowledge ascribed to the interpretation procedures undertaken related to the integrated findings to generate the mixed insights.

Complex adaptive system refers to phenomena that defy simplistic analyses of cause and effect and that have the capacity to adapt to contextual changes (Weaver, 1948).

Complex mixed methods research contexts refer to research systems that are dynamic, unpredictable, interrelated and involve imperfect understandings about the environmental influences.

Complex mixed methods research integrations refer to research procedures that reflect dynamic, agile, and imperfect understandings about the feasibility influences.

Complex mixed methods research interactions refer to research capacity that reflects dynamic, unpredictable, integrative, and imperfect understandings about the social influences.

Complex mixed methods research outcomes refer to research evidence that reflects dynamic, unpredictable, emergent, and imperfect understandings about the practical influences.

Complex mixed methods research problems refer to problems that involve multiple interacting systems, social and disciplinary uncertainties, and imperfect understandings about their background influences.

Complexity refers to conditions in which the research system is integrated and yet too varied for understanding using simple, mechanistic and linear methods.

Complexity effects refer to the deepened understandings of the relevant issues and considerations gained from engaging in progressive learning about the research conditions.

Complexity lens refers to a new view of how to see, understand, and influence research in which we assume nonlinearity and which is reflective of the principles of complexity science.

Complexity science refers to a collective of theories and conceptual tools used to study a system and problems that are dynamic, unpredictable, and multidimensional.

Complexity-sensitive mixed methods research approach refers to an innovative approach to mixed methods research guided by six adaptive practices.

Complexity study profile refers to a tool developed for diagnosing and representing the levels of complexity of research conditions across five dimensions: intentions of research problems, systems within research contexts, designs of research integrations, capacity of research interactions, and evidence of research outcomes.

Conditions of complexity refer to the environment surrounding research and are defined by five dimensions of complexity.

Data strands refer to the qualitative or quantitative data procedures.

Descriptive design approach refers to an approach to describing designs based on four inter-dependent and iterative tasks: articulating the framing considerations guiding the study, examining the logic considerations underpinning the design, attending to the ethical con-siderations during the research, and assimilating procedural adaptations throughout the implementation.

Design orientation refers to the point of reference for the research design.

Dimensions of complexity refer to the aspects from which the conditions of research complex-ity are described and assessed.

Emergence refers to the capacity of members and teams to accommodate the products of their integrative interactions.

Emergent mixed methods research designs refer to the designs guiding mixed methods research when its use arises due to issues that develop during the process of conducting the research (Creswell & Plano Clark, 2018).

Environmental influences refer to the dynamic and unpredictable influences that arise and their effects within and across the interrelated research systems.

Evolving mixed methods research designs refer to designs guiding mixed methods research that adjust over time by assimilating to changing conditions.

Fixed mixed methods research designs refer to designs guiding mixed methods research when the predetermined designs at the beginning of the research are implemented as planned (Creswell & Plano Clark, 2018).

Framing perspectives refer to the differing points of view when presenting information about the same topic.

Grand challenges describe research problems that arise from 'environmental degradation and climate change, poverty, health, social and economic inequality, and geopolitical instability, among many others' (Mertens et al., 2016b, p. 12). See also *wicked problems*.

Grey literature is considered to lack a system of bibliographic control, which renders searches more challenging for materials not published by a commercial entity and instead generated by government departments, scholarly societies and associations, and industry (Alberani, Pietrangeli, & Mazza, 1990). Also described as non-conventional, and some-times transient, publications found by being cited in journal articles, within collections, on web pages, or referred to on author's curricula vitae.

High complexity refers to conditions where there is no assumption of stability, a high degree of uncertainty, and evidence of nonlinear and dynamic influences. See also *low complexity*, *moderate complexity*.

Innovation refers to the creation of something new, pioneering, and perhaps transformative.

Integrated findings refer to the products of mixed analysis in mixed methods research.

Integration procedures refer to the strategies involved in the mixing of qualitative and quan-titative in mixed methods research.

Integrative interactions refer to the type of collaborations that are generative of outcomes greater than the sum of the individual contributions.

Integrative thinking is bringing a complexity lens to bear on what works in traditional mixed methods research practice tendencies to develop adaptive practices for use under varying conditions of complexity.

Intensity of mixing refers to the degree to which the qualitative and quantitative data strands are integrated during mixed methods research.

Interactive, system-based design approach refers to an approach to designing mixed methods research in which the quantitative and qualitative data strands interact with each other throughout the research process (Creswell & Plano Clark, 2018).

Interpersonal contexts refer to the community-level details of the interrelations among those actively involved in the research, such as the theoretical approach and ethical standards guiding researchers in their interactions with one another and with their participants.

Leader-centric effects refer to the influence from a single researcher directing research team interactions.

Literature search parameters refers to the boundaries-related criteria such as keywords and dates when examining published and grey literature.

Low complexity refers to conditions where there is an assumption of stability and a high degree of agreement and certainty. See also *moderate complexity, high complexity*.

Messiness refers to the mixed methods research construct that 'recognize[s] the inherent complex, dynamic, and undetermined nature of mixed methods research practice' (Plano Clark & Ivankova, 2016, p.277).

Methodological congruence refers to the goal of maintaining fit among the tasks involved in the organic mixed methods research process.

Methodological rigour refers to the strength of the underlying logic of the research and the confidence with which conclusions can be drawn.

Mixed insights refer to the interpretations generated from the integrated findings in mixed methods research.

Mixed methods research requires the integration of quantitative and qualitative data and assumes that the collective contribution mitigates inherent weaknesses in either type of data.

Mixing purpose refers to the rationale for integrating qualitative and quantitative data in mixed methods research.

Moderate complexity refers to conditions where some assumption of stability and degree of agreement and certainty exist. See also *low complexity, high complexity*.

Organic mixed methods research process refers to explicitly depicting the research process as more creative, evolving, and emergent than might be assumed. The six practices may be revisited and outcomes revised at any time in the process. There is no assumption of linearity or of rigidly following a preconceived plan for the six iterative practices: determining if the study need or research problem is suitable for mixed methods research; articulating and specifying mixing purposes; identifying and describing the research contexts; distinguishing and specifying the required research capacities; designing and conducting the research procedures guiding data collections, analyses, and integrations; and generating and evaluating evidence of research outcomes.

Personal contexts refer to individual-level details of the orientations of those actively involved and the influences shaping their backgrounds.

Point of interface refers to the point or points where mixing of qualitative and quantitative data strands occurs in a mixed methods research design.

Practical influences refer to the dynamic and unpredictable influences that arise and affect the processes involved in generating evidence of mixed methods research outcomes.

Proximity focus refers to the emphasis of traditional definitions of research contexts on pre-determining the contextual boundaries based on proximity to the study problem.

Published literature is considered to be materials accessed through publishers with assigned locators to assist access; for example, the International Standard Book Number (ISBN) and, more recently, the Digital Object Identifier (DOI) system.

Qualitative data refers to evidence that is text- and image-based.

Quality criteria are study techniques justifying the study's outcomes are warranted and the researcher's inferences are defensible (Collins, 2015).

Quantitative data refers to evidence that is numeric-based.

Relational systems approach refers to an approach to defining mixed methods research contexts involving a focus on the way two or more research systems are connected.

Research design refers to the types of inquiry that provide specific direction for procedures in a research study (Creswell, 2014).

Research design typology refers to a system of categorization of designs.

Research ethics refer to application of fundamental ethical principles to the planning and implementation of research. Researchers are often guided by three principles for conduct of ethical research: respect for persons, concern for welfare, and concern for justice.

Research outcomes refer to the many products that are produced by mixed methods research.

Research problem refers to an issue that leads to a need to conduct a study. Typically, a researcher introduces a mixed methods study by framing the research problem by situating the background and motivations for the study.

Research purpose refers to the rationale for conducting research.

Research question refers to the questions guiding the study.

Research team refers to the people involved in the research process.

Research topic refers to a broad subject area in which a research problem is situated.

Self-organization refers to the capacity of members and teams to accommodate the products of their integrative interactions. See also *emergence*.

Social contexts refer to the global-level details of the influences on both interpersonal and personal contexts involved in the study, such as traditions of the fields or disciplines of study, the historical, political, and economic landscape of countries or institutions involved, as well as societal priorities such as funding or pressing foci.

Systems perspective refers to the viewpoint which allows monitoring and describing the environmental influences and subsequent effects on the systems over time. Only once environmental influences are recognized can the influences in a system matter, how they interact, and to what effect be discerned.

Team-centric leadership style refers to a distributed leadership style where the team adopts mutual accountability for their interactions.

Traditional mixed methods research practices refer to the established routines and tasks performed by researchers undertaking a mixed methods research process.

Typology-based design approach refers to a strategy for designing mixed methods research that is based on selecting among established designs.

Wicked problems arise from 'environmental degradation and climate change, poverty, health, social and economic inequality, and geopolitical instability, among many others' (Mertens et al., 2016b, p. 12). See also *grand challenges*.

APPENDIX B

APPENDIX B

TEMPLATES FOR RESEARCH PRACTICE INNOVATIONS

This appendix provides templates for some of the figures and tables in this book. Editable versions of templates denoted with an asterisk are also available on the companion website.

*Table B.1 Template for creating mixed methods study complexity profile (Chapter 4)

Dimension of complexity	Dimension characteristics	Level of complexity			
		Low	Moderate	High	Rationale/description
Intentions of research problems	Stability of background influences				_____
	Clarity of mixing purpose				_____
	Certainty of study outcomes				_____
Systems of research contexts	Dynamics of environmental influences				_____
	Range of geographical dispersion				_____
	Diversity of participants				_____
Designs of research integrations	Predictability of feasibility influences				_____
	Nature of design approach				_____
	Definition of timeframes and resources				_____
Capacities of research interactions	Diversity of social influences				_____
	Extent of role definition				_____
	Nature of interpersonal outcomes				_____
Evidence of research outcomes	Familiarity of practical influences				_____
	Transparency of integration strategy				_____
	Nature of study impacts				_____
Overall study complexity rating					
Rationale for study's complexity rating					

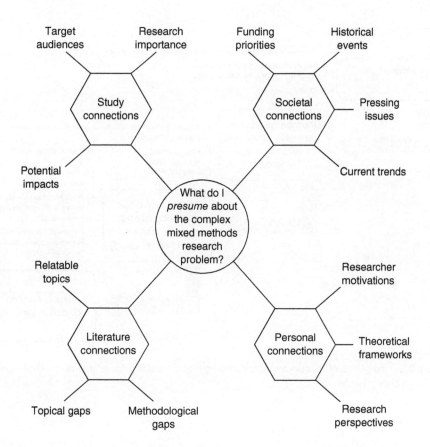

*Figure B.1 Template for visual mapping informing framing a complex mixed methods research problem (Chapter 5)

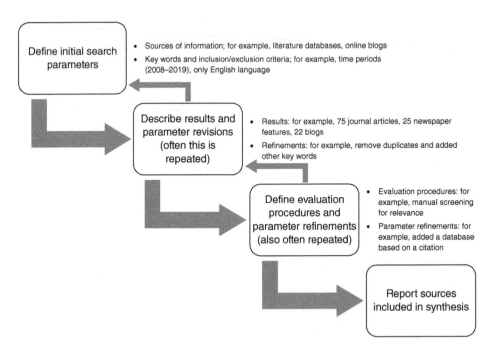

*Figure B.2   Template for flow diagram for documenting literature search for a complex mixed methods research problem (Chapter 5)

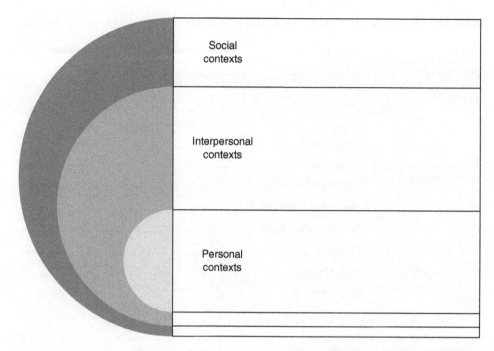

*Figure B.3   Template for conveying interrelated societal, interpersonal and personal systems defining the complex mixed methods research contexts (Chapter 6)

*Table B.2 Template for conveying initial understandings for guiding descriptive design approach (Chapter 7)

Tasks	Considerations	Initial understandings	Evolutions
Articulate framing sensitivities guiding study foundations	Guiding theoretical framework	_____	
	Study's need for integration	_____	
	Intensity of mixing (research stage)	_____	
Examine logic features guiding data integrations	Timing of data strands	_____	
	Weighting of data strands	_____	
	Mixed sampling strategies	_____	
	Generating data strategies	_____	
	Mixing strands strategies	_____	
Attend to ethics concerns guiding research procedures	Respect for persons	_____	
	Concern for welfare	_____	
	Justice	_____	
Assimilate procedural adaptations guiding researcher responses	Design typology (if appropriate)	_____	
	Potential procedural adaptations	_____	
Other?		_____	

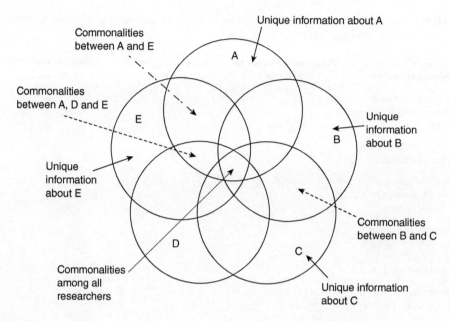

*Figure B.4   Template for conveying unique and common backgrounds and expertise of research members (Chapter 8)

*Table B.3   Template for conveying desirable evidence for methodological rigour of qualitative, quantitative and mixed methods research (Chapter 9).

Desirable evidence	Mixed methods research evidence	Quantitative research evidence	Qualitative research evidence
Describe the participants and mixed sampling strategies			
Convey the data collection for the data strands			
Outline the qualitative, quantitative, and mixed analysis processes			
Represent the integrated findings and, if applicable, separate qualitative and quantitative findings as well			
Describe the interpretation approaches for generating mixed insights			
Discuss mixed insights and point to implications, limitations, and future directions			

APPENDIX C

APPENDIX C

BIOGRAPHIES OF RESEARCHER SPOTLIGHT CONTRIBUTORS

Christo Ackermann, PhD is a faculty member at the University of South Africa (South Africa). Before joining academia, he worked as an internal auditor, having qualified as a certified internal auditor, certified government auditing professional, and certified in control self-assessment. Apart from teaching auditing to third-year students, he is currently involved in postgraduate supervision at master's and doctoral level. He published the data transformation triangulation design from his doctoral programme completed in 2016, and joined the Mixed Methods International Research Association in 2017.

Mandy Archibald, PhD currently holds a research-only postdoctoral position as a Canadian Institute for Health research fellow and National Health and Medical Research Council post-doctoral research officer in the College of Nursing and Health Sciences, Flinders University (South Australia). She received her doctorate in nursing from the University of Alberta in 2016 and is also a registered nurse, multimedia artist, and advocate and practitioner of transdisciplinary research. She describes these diverse facets of clinical care, science, and artistic practice as influential in shaping her personal and research identity. She has contributed to conceptualizing the interrelationship, practice, and intersection of arts-informed/arts-based research and mixed methods research, and to conceptualizing collaborative relationships for research and impact. She serves as associate editor of the *International Journal of Multiple Research Approaches*, reviews for the *Journal of Mixed Methods Research*, and was elected to the executive MMIRA board in 2014 where she established a successful mixed methods webinar series in collaboration with the International Institute for Qualitative Methodology. She mentors and co-supervises higher-degree students across clinical and methodological areas (not limited to health communication and visual methods). Her work can be found in such journals as *Implementation Science* and the *Journal of Mixed Methods Research*.

Pat Bazeley, PhD at present is focusing on passing on what she has learned from over 40 years of doing and teaching research through writing methods-based articles and books. More formally, she is an adjunct professor at Western Sydney University (Australia), after many years as a (very) part-time associate professor at the University of New South Wales. During that time, she has supervised students using qualitative or mixed methods in psychology, public health, and primary health. Additionally, she has run a training and consulting business (Research Support P/L) since 1998 which, for 14 years, was based at a 10-acre research retreat in the Southern Highlands of NSW. People who came to learn (and sometimes to be rescued) over that period were from all academic disciplines, but especially social sciences and the professions. Her 1970s doctorate, based on a mixed methods, action research project, proposed that community development was an effective strategy for promoting mental health in a disadvantaged population. She describes this work as both conceptually and methodologically innovative, especially for 1970s psychology in Australia! After a period as a community worker, a builder, and a mother, she focused more on consultant research, then moved into an academic research development role during the 1990s. It was during the early 1990s that she began experimenting with linking qualitative and quantitative data sets using computer software. Since then she has published articles and books on qualitative and mixed methods, focusing especially on integrative analysis. She has also served as an associate editor for the *Journal of Mixed Methods Research* and as the second president of the Mixed Methods International Research Association.

Kathleen Collins, PhD is a professor in the Department of Curriculum and Instruction in the College of Education & Health Professions at the University of Arkansas – Fayetteville (USA). She earned her doctorate in education with an emphasis on special education and research methodology in the areas of design and qualitative methods at the University of California Santa Barbara. She has given over 100 presentations at international, national, regional, and university venues. She has published over 80 articles, book chapters, and encyclopaedia chapters, and co-edited a book on the application of mixed methods research to the study of stress and coping. The topics addressed in her mixed methods research publications are in the areas of sampling and validity designs, mixed data analysis techniques, choice of method towards enhancing integration, application of mixed methods research in empirical studies, and approaches to teaching a mixed methods research course. She teaches graduate-level courses and presents workshops on design and application of mixed methods research at selective universities and conferences. Dr. Collins serves on the Executive Board of the Mixed Methods International Research Association as the Conference Chair (2016–2018).

Dr. Elizabeth G. Creamer is professor emerita from the Educational Research and Evaluation Program in the School of Education at Virginia Polytechnic Institute and State University (United States) and visiting senior scholar at the University of Michigan. She received a Bachelor of Arts degree in English education at Northwestern University, a master's degree in English and reading instruction at Colorado State University, and a doctorate from Virginia Tech. Over the course of her 40-year career as both a faculty member and an administrator, Creamer authored four books or monographs, 124 journal articles and book chapters, and 95 conference presentations and workshops, many at international venues. She is the author of the 2018 SAGE textbook, *An Introduction to Fully Integrated Mixed Methods Research*, which builds a framework for the integration of qualitative and quantitative data and analytical procedures across all phases of the research process. Creamer is the fifth president of the Mixed Methods International Research Association. Building on over 15 years of teaching graduate-level courses in qualitative and mixed methods research design, her recent writing projects have addressed the value-added of the search to explain conflicting findings, and mixed methods approaches to developing grounded theory with intervention and evaluation research.

Jessica DeCuir-Gunby, PhD is a professor of educational psychology and a university faculty scholar in the Department of Teacher Education and Learning Sciences at North Carolina State University in Raleigh (USA). She attended Louisiana State University and earned a Bachelor of Science degree with a double major in psychology and Spanish. She then attended the University of Georgia where she earned both her Master of Arts and doctoral degrees in educational psychology. She teaches several graduate courses, including courses in adolescent development, multicultural lifespan development, mixed methods research, diversity and equity, and critical race theory. Her research programme focuses on two areas: race and racial identity, including critical race theory, and research methods with an emphasis on mixed methods. The majority of her research explores how issues of race and racism, often using a critical race theory lens, impact African Americans across the lifespan and in various educational contexts. Additionally, as a practical/applied methodologist, she writes about the research process, teaching others how to utilize specific methodological approaches. For instance, she led a research team in the creation of a team-based interview codebook development process (see DeCuir-Gunby, Marshall, & McCulloch, 2011). Similarly, she helped the same research team to develop a mixed methods approach to analysing teacher classroom video data (see DeCuir-Gunby, Marshall, & McCulloch, 2012). Furthermore, her passion for teaching others how to engage in research, particularly mixed methods research, was also demonstrated in her co-authored book (with Paul Schutz), *Developing a mixed methods proposal: A practical guide for beginning researchers*.

Amrit Dencer-Brown (Imi) is a doctoral candidate at Auckland University of Technology (AUT, New Zealand). She is a Commonwealth scholar from the UK, with a masters in marine biology, advanced diploma in environmental conservation, and a Bachelor of Science (Honours) in zoology. She tutors high school students in biology and chemistry and works as a teaching assistant at AUT in marine ecology and social ecology. She recently ran a two-hour workshop on mixed methods in social-ecological systems for second- and final-year undergraduates. Her research in social-ecological trade-offs between removing and preserving mangrove ecosystems in New Zealand uses a multiphase mixed methods design. She is currently writing a paper for publication on her mixed methods framework.

Professor Dawn Freshwater is vice chancellor of the University of Western Australia, Perth (Australia) and professor of mental health at the University of Leeds (UK). She earned her doctorate from Nottingham and her Bachelor of Arts (Honours) from Manchester. She is a registered nurse, registered nurse teacher, and a Fellow of the Royal College of Nursing, as well as a mental health researcher and practitioner, and a psychotherapist. Dr. Freshwater has taught undergraduate and postgraduate courses relating to mixed methods research, and supervised 18 doctoral students to completion in the field of health using multiple approaches, including mixed methods. She served as editor of the *Journal of Mixed Methods Research* for a period of 4 years. She has been a proponent and advocate of mixed methods research conferences and the MMIRA for over a decade. She has been a reviewer of Medical Research Council and National Institute of Health Research grants using mixed methods approaches. She has published numerous papers and reports using mixed methods research.

Tim Guetterman, PhD is an assistant professor in the Department of Family Medicine at the University of Michigan (USA). He completed his doctorate in the Quantitative, Qualitative, and Psychometric Methods Program at the University of Nebraska-Lincoln. He specializes as an applied research methodologist in mixed methods. His training is in education, and he sees his work as entirely interdisciplinary, working with fields such as assessment, evaluation, education, health sciences, leadership, business, and others. Every year, he teaches multiple short mixed methods courses and workshops at his university, and others internationally, where his students are typically at the graduate or post-doctoral level, and from diverse disciplines. He has also taught numerous graduate courses online, mainly general research design and statistics. To date, he has published 30 peer-reviewed journal articles and five book chapters, and nearly all of them involve mixed methods. As a methodologist, he consults on many projects, but he also does research to advance methodology. Projects that he is most excited about examine issues such as the use of visual joint displays in mixed methods, qualitative sampling, and, most recently, the intersection of qualitative designs with mixed methods designs. Much of his empirical mixed methods research has involved using technology to improve communication and information dissemination. His real passion is methodology, and he keeps a list of future projects and papers he would like to write!

Hisako Kakai, PhD is a professor of international communication at Aoyama Gakuin University, Tokyo (Japan). She obtained her doctorate in educational psychology from the University of Hawaii, Manoa. Currently, she teaches courses at both undergraduate and graduate level in research methods and communication theories in areas such as intercultural and health communication. She also supervises students' theses and dissertation projects. Her history in mixed methods research began in the late 1990s when she was involved in several cancer research projects at the Cancer Research Center of Hawaii. Her experience in mixed methods research at the Cancer Research Center led her to carry out her own dissertation project using this approach. Since its launch in 2007, she has been serving as an editorial board member for the *Journal of Mixed Methods Research*. She has published numerous journal articles and books on mixed methods research in Japanese. Her book, *Introduction to Mixed Methods Research: The Art of Integration between Qualitative and Quantitative Methods* (Kakai, 2015), is the first and sole methodological book on mixed methods research written by a Japanese scholar in Japanese. She recently translated John Creswell's (2015a) *A Concise Introduction to Mixed Methods Research* into Japanese. From its inauguration in 2015 until August 2017, she served as president of the Japan Society for Mixed Methods Research, the first and sole mixed methods academic association in Japan. She has given talks and conducted workshops on mixed methods for academic associations as well as research universities, especially in the field of nursing.

Donna Mertens, PhD is professor emeritus at Gallaudet University in Washington, DC (USA). She taught research and evaluation methods for over 30 years to deaf and hearing graduate students in education, psychology, social work, and international development. She served as editor of the *Journal of Mixed Methods Research* from 2009 to 2014. She served as president and board member of the American Evaluation Association from 1997 to 2002, and is a founding member of the Mixed Methods International Research Association. She has authored several books that include mixed methods: *Mixed Methods Design in Evaluation* (Sage, 2018), *Research and Evaluation in Education and Psychology* (Sage, 2015), and *Program Evaluation Theory and Practice* (Guilford, 2018). She used the transformative paradigm to frame her mixed methods research and evaluation work because she is committed to social change that reduces inequities in society. Work of this nature led her to reflect on the role of complexity theory in the design of research and evaluation studies. Her work in the deaf community taught her the importance of developing respectful relationships with members of the community who are affected by research findings. From the deaf community, she also learned the importance of being aware of diversity within communities, that deaf people are not homogeneous, and that they differ on the basis of communication mode, country of origin, economic status, racial and ethnic group, and sexual identity. The transformative mixed methods approach consciously addresses these dimensions of diversity to challenge societal practices of discrimination and marginalization.

Alicia O'Cathain is professor of health services research at the School of Health and Related Research at the University of Sheffield (UK). She undertakes mixed methods studies in a range of topics, including patient experience of health services, variation in health care practice, evaluation of policy initiatives, and the development and evaluation of complex interventions. She is very interested in the practice of mixed methods research in the real world. Since 2007, she has written many journal articles and book chapters on key practical issues facing researchers. These include how to assess quality (introducing the six-item GRAMMS on Good Reporting of a Mixed Methods Study), how to integrate findings and data, how team working affects the products of mixed methods studies, and how to report mixed methods studies. Recently, she has focused her writing on how to combine qualitative research and randomized controlled trials, and she has written a book about this (published in 2018). She also runs workshops on mixed methods research and supervises mixed methods PhDs.

Bephyer Parey holds a BSc in Mathematics and a MSc in Statistics from the University of the West Indies, Trinidad and Tobago, and is currently a PhD candidate in Social Policy at the Sir Arthur Lewis Institute of Social and Economic Studies at the same institution. Her area of research is disability in Trinidad and aims to provide recommendations regarding the inclusion of children with disabilities in regular schools, persons of working-age with disabilities in open employment, and older persons with disabilities within the household. Importantly, in 2015 she was introduced to mixed methods research and the Mixed Methods International Research Association. Through this, she recognized the importance of mixed methods research in addressing global problems and decided to employ a mixed methods approach to her doctoral research.

Norma Romm, PhD is a research professor in the Department of Adult Education and Youth Development at the University of South Africa. Her master's and doctoral theses (1982, 1986) were both in the field of sociology. In the theses, and in her book *The Methodologies of Positivism and Marxism* (Romm, 1991), she dealt with methodological issues, exploring a variety of Marxist-oriented positions concerning the role of research in society. Her interest has always been in how research can make a difference by constructively changing the world. When using mixed methods research, and justifying its use, her concern is to utilize/adapt methods combined with one another, to forward social justice (as defined in the context of application). Her projects have contributed to our understandings of how mixed methods research can facilitate the involvement of research in unfolding social outcomes, and how focus group sessions can be actively facilitated to reconsider the status and import of the 'results' from a questionnaire that had been administered during an earlier phase of the research. Her most recent book, *Responsible Research Practice* (Romm, 2018), advocates, inter alia, the 'stretching' of various paradigmatic/philosophical underpinnings of mixed methods research to make room for increased reflection on the responsibilities of professional researchers, research participants, and concerned stakeholders for activating improvements in the quality of social and ecological life.

Judith Schoonenboom, PhD has been engaged in education and educational research since she started peer-teaching at the age of 6 in Amstelveen, the Netherlands. She began her career as a linguist. In the 1990s, she became involved in educational innovation projects. She switched to education as her main discipline, specializing in research methodology. In 2010, she discovered the mixed methods community, where she was able to finally combine her interests in methodology, language, numbers, education, and technology. Three years ago, she migrated to Vienna, Austria, and became professor of empirical pedagogy, with an emphasis on mixed methods research. On various occasions, she has held workshops related to mixed methods in educational research. Her key publications include an article with Burke Johnson and Dominik Froehlich, 'Combining Multiple Purposes of Mixing within a

Mixed Methods Research Design', in the *International Journal of Multiple Research Approaches*; the sole-authored chapter 'Mixed Methods in Early Childhood Education' in M. Fleer & B. van Oers (Eds.), *International Handbook of Early Childhood Education* (pp. 269–293) published by Springer Netherlands; and the sole-authored articles 'A Performative Paradigm for Mixed Methods Research' in the *Journal of Mixed Methods Research* and 'Designing Mixed Methods Research by Mixing and Merging Methodologies: A 13-Step Model' in *American Behavioral Scientist*.

Dr. Emma Uprichard is an associate professor at the Centre for Interdisciplinary Methodologies, University of Warwick (UK). She is also a Fellow at the Alan Turing Institute, the UK's national data science centre, and a member of the National Statistician's Data Ethics Advisory Committee. Previously, she was a lecturer in quantitative methods at Durham University, a lecturer in social research methods at the University of York, and senior lecturer in sociology at Goldsmiths University of London. She studied sociology with education as an undergraduate before going on to do a masters and doctorate in sociology. Her doctorate was on the methodological implications of a critical realist and complex systems approach to studying cities as complex systems; it involved five different methods over time and in two countries. Since then, she has been involved in a number of mixed methods projects. Throughout her research, she has been interested in three main questions: how do we empirically study a nonlinear social entity that itself changes as we research it; how might we study that social entity in a way that also produces useful knowledge for policy and planning purposes; and how do we study complex social change over time and space in a way that also preserves the notion of the ageing human agent, intergenerationally, while appreciating the importance of context? These questions not only demand mixed methods approaches, but also raise challenges about how to study complex open systems, which are always changing (and not changing) across time and space.

Elaine Van Melle, PhD is a senior educational scientist at the Royal College of Physicians and Surgeons of Canada. She holds a doctorate and masters in education (Queen's University, Kingston, Ontario), a Master of Health Science in health administration (University of Toronto), and a Bachelor of Science (Honours) specializing in microbiology and immunology (Western University, London, Ontario). The Royal College is currently leading a national transformation of residency education to a competency-based approach. Her role is to facilitate a multi-year programme evaluation initiative. Due to the complexity of both the project and the innovation, using mixed methods is an important skill that she brings to the table as well as during her graduate degrees. Over the past 10 years, she has led numerous workshops on getting started with mixed methods.

REFERENCES

Aboela, S. W., Larson, E., Bakken, S., Carrasquillo, O., Formicola, A., Glied, S. A., …, Gebbie, K. M. (2007). Defining interdisciplinary research: Conclusions from a critical review of the literature. *Health Services Research, 42,* 329–346. doi: 10.1111/j.1475-6773.2006.00621.x.

Adams, D. (1985). *The hitchhiker's guide to the galaxy.* London: Pan Books.

American Educational Research Association (AERA). (2006). Standards for reporting on empirical social science research in AERA publications. *Educational Researcher, 35*(6), 33–40.

Anderson, P. (1999). Perspective: Complexity theory and organization science. *Organization Science, 10*(3), 216–232. doi:10.1287/orsc.10.3.216.

Appelbaum, M., Cooper, H., Kline, R. B., Mayo-Wilson, E., Nezu, A. M., & Rao, S. M. (2018). Journal article reporting standards for quantitative research in psychology: The APA Publications and Communications Board Task Force report. *American Psychologist, 73*(1), 3–25. doi: 10.1037/amp0000191.

Arnault, D., & Fetters, M. D. (2012). R01 funding for mixed methods research: Lessons learned from the mixed-method analysis of Japanese depression project. *Journal of Mixed Methods Research, 5*(4), 309–329. doi: 10.1177/1558689811416481.

Bazeley, P. (2003a). Teaching mixed methods. *Qualitative Research Journal, 3*(3), 117–126.

Bazeley, P. (2003b). Computerized data analysis for mixed methods researchers. In A. Tashakkori & C. Teddlie (Eds.). *SAGE handbook of mixed methods in social & behavioral research.* Thousand Oaks, CA: Sage.

Bazeley, P. (2018). *Integrating analyses in mixed methods research.* London: Sage.

Bazeley, P., & Kemp, L. (2012). Mosaics, triangles, and DNA metaphors for integrated analysis in mixed methods research. *Journal of Mixed Methods Research, 6*(1), 55–72. doi: 10.1177/1558689811419514.

Boote, D. N., & Beile, P. (2005). Scholars before researchers: On the centrality of the dissertation literature review in research preparation. *Educational Researcher, 34*(6), 3–15. http://www.jstor.org/stable/3699805.

Bowers, B., Cohen, L. W., Elliot, A. E., Grabowski, D. C., Fishman, N. W., Sharkey, S. S., ..., Kemper, P. (2013). Creating and supporting a mixed methods health services research team. *Health Services Research, 48*, 2157–2180. doi: 10.1111/1475-6773.12118.

Braithwaite, J., Churruca, K., Ellis, L. A., Long, J., Clay-Williams, R., Damen, N., ..., Ludlow, K. (2017). *Complexity science in healthcare – Aspirations, approaches, applications and accomplishments: A white paper*. Sydney: Australian Institute of Health Innovation, Macquarie University. Retrieved from http://bit.ly/2If4KMG.

Bridges, W., & Bridges, S. (2016). *Managing transition* (4th ed.). Boston: Da Capo Press.

Bronfenbrenner, U. (1979). *The ecology of human development*. Cambridge, MA: Harvard University Press.

Bryman, A. (2006). Integrating quantitative and qualitative research: How is it done? *Qualitative Research Journal, 6*(1), 97–113. doi: 10.1177/1468794106058877.

Bryman, A. (2007). The research question in social research: What is its role? *International Journal of Social Research Methodology, 10*, 5–20. doi: 10.1080/13645570600655282.

Bryman, A. (2014). June 1989 and beyond: Julia Brannen's contribution to mixed methods research. *International Journal of Social Research Methodology, 17*(2):121–131. doi: 10.1080/13645579.2014.892653.

Byrne, D. (1998). *Complexity and the social sciences*. London: Psychology Press.

Byrne, D., & Callaghan, G. (2014). *Complexity theory and the social sciences: The state of the art*. New York: Routledge.

Capra, F. (2002). *The hidden connections: Integrating the biological, cognitive, and social dimensions of life into a science of sustainability*. New York: Doubleday.

Caracelli, V. J., & Greene, J. C. (1997). Crafting mixed-method evaluation designs. In J. C. Greene & V. J. Caracelli (Eds.), *Advances in mixed-method evaluation: The challenges and benefits of integrating diverse paradigms* (pp. 19–32). San Francisco: Jossey-Bass.

Castellani, B. (2014). Complexity and the failure of quantitative social science. *Focus, 14*. https://discoversociety.org/2014/11/04/focus-complexity-and-the-failure-of-quantitative-social-science/

Christ, T. (2009). Designing, teaching, and evaluating two complementary mixed methods research courses. *Journal of Mixed Methods Research, 3*, 292–325. doi: 10.1177/1558689809341796.

Chui, W. H., & Cheng, K. K.-Y. (2017). Perceptions of fairness and satisfaction in lawyer–client interactions among young offenders in Hong Kong. *Journal of Mixed Methods Research, 11*(2), 266–285. doi: 10.1177/1558689815593834.

Colditz, J. B., Welling, J., Smith, N. A., James, A. E., & Primack, B. A. (2017). World vaping day: Contextualizing vaping culture in online social media using a mixed methods approach. *Journal of Mixed Methods Research*. doi: 10.1177/1558689817702753.

Collins, K. M. T. (2015). Validity in multimethod and mixed research. In S. N. Hesse-Biber & R. B. Johnson (Eds.), *The Oxford handbook of multimethod and mixed methods research inquiry* (pp. 240–256). Oxford: Oxford University Press.

Collins, K. M. T., & O'Cathain, A. (2009). Ten points about mixed methods research to be considered by the novice researcher. *International Journal of Multiple Research Approaches, 3*(1), 2–7.

Collins, K. M. T., Onwuegbuzie, A., & Johnson, B. (2012). Securing a place at the table: A review and extension of legitimation criteria for the conduct of mixed research. *American Behavioral Scientist, 56*, 849–865. doi:10.1177/0002764211433799.

Creamer, E. G. (2016). A primer about mixed methods research in an educational context. *International Journal of Learning, Teaching, and Education Research, 15*(8), 1–13.

Creamer, E. (2018). *An introduction to fully integrated mixed methods research*. Thousand Oaks, CA: Sage.

Creswell, J. (2009). *Research design: Qualitative, quantitative and mixed methods approach* (3rd ed.). Thousand Oaks, CA: Sage.

Creswell, J. W. (2011). Controversies in mixed methods research. In N. K. Denzin & Y. S. Lincoln (Eds.), *The SAGE handbook of qualitative research* (4th ed., pp. 269–284). Thousand Oaks, CA: Sage.

Creswell, J. W. (2014). *Research design: Qualitative, quantitative, and mixed methods approaches* (4th ed.). Thousand Oaks, CA: Sage.

Creswell, J. W. (2015a). *A concise introduction to mixed methods research.* Thousand Oaks, CA: Sage.

Creswell J. W. (2015b). Revisiting mixed methods and advancing scientific practices. In S. Hesse-Biber & B. Johnson (Eds.), *The Oxford handbook of multimethod and mixed methods research inquiry* (pp. 57–71). Oxford: Oxford University Press.

Creswell, J. W., Fetters, M. D., & Ivankova, N. V. (2004). Designing a mixed methods study in primary care. *Annals of Family Medicine, 2*(1), 7–12.

Creswell, J. W., Klassen, A. C., Plano-Clark, V., & Smith, K. C. for the Office of Behavioral and Social Sciences Research (2011). *Best practices for mixed methods research in the health sciences.* National Institutes of Health. Retrieved from https://obssr.od.nih.gov/training/online-training-resources/mixed-methods-research/.

Creswell, J., & Plano Clark, V. (2007). *Designing and conducting mixed methods research.* Thousand Oaks, CA: Sage.

Creswell, J., & Plano Clark, V. (2011). *Designing and conducting mixed methods research* (2nd ed.). Thousand Oaks, CA: Sage.

Creswell, J., & Plano Clark, V. (2018). *Designing and conducting mixed methods research* (3rd ed.). Thousand Oaks, CA: Sage.

Creswell, J. W., Plano Clark, V. L., Gutmann, M., & Hanson, W. (2003). Advanced mixed methods research designs. In A. Tashakkori & C. Teddlie (Eds.), *Handbook of mixed methods in social & behavioral research* (pp. 209–240). Thousand Oaks, CA: Sage.

Creswell, J. W., & Poth, C. N. (2017). *Qualitative inquiry and research design: Choosing among five approaches* (4th ed.). Thousand Oaks, CA: Sage.

Curry, L. A., Krumholz, H. M., O'Cathain, A., Plano Clark, V. L., Cherlin, E., & Bradley, E. H. (2013). Mixed methods in biomedical and health services research. *Circulation: Cardiovascular Quality and Outcomes, 10*(1), 119–123.

Curry, L. A., & Nunez-Smith, M. (2015). *Mixed methods in health sciences research.* Thousand Oaks, CA: Sage.

Curry, L. A., O'Cathain, A., Plano Clark, V. L., Aroni, R., Fetters, M., & Berg, D. (2012). The role of group dynamics in mixed methods health sciences research teams. *Journal of Mixed Methods Research, 6*(5), 5–20. doi: 10.1177/1558689811416941.

Dahlberg, B., Wittink, M. N., & Gallo, J. J. (2010). Funding and publishing integrated studies: Writing effective mixed methods manuscripts and grant proposals. In A. Tashakkori & C. Teddlie (Eds.), *SAGE handbook of mixed methods in social & behavioral research* (pp. 775–802). Thousand Oaks, CA: Sage.

Davis, B., & Sumara, D. J. (2006). *Complexity and education: Inquiries into learning, teaching, and research.* Mahwah, NJ: Lawrence Erlbaum Associates.

Davis, B., Sumara, D. J., & Luce-Kapler, R. (2000). *Engaging minds: Changing teaching in complex times.* Mahwah, NJ: Lawrence Erlbaum Associates.

Day, C., Sammons, P., & Gu, Q. (2016). Combining qualitative and quantitative methodologies in research on teachers' lives, work, and effectiveness: From integration to synergy. *Educational Researcher, 37*(6), 330–342. doi: 10.3102/0013189X0832409.

De Bono, E. (1999). *Simplicity.* London: Penguin.

DeCuir-Gunby, J. T., & Schutz, P. A. (2017). *Developing a mixed methods proposal: A practical guide for beginning researchers.* Thousand Oaks, CA: Sage.

Dickson, V., Lee, C. S., & Riegel, B. (2011). How do cognitive function and knowledge affect heart failure self-care? *Journal of Mixed Methods Research, 5*(2), 167–189. doi: 10.1177/1558689811402355.

Enosh, G., Tzafrir, S. S., & Stolovy, T. (2014). The development of Client Violence Questionnaire (CVQ). *Journal of Mixed Methods Research, 8*(1), 273–290. doi: 10.1177/1558689814525263.

Fàbregues, S., & Molina-Azorin, J. F. (2017). Addressing quality in mixed methods research: A review and recommendations for future agenda. *Quality & Quantity, 51*(6), 2847–2863. doi: 10.1007/s11135-016-0449-4.

Fenner, M., Scheliga, K., & Bartling, S. (2013). Reference management. In S. Bartling & S. Friesike (Eds.), *Opening science: The evolving guide on how the internet is changing research, collaboration and scholarly publishing* (pp. 125–137). Heidelberg: Springer Open. doi: 10.1007/978-3-319-00026-8_8.

Fetters, M. D., Curry, L. A., & Creswell, J. W. (2013). Achieving integration in mixed methods designs – principles and practices. *Health Services Research, 48*(6), 2134–2156. doi: 10.1111/1475-6773.12117.

Fetters, M. D., & Freshwater, D. (2015). Publishing a methodological mixed methods article (Editorial). *Journal of Mixed Methods Research, 9*(3), 203–213.

Fetters, M. D., & Molina-Azorin, J. F. (2017). The journal of mixed methods research starts a new decade: Principles for bringing in the new and divesting of the old language of the field. *Journal of Mixed Methods Research, 11*, 3–10. doi: 10.1177/1558689816682092.

Fink, A. G. (2013) *Conducting research literature reviews: From the internet to paper* (4th ed.). Thousand Oaks, CA: Sage.

Flyvbjerg, B. (2006) Five misunderstandings about case-study research. *Qualitative Inquiry, 12*(2), 219–245. doi: 10.1177/1077800405284363.

Freshwater, D. (2007). Reading mixed methods research: Contexts for criticism. *Journal of Mixed Methods Research, 1*(2), 134-146. doi: 10.1177/1558689806298578.

Greene, J. C. (2007). *Mixed methods in social inquiry*. San Francisco: Jossey-Bass.

Greene, J. C. (2008). Is mixed methods socil inquiry a distinctive methodology? *Journal of Mixed Methods Research, 2*(1), 7–22. https://doi.org/10.1177/1558689807309969.

Greene, J. C. (2015). Preserving distinctions within the multimethod and mixed methods research merger. In S. Hesse-Biber & B. Johnson (Eds.), *The Oxford handbook of multimethod and mixed methods research inquiry* (pp. 606–615). Oxford: Oxford University Press.

Greene, J. C., & Caracelli, V. J. (Eds.) (1997). *Advances in mixed-method evaluation: The challenges and benefits of integrating diverse paradigms* (New Directions for Evaluation, No. 74). San Francisco: Jossey-Bass.

Greene, J. C., Caracelli, V. J., & Graham, C. R. (1989). Toward a conceptual framework for mixed-method evaluation designs. *Educational Evaluation and Policy Analysis, 11*(3), 255–274. doi: 10.3102/01623737011003255.

Greenhalgh, T., Hawe, P. & Lykum, L. (2017) Preface (pp. v–vi). In J. Braithwaite, K. Churruca, L. A. Ellis, J. Long, R. Clay-Williams, N. Damen, …, K. Ludlow, *Complexity science in healthcare – Aspirations, approaches, applications and accomplishments: A white paper*. Sydney: Australian Institute of Health Innovation, Macquarie University. Retrieved from http://bit.ly/2If4KMG.

Guest, G. (2013). Describing mixed methods research: An alternative to typologies. *Journal of Mixed Methods Research, 7*, 141–151. doi: 10.1177/1558689812461179.

Guetterman, T. C. (2017). What distinguishes a novice from an expert mixed methods researcher? *Quality & Quantity, 51*(1), 377–398.

Guetterman, T. C., Fetters, M. D., & Creswell, J. W. (2015). Integrating quantitative and qualitative results in health science mixed methods research through joint displays. *Annals of Family Medicine, 13*, 554–561. doi: 10.1370/afm.1865.

Guetterman, T. C., Creswell, J. W., & Kuchartz, U. (2015). Using joint displays to Maxqda software to represent the results of mixed methods research. In M. T. McCrudden, G. Schraw, & C.W. Buckendahl. *Use of visual displays in research and testing* (pp. 145–175). US: Information Age Publishing.

Hall, B., & Howard, K. (2008). A synergistic approach: Conducting mixed methods research with typological and systemic design considerations. *Journal of Mixed Methods Research, 2*(3), 248–269. doi: 10.1177/1558689808314622.

Hemmings, A., Beckett, G., Kennerly, S., & Yap, T. (2013). Building a community of research practice: Intragroup team social dynamics in interdisciplinary mixed methods. *Journal of Mixed Methods Research, 7*(3), 261–273. doi: 10.1177/1558689813478468.

Hesse-Biber, S. N. (2010). *Mixed methods research: Merging theory with practice*. Thousand Oaks, CA: Sage.

Hesse-Biber, S. N. (2015). Introduction: Navigating a turbulent research landscape: Working the boundaries, tensions, diversity, and contradictions of multimethod and mixed methods inquiry. In S. N. Hesse-Biber & R. B. Johnson (Eds.), *The Oxford handbook of multimethod and mixed methods research inquiry* (pp. xxxiii–liii). Oxford: Oxford University Press.

Hesse-Biber, S. (2016). Doing interdisciplinary mixed methods health care research: Working the boundaries, tensions, and synergistic potential of team-based research. *Qualitative Health Research, 26*(5), 649–658. doi: 10.1177/1049732316634304.

Hesse-Biber, S., & Johnson, R. B. (2013). Coming at things differently: Future directions of possible engagement with mixed methods research. *Journal of Mixed Methods Research, 7*, 103–109. doi: 10.1177/1558689813483987.

Heyvaert, M., Hannes, K., & Onghena, P. (2017). *Using mixed methods research synthesis for literature reviews*. Thousand Oaks, CA: Sage.

Holland, J. H. (1999). *Emergence: From chaos to order*. Cambridge, MA: Perseus Books.

Ivankova, N. V., Creswell, J. W., & Stick, S. (2006). Using mixed methods sequential explanatory design: From theory to practice. *Field Methods, 18*(1), 3–20. doi: 10.1177/1525822X05282260.

Johnson, B., & Christensen, L. (2016). *Educational research: Quantitative, qualitative, and mixed approaches* (6th ed.). Thousand Oaks, CA: Sage.

Johnson, R. B., & Onwuegbuzie, A. J. (2004). Mixed methods research: A research paradigm whose time has come. *Educational Researcher, 33*(3), 14–26. doi: 10.3102/0013189X033007014.

Johnson, S. (2001). *Emergence: The connected lives of ants, brains, cities, and software*. New York: Scribner.

Jones-Rooy, A., & Page, S. E. (2012). The complexity of system effects. *Critical Review, 24*(3), 313–342. doi: 10.1080/08913811.2012.767045.

Kauffman, S. (1995). *At home in the universe*. New York: Oxford University Press.

Kossiakoff, A., Sweet, W. N., Seymour, S. J., & Biemer, S. M. (2011). *Systems engineering principles and practice*. Hoboken, NJ: John Wiley & Sons.

Leech, N. L., Dellinger, A. B., Brannagan, K. B., & Tanaka, H. (2010). Evaluating mixed methods studies: A mixed methods approach. *Journal of Mixed Methods Research, 4*, 17–31. doi: 10.1177/1558689809345262.

Levitt, H.M., Bamberg, M., Creswell, J. W., Frost, D. M., Josselson, R., & Suárez-Orozco (2018). Journal article reporting standards for qualitative primary, qualitative meta-analytic, and mixed methods research in psychology: The APA Publications and Communications Board Task Force Report. *American Psychologist, 73*(1), 26–46. http://dx.doi.org/10.1037/amp0000151.

Lewin, R. (1993) *Complexity: Life at the edge of chaos*. Chicago: University of Chicago Press.

Lewin, R. (1999). *Complexity: Life at the edge of chaos* (2nd ed.). Chicago: University of Chicago Press.

Lewin, R., & Regine, B. (2001). *Weaving complexity and business*. New York: Texere.

Manson, S. M. (2001). Simplifying complexity: A review of complexity theory. *Geoforum, 32*(3), 405–414. https://doi.org/10.1016/S0016-7185(00)00035-X.

Marshall, P. L., DeCuir-Gunby, J. T., & McCulloch, A. W. (2015). *When critical multiculturalism meets mathematics: A mixed methods study of professional development and teacher identity*. Lanham, MD: Rowman & Littlefield.

Maxwell, J. A. (2012). *A realist approach for qualitative research*. Thousand Oaks, CA: Sage.

Maxwell, J. A. (2013). *Qualitative research design: An interactive approach* (3rd ed.). Thousand Oaks, CA: Sage.

Maxwell, J. A., Chmiel, M., & Rogers, S. E. (2015). Designing integration in multimethod and mixed methods research. In S. N. Hesse-Biber & R. B. Johnson (Eds.), *The Oxford handbook of multimethod and mixed methods research inquiry* (pp. 223–229). Oxford: Oxford University Press.

Maxwell, J. A., & Loomis, D. M. (2003). Mixed methods design: An alternative approach. In A. Tashakkori & C. Teddlie (Eds.), *Handbook of mixed methods in social & behavioral research* (pp. 241–271). Thousand Oaks, CA: Sage.

Mertens, D. M. (2003). Mixed methods and the politics of human research: The transformative-emancipatory perspective. In A. Tashakkori & C. Teddlie (Eds.), *Handbook of mixed methods in social & behavioral research* (pp. 135–164). Thousand Oaks, CA: Sage.

Mertens, D. M. (2014). A momentous development in mixed methods research. *Journal of Mixed Methods Research, 8*, 3–5. doi: 10.1177/1558689813518230.

Mertens, D. M. (2015). Mixed methods and wicked problems. *Journal of Mixed Methods Research, 9*, 1–6. doi: 10.1177/1558689814562944.

Mertens, D. M., Bazeley, P., Bowleg, L., Fielding, N., Maxwell, J., Molina-Azorín, J. F., & Niglas, K. (2016a). Expanding thinking through a kaleidoscopic look into the future: Implications of the Mixed Methods International Research Association's task force report on the future of mixed methods research. *Journal of Mixed Methods Research, 10*(3), 221–227. doi: 10.1177/1558689816649719.

Mertens, D. M., Bazeley, P., Bowleg, L., Fielding, N., Maxwell, J., Molina-Azorín, J. F., & Niglas, K. (2016b). *The future of mixed methods: A five year projection to 2020*. MMIRA. Retrieved from http://mmira.wildapricot.org/resources/Documents/MMIRA%20task%20force%20report%20 Jan2016%20final.pdf.

Mitleton-Kelly, E. (2003). Ten principles of complexity & enabling infrastructures. In E. Mitleton-Kelly (Ed.), *Complex systems and evolutionary perspectives on organisations: The application of complexity theory to organisations* (pp. 21–50). Oxford: Elsevier Science.

NIH Office of Behavioral and Social Sciences (2018). *Best practices for mixed methods research in the health sciences* (2nd ed). Bethesda: National Institutes of Health. Retrieved from https://www.obssr.od.nih.gov/wp-content/uploads/2018/01/Best-Practices-for-Mixed-Methods-Research-in-the-Health-Sciences-2018-01-25.pdf.

Molina-Azorin, J. F., & Fetters, M. D. (2016). Mixed methods research prevalence studies: Field-specific studies on the state of the art of mixed methods research. *Journal of Mixed Methods Research, 10*(2), 123–128. doi: 10.1177/1558689816636707.

Morgan, D. L. (1998). Practical strategies for combining qualitative and quantitative methods: Applications to health research. *Qualitative Health Research, 8*(3), 362–376.

Morgan, D. L. (2014). *Integrating qualitative and quantitative methods: A pragmatic approach.* Thousand Oaks, CA: Sage.

Morse, J. (1991). Approaches to qualitative-quantitative methodological triangulation. *Nursing Research, 40*(2), 120–123.

Morse, J. M., & Niehaus, L. (2009). *Mixed method design: Principles and procedures.* Walnut Creek, CA: Left Coast Press.

Morse, J., & Richards, L. (2002). *Readme first for a user's guide to qualitative research.* Thousand Oaks, CA: Sage Publications.

Nicolson, D. J., Knapp, P., Gardner, P., & Raynor, D. K. (2011). Combining concurrent and sequential methods to examine the usability and readability of websites with information about medicines. *Journal of Mixed Methods Research, 5*, 25–51. doi: 10.1177/15586898103 85694.

O'Cathain, A. (2010). Assessing the quality of mixed methods research: Towards a comprehensive framework. In A. Tashakkori & C. Teddlie (Eds.), *SAGE handbook of mixed methods in social & behavioural research* (2nd ed., pp. 531–555). Thousand Oaks, CA: Sage.

O'Cathain, A., Murphy, E., & Nicholl, J. (2008). Multidisciplinary, interdisciplinary, or dysfunctional? Team working in mixed-methods research. *Qualitative Health Research, 18*, 1574–1585. doi: 10.1177/1049732308325535.

Onwuegbuzie, A. J., & Collins, K. M. T. (2007). A typology of mixed methods sampling designs in social science research. *The Qualitative Report, 12*(2), 281–316.

Onwuegbuzie, A., Collins, K. M. T., & Frels, R. K. (2013). Foreward: Using Bronfenbrenner's ecological systems theory to frame quantitative, qualitative, and mixed research. *International Journal of Multiple Research Approaches, 7*(1), 2–8. doi: 10.5172/mra.2013.7.1.2.

Onwuegbuzie, A., & Combs, J. P. (2010). Emergent data analysis techniques in mixed methods reserach: A synthesis. In A. Tashakkori and C. Teddlie (Eds.) *Sage Handbook of Mixed Methods in Social and Behavioural Research* (pp. 397–430). Thousand Oaks, CA: Sage.

Onwuegbuzie, A., & Corrigan, J. A. (2014). Improving the quality of mixed research reports in the field of human resource development and beyond: A call for rigor as an ethical practice. *Human Resource Development Quarterly, 25*, 273-299. doi:10.1002/hrdq.21197.

Onwuegbuzie, A. J., & Frels, R. (2016). *7 Steps to a comprehensive literature review.* London: Sage.

Onwuegbuzie, A. J., & Hitchcock, J. H. (2017). A meta-framework for conducting mixed methods impact evaluations: Implications for altering practice and the teaching of evaluation. *Studies in Educational Evaluation, 53*, 55–68. doi: 10.1016/j.stueduc.2017.02.001.

Onwuegbuzie, A. J., & Hitchcock, J. H. (2015). Advanced mixed analysis approaches. In S. Hesse-biber & B. Johnson (Eds.), *Oxford handbook of multimethod and mixed methods research inquiry* (pp. 275–295). New York: Oxford University Press.

Onwuegbuzie, A. J., Johnson, B., & Collins, K. M. T. (2009). Assessing legitimation in mixed research: A new framework. *Quality & Quantity, 45*(6), 1253–1258. doi: 10.1007/s11135-009-9289-9.

Onwuegbuzie, A. J., & Leech, N. L. (2006). Linking research questions to mixed methods data analysis procedures. *The Qualitative Report, 11*, 474–498.

Onwuegbuzie, A. J., & Poth, C. (2016). Editors' afterword: Toward evidence-based guidelines for reviewing mixed methods research manuscripts submitted to journals. *International Journal of Qualitative Methods, 15*(1), 1–13. doi: 10.1177/1609406916628986.

Pagels, H. (1985) *Perfect symmetry: The search for the beginning of time*. New York: Simon & Schuster.

Patton, M. Q. (2010). *Developmental evaluation: Applying complexity concepts to enhance innovation and use*. New York: Guildford Press.

Peck, M.S. (1998). *Further along the road less traveled*. New York: Simon & Schuster.

Pei, J., Denys, K., Hughes, J., & Rasmussen, C. (2011). Mental health issues in fetal alcohol spectrum disorder. *Journal of Mental Health, 20*(5), 473–483. doi: 10.3109/09638237.2011.577113.

Pincus, T., Vogel, S., Breen, A., Foster, N. & Underwood, M. (2006). Persistent back pain – why do physical therapy clinicians continue treatment? A mixed methods study of chiropractors, osteopaths and physiotherapists. *European Journal of Pain, 10*, 67–76. doi: 10.1016/j.ejpain.2005.01.008.

Plano Clark, V. L., & Ivankova, N. V. (2016). *Mixed methods research: A guide to the field*. Thousand Oaks, CA: Sage.

Plano Clark, V. L., Schumacher, K., West, C., Edrington, J., Dunn, L. B., Harzstark, A., Miaskowski, C. (2013). Practices for embedding an interpretive qualitative approach within a randomized clinical trial. *Journal of Mixed Methods Research, 7*, 219–242. doi: 10.1177/1558689812474372.

Poth, C. (2008). *Promoting evaluation use within dynamic organizations: A case study examining evaluator behaviour*. Unpublished PhD dissertation, Queen's University, Kingston, Ontario.

Poth, C. (2010). Examining the contributions of a mixed methods exploratory sequential design: A qualitative perspective. In M. Pourkos & M. Dafermos (Eds.), *Qualitative research into social sciences: Epistemological, methodological and ethical issues* (pp. 525–539). Athens: Topos.

Poth, C. (2012). Exploring the role of mixed methods practitioner within educational research teams: A cross case comparison of the research planning process. *International Journal of Multiple Research Approaches, 6*(3), 315–332. doi: 10.5172/mra.2012.6.3.314.

Poth, C. (2014). What constitutes effective learning experiences in a mixed methods research course? An examination from the student perspective. *International Journal of Multiple Research Approaches, 8*(1), 74–86. doi: 10.5172/mra.2014.8.1.74.

Poth, C. (2018a). The curious case of complexity: Implications for mixed methods research practices. *International Journal of Multiple Research Approaches, 10*(1). 403–411. doi:10.29034/ijmra.v10n1a27.

Poth, C. (2018b). The contributions of mixed insights to advancing technology-enhanced formative assessments within higher education learning environments. *International Journal of Educational Technology in Higher Education, 15*(9) 1–19. doi: 10.1186/s41239-018-0090-5.

Poth, C. N., Fetters, M. D., & Molina-Azorin, J. F. (2018). Distinct yet synergetic contributors to mixed methods research: Intersections for MMIRA and JMMR. *Journal of Mixed Methods Research, 12*(1), 3–10. doi: 10.1177/1558689817743581.

Poth, C., McCallum, K., & Atkinson, E. (2014, June). *Towards enhanced online teacher professionalism: A mixed methods examination of pre-service teachers' perspectives*, Conference paper presented at the inaugural biannual global meeting of the Mixed Methods International Research Association, Boston.

Poth, C., & Onwuegbuzie, A. J. (2015). Special issue: Mixed methods. *International Journal of Qualitative Methods, 14*(2), 1–4.

Poth, C., & Onwuegbuzie, A. J. (2016). Editor's introduction: Special issue: Mixed methods Part II. *International Journal of Qualitative Methods, 15*(1), 1–2. doi: 10.1177/1609406916628985.

Poth, C., Pei, J., Job, J., & Wyper, K. (2014). Towards intentional, reflective, and assimilative classroom practices with students with FASD. *The Teacher Educator, 49,* 247–264. doi: 10.1080/08878730.2014.933642.

Prigogine, I., & Stengers, I. (1984). *Order out of chaos.* New York: Free Press.

Richards, L. & Morse, J (2013). *Readme first for a user's guide to qualitative methods* (3rd ed.). Thousand Oaks, CA: Sage.

Rittel, H. W. J., & Webber, M. M. (1973). Dilemmas in a general theory of planning. *Policy Sciences, 4,* 155–169.

Robins, C. S., Ware, N. C., dosReis, S., Willging, C. E., Chung, J. Y., & Lewis-Fernández, R. (2008). Dialogues on mixed-methods and mental health services research: Anticipating challenges, building solutions. *Psychiatric Services, 59*(7), 727–731.

Salas, E., Dickinson, T. L., Converse, S. A., & Tannenbaum, S. I. (1992). Toward an understanding of team performance and training. In R. W. Swezey & E. Salas (Eds.), *Teams: Their training and performance* (pp. 3–29). Westport, CT: Ablex Publishing.

Salas, E. Fiore, S. M., & Letsky, M. P. (2012). Why cross disciplinary theories of team cognition? In E. Salas, S. M. Fiore, & M. P. Letsky (Eds.), *Theories of team cognition: Cross-disciplinary perspectives* (pp. 3–18). New York: Routledge.

Sandelowski, M. (2000). Combining qualitative and quantitative sampling, data collection, and analysis techniques in mixed-methods studies. *Research in Nursing & Health, 23,* 246–255. doi: 10.1002/1098-240X(200006)23:3<246::AID-NUR9>3.0.CO;2-H.

Seltzer-Kelly, D., Westwood, S. J., & Peña-Guzman, D. M. (2012). A methodological self-study of quantitizing: Negotiating meaning and revealing multiplicity. *Journal of Mixed Methods Research, 6*(4), 258–274. doi. 10.1177/1558689811425798.

Sharp, J. C., Mobley, C., Hammon, C., Withington, S., Drew, S., Stringfield, S., & Stipanovic, N. (2012). A mixed methods sampling methodology for a multisite case study. *Journal of Mixed Methods Research, 6,* 34–54. doi: 10.1177/1558689811417133.

Shipler, D. (2005). *The working poor: Invisible in America.* Toronto: Random House of Canada.

Sincero, J. (2013). *You are a badass: How to stop doubting your greatness and start living an awesome life.* Philadelphia: Running Press.

Snelson, C. L. (2016). Qualitative and mixed methods social media research: A review of the literature, *International Journal of Qualitative Methods, 15,* 1–15. doi: 10.1177/1609406915 624574.

Stacey, R., Griffin, D., & Shaw, P. (2000). *Complexity and management: Fad or radical challenge to systems thinking?* London: Routledge.

Streiner, D. L., & Sidani, S. (Eds.) (2010). *When research goes off the rails: Why it happens and what you can do about it.* New York: Guilford Press.

Strudsholm, T., Meadows, L. M., Robinson Vollman, A., Thurston, W. E., & Henderson, R. (2016). Using mixed methods to facilitate complex, multiphased health research. *International Journal of Qualitative Methods, 15*(1), 1–11. doi: 10.1177/1609406915624579.

Szostak, R. (2015). Interdisciplinary and transdisciplinary multimethod and mixed methods research. In S. N. Hesse-Biber & R. B. Johnson (Eds.), *The Oxford handbook of multimethod and mixed methods research inquiry* (pp. 128–143). Oxford: Oxford University Press.

Tashakkori, A., & Teddlie, C. (1998). *Mixed methodology: Combining qualitative and quantitative approaches.* Thousand Oaks, CA: Sage.

Tashakkori, A., & Teddlie, C. (2003). *SAGE handbook of mixed methods in social & behavioral research.* Thousand Oaks, CA: Sage.

Tashakkori, A., & Teddlie, C. (2010). Epilogue: Current developments and emerging trends in integrated research methodology. In A. Tashakkori & C. Teddlie (Eds.), *SAGE handbook of mixed methods in social & behavioral research* (2nd ed., pp. 803–826). Thousand Oaks, CA: Sage.

Taylor, L. K., Merrilees, C. E., Corkalo Biruski, D., Ajdukovic, D., & Cummings, E. M. (2017). Complexity of risk: Mixed-methods approach to understanding youth risk and insecurity in postconflict settings. *Journal of Adolescent Research, 32*(5), 585–613. doi: 10.1177/0743558416684950.

Teddlie, C., & Tashakkori, A. (2009). *Foundations of mixed methods research: Integrating quantitative and qualitative approaches in the social and behavioral sciences*. Thousand Oaks, CA: Sage.

Tversky, A., & Kahneman, D. (1981). The framing of decisions and the psychology of choice. *Science, 211*(4481), 453–458. doi: 10.1126/science.7455683.

Ungar, M., & Liebenberg, L. (2011) Assessing resilience across cultures using mixed methods: Construction of the Child and Youth Resilience Measure. *Journal of Mixed Methods Research, 5*(2), 126–149.

Uprichard, E. (2012). Narratives of the future: Complexity, time and temporality. In M. Williams & W. P. Vogt (Eds.), *SAGE handbook of innovation in social research methods* (pp. 103–119). Thousand Oaks, CA: Sage.

Uprichard, E., & Dawney, L. (2016). Data diffraction: Challenging data integration in mixed methods research. *Journal of Mixed Methods Research*. doi: 10.1177/1558689816674650.

Waldrop, M. M. (1992). *Complexity: The emerging science at the edge of order and chaos*. New York: Simon and Schuster.

Weaver, W. (1948). Science and complexity. *American Scientist, 36*, 536–544.

Wheeldon, J., & Åhlberg, M. (2012). *Visualizing social research*. Thousand Oaks, CA: Sage.

Wilson, A. T., & Winiarczyk, R. E. (2014). Mixed methods research strategies with deaf people: Linguistic and cultural challenges addressed. *Journal of Mixed Methods Research, 8*(3), 266–277. doi: 10.1177/1558689814527943.

Zaccaro, S. J., Heinen, B., & Shuffler, M. (2009). Team leadership and team effectiveness. In E. Salas, G. F. Goodwin, & C. S. Burke (Eds.), *Team effectiveness in complex organizations: Cross-disciplinary perspectives and approaches* (pp. 83–111). New York: Psychology Press.

Zea, M. C., Aguilar-Pardo, M., Betancourt, F., Reisen, C. A., & Gonzales, F. (2014). Mixed methods research with internally displaced Colombian gay and bisexual men and transwomen. *Journal of Mixed Methods Research, 8*(3), 212–221. doi: 10.1177/1558689814527941.

Zhou, X., & Hall, J. N. (2016). Mixed methods papers in first-person and third-person: Writing voices in dialogue. *Journal of Mixed Methods Research, 2*, 344–357. doi: 10.1177/1558689816652755.

INDEX